LIFELINES

Lifelines

A Viennese Family's Letters
from Home and Exile,
1938–1947

Patricia Haim

Copyright © 2024 Patricia Haim

Lifelines: A Viennese Family's Letters from Home and Exile, 1938–1947

All rights reserved.

ISBN: 979-8-218-45547-7
Library of Congress Control Number: 2024914634

Developmental editing, line editing, proofreading, and
interior book design provided by Indigo: Editing, Design, and More:
Developmental and line editor: Kristen Hall-Geisler
Proofreaders: Bailey Potter and Sarah Currin
Interior book designer: Olivia M. Hammerman
www.indigoediting.com

Cover Design: Joan Julian
Map: Carol L. Couch
Author Photo: Dorothy Freudenberg

To the memory of Tim McNamara and Edith Liebenthal, in thanks for their lifelong friendship. Without them, these stories could not have been brought back from Lethe's edge into the light.

πάντα ῥεῖ
"Everything flows."
Paul Kurz's signature saying,
after Heraclitus.

CONTENTS

Notes on the Text i

Vienna Inner Districts Map ii

Key Addresses in Vienna, 1938–1947 iii

Beginnings 1
   Chapter 1: How the Project Began 3
   Chapter 2: Who Was Who—Memories and Facts 9
   Chapter 3: Some History: The End of Austria 29

The Letters Begin 43
   Chapter 4: Lilly in England 45
   Chapter 5: At the Canfields 53
   Chapter 6: Kristallnacht and Beyond 63
   Chapter 7: Walter Leaves Home—A Passport and Visit to England . . 81
   Chapter 8: Life at the Canfields Continues 91
   Chapter 9: Walter in America—Letters from the Haim Family 127

Refugees in England, Then Enemy Aliens 147
   Chapter 10: Paul and Paula in Vienna 149
   Chapter 11: Paul in the Midlands 161
   Chapter 12: Internment in England 187
   Chapter 13: Britain Attempts to Export Its Internees 199
   Chapter 14: Internment in Australia 209

Parallel Threads—The Families in Vienna 1939–1941 245
   Chapter 15: The Extended Haim Family 247
   Chapter 16: 1940—Moves and Loss 261
   Chapter 17: The Neuhaus Parents' Emigration Saga 281
   Chapter 18: 1941 299

After the Letters from Vienna Ended **311**
   Chapter 19: Restrictions Upon Restrictions 313
   Chapter 20: Into the Maw of Theresienstadt 327
   Chapter 21: The End of the War in Vienna 367
   Chapter 22: Survivors in Vienna 381
   Chapter 23: Paul and Paula—Refocus 411
   Chapter 24: New Light 447

Appendix: Who Was Who 451

Acknowledgments **459**

About the Author 461

NOTES ON THE TEXT

Most of the letters quoted in this book were written in German and were translated by the author. Words in German letters that were originally written in English are noted with italics, and vice versa for German words in letters originally written in English. Original emphasis has been retained. Austrian colloquialisms and words and phrases from languages other than German or English are generally noted in the text. Minor spelling, punctuation, and capitalization inconsistencies have been silently regularized.

Vienna Inner Districts Map
With Some Locations, 1938–1947

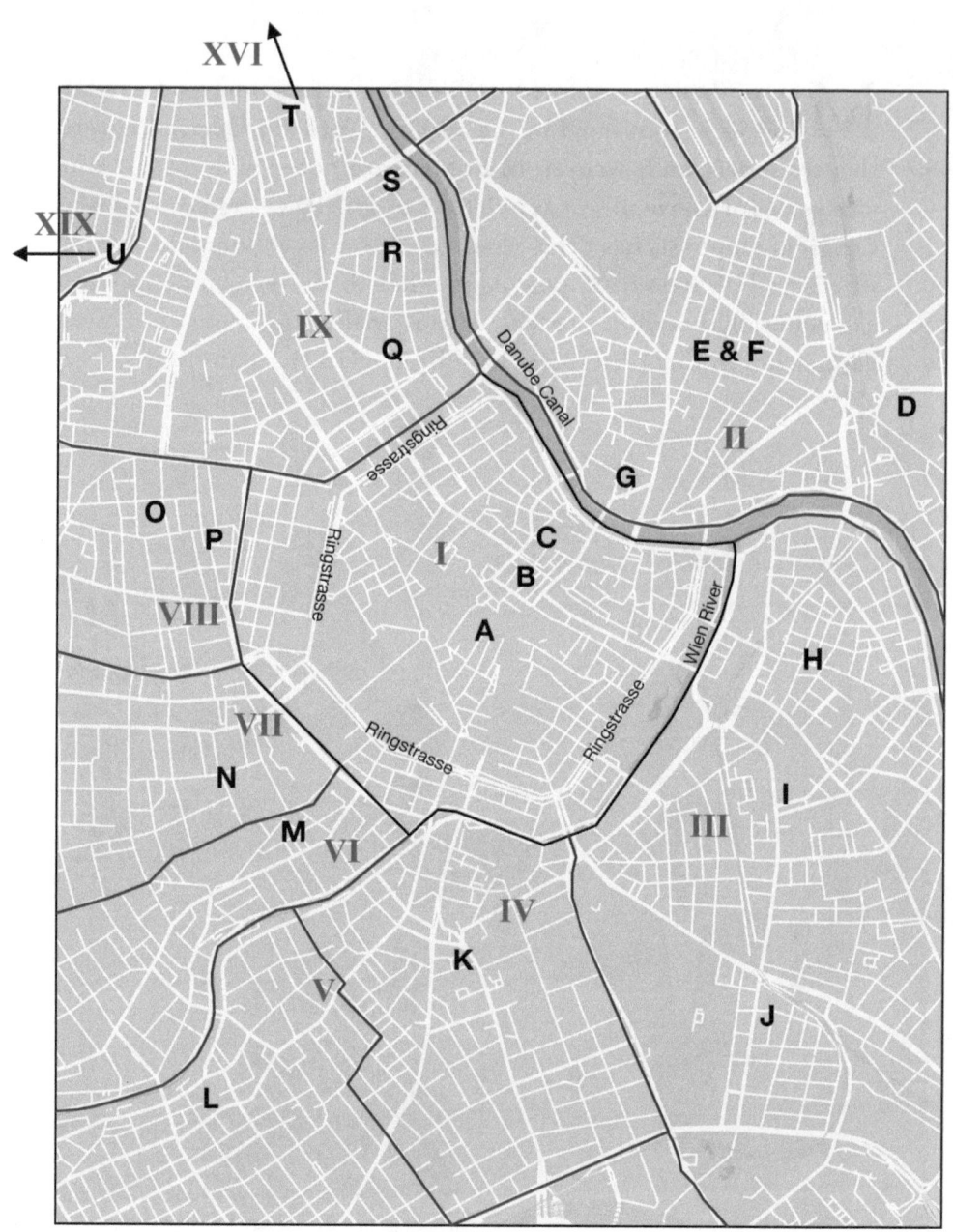

Key Addresses in Vienna, 1938–1947

These are the Vienna addresses between 1938 and 1947 for the most significant places noted in this book. For ease in locating them on the map, addresses are arranged by district. Apartment numbers are included where known.

I District, Inner City
- A. St. Stephen's Cathedral. This gothic structure at the center of the Inner City is Vienna's most recognizable historic landmark.
- B. Hotel Wandl, Petersplatz 9. Walter Haim worked at the Hotel Wandl from 1932 until the spring of 1938.
- C. Lazenhof 2, apartment 10. Paula Kurz and Antoinette Haim lived in a communal apartment in this building, which was owned by the Jewish community, from March 1943 to May 1945.

II District, Leopoldstadt

Now a trendy area, Leopoldstadt was historically a heavily Jewish district. It is located on the island that lies between the Danube Canal and the Danube River.
- D. The Riesenrad. This giant Ferris wheel in the Prater amusement park is another Vienna landmark, visible at the end of Novaragasse.
- E. Novaragasse 39. Ignaz and Mathilde Kurz lived in an apartment and ran a grocery store in this building, and Paul and Olga Kurz grew up there.
- F. Novaragasse 40, apartment 28. Paula Kurz, Antoinette Haim, Mathilde Kurz, and Dr. Martha Müller lived here in a communal apartment with three unrelated people beginning in February 1942. After Mathilde and Martha were deported to Theresienstadt in the summer of 1942, Paula and Antoinette remained at this address into 1943.
- G. Lilienbrunngasse 5, apartment 10. Hans and Lisl Haim

lived in a communal apartment in this building from September 1939 into April 1945.

III District, Landstrasse

H. Salmgasse 3. Hans and Lisl Haim lived here in a comfortable apartment (previously the home of Hans's maternal grandparents) until September 1939, when they were forced to move to "Jewish" communal housing in Leopoldstadt.

I. Sechskrügelgasse 2, apartment 9. Paula Kurz, her parents Martin and Antoinette Haim, Mathilde Kurz, and Dr. Martha Müller all lived in a room in this communal apartment for a short time, from December 1940 into January 1941.

J. Aspang railroad station. Between 1939 and 1942, trains leaving from this station were used to deport 47,000 Jews (including Regine Landsmann, Mathilde Kurz, and Dr. Martha Müller) from Vienna to ghettos and concentration camps.

IV District, Wieden

K. Favoritenstrasse 12, apartment 4. Paula Kurz, Antoinette and Martin Haim, Mathilde Kurz, and Dr. Martha Müller shared a room in this communal apartment from January 1941 through February 1942.

V District, Margareten

L. Margaretenstrasse 121, apartment 8. Since 1918, this had been the home of Martin and Antoinette Haim and their children Alice, Paula, and Walter. They were forced to leave it in November 1940.

VI District, Mariahilf

M. Linke Wienzeile 138. Paula and Paul Kurz and Paul's aunt Grete Wilheim shared an apartment in this Jugendstil (art nouveau) building from 1932 until January 1939, when Paula and Paul moved to the Haim family apartment at Margaretenstrasse 121 in preparation for emigration.

VII District, Neubau

N. Neustiftgasse 55, apartment 7. This was Olga Kurz's apartment and consulting rooms after her return from England in 1946. Paula Kurz lived there with Olga until she was able to emigrate to Australia in 1947.

VIII District, Josefstadt

O. Albertgasse 38. Lilly Neuhaus graduated from this demanding girls' academic high school, informally known as "Albertgasse," in 1937. Edith (née Friedler) Liebenthal was a student there until the spring of 1938.

P. Zeltgasse 1, apartment 2. Paula Kurz and Antoinette Haim lived here for a few months beginning in May 1945.

IX District, Alsergrund

Q. Grünentorgasse 4, apartment 5. This was the longtime apartment of Regine Landsmann (Omama) and Arthur, Pauline, and Lilly Neuhaus. The Neuhaus parents had to leave this apartment in August 1940.

R. Seegasse 9. This was the Jewish old age home where Regine Landsmann lived from April 1940 until she was deported to Theresienstadt in August 1942.

S. Rögergasse 34, apartment 12. Arthur and Pauline Neuhaus lived here from October 1940 until they were able to leave Vienna in March 1941.

XVI District, Ottakring

T. Sandleitenhof municipal apartments, Matteottiplatz 34. The large Sandleiten housing complex was a product of the "Red Vienna" years. Its central square was named for Giacomo Matteotti, an Italian socialist who was murdered by the fascists in 1924.

XIX District, Döbling

U. Iglaseegasse 51, apartment 3. Hans and Lisl Haim lived in this outer suburb beginning in June 1945.

PART 1

Beginnings

CHAPTER 1

How the Project Began

I grew up as an all-American child in 1950s New York City. For my first eleven years, my parents, brother, and I lived in a three-room apartment in Jackson Heights. We had a living room with walls painted dark green—always dim because the room's two windows faced an airshaft between ours and the next row of apartments—plus one bedroom, a kitchen, and a bathroom. A long, windowless foyer led from the front door to the kitchen. My mother's Singer sewing machine stood there in a maple cabinet under a square mirror set in an angled, green glass frame (mid-century modern before the style had a name).

Two closets opened from the foyer. My father's closet, the slightly narrower one, held his hats, suits, and shoes, always put away with wooden shoe trees. It also contained modest mysteries that my brother and I were never allowed to approach: stacks of the little pocket diaries that my father always carried, one for each year; two aluminum boxes, about twelve by ten inches and three inches high, with rounded corners and an aster-like pattern of air holes; and dark-red manila folders filled with stamps and letters, each folder tied with a woven flat tape that was stapled to the front flap.

Stamps and Letters

A couple of times, my father showed me a few of the stamps that were in the red folders, some still attached to their envelope corners, others with their entire envelopes. I knew that my father sent for and saved first-day covers of US stamps that interested him, but he never kept a stamp album that I saw, never organized or sorted them. Still, he religiously saved unusual stamps from letters that arrived at our apartment or his office. Later, when our mother went back to work for a company that imported machine tools from Germany, Hungary, and Spain, she sometimes brought stamps home for him. He kept them, too, in the dark-red folders in his closet.

My parents gave me a beginner's stamp album when this hobby became popular with my grade school class at Public School 149. We could even bring the albums to school some Friday afternoons and trade stamps. My classmates regularly saved stamps that had been soaked off their envelopes, but when I tried to do that at home, it tapped into a well of my father's standards that I hadn't known existed. I was told earnestly that this was not acceptable; soaking removed the glue and made a stamp less valuable. It also destroyed the postmark. Only mission stamps, a lower form of stamps sold by Roman Catholic organizations to raise money, were treated this way.

My collection included a few older German stamps, identifiable by "Deutsches Reich" written in spiky letters. Some of them were worth millions of marks, with black numbers denoting even more millions rubber-stamped over the original engraving. My father told me that those stamps were issued during the hyperinflation in Germany after World War I, when money lost its value by the hour. He told me that for a time when he was a very young man, he would be paid twice a day in stacks or bags of paper money and immediately go out to buy things because if he waited for the end of the day, that money would buy even less. He said that people would bring a suitcase of money and might be able to buy a loaf of bread with it. Only the peasants—the farmers—did well in those times because they would come into the city with food that they grew for next to nothing and barter it for furniture, gold, art. This all seemed to have happened to him in some unlocated past, with no anchoring place names. My father certainly never talked about the politics that had led to his experience with hyperinflation or its results.¹

Here is a story about stamps that captures what a veiled presence Austria formed in my childhood. One day I came home from school with a new stamp. The girl who had traded it to me did not herself know where it was from. Someplace exotic and complicated, she said. I reported this to my father and then showed him the stamp, marked "Österreich." While I don't recall what he said, I know I felt embarrassed by the incident and he seemed unsettled. Instead of asking more, I added "Österreich" to my mental list of off-limits topics.

My father saved not only stamps and their envelopes, but also old letters. He kept almost every letter that he received from his extended family beginning in late 1938 and continuing through the war years and after. My father never told me that he had this trove of letters, never brought them out, probably never reread them because that was not necessary. Independent of their contents, the letters as physical objects embodied their writers, overcoming the limitations of distance and mortality. One linguist explained this phenomenon, analyzing letters written by a Slovak family during the war years: "As forms of written communication, letters not only replace oral conversations, but they replace or represent the person writing them. For both the writer and receiver of the letters, they cross borders; for them, they open their arms; for them, they hold hands."²

My father died in New York in the summer of 1979. When my parents' house was sold, the red folders were bundled into plastic garbage bags that sat for more than two decades in my brother's

---

1   The Austrian hyperinflation of 1921–23 was not simply an economic disaster. Old peoples' pensions became worthless overnight, while wider social bonds and ethical norms that had been seen as part of the eternal natural order were shredded. Stefan Zweig, Austria's best-known writer of the inter-war period, recalled the hyperinflation's disintegrating effect: "Standards and values disappeared during this melting and evaporation of money; there was but one merit: to be clever, shrewd, unscrupulous, and to mount the racing horse instead of being trampled by it" (Stefan Zweig, *The World of Yesterday* [New York: Viking Press, 1943], 291–292).

2   Jozef Tancer, "Glimmers of Light in Existence: Communication Strategies and Language Reflection in the Holocaust Letters of the Sachsel Family in Bratislava," in *In the Supermarket of History: Forms of Modern History and Society in the Central European Area*, G. Dudelova and D. Kodajova, eds. (Bratislava, Slov.: Veda, 2021), 505.

basement. After our mother died in 2002, my brother wanted finally to discard all the seemingly meaningless relics. I asked him to send them to me instead, and the letters, in their decrepit folders, were shipped across the country to Oregon. At first they seemed to have become my albatross. Eventually I began to feel that they carried an imperative to make something of them, to tell the stories.

Unearthing the Past

There was no easy entry into this mass of old paper. I began with the most mechanical tasks. First stamps and empty envelopes had to be separated from letters. Then I sorted the heaps of as-yet unread letters by writer and arranged them chronologically in file folders. It was all a trial. The translucent airmail paper was brittle, stacks of the letters had been damaged by the basement's dampness and an ill-behaved cat, many of the handwritings looked as incomprehensible as EKG tracings, and my high school German had receded to the back of my brain. Still, even this bare sorting offered periscope glimpses into the previously unapproachable past. My father's parents and sisters had written regularly to him, usually twice a week, beginning the day after he left Vienna in January 1939. My mother had written dozens of letters to him during the ten months when she was in England, engaged in unequal combat with visa officials at the US consulate in London. My father's older brother Hans, previously just a name to me, wrote regular letters before, during, and after the war. There were many letters from my uncle Paul Kurz, first from Vienna, then England, and finally Australia, his handwriting instantly recognizable. There were even letters with Filipino stamps from an aunt of my father's who had escaped to Manila.

Organizing the letters had begun as something of an evening pastime, like knitting. It grew into a quest as I started to read and transcribe the more accessible ones. Paul's letters offered a good start. He often typed his letters and switched from writing in German to English shortly after the war began so that the censors, first in the

UK and then in Australia, would pass them more quickly. Most of Hans's letters were typed as well, though that advantage was offset by his long, convoluted German sentences.

Simultaneously, I entered the rabbit warren of genealogical research. I scrolled through microfilms of Viennese records ordered through the local Latter-day Saints' reading room. Then I corresponded with the Israelitische Kultusgemeinde (IKG, or Jewish Community) in Vienna and the Austrian War Archives. As the years passed, online sources proliferated. In 2008 I traveled to Vienna and spent a couple of afternoons at the IKG. At the time, their archives were still so informal that a visitor could pull from the shelves original ledgers recording 150 years of the community's births, marriages, and deaths, and leaf through them with ungloved hands. For that visit I had compiled a list of the letters' return addresses and marked them on a Google map. I walked through Vienna's 1st, 2nd, 5th, and 9th Districts, map in hand, photographing building numbers and street names that became more resonant the more I read.

What had begun as a slash pile of brambles began to put out recognizable roots and branches. The letters told parallel stories of the Haim, Kurz, and Neuhaus families as they unfolded day by day in Vienna, England, and Australia and were recounted in letters to my father in New York. While piecing together the letters' narratives, I began to excavate my own childhood memories. Like the letters, those memories were shot through with themes of identity, language, and a mythical place called Vienna, a sunken Atlantis. As I gathered these shards of memories and annotated the letters, it became ever clearer how walled off this history had been. I began to notice how often I had glimpsed clues from my parents, grandparents, aunt, and uncle, and how consistently I had failed to pursue them because, inadvertently but quite effectively, I had been conditioned not to.

Individual memory is necessarily subjective and shifting, and second-generation Holocaust survivors have written a great deal about the process and psychic results of unearthing memories of the taboo past. I had something more objective than memories. The letters that my father saved had recorded, in what would now be called "real time," their writers' minute-by-minute thoughts, awareness, hopes, and voices, uncontaminated by later nostalgia or foreshadowing. They revealed the writers as remarkable people who heroically continued to write through traumas of separation and exile. They wrote during daily ups and downs over which they had no control and counseled my father not to look back at the lost past. (Looking backwards has ended badly in all our familiar mythologies, from Lot's wife to Orpheus.) They wrote knowing there was much that they could not say directly. Subjectively, my father, Walter, needed to be supported, and objectively, letters had to pass the censors. Every word of wartime letters from Vienna was scrutinized by Wehrmacht censors, while letters from England and Australia were subject to similar review by the British and Australian military.

What emerged from the letters was an improbable story of loss, separation, and sometimes reunion. The goal of this book is to remember—or more accurately to excavate and reconstruct—the remarkable people who wrote these letters during appalling times. I have tried to bring this history to light in their own words from their letters and to sketch in the historical context that is not common knowledge today.

CHAPTER 2

Who Was Who—
Memories and Facts

The Haim Family—Martin Haim

My father told me only a few stories about his father. I knew from an early age that his name was Martin (my father insisted on using Craig Martin toothpaste, a long-defunct brand, because of the name). Beyond his name, here is all that my father told me about his father: Martin was born on the day of the spring equinox, March 21. As a young man, he supposedly made himself a year older by giving out 1859 as his year of birth instead of 1860 because in those days, age was respected and young people weren't taken seriously. (That seems to have been folklore. The Vienna records concur that Martin Haim was born there in 1859.) On the other hand, a young man's trying to make himself seem older would have been entirely plausible in 1880s Austria. "Gray hair was merely a new sign of dignity," Stefan Zweig wrote in his memoir, *The World of Yesterday*. Zweig recalled, "My father, my uncle, my teacher, the salesmen in the shops, the members of the Philharmonic at their music stands were already, at forty, portly and 'worthy' men. They walked slowly, they spoke with measured accent, and, in their conversation, stroked their well-kept beards, which often had already turned gray."[3]

There were more bits of stories. Martin had collected stamps and as a young man lived for a time in Cairo, working as an accountant.

---

3   Zweig, *The World of Yesterday*, 25.

Residents of Cairo then had the advantage of three holy days off per week: Friday for the Muslims (whom my father called Mohammedans), Saturday for the Jews, Sunday for the Christians. Martin became very "impressed" (this was my father's word) by Islam while in Cairo and may even have thought briefly of converting, though converting from what remained unspoken. In letters written after his death, Martin's children recalled him as the most well-traveled and adventurous member of the family.

Martin, Alice, and Paula Haim, Bucharest, August 1911.

A moment in Martin's midlife was captured in a photographer's studio in Bucharest in August 1911. Martin, as the patriarch, sits in a chair while his teenaged daughters, Alice and Paula, stand next to him. Martin is wearing a dark, tailored suit with a matching vest, a collared white shirt with French cuffs and cufflinks, and a tie. A substantial gold watch chain is looped across the front of his vest. He wears two rings on the fourth finger of his right hand and holds a walking stick in his left. Alice and Paula are dressed modestly. Although the photo was taken

Martin and Antoinette Haim, late 1930s.

in summer, they wear white blouses with high lace collars and gloves. Their hair is still long, arranged in updos. This was the era before bobbed hair became an acceptable norm. I can't detect any indication of nationality or religion in this solidly middle-class trio.

Two pieces of my Martin Haim's jewelry from this photo survived. One is the star and crescent moon pinned to the knot of his tie. In an ironic amalgam of cultures, this motif—a traditional icon for both Turkey and Islam—had become a symbol of the Turkish Jewish community in Vienna. The second is the watch charm, a sliver of which can be seen near his waist, containing a photo of a young woman with flowers in her upswept, wavy hair. Many years later, I found it resting in one of the tin boxes from my father's closet.

Back home in Vienna, the Haim family was visibly urban and middle class. Photos from the late 1930s show Martin as a well-dressed city gentleman. He still had a trimmed, pointed beard and moustache, although they had gone grey. In snapshots taken at resorts in the country, Martin wore suits or a tailored jacket and dark dress pants, a vest, a topcoat, a gold watch chain, a walking stick, a city-style hat, and polished shoes.

There are very few traces of the previous Haim generation, but they seem to have been part of the comfortable bourgeoisie. An undated photo of Martin's parents shows them both in opera-worthy evening dress. Johann Haim wears a starched shirt and white tie, and Flora an

Martin and Antoinette at a mountain resort, late 1930s.

Martin's parents Johann and Flora Haim in evening dress, undated.

elaborate gown with a confection of ostrich feathers on her head.⁴

The archives confirm the Haim family's Turkish roots. Not simply an exotic land to the east, for centuries Turkey had been a threatening rival empire. Every Austrian schoolchild learned that the Muslim Turks had twice been defeated by Christian knights at the gates of Vienna, first in 1529 and again in 1683, leaving behind sacks of coffee beans as they fled. Martin's birth in 1859 was registered with the Turkish Sephardic (that is, Jewish) community in Vienna, which noted that his father, Johann Jochanan Haim, had been born in the ancient Turkish city of Adrianople (now Edirne) in about 1822, and that his mother, Flora (née Eskenasy), was born in Vienna in about 1826 but was "zuständig" to Turkey.⁵

Antoinette (Née Feder) Haim

I know less about my father's mother because he talked about her even more rarely than he did Martin. My father told me that his mother's given name was Antoinette (though official records often use the less francophone name "Antonie"), and her maiden name was Feder, meaning a feather or plume, and by extension a pen. I don't know the extent to which she attended school or what talents and interests she had beyond her extensive family.

---

4 Johann Haim must have done well in business as a "Turkish merchant." In 1905 the family paid to have a death notice printed in the *Neue Freie Presse*, at the time Vienna's chief liberal newspaper, "regarded by many as *The Times* of central Europe" (Steven Beller, *Vienna and the Jews 1867–1938* [Cambridge, UK: Cambridge University Press, 1989], 38).

5 The term "zuständig" was a staple of Austrian imperial recordkeeping. Not fully equivalent to modern citizenship, it denoted the jurisdiction which was legally responsible for an individual if they should become impoverished and where the person had a right of residency.

Unlike his three older siblings, Martin married outside the Sephardic community. Antoinette came from an Ashkenazi family, though hints in the letters suggest that she effectively became a "Spaniolen," a Sephardi. She cooked Eastern European and Middle Eastern specialties, like the stuffed grape leaves of my mother's memory. This culinary leaning could have come about because of Martin's preferences, reinforced by the family's sojourns in Bucharest. (Bucharest was a repeated term in family mythology. My aunt Paula was born there in 1896, and my father attended a German language primary school there from 1909 to 1913.) In 1940, Antoinette sent Walter and Lilly a page of Middle Eastern recipes for aubergines, not a typical Viennese vegetable.

Like Martin, Antoinette was a native of Vienna, where the Feder family registered their milestone events with the Ashkenazi Jewish community. The IKG recorded her birth on March 12, 1868, to parents Ignaz and Rosa (née Horowitz) Feder. The Feder parents came from Pressburg, a town that was then governed by Hungary and is now Slovakia's capital city of Bratislava. They were part of the large, mid-nineteenth-century migration of Jews from western Hungary and the Austrian provincial lands to Vienna that was spurred by the partial lifting of legal restrictions on their travel and occupations. One historian summarized the statistics:

> The first mass convergence [of Jews] on Vienna coincided with the breaking down of the legal barriers to full emancipation in Austria and the golden age of liberal hegemony....According to a sample study of the social structure of Viennese Jewry in the year 1857 (based in particular on the Leopoldstadt [Vienna's heavily Jewish 2nd District]), 25 per cent of its Jews were born in Hungary (mainly Pressburg), 20 per cent in Vienna itself, 15 per cent in the many small Jewish communities of Moravia, 10 per cent in Galicia, and only 4 per cent in Bohemia.[6]

---

6   Robert S. Wistrich, *The Jews of Vienna in the Age of Franz Joseph* (Lexington, MA: Plunkett Lake Press, 1989, Kindle edition 2016), 1077–1078.

My father mentioned that his mother's mother was named Rose and that he recalled her as a very old lady. Once when we passed a package of Horowitz Margareten brand Passover matzos in a supermarket in Jackson Heights, he told me that his grandmother's maiden name had been Horowitz. Unsaid at the time was anything about the family's having been Jewish or that the brand name on this package of matzos was doubly resonant because the Haim family's address for decades had been Margaretenstrasse in Vienna.

My uncle Paul Kurz spoke fondly of his mother-in-law, whom he called "Tonie." He told me that he had designed an apparatus for her to brew coffee using cold water so that it would not be bitter. Tonie made a point of showing her cold coffee brewer to Gustl Landsmann, one of my maternal grandmother Pauline Neuhaus's two brothers, shortly before he emigrated in 1940. She explained the system to Gustl and wrote to my father: "The idea is very good and the execution simple and practical, coffee made by a cold method." Paul also liked Antoinette's cooking and would describe a dish that she made as "à la Tonerl," using an Austrian diminutive.

Antoinette was the oldest of Rosa and Ignaz Feder's nine children, all born in Vienna. My father thus would have grown up among numerous aunts, uncles, and cousins on the Feder side of the family. He kept some letters from two of his aunts, Antoinette's sisters Helene, the youngest, and Malvine.

Antoinette wrote letters at least weekly to my father after he left Vienna and then to my parents jointly. I can read very little of her old-fashioned handwriting beyond a few names and her invariable signature, "Mama."

During the years of frantic emigration that began in 1938, and no doubt before that, Antoinette was a source of cohesion for the extended family—the Haims, the de Majos, and after Paula's marriage, the Kurzes and Wilheims. Once my parents were in New York, that web of relations, all of whom were family even if they were not related by blood, gradually eroded. We did not know who or where they were, and we did not try to find out. Here is a concrete example: In the 1950s and 1960s, two adult granddaughters of Martin Haim's older sister Sophie (née Haim) de Majo lived with their families in Elmhurst, the neighborhood directly across Roosevelt Avenue from us in Jackson Heights. Others of Sophie's grandchildren and their families landed in the Chicago area. I never knew that, never heard of any of them, and have no reason to think that my father or his sister Paula knew about them either.

This seems part of a common pattern. A recent scholar (and third-generation Viennese survivor) identified "permanent family separation" as the "defining aspect" of the Nazi era's effect on the Vienna Jewish community, even though about two thirds were able to escape and survived.[7] Without continuing shared ties —years of joint family dinners, holidays, and milestones—even documented blood connections fade into nothingness.

My Father—Walter Haim

My childhood memories of my father are of a quiet man who loved classical music, art, and languages. When he was home or in the car, the only radio station that could be played was WQXR, New York City's classical music broadcaster. Because of him, our bookcase, off limits to the children, held volumes of Goethe, Dante (in German), and Shakespeare, as well as a set of Langenscheidt's bilingual pocket dictionaries: German-French, German-Italian, German-Spanish, even German-Romanian. My father told a story that when he was a schoolboy in Bucharest, one spoke German at school, French at home so the maid wouldn't understand, a bit of Turkish to the sweet sellers on the street, and some Romanian to the locals. The message was that acquiring languages was something educated people did, a form of noblesse oblige.

---

7   Ilana Fritz Offenberger, *The Jews of Nazi Vienna, 1938–1945: Rescue and Destruction*, (New York: Plagrave Macmillan, 2017), xii -xiv, 293–305. About two thirds of the community, or over 136,000 people, were able to emigrate between 1938 and 1941.

Hiking and the Outdoors

Not all the family's pleasures were indoors. In his early life, Walter loved skiing, hiking, and mountains. "Glacier" remained a resonant word for him, though once in New York, all this was out of reach. Paul, his brother-in-law, said that in the old days my father had a perfect physique. My father told me the story that he sometimes got to carry the mail from the post office up to an alpine hut or shelter. When he hiked, his goal was to get from a marked trailhead to the next junction or town faster than the times given on the signposts, where distances were realistically noted in hours of walking rather than kilometers.

Walter's sister and brother-in-law, Paula and Paul, were also drawn to the outdoors. Walter brought with him several photos of them hiking in the mountains. They are wearing country clothes: shorts with suspenders and heavy knee socks for Paul, white collared blouses, thick socks, and solid shoes for the women.

Paula, Paul, and possibly Alice at a country inn after a hike, 1930s.

What does not appear in any of the photographs is tracht, the Austrian national costume most recognizable as dirndls and lederhosen. Originally modeled on Alpine peasants' clothing, tracht was adopted in the late nineteenth century by the upper and middle classes for vacations in the country. A famous photo from 1911 shows Sigmund Freud's daughter Anna wearing tracht while walking with her father in the Dolomites, at the time Austrian Südtirol. Even Theodor Herzel, the founder of modern political Zionism, was photographed with his three children in his study, all wearing tracht.[8] After WWI, tracht became a political emblem of German nationalists.[9] Finally in 1938, Jews in Greater Germany were expressly prohibited from wearing tracht.

Walter's Touring Club ID photo, about 1917–1920.

For a time Walter was a member of the Austrian Touristenverein (Touring Club). He brought with him a photo that had been attached to his club identification document. In it he looks a bit impish, relaxed, slim, and well-dressed, wearing the round steel-framed glasses that he still had many years later in New York. The Touristenverein stamp shows that Walter was a member of the club's "academic" or student section. This would date the photo to between 1917 and 1920, while Walter attended Vienna's business academy. The photo was peeled off from some sort of document, leaving a patch of print and a signature on the back.

The Touring Club may have been one of Walter's formative experiences of exclusion. It had been founded in 1908 as the

---

8 The photo is not dated, but Herzel died in 1904. Both photos can be found in Hilde Spiel, *Vienna's Golden Autumn: From the Watershed Year of 1866 to Hitler's Anschluss, 1938* (Weidenfield & Nicholson, New York: 1987), 156–157.

9 See, e.g., Marjorie Perloff, *The Vienna Paradox: A Memoir* (New York: New Directions, 2004), 41; and Shira Rubin, "A New Spin on Traditional German Clothes," *Tablet*, September 15, 2019, tabletmag.com/sections/community/articles/a-new-spin-on-traditional-german-clothes.

Christian Worker Tourist Club.[10] Then in the early 1920s, numerous Austrian associations, in particular sports and Alpine groups, adopted rules excluding Jews from membership.[11] It seems reasonable that Walter joined the student section of the Touring Club before the wave of postwar antisemitic exclusions and expulsions. His association with the club probably ended shortly after the new rules were adopted, as he was sensitive to social cues and not one to challenge group boundaries. Nevertheless, the photo must have been meaningful to Walter. He kept this picture of his teenaged self and brought it with him to America, detached from the document showing that he had been a member of a club that no longer welcomed him.

Once in New York, my father's life was more constricted. He was much older than my mother and visibly older than my friends' parents. He was introverted and had no separate friends of his own. He listened to classical music on the radio but did not go to concerts or the theater. New York had no equivalent to walks in the Vienna Woods. Socializing was limited to Sunday afternoons of coffee and cake at my grandparents' apartment. For decades, without complaint, he made the long subway commute during morning and evening rush hours between Queens and Lower Manhattan, where he did some sort of accounting for an insurance company. During "annual statements" season, he worked even longer hours, arriving home long after dark.

My father is the hub at the center of this story, as the surviving letters are ones that were written to him. The red folders contained only one letter that he himself wrote. Thus he largely remains a negative space, defined by what others wrote to him.

---

10 See *Der Tourist*, http://www.touristenverein.at/Index/Zeitung/2008%20Der%20Tourist%204.pdf. Not surprisingly, this newsletter's timeline says nothing about the club's racial or religious membership policies.

11 Bruce F. Pauley, *From Prejudice to Persecution: A History of Austrian Anti-Semitism* (Chapel Hill, NC: University of North Carolina Press, 1998), 118.

Travel

Walter had traveled to France at least once. Somehow he saved a postcard that he had written to Paul. It is postmarked Versailles, dated May 23, 1935, and addressed to "Herrn Ing. Paul Kurz, II, Novaragasse 39, Vienne, Autriche," using the French spellings of the city and country. The front of the card is a black-and-white photo of the Dome des Invalides, looking monumental as it rises from a base of formal plantings to an airy cross above the dome. Why Walter would have written to Paul alone, and at Paul's parents' address when he and Paula had been married since March 1932 and were living at the Linke Wienzeile, I don't know. Nor do I know if Walter was alone in Paris or with a group, on a business trip or simply vacation. Whatever the circumstances, Walter was happy to be in Paris:

> Dear Paul, it is so beautiful here that I just cannot leave—You know it yourself. My travel purpose is as good as if it had fallen in the water [i.e., no good at all], but now I don't care and will stay here as long as possible. So in the meantime many heartfelt greetings to you and everyone who may read this card.

Anxiety

By 1939 when he left for the United States, Walter had become more anxious, prone to nervous conditions like eczema, headaches, and neuralgia. Among the items that he brought to New York from Vienna are prescriptions for aspirin, Vaseline, and a skin ointment called Cehasol, the last written by a doctor whose prescription form was marked with a star of David and the limitation that he was "licensed for medical treatment for Jews only." Walter had worn glasses since his grade school days and was quite nearsighted. Paula worried in her letters about his eyestrain from work: "Bibolein, that your eyes have become worse troubles me a lot, though unfortunately that doesn't help you. Your eyes were the constant anxiety of our dear Mama."

Walter's 1938 passport photo shows the change from his confident Touring Club photo. He appears worried and closed off, with head tilted down, vulnerable, turned inward, no longer looking the world in the eye. To the right, ink from the stamped red "J" bleeds through the page.

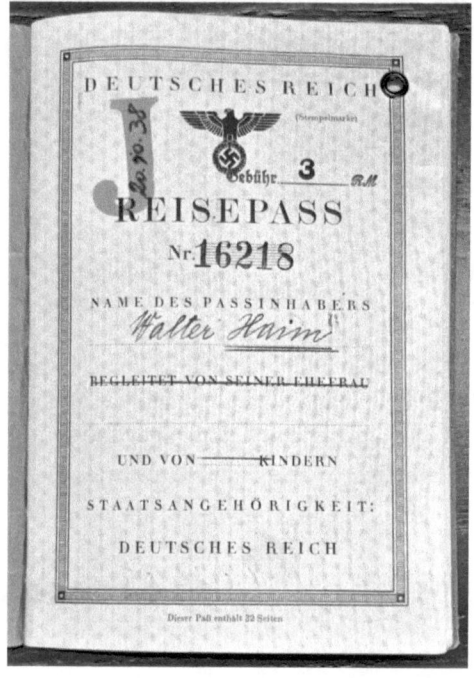

Walter's German passport cover page with the added red "J," October 1938.

Walter's passport identification page.

"Bobby"

From a child's perspective, my father always seemed to have been old, but he had grown up as the perpetual youngster in a much older family. His siblings were six, eight, and thirteen years older than he, and his father was forty-three when this youngest son was born. Walter's oldest sister Alice called him "Bobby," a gesture of affectionate Anglophilia. For example, in an early family letter from 1939, Alice signed off, "Bye-bye Bobby dear, be a good boy and don't forget that there are some people in faraway Vienna who love you dearly." Paula, his next older sister, teasingly inverted that pet name and he became "Bibo" or "Bibolein," a diminutive. Paula remarked on it when Lilly began to write about her husband as Bibo:

> So you also call Walter Bibo! He should tell you how indignant he was the first time that I twisted "Bobi" around.

Walter's brother-in-law, Paul, also usually addressed him as Bobby and wrote as though he were a generation older, although Paul and Walter had been born only seven months apart.

Shadows of Homesickness

Homesickness was never mentioned, but it was an ineradicable substratum. When my father left Vienna early in 1939, he brought with him several pillow shams and a red table cover with cross-stitched Jugendstil (art nouveau) flowers that his mother Antoinette had embroidered. They were never used but remained untouchable relics.

When we still lived on 89th Street, my father once showed me the tin boxes. He pointed to tiny glass vials filled with tea leaves, which looked like little test tubes with metal caps. He said that his mother had given them to him as a parting gift. Both Walter and Antoinette recalled them as talismans of home and possible reunion.

Antoinette wrote in June 1941, after Walter had been gone for two and a half years:

> Yes, I recall forcing sugar and tea on you before your departure. Just hang on to those things, someone will make them some time, perhaps even I!

Another story was that when my father left Vienna, his father had advised him always to keep enough money to buy a return ticket, and that way he wouldn't be homesick. Perhaps Walter didn't have enough money to set aside, or the mental trick didn't work. Before I learned to read, my bookshelf included a Little Golden Book edition of *The Cold-Blooded Penguin*. Early on, I sensed that this was an awkward story for my father to read to me. Pablo the penguin was always cold and so could not bear to live in his native country with all the other penguins. Pablo crossed the ocean by himself in a jet-propelled bathtub and reached his dream land, a warm tropical isle where he basked in the sun, at ease in his hammock. Still, Pablo sometimes thought of his cold snowy home and his former companions far away, never to be seen again. The metaphor could not have been sharper.

Despite an undercurrent of losses, neither of my parents could have been accused of being a "beiunski," the sort of obnoxious immigrant who complained that things had been better "bei uns," back home. This was a recognized type. The German-language newspaper in New York, *Aufbau* (the name means "rebuild"), ran a satiric article in 1936, even before the wave of post-Anschluss Austrian immigration, titled "Ten Commandments for New Immigrants." It advised German-speaking newcomers in through-the-looking-glass fashion how to avoid being a beiunski:

> When you're invited for dinner, make fun of the poor American cuisine, the cheap Woolworth knives, the poor table manners of the Americans who even cut their potatoes with a knife, and do not forget to mention that you used to have sterling silver at home....Do not forget to make a

point that people in Germany know how to live better than Americans do, and please don't forget to mention that the entire American culture has been imported from Europe.[12]

Walter's Siblings—Hans Haim

My father's older brother was called "Hans." I knew that even though he had died before I was born. I also knew that when my father was offered a job by a company located on John Street in Lower Manhattan's financial district, he took that as a good omen, since "Hans" translates to "John."

Hans was a native Viennese through and through, born there in 1889. Although he had been formally named Johann Jochanan after his paternal grandfather, he was always Hans to everyone, and that is the name on his gravestone.

Like a typical Viennese, Hans vacationed in the Austrian countryside, but he had never traveled farther than Berlin and saw no attraction in doing so. He had served in the Austro-Hungarian army during World War I, and a story survives from that time. Hans wrote home to thank his parents for sending him a care package, mentioning that the canned butter was a bit rancid, but that he and his comrades enjoyed it anyway. Not butter at all—that had been a tin of anti-louse cream. A posed photo of the Haim children taken in 1918 shows Hans in uniform, the two stars on his collar indicating a rank of corporal. His blonde wife, Lisl (Elisabeth Auguste, née Ricker), dressed in brocade with a cameo pin, stands beside him. Young Walter has a slight twinkle in his eyes, while everyone else looks grim.

Hans was a businessman. He worked at a bank after the Great War then left in about 1930 to form a partnership with a furniture maker and his brother. Their company, Bucek & Haim, advertised in Lehmann's Vienna City Directory that it offered "art and furniture

---

12 Monroe Price, *Objects of Remembrance: A Memoir of American Opportunities and Viennese Dreams* (Budapest: Central European University Press, 2009), 57.

woodworking and workshops for complete home furnishing." This was an inauspicious time to start a business. Austria had been hit hard by the depression, bank failures, and political unrest between Socialists and far right forces, culminating in the short civil war of February 1934 that ended the First Republic. Bucek & Haim lasted only four years. Eventually Hans landed the position of cashier with the IKG, Vienna's Jewish Community. It was a good fit for him, requiring solo work, scrupulous honesty, and a love for detail.

The younger Haim family in 1918. From the left: Hans, his wife Lisl, Paula, Walter, and Alice.

Alice Haim

My father's older sister, Alice, was also a native Viennese, born in 1891. There are few remaining traces of Alice, and my father very rarely spoke of her. Her name was written on the brown paper cover that protected our prime linguistic resource, *The Concise Oxford English Dictionary*. Alice may have lived in Bucharest for a time, or at least visited the family there, as she appears in the 1911 photograph with her father and younger sister, Paula.

I've found no records of Alice's education, but somehow she acquired the language skills to make a living giving private English lessons. After the Anschluss, she was listed in Lehmann's Vienna City Directory as a language teacher, her business address the family's apartment at Margaretenstrasse 121. Alice never married and continued to live with her parents. She had a "weak heart," a family condition.

Paula (Née Haim) Kurz

The younger of my father's two sisters was Paula. She was born in Bucharest in 1896 during one of the family's sojourns there. (I imagine that the family had relatives in Bucharest, though I have not found traces of them.) As with her older sister Alice, there is no evidence that Paula had a formal education, but she learned bookkeeping and accounting and worked successfully with her father. Beginning in 1924 Paula had her own entry in Lehmann's annual Vienna City Directory as an auditor, with the same address and telephone number as Martin, suggesting that his accounting business, and Paula's role in it, had expanded.

Within a large circle of relatives and acquaintances, one of Paula's closest friends was Olga Kurz, a pediatrician. Olga had a younger brother, Paul Kurz, a chemical engineer. When and how Paula and Paul met is unknown; perhaps they became acquainted through Olga. They married in 1932.

Despite their later closeness, the relationship between Paula and her younger brother, Walter, was contentious when they were younger. Paula was the overbearing older sister, and Walter did not always stand up for himself. Paula signed one of the earlier letters, "Your old dragon." Years later she wrote, thanking Walter for a Valentine's Day card, "Yes I believe that you have already endured all sorts of things from your big sister. Paul said that instead of going to Dr. Fischer [probably for nerves], you should have thrashed me at the time."

My Mother—Lilly (Née Neuhaus) Haim

My mother Julianne—always "Lilly" to the family—was the only child of a career Austrian military officer, my grandfather Arthur Neuhaus, and an elegant Frau Offizier, my grandmother Pauline (née Landsmann) Neuhaus. Lilly was born in Vienna on February 25, 1919. She was "ein Kind der Republik," "a child of the Republic," as she told my daughter after being asked something about the old monarchy.

Lilly, about 1920.

Lilly and her mother, who is called "Mutti" in the letters, were always very close. One of the stories my mother told me about her mother would have taken place when she herself was still a very young child, in the early 1920s. Vienna suffered from serious food and fuel shortages for years after the country was defeated and dismembered in 1918. One day Lilly heard on the radio that people had been arrested for diluting milk. She began crying the next time that she saw her mother preparing farina, a favorite comfort food, in the usual way—half milk, half water—because she was afraid that this was a crime for which her mother would be taken away.

Pauline maintained a warm relationship with her older brother Sigl Landsmann and sister-in-law Irma, but there always seems to have been a rivalry, at least on one side, between Lilly and her younger cousin

Pauline and Lilly Neuhaus, late 1920s.

Anneliese, called Lissy. In photographs of the cousins taken when my mother was fourteen, she is invariably stiff and looks put-upon, while Lissy, age ten, is perky and smiling.

Pauline had had to end her schooling at about age sixteen for reasons never explained, perhaps to go to work. Lilly, in contrast, was always encouraged to be a good student, first at the neighborhood Schubertschule in the 9th District, then at Albertgasse Gymnasium (a demanding academic girls' high school) in the neighboring 8th District. My mother told me that her mother was disappointed whenever she didn't get the top grade of five, at least in the subjects she was good at, like math. She was required to take four years of Latin at Albertgasse, which she claimed to have hated and not done well at, though she was always my unfailing Latin resource in high school. Her Kleine Stowasser Latin-German dictionary was a family staple. I still have it, with "Eigentum: Lilly Neuhaus!" (Property of Lilly Neuhaus!) written on the flyleaf.

Cousins Lissy and Lilly, August 1933.

CHAPTER 3

Some History: The End of Austria

My father's dark red folders did not contain anything dating back to the Anschluss, Germany's annexation of Austria in March 1938. That was when the family's recognizable world crumbled. Here is a rapid overview of the preceding decades.

The venerable Habsburg monarchy collapsed in November 1918, the month of the armistice that ended what was then called the Great War. A Republic of German-Austria existed for a short time, and the First Republic of Austria was established the following year. The fledgling republic was beset by overwhelming financial, political, and social problems, including the hyperinflation of 1921–1923.

Things deteriorated over the next decade. In July 1927, a riot in Vienna between left and right paramilitary forces left dozens of workers dead and hundreds of protesters and police injured. In neighboring Germany, Hitler was appointed chancellor in January 1933. That March, he and the Nazi Party seized power, ending the tottering Weimar Republic. In May 1933 Engelbert Dollfuss united conservative Austrian political groups in the newly established Fatherland Front. That August, Mussolini announced that Italy would guarantee Austria's independence in the face of German expansionism. (Not altruism, this was one move in complex international jockeying among the European powers.)

Early in 1934, Austrian left-wing parties staged a civil uprising. Government forces crushed it, and the Federal State of Austria took over from the Republic. Dollfuss's Fatherland Front became the single ruling party. It banned all other parties—including the Social Democrats and Communists on the left, and the Austrian Nazi Party on the far right—adopted a new constitution, and governed without parliament. Dollfuss became chancellor, but after only a few months in office, he was assassinated in July 1934 by illegal Austrian Nazis supported by Germany. Dollfuss's successor as chancellor was Kurt Schuschnigg. Schuschnigg and the Fatherland Front ruled the Austrian "corporate state" in close alliance with the always-powerful Catholic Church. After Dolfuss's murder and with Germany threatening to take over Austria, Mussolini made good on his earlier commitment and sent troops to the alpine border between Austria and Italy at Brenner Pass. The chess move worked. Hitler backed down, and Mussolini again promised to support an independent Austro-Fascist state against future encroachment by Nazi Germany. Schuschnigg's Fatherland Front continued to oppose a union with Germany, which it saw as too Prussian and too anti-clerical, contrary to the desire of both many Social Democrats and the illegal Austrian Nazi Party.

Anschluss

The Austrian corporate state muddled on for a few years. Early in 1938, Hitler began to exert renewed pressure on Austria to become a part of "Greater Germany," a goal that he'd laid out thirteen years earlier in *Mein Kampf*. Chancellor Schuschnigg scheduled a plebiscite for Sunday, March 13, for Austrians to vote on whether to remain independent. The plebiscite was preempted when Schuschnigg resigned near midnight on March 11 after being confronted with an impossible ultimatum from Hitler. This time Mussolini, Austria's erstwhile Fascist protector to the south, refused to step in to shield Austria from Nazi Germany to the northwest.

Austrian radio broadcast Schuschnigg's final speech as chancellor on the night of Friday, March 11, 1938. He summarized Hitler's demands to appoint a new cabinet of Nazi ministers in Austria and characterized as lies Hitler's claims that "German" people within Austria were being threatened by left-wing violence. The finale came as a surprise. Despite Hitler's falsehoods, Schuschnigg announced that he would not resist Germany's superior armed force. Hitler could simply walk in and take over Austria. Here is the core of Schuschnigg's speech:

> This day has placed us in a tragic and decisive situation. I have to give my Austrian fellow countrymen the details of the events of today.
>
> The German Government today handed to President Miklas [the Austrian head of state] an ultimatum, with a time limit, ordering him to nominate as chancellor a person designated by the German Government and to appoint members of a cabinet on the orders of the German Government; otherwise German troops would invade Austria.
>
> I declare before the world that the reports launched in Germany concerning disorders by the workers, the shedding of streams of blood, and the creation of a situation beyond the control of the Austrian Government are lies from A to Z. President Miklas has asked me to tell the people of Austria that we have yielded to force since we are not prepared even in this terrible situation to shed blood. We have decided to order the troops to offer no resistance.
>
> So I take leave of the Austrian people with the German word of farewell uttered from the depth of my heart: God protect Austria.[13]

The next morning, Saturday, March 12, German troops crossed Austria's western border unopposed. There, Hitler and other Nazi

---

13 "Anschluss," Spartacus Schoolnet, accessed January 31, 2022, https://spartacus-educational.com/2WWanschluss.htm.

leaders were welcomed with now-infamous popular jubilation. Three days later, on March 15, Hitler made a triumphal entry into Vienna, where he was received joyously by an overwhelming majority of the Austrian population. (They were a fickle group. Current scholarship agrees that if Schuschnigg's plebiscite had been held on March 13, the popular vote would have gone against union with Germany.)

The myth of Austria as Nazism's "first victim" claims that Schuschnigg was forced to capitulate to an external force majeure. This is far from the whole story. Since 1934 the Austrian government had diligently persecuted the workers' parties, including the illegal but formerly mainstream Social Democrats, while the illegal Nazi party remained active, and individuals with open Nazi leanings, like Arthur Seyss-Inquart, served in the government. By 1938 the left no longer had the means to resist right-wing violence. The night before Austria opened its borders to the Wehrmacht, a fifth column of German-supported illegal Nazi cells instigated "pogrom-like riots" Vienna, initiating the violence that "would dominate the city for the following weeks and irreversibly change the lives of those affected by them."[14] Beginning on March 13, the day after German troops occupied Vienna, Jews in the city were seized at random and, among other humiliations, made to scrub painted pro-Schuschnigg election slogans off walls and streets.[15] These incidents were widely reported and piously deplored in the Western press, though no country intervened.

Shortly after the Anschluss, on May 20, the Nuremberg "racial" laws were extended to Austria. Originally enacted in 1935 in Germany, these laws had been gradually broadened during the intervening years, but in Austria they were put into effect all at once.[16] They deprived Jews of their citizenship and basic rights. They defined

---

14   Florian Freund and Hans Safrian, *Expulsion and Extermination: The Fate of the Austrian Jews 1938–1945* (Vienna, Austria: Documentation Center of Austrian Resistance, 1997), 10.

15   Jürgen Matthäus and Mark Roseman, *Jewish Responses to Persecution: 1933–1938*, vol. 1 (Lanham, MD: AltaMira Press, 2010), 278 and 278n8, citing a Jewish World Congress report from Trieste dated April 5, 1938.

16   Matthäus and Roseman, *Jewish Responses*, 449.

a citizen of the Reich to exclude anyone who was not of "German or related blood" and defined who would be considered a Jew based on ancestry as well as religious affiliation. Marriages and extramarital relations between Jews and "Germans" were prohibited. Playing on stereotypes of Jews as rapacious sexual predators, Jews were forbidden from employing any "German" female under age forty-five in their households. To prevent Jews from defensively camouflaging themselves or their apartments, they were prohibited from displaying the Reich flag or colors.[17]

"Emigration or Annihilation"

On June 20, 1938, the *New York Times* printed a seven-column article with the dateline London based on a report from an unnamed correspondent, headlined "Vienna Nazis Widen Drive on Jews; Every Family Reported Suffering." The correspondent wrote:

> Since 1933 the policy of the Reich towards the Jews has been summed up as emigration or annihilation....In Vienna and Austria no vestige of decency or humanity has checked the will to destroy, and there has been an unbroken orgy of Jew-baiting such as Europe has not known since the darkest days of the Middle Ages.
>
> In Czarist Russia pogroms against the Jewish population were frequent, but at least they were intermittent, and the Jews were able to carry on life. In Vienna they are rapidly forced out of every economic activity, and what once was a community outstanding in intellect and culture is being turned into a community of beggars.[18]

---

17 Matthäus and Roseman, *Jewish Responses*, 444–445.

18 "Vienna Nazis Widen Drive on Jews; Every Family Reported Suffering," *New York Times*, June 20, 1938, https://www.nytimes.com/1938/06/20/archives/vienna-nazis-widen-drive-on-jews-every-family-reported-suffering.html.

Once Adolf Eichmann was installed as head of the Central Office for Jewish Emigration in Vienna in August 1938, it took no special insight, no seer-like qualities, for Austrian Jews to understand that the new government's policy was to force them all to leave and as soon as possible: emigration or annihilation.

Emigration was far easier said than done. Aside from psychological resistance and inertia, there were enormous practical barriers. First, Jews in what had become the Ostmark, a province of Greater Germany, had to find some country that would give them a visa allowing emigration. Then they had to obtain a German passport and exit visa and pay confiscatory emigration taxes.

The dehumanizing process has been described over and over by later historians. Here is one example:

> Those who wanted to leave the Ostmark had to spend hours—sometimes an entire day—waiting in line for a passport at the Polizeikommisariat Wehrgasse (Vienna, 5th District), where the authorities often mistreated the applicants....To secure all the necessary documents, one had to pass through the hand[s] of the merciless authorities. Dozens of formalities for every kind of official had to be contended with, and senseless instructions followed.[19]

Eichmann's process was astoundingly effective; it disposed of unwanted Jews and made money for the Reich. One historian described his Central Office for Jewish Emigration as "a conveyor belt system":

> People were systematically processed. They left the office divested of their property but with an emigration visa and a fixed date for leaving the country. If they did not leave the Third Reich within ten days, they were likely to be arrested and deported to a concentration camp.[20]

---

19 Freund and Safrian, *Expulsion and Extermination*, 12–13.

20 Doron Rabinovici, *Eichmann's Jews: The Jewish Administration of Holocaust Vienna, 1938–1945* (Cambridge, UK: Polity Press, 2011), 52.

Eichmann's "Vienna system" was such a success that it was copied in Berlin, Prague, and other cities occupied by Germany.[21]

The Western democracies understood both that the Nazi regime intended to expel former Austria's Jews and that there were nowhere near sufficient numbers of countries that would admit them. The *New York Times*, a voice of moderate conservatism, addressed the conundrum of "impossible immigration" in an article on June 20, 1938:

> The authorities demand rapid and impossible emigration. The Jews would welcome evacuation, but for most it is impossible. Only a few still own any considerable property and they cannot take out even that tithe that hitherto Jews leaving Germany have been able to save. Thousands turn in despair to relatives and friends abroad, beseeching them to obtain permanent or temporary visas. Thousands stand outside the consulates of America, England and other countries, waiting through the night for admission so that they may register their name.

These are the circumstances under which Lilly, still a teenager, and Walter were fortunate enough to escape Vienna, leaving behind their parents and extended families, friends and colleagues, language and culture.

Lilly at School and University

Lilly graduated from Albertgasse Gymnasium in 1937 in what were still normal times. A few stories survive. Her Latin instructor was a fearsome martinet. The girls went to the mountains for a week every winter where they were taught to ski. Their alpine lodgings were terribly cold, so cold that the only way the girls could warm

---

21 Rabinovici, *Eichmann's Jews*. See also Steven Beller, *Antisemitism: A Very Short Introduction* (Oxford, UK: Oxford University Press, 2015), 92 ("Adolf Eichmann's job in Vienna after March 1938 was devoted to forcing Jews to emigrate, while fleecing them of as much of their property as possible.").

their hands was to pee on them. When the girls at Albertgasse took the oral portions of their "Matura" final exams, they wore evening gowns to mark the solemnity of the occasion.

Lilly's life was not all schoolwork. One snapshot that I recall seeing as a kid, probably at my grandparents' apartment, was of my mother dressed as an Austrian army officer holding a cigarette while another officer lights it for her. She is wearing a military greatcoat, gloves, and a cylindrical shako hat with a brim. This playful scene dates from about 1936.

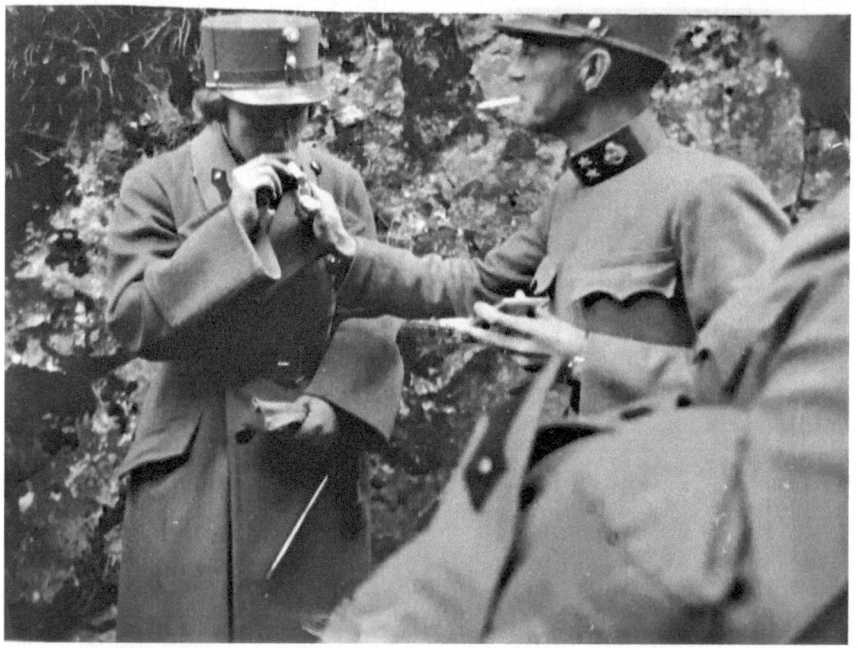

Lilly dressed as an officer.

From a similar military outing, a photo survives of Lilly dressed in peasant costume with a cage of carrier pigeons on her back, Papagena-style. Her father Arthur, in uniform, stands beside her.

A bright, diligent, and mathematically inclined student, Lilly attended the University of Vienna for two terms, fall 1937 and winter 1938, according to her official student booklet. She was expelled along with all the other Jews in April 1938. Even before the official

Chapter 3: Some History: The End of Austria 37

Lilly carrying a cage of carrier pigeons, late 1930s.

expulsion order, harassment by antisemitic German nationalist student groups had made attending university impossible for many Jewish students.²²

Antisemitic changes were made in the secondary schools as well. In May 1938, the year after Lilly had graduated, Albertgasse's students were separated by "race," with Jewish students being assigned to "parallel classes."²³ Among the girls in these divided classes was Edith (née Friedler) Liebenthal, a close family friend during our Jackson Heights days and beyond.

In September 2018, at the age of ninety-four, Edith wrote out her "long-buried memories" of Albertgasse for me, particularly her return to school after the Anschluss:

> The full name of our school was Mädchen-Realgymnasium und Oberlyzeum des Vereines für Realgymnasialen Mädchenunterricht [essentially girls' modern academic high school and upper secondary school of the association for girls' secondary education] in Wien 8, Albertgasse 38. Quite an impressive title. Your mom and I often talked about our

---

22 Rabinovici, *Eichmann's Jews*, 29. Discrimination and violence against Jewish students at Vienna's universities predated the Anschluss. A well-known photograph from 1933 shows Jewish students climbing out the windows of the Julius Tandler Anatomical Institute to escape rampaging German nationalist students. https://geschichte.univie.ac.at/en/articles/terror-against-anatomical-institute-julius-tandler. See also https://geschichte.univie.ac.at/en/articles/expulsion-teachers-and-students-1938 ("Of the 9,180 students at the university in the winter semester of 1937/38, 2,230 students were expelled [in 1938] as 'Jews.'").

23 "Geschichte der Schule," BGRG 8, Albertgasse, accessed March 23, 2022, https://www.grg8.at/HP_GRG8_2016/seit1.html. See also: about 66 percent of the female students had to leave the school in 1938 because of "racial and political persecution" ("Realgymnasium und Wirtschaftskundliches Realgymnasium Feldgasse," Wikipedia, accessed May 26, 2023, https://de.wikipedia.org/wiki/Realgymnasium_und_Wirtschaftskundliches_Realgymnasium_Feldgasse#Schulgeschichte).

common experiences at Albertgasse while strolling down 37th Avenue to 82nd Street [in Jackson Heights] with our kids in tow.

It was March of 1938 and Vienna was now part of Germany. I had just recently turned fourteen, the official age when Jewish education came to an end. We were, however, allowed to finish the school year. I returned to Albertgasse, not knowing what to expect. At first glance it seemed unchanged but soon it became obvious that many teachers were conspicuously absent, among them Dr. Ritter, our Klassenvorstand [homeroom teacher], and Dr. Singer, the dreaded math teacher. New faces could be seen everywhere. All teachers, old and new, wore swastika pins of a certain design that, we learned, indicated that they had been members of the illegal Austrian Nazi Party. Not only the teachers, also the merchants and the man on the street; it seemed that everyone had been a party member.[24] These same people wanted you to believe later that they had been Hitler's first victims. Hah! There was just one old-time teacher who did not wear the pin, Prof. Wahrman, a history teacher whose specialty was ancient history, and she looked the part. It was said she was still a monarchist.

Our old classroom was not the same anymore. It had been divided into two parts with an aisle separating them. Facing the teacher on her right were the Christian students, on her left the Jewish ones. The proportion was roughly fifty-fifty; no surprise considering the eternal Jewish drive for education. There was little, if any, communication between the two groups. Old friendships no longer existed. As the days passed we became aware that two girls had not returned. One, a Jewish

---

24   The Vienna Philharmonic Orchestra recently acknowledged that before the Ansculuss, 20 percent of its members were members of the illegal Nazi party ("4. National Socialism: The Vienna Philharmonic under National Socialism [1938–1945]," Wiener Philharmoniker, accessed December 30, 2022, https://www.wienerphilharmoniker.at/en/orchestra/history/nationalsozialismus#the-first-republic-and-austrofascism-enhancing-references-to-vienna-as-the-city-of-music-and-strengthening-internal-authoritarian-structures-10574).

girl, Marietta, was supposedly dead. Eventually this was confirmed. Her whole family had committed suicide. The other absentee was a puzzle. Liesl was a Christian. Where was she? She had a younger sister in the third grade who clued us in. Their father, a well-known physician in Vienna, had traveled to England to attend a conference and Liesl, his oldest daughter, had begged to be taken along. She never returned to Vienna. Actually she was a *mischling* [person of mixed "German" and non-"German" "race"], a term we just began to understand.

English Classes and an Engagement

Sometime after graduating from Albertgasse, Lilly enrolled in an English course at the University of Vienna. There she met Walter Haim, a fellow student. Walter was seventeen years older than Lilly, but they seem to have quickly established a companionable relationship, going to class, studying, and spending Sundays together. By May 1938, when Walter completed an IKG emigration questionnaire, they had become engaged. Their courtship was so compressed that Lilly did not get to meet all of Walter's immediate family. Hans wrote teasingly on April 30, 1939: "That we don't know Lilly is all in all only your fault, but you can make up for that in New York!" Eight years later, in 1947, Hans's wife Lisl sent Lilly birthday greetings and noted that they had never met in person.

Lilly cannot have felt much instinctive ease with her prospective parents-in-law, whom she would have visited only a few times before leaving for England. If nothing else, there was a generation gap. Walter's parents were two generations older than she was, the age of Lilly's grandmother. Paula, the younger of Walter's two sisters, had been born in 1896, the same year as Lilly's mother, Pauline. Hans was as old as Lilly's father. My mother once described a dinner with my father's parents. They were both immensely old and dignified, she said, Martin looking like George Bernard Shaw and Antoinette like the aged Queen Victoria. They served foods that Lilly was not familiar with, memorably stuffed grape leaves. Lilly could barely choke them down though, unlike Walter, she was not at all a picky eater.

Lilly Gets a UK Visa

Lilly's parents had the luck and means to be able send her to England in the fall of 1938, escaping what, since March 1938, had become "Vienna, Germany." Her father, the major, was a pragmatist and something of a "macher" (someone who got things done). With his urging, and no doubt with some help from the Jewish communities in Vienna and the UK, Lilly obtained the job offer that was essential for a "domestic service" visa. She would go to England as a nanny and tutor for an observant Jewish family. The UK had created the "domestic service" visa category in the 1920s, long before the refugee crush, "to alleviate the chronic shortage of maid servants despite otherwise very strict immigration restrictions."[25] About twenty thousand young Jewish women fled to England this way. There is some anecdotal evidence that British mistresses preferred Austrian to German maids because the Austrians "had a reputation as excellent cooks."[26]

Lilly's German passport was issued in September 1938,[27] and she left a few days later by train. The passport was issued under her formal name of Julianne, though she had been called Lilly in school and by the family from the time she was an infant. German passports for Jews were not yet marked with a large red "J"; that began the following month.

---

25   Suzann Wurm, "Maid Servants in England: Austrian Jewish Women in Emigration 1938–39," Central European Economic and Social History, October 8, 2017, http://central-europeaneconomicandsocialhistory.com/maid-servants-in-england-austrian-jewish-women-in-emigration-193839.

26   Wurm, "Maid Servants in England."

27   This was several months before the Kindertransports (children's transports), which began only after the Kristallnacht pogrom of November 9–10, 1938. In any case, at age nineteen, Lilly would have been too old for the Kindertransports, which accepted children only up to age eighteen. Edith Liebenthal was one of the ten thousand or so Austrian children for whom the Kindertransports were a lifeline to England.

Lilly's UK registration certificate, September 1938.

Lilly arrived at Dover after a sea crossing from France and was admitted on September 30, 1938, looking very much like the young university student that she had been. She paid a mandatory shilling and was issued a Certificate of Registration by the Aylesbury Constabulary bearing her photograph, her "profession or occupation" identified as "Domestic Servant," and noting her English and former addresses. In minor protest against the annexation of Austria into Germany, on the line for "Nationality," Lilly wrote "Austrian (In possession of German Passport)." She left the line for "Previous Nationality (if any)" blank. Those entries were corrected by another hand in red pen, so that her "Nationality" became "German" and "Previous Nationality" "Austrian."

The conditions of entry typed into the registration booklet and underlined in red ink allowed Lilly to work in the UK. She was permitted to remain for one year. This limit could be extended if she continued in domestic service. As further conditions of entry, she had to register with the local police and report any change in address or employment to them and have the details entered into the booklet.

While Lilly was in England, her father, Arthur, sent her several photos of himself. In one, he is sitting comfortably on a bench

Arthur Neuhaus in Austrian uniform with Wehrmacht insignia, early 1938.

in the 9th District wearing a light-colored suit and tie, civilian clothes. According to the caption, he is reading a letter from Walter. There is also a photo of Arthur in uniform. This would have been taken around March or April 1938, shortly after the Anschluss when the Austrian army was immediately incorporated wholesale into the Wehrmacht. A Wehrmacht eagle and swastika are sewn over his right breast pocket, while the collar still retains his Austrian rank insignia. The photo is captioned on the back in Arthur's handwriting, "Don't forget when far away" (Vergiss auch in der Ferne nicht an….). There is no overt mention of the underlying irony—an Austrian, or formerly Austrian, Jewish officer wearing a swastika. Another print of the same photo survives. Dated October 1938, the bottom portion was cut off to remove the German insignia.

Edith Liebenthal commented in an email to me eighty years later, "Your grandfather's picture wearing his Austrian army uniform but with the Wehrmacht insignia on his chest is comical indeed. If it had not been the first sign of the catastrophe to hit him and all of us, it would have been funny, very funny."

PART 2

The Letters Begin

CHAPTER 4

Lilly in England

I have unearthed records with names, dates, and places for the family back into the early 1800s, but their voices begin only in late 1938 with Lilly's letters from London.

The Journey and First Days in England

Once in England, Lilly reported in a letter sent on October 5, 1938,[28] to her fiancé Walter, still in Vienna, that the train journey was "really very unpleasant, so long." While traveling through southeastern Germany, she had had to evade the salacious intentions of a fellow passenger:

> My travel companion, Mr. Pege, talked to me from Wurzburg to Frankfurt, he suggested I get off with him and travel further on the next day. Really! But don't say anything at home, otherwise they will think that I am a sought-after article for girl-traffickers.

From the first, Walter served as her sounding board, her "confessor," because she could not "write the truth to everyone else, that is, especially at home." Lilly's mother in particular had anticipated all

---

28   Lilly generally noted only the day of the week on her letters rather than the whole date. This letter, which was postmarked October 5, 1938, but written in bits during the previous week, is the earliest one that Walter saved.

sorts of trouble, and Lilly wanted to shelter her from the inevitable unpleasantnesses she encountered:

> Don't be angry that I harangue you so, but finally I have to write someone the truth, no!?

On her first weekend in England, Lilly thought back to their Sundays together in Vienna:

> Tomorrow is Sunday, so already a long time that we have been so far from each other, but hopefully, perhaps this also won't last long until we get back together again.

A Short Stay with the Levys

Lilly spent the first two nights in England, Friday to Sunday, at a hostel for Jewish refugees in London. She then moved in with the Levys, the family who had offered her a position as a nanny. They lived in Aylesbury, a sizable town in the South Midlands about fifty miles from London. Observant Jewish families in communities outside Greater Germany had been urged to hire young (even if secular) refugees from Austria and Germany as domestic workers as a good deed, a mitzvah.[29]

Lilly's situation with the Levys did not go well. In that same first letter to Walter, she wrote:

> The house is a pig sty,...everything with the exception of my room. The children, 4, 6, 7, 8, are very cute but also not chemically clean. You see, once again Mutti's premonitions have been proved right, but you know: no word about it!!

---

29 A parallel situation appears in a letter written to Walter by Grete Ullman, perhaps a cousin, in February 1939, addressed to him on the *Queen Mary*. She wrote that she had found a post in Budapest as a nanny to two young children in a religious family. She described the parents as "particularly young, very pious." There are no more saved letters from Grete Ullmann, so I know nothing of her fate or that of her young employers. They applied for immigrant visas to El Salvador between 1942 and 1944 and then disappear from the online records.

[My] stomach...growls just as though possessed because I am fasting today. Which is not a big difference because the food is too nasty for me, but at least it's good for the figure.

Along with the food, the Levys' toilet fell dismally short of Viennese standards:

There isn't even a decent loo, there is a shed with a partitioned area at the other end of the yard, that is all.

Cultural Dissonances

Contemporaries and later historians have noted the cultural incompatibilities between German-speaking Jewish refugees of 1938 and 1939, most of them solidly middle class, and their English employer-hosts. Many of the latter were lower-middle or working class, their forebears having arrived in the UK a generation or two earlier from Eastern Europe, and by and large they had remained religiously observant. The young Austrian and German women who came to work as their maids or nannies tended to be more bourgeois, more assimilated, less pious, better educated, and used to a higher (i.e., continental) standard of living. This was no recipe for harmony.

An editor of the UK's Association of Jewish Refugees recalled the meeting between "a poor Anglo-Jewish family from the East End" and a young refugee that "encapsulated that divide in social class and lifestyle, in Jewishness and religious observance":

After the pogroms of November 1938, the family had taken in a young refugee girl. Expecting "a downtrodden impoverished child," they were surprised when their guest arrived with several cases full of expensive clothing. Her first request was for a hot bath—in a house that probably had no proper bathroom. Worse still, when the family sat down to the Friday evening meal, the girl had never heard the Sabbath blessings. The family...was outraged: "There we are told of the poor Jews in Germany, who are persecuted because they are Jews, and now we learn to our dismay that they still lived in comfort and had no Jewish bonds though their Jewishness was the reason of their plight."[30]

Historian Walter Laqueur, himself a member of the "Generation Exodus" that he wrote about, commented on the culture shock that many young, bourgeois refugees from Austria and Germany experienced when they arrived in the English homes where they had come to work as servants:

> They had been accustomed at home to some elementary comforts that were not yet known in middle-class (let alone working-class) Britain, such as central heating. Nor were indoor toilets frequently found in working-class quarters.... They found the food virtually inedible (except Cadbury chocolate, which they preferred to the German brands).[31]

Moreover, these young Austrian women were "not ideal domestics" in class-bound England:

> Very often they had been of a higher social standing and better educated than those they were working for in Britain. They felt that they were cleverer than their mistresses and when upbraided they were likely to talk back. They forgot that they had been hired to wash dishes, not to play the piano.[32]

Jews whose grandparents or great-grandparents had come from the east—Galicia, Poland, and what had been the Habsburg crown lands—were no novelty in the Vienna of the 1930s, but after a couple of

---

30 Anthony Grenville, "Anglo-Jewry and the Jewish Refugees from Nazism," *AJR Journal* 12, no. 12 (December 2012), https://ajr.org.uk/wp-content/uploads/2018/02/2012_December.pdf.

31 Walter Laqueur, *Generation Exodus: The Fate of Young Jewish Refugees from Nazi Germany* (New York: I. B. Tauris, 2001), 193–194.

32 Laqueur, *Generation Exodus*, 201–202.

generations, their communities had evolved quite differently from those in England. Jewish migrants to Vienna had by and large become secularized and risen into the middle or at least lower-middle classes. They also had abandoned ancestral Yiddish for standard (Austrian) German. Historian Robert Wistrich identified the cultural and economic roots of the class differences between Jewish communities in Vienna and London:

> Vienna did not…provide a fertile ground for the emergence of a working-class, Yiddish-speaking subculture such as existed in the far-flung Russian and Polish Jewish diasporas at the turn of the century—from Vilna and Minsk to London's East End.…The dominance of the German language and *Kultur* in Vienna, and the absence of a Jewish proletariat economically rooted in the clothing industry and the sweatshops, seemed to preclude this development.[33]

Lilly's uneasy experience with the Levys echoed these cultural and class dissonances.

Living with the Levys

Things looked a bit brighter to Lilly on her first morning at the Levys' house. She wrote to Walter:

> The story is not at all so bad. Today "She" brought me tea in bed and said that she does not want me to do housework but to teach the children manners, do homework, instruct, etc. They had a *boarding house* in London, became kosher and have been here [in the Midlands] for 1 ½ years.

Math rather than languages had been Lilly's strong suit at school and university, but now she had to translate that knowledge into English. She complained to Walter:

---

33 Wistrich, *The Jews of Vienna*, 1234.

Although I give diligent *lessons*, you can't imagine at all how hard mathematics expressions are in English.

Lilly referred to Paul Kurz twice in this early letter, though not by name. First she asked Walter to "tell your brother-in-law that I will write to him first when I have a secure income, and now I am looking at unemployment!" and she included him in a broad question about the families' uncertain future:

Say, what sort of plans and hopes do my parents have, your sister and brother-in-law? (and we ???)

During these first days, Lilly was so strapped for cash that she asked relatives of her future in-laws in England for small loans. She even borrowed £3.10 from Gertrud Wilheim, a cousin of Paul's. She didn't repay it, which rankled with Gertrud. Nearly two years later, in April 1940, a fur broker in New York who identified himself as Gertrud's brother-in-law sent Walter a letter on Gertrud's behalf, asking Walter to repay the money that she "had advanced to your fiancée" back in 1938 because Gertrud, by then in Sao Paulo, needed funds to help her husband set up a photography studio.[34] The disparate individuals and scattered locations in this little vignette offer a diaspora microcosm.

Despite having been brought tea in bed, it took Lilly only a day or so to start extricating herself from the Levys. She wrote to Dorothy Canfield in London, whose earlier job offer as a maid Lilly had turned down, asking if a place was still available. She was very pleased when Mrs. Canfield answered quickly and arranged to meet her the following weekend, seeding her account to Walter with English words:

---

34 Gertrud's husband, Peter Scheier (1908, Germany–1979, Germany) became a respected photographer in Brazil. See, e.g., https://www.academia.edu/42763402/Peter_Scheier_and_Marcel_Gautherot_Bras%C3%ADlia_Lyric_and_Epic. For more information, see also https://ims.com.br/titular-colecao/peter-scheier/; and https://www.academia.edu/41934089/Peter_Scheier_A_modern_photographer_and_the_idea_of_the_city.

She writes that what I did is very *unusual*. But that she *sympathized* with me and in short, if she can meet me on Saturday or Sunday in Aston Clinton [the area where the Levys lived], though she is already in negotiations with another *maid*.

Lilly's boldness paid off. She wrote to Walter:

But now I get to the serious side of life. So listen *prick your ears (or rather eyes)*! I answered her immediately, *nervous tension ect. ect.*,[35] but only shortly, to which she responded on the same day with 3 degrees friendly. The first sentence: *Now you have explained further I understand more clearly....your appointment suits us very well* and if she can't come, she will telegraph....Now I hope and will try *"to make an impression."* So today it will be decided at 6.

Looking back in the midst of a legal squabble over Lilly's wages, Dorothy's husband Alexander Canfield recalled that first encounter. They met, he wrote in a letter:

...at the Bell Hotel, Aylesbury on 8.10.38 when she told us she was very unhappy in her present situation and begged us to take her even if it was "au pair."

Still, Lilly was quite definite about what she would and would not do—no floor scrubbing or window washing, according to Alexander's letter.

In the meantime, Lilly received an eight-page letter from Walter. She called him a wonder, a "golden boy," and asked him to continue writing as "the letters from you are my entire evening reading."

Escape from the Levys was finalized rather quickly. On October 9, 1938, Lilly moved to Mr. and Mrs. Canfield's residence in Croydon,

---

35 Lilly consistently used the abbreviation "ect." rather than "etc." I found this error amusing, as Lilly's schooling had included years of mandatory Latin, and have retained this quirk in the translations of her letters.

a town south of London and the site of England's first international airport. She reported to the Metropolitan Police on October 12, who duly entered the details into her registration booklet.

CHAPTER 5

At the Canfields

Dorothy and Alexander Canfield were English through and through. When I was a child, they sent wonderful Christmas presents—a pearl shell pen and pencil set, a box of Winsor & Newton watercolors, a set of stationery in a pigskin case, for which I dutifully wrote thank-you notes addressed to Aunt Dorothy and Uncle Alex. Alexander Canfield visited once in New York when I was still in grade school (though I cannot recall a single detail of what he looked like) and gave me a white beaded evening purse with embroidered butterflies. He worked for Schweppes, then a thoroughly British company. A family skeleton to be whispered about was that Dorothy Canfield's mother at one time had been "in service"—that is, a maid.

Lilly in Croydon, November 1938.

In November 1938 Lilly went to a photographer in Croydon and sent copies of a portrait back to her family and Walter in Vienna. No longer a schoolgirl, she looked elegant in a tailored top, her hair permed.

Lilly regarded Dorothy Canfield as a "snob" but found her husband, Alex, much more down to earth. In June 1939 she wrote about his having been chosen to represent his employer at some local festivities for King George VI's birthday celebrations:

Yesterday there were ____ [?] *luncheons* in honor of the king's birthday, and Mr. Canfield was called to one as the representative of his company "Pascall." She is really such a *snob*, you can imagine how proud she is of him now!!! He's not at all like that.

One of Lilly's letters from February 1939 offers a possible answer to the question of why Dorothy Canfield hired a foreign maid: her father was, or had been, Jewish. Lilly wrote to Walter:

Sunday evening: this afternoon their parents were here, now at 7:30 p.m. they left and as usual left me alone with the dishes. Her [Dorothy Canfield's] mother is very nice, reminds me of yours. One can see the Jewish origins in her father, that is, I see it, but here in England one takes no notice of that!

Lilly noted Dorothy Canfield's Jewish connection casually, so it seems not to have been something that had been hidden from her or that Lilly had just discovered. Perhaps not only the pious Levy family and Arde Bulova, the watch magnate in Queens (more on him later), had volunteered to help Jews escape Nazi Germany, but also Dorothy Canfield, the suburban English housewife.

Lilly's time with the Canfields began very brightly. She reported to Walter in October 1938, "Things are going wonderfully well for me," and described how the Canfields had taken her on a weekend driving trip to an A-list of historic sites—Eton, Windsor, Runnymede, Hampton Court. I was surprised to learn that this wasn't her first trip to England. Lilly apparently had visited the previous year, probably on a student trip. After the drive with the Canfields through Eton and Windsor, she wrote, "A year ago I was here too, but at that time I hadn't even dreamed of some things." Lilly was amused by the young gentlemen students at Eton in their top hats: "I tell you the *Eton boys* with their *tophats* are hilarious! Short pants, *sweater*, but *tophat!*"

She was sufficiently impressed by Hampton Court, a grand palace that had been built by Cardinal Wolsey in the early sixteenth century and was subsequently a residence of English monarchs from Henry VIII through George II, to write, "Now for the first time I will take note of history!" Lilly had not been much of a history student. In her first term at the University of Vienna, she got a grade of only two out of five in a course on the ideological and historical bases of the Austrian state. In contrast, she earned a five in differential and integral calculus.

The next weekend Lilly went with the Canfields to Streatham, the Victoria and Albert Museum, the Albert Memorial, Albert Hall, ending with a gallop through Westminster Abbey. Lilly used the little time she had at the Abbey to visit Poet's Corner, though "in the hurry I could not find Chaucer." She asked how her parents were progressing with the English lessons that Walter was giving them ("Are they actually learning something?") and alerted him to a tricky homonym:

> If you ask what "mandeln" means in English, then they say *tonsils* and not *almonds, silly fool*.

Lilly cautioned Walter about the traffic in England: "But you could not drive here, I tell you that! Such traffic, indescribable." She did not mention left- versus right-hand driving, which had political implications. Vehicles had driven on the left side of the road in Austria (except for Tyrol) until the Anschluss, when the Nazi government decreed an immediate switch to right-hand driving, consistent with the rest of Germany.

In her next letter of October 1938, Lilly let Walter in on "a very big, big secret" and urged him, "Don't tell anyone, really no one at all." She had signed up to take the Cambridge External English exam. She was very happy about having committed herself to that goal:

> Thus already paid, so no more going back! Please don't say that this is imbecility, I have such an *immense* inner happiness from it. It cost 30 shillings, my entire money, but I don't regret it. At least the time here is not <u>only</u> a wait, but I can

achieve something also—hopefully, I would be heartbroken if it went wrong.

The test is on the 6 and 7th of December. Results a month later (cruelty to animals noted by the way). But I am as happy as a small child.

Three texts were assigned for the exam: Shakespeare's *Julius Caesar* and two more modern ones, John Galsworthy's novel *The Man of Property* and Shaw's recent play *St. Joan*, which had premiered in 1923, only three years after Joan's belated canonization. Walter sent Lilly a small-format 1924 Tauchnitz edition of *St. Joan* in early November 1938. Decades later, this volume of *St. Joan* remained a fixture in the family bookcase, and I first read it in junior high school. Though published in Leipzig, the book was entirely in English, including an extensive preface by Shaw, with my mother's shorthand notes (completely illegible) penciled in the margins.

Lilly, who knew how to be an effective student, devised a study schedule. She realized that being able to study in safety in England was a luxury compared to Walter's and the family's situation in Vienna:

Now I need your *outlines* again! I have already made myself a lesson plan, every day something different. Nice of the Canfields that they allow it, no? A shame that we can't study together again! Most important, I feel so mean at times. I sit here in England, things are going well for me, and you....

During these early weeks, Lilly wrote to Walter every few days. On October 22, her topics were visa issues and worry about her mother. Mutti's letters made Lilly feel "very desperate" as she deduced from them how "really terribly miserable" her mother must be back in Vienna. Lilly was keeping up with international immigration politics and wrote that an agreement was about to be signed raising the American quota for Germans, which then included former

Austrians, to twenty-five thousand per year. (The actual number was a bit over twenty-seven thousand per year.) She asked Walter whether her father had filled out the initial form for a US visa, as "I believe that there would now be a place."

On matters other than her helpless inability to do anything for her parents, Lilly remained solidly practical. She didn't mince words about her view that no more help was to be had from Arde Bulova, a businessman in New York who had provided affidavits of support for her and Walter. The Haim family had then asked him for additional affidavits, but Lilly disagreed with that tactic: "No well is inexhaustible." She was willing to consider just about any escape, even to remotest Africa:

> So many are now talking about Tanganyika as a possibility, please—I know you have a lot to do—but perhaps you can find out, for the moment, for my parents and your brother-in-law, until we can bring them to America, *if* and *when* we are there.

In the fall of 1938, Lilly still hoped that her own and Walter's American visas would come through in time for them to travel together. She wanted to be frugal about their next steps too:

> If it isn't <u>very</u> premature, I would like to say the following to you about the journey. The crossing on an ordinary ship is about £20, on the *Queen Mary* £30, so why? In any case we won't be luxury travelers.

She closed with the reassurance, "Walter, I think a lot about you now."

A couple of days later, Lilly sent Walter a clipping from the London *Daily Telegraph* with the headline, "Roosevelt's Policy on Palestine—Open Door for Jews." The short article read:

> President Roosevelt's anxiety to prevent any curtailment of Jewish immigration to Palestine was disclosed by Senator

Wagner after an interview with the President at his Hyde Park home yesterday.

"The President is greatly concerned about Palestine," he said, "and he favours its continued use as a Jewish National home without limitation.

"He is watching the situation from day to day and will do everything in his power to prevent limitations being placed on immigration."

After seeing the article with its flicker of hope, Mrs. Canfield had phoned the Palestine Information Service, but what they told her was discouraging. Legal immigration to Palestine was out of practical reach. The British government required intending immigrants to Palestine put up £1,000 (that is, fifty times the cost of a regular ship ticket from the UK to New York) or obtain a British subject as a sponsor. Still, Lilly urged Walter to find out what he could:

Please inquire immediately about Palestine and you can use the Canfields as an English reference or guarantor everywhere....

At the same time, Lilly was forging ahead with her preparation for the Cambridge English exam:

I am already studying well for the test. I have already read through Caesar, the devil should fetch him—English—and taken notes. Say, what can they ask about that? Go, please find out which battle it takes place after. And I have already looked at a dictation from 1936: A mistake *indefinitely* I wrote donkeys! Today I am doing a translation, but it is horribly difficult [sauschwer]!

In Vienna Lilly's father had had some sort of "shock again about retirement" from the army. She prescribed increased English lessons, advising Walter to "give him a lot to study, so that he will be distracted." Arthur would have been one of many career military officers in his situation. After absorbing the Austrian army into the Wehrmacht after the Anschluss, the Nazi government then forcibly retired officers who were Jewish or considered too loyal to the former government.[36] Jewish officers in particular were then deprived of part of their pensions.

On the positive side, Lilly had used her day off to visit Viennese connections in London:

> Sunday afternoon I was in London with the Mayers[37] and walked in Kensington Garden. I am just happy if I can speak German and get Viennese cooking! But toi toi toi I really can't complain.

Lilly also asked about Paul's emigration hopes for Australia:

> What is happening with your brother-in-law's Australia plan?

Settling In

By the end of October the first euphoria had worn down, and Lilly wrote about her difficulties studying in the Canfields' house. Whenever she sat down to study or work on a translation, "the fireplace needs coal, or it is time for a snack, ect., ect., and you know how disturbing it is and I cannot say: quiet, I am studying now!!!!" London was still exciting, though, its streets and landmarks resonant with associations from Lilly's reading:

> Yesterday midday I was in London, Mutti can tell you additional *details* because I can't repeat the entire litany again,

---

36 Walter Maass, *Country without a Name: Austria under Nazi Rule 1938–1945* (New York: Frederick Ungar Publishing, 1979), 21.

37 Fritz Mayer, his wife Julie, and their two young daughters were living in Golders Green, London. Fritz was a second cousin of Pauline Neuhaus, though Lilly wrote about him as her uncle.

> it is <u>too</u> complicated. But take note, I went by foot from Victoria to Marble Arch: Grosvenor Place, Park Lane. The entire time I had to think of the Forsythes, and imagine *Stanhope Gate*, it really exists, I always believed that dear Galsworthy invented it! Mostly if I go walking in London, it seems so funny to me, like a museum. I look forward to each cornerstone!

London, Lilly wrote, was "the city of my dreams." I read this as an ironic reference to an old, unabashedly sentimental song that glorified Vienna: "Wien, du Stadt meiner Träume" (Vienna, City of My Dreams).[38] A month later, Lilly still felt the same excitement about London:

> I feel always so wonderful in Piccadilly or Hyde Park Corner, and now I can already say that I know it a very little bit.

Lilly noted tartly that Walter as a male should not have a problem obtaining passage to America quickly from the Jewish aid organization which was then based at Woburn House in London: "They only make difficulties for girls, saying that they should remain there and work, and their permits [allowing them to work as domestic servants] will be extended." Woburn House, and the subsequent location at Bloomsbury House, figure large in refugee accounts. Before the war, Woburn House in central London housed the main office of the Board of Deputies of British Jews, as well other Jewish refugee aid organizations.[39] Partly because of its unavoidable red tape, partly because of the impossibility of its overwhelming task, it was viewed with great ambivalence by the multitudes who sought help there:

---

38 "Rudolf Sieczy," Wikipedia, accessed January 19, 2022, https://en.wikipedia.org/wiki/Rudolf_Sieczy%C5%84ski. The song was written in 1914.

39 "Bloomsbury House," Kitchener Camp, accessed January 19, 2022, http://www.kitchenercamp.co.uk/research/bloomsbury-house/.

Woburn House, to some extent then, symbolised escape and rescue from National Socialist Germany. Almost inevitably, perhaps, it also became known for delays and bureaucracy as the numbers of people trying to leave increased, especially after the events of November 1938....

In fact, by December 1938, Woburn House was receiving around 1,500 letters and 1,000 people calling in person at the offices each day. By the end of March this had risen to 17,000 letters and around 6,000 personal interviews per week. By July 1939, over 400 staff were receiving 21,000 letters a week....[40]

Lilly ended her letter in late November with the usual fatalistic comment, "But we will see," then added with an edge, "the question is only <u>what</u> we will see."

In Vienna Walter regularly visited his prospective in-laws, or at least his mother-in-law. Seven months after the Anschluss, the stream of emigrants from Vienna was hollowing out families and social circles, leaving those who could not emigrate increasingly isolated and anxious. Lilly wrote that fall:

> And I am also very happy that you go so often to Mutti, the poor thing is certainly very very much alone and lonesome. It is really terrible for her when one after the other steams away, and her hopes unfortunately are not very good. But Walter, if we two once are somewhere they simply <u>must</u> follow, agreed?!

Lilly's ambiguous position as a maid vs. lady's companion was a sensitive topic, and she tried to keep her disappointment hidden from her mother. One day in November, she visited the Tate Gallery with the Canfields, but the next evening they went off to the theater without her. Lilly wrote:

---

40 "Bloomsbury House," accessed July 25, 2022, https://kitchenercamp.co.uk/research/bloomsbury-house/.

Your letter to Mr. C[anfield] also arrived, but they are at the theater, I am alone. Don't tell Mutti, otherwise she will perhaps be annoyed.

The world seemed to be proceeding normally on November 4, the eve of Guy Fawkes Day, a quintessentially British holiday. Neighborhood children had been soliciting pennies to buy firecrackers and materials to construct a large bonfire and flammable dummy of Guy Fawkes, the traitor who had attempted to blow up Parliament with barrels of gunpowder in 1605. There were no particular signs that foreshadowed war. Lilly wrote:

I just came home from the barber and beauty shop, sat at the table, and Mrs. Canfield said, "*O, I am awfully sorry, I forgot to tell you there is a letter from Walter.*" So I devoured the sausages and your letter together....

Today it is *Guy Fawkes day* here, everywhere there are fireworks and the children have been coming already for two weeks: "*Anything for the Guy!*"

Lilly was not pleased with English texts that she had to read and translate for the Cambridge exam. At the moment, Galsworthy was not a favorite. Following the Victorian tradition, his novels were long doorstoppers. She complained, "I certainly will never get finished with *The* "blessed" *Man of Property*. It attracts like a liverwurst."

CHAPTER 6

Kristallnacht and Beyond

On November 9, 1938, Lilly was in a good mood, girlish and chattering. The previous day she had written a second stiffly formal thank-you letter to her future mother-in-law Antoinette Haim, and now she crowed to Walter about her English progress and translations:

> Eetsch! Mrs. Canfield said that my translation was better, eetsch! No joke, she really said it....But you, sloppy-Joe [Schlampertatsch], you made a blunder: *selfcontroll* [sic] is properly Selbstbeherrschung and not Selbstkontrolle. Are you crying, that you have a secret grudge against me because I always knew....

There was nothing new, and she counseled optimism:

> But hope hope hope is all that one has. Be very well, count my letters only a little longer and many kisses from your Lilly.

While it was a sunny November in England, the situation had become critically worse for the Jews throughout Greater Germany, including Vienna. The Kristallnacht pogrom of November 9–10, 1938, began on the day that Lilly mailed this letter. Two days later, on November 11, which coincided with the twentieth anniversary of the armistice that had ended the Great War, British newspapers reported on shocking riots and destruction across Greater Germany, complete with photographs.⁴¹ The right-leaning London *Times* ran an article titled "Nazi Attacks on Jews—Orgy of Hitler Youth—Synagogues Burnt—Destruction and Plunder," but relegated it to page 14 rather than giving it space on the first page. The London *Times* reported specifically: "In Vienna the synagogues were blown up with bombs and thousands of Jews were arrested." The *Times* also wrote, without pinpointing any source or location, "Army officers in uniform did try to bring the fanatics to reason but were forced to leave because of threats."⁴²

Lilly would have read these news reports at breakfast in Croydon, and on November 11 she sent Walter a one-sentence letter:

> I haven't had any news from you in for very long, please write immediately.

The next day, November 12, a reassuring letter arrived from Walter in Vienna; everyone in the two families was okay. Lilly wrote back immediately:

> I can hardly tell you how thankful I am to you for your letter. Now at least I cry because yesterday morning you all were healthy and together. God protect you [pl.] further. Your letter arrived like a deliverance from the last two days of shaking from fear for you [pl.] and self-reproaches, I can't tell how you must feel. Now after the receipt of the letter I am completely shattered, as if after a difficult, difficult operation.

After being reassured that Walter and the families had come through the November pogrom, Lilly's letters returned to the

---

41 See, e.g., Richard Nelsson, "From the Archive: Kristallnacht," *The Guardian*, November 8, 2013, https://www.theguardian.com/theguardian/from-the-archive-blog/2013/nov/08/kristall-nacht-guardian-archive-1938, and "Daily Express Report on Kristallnacht, November 11, 1938," Facing History and Ourselves, accessed January 19, 2022, https://www.facinghistory.org/resource-library/text/daily-express-report-kristallnacht-november-11-1938.

42 "Nazi Attacks on Jews—Orgy of Hitler Youth—Synagogues Burnt—Destruction and Plunder," *Times*, November 11, 1938.

dominant themes of the approaching Cambridge English exam and frustrations with the US visa process.

Piecing Together the November Pogrom

November 9–10, 1938, remained a lasting memory for Walter and his family. During that horrific night, all but one of Vienna's synagogues were burnt to rubble, and about 6,500 Jews were arrested there, with 3,700 of them sent to Dachau.[43] Nine years later, in November 1947, when the Haim siblings were dispersed across three continents, Walter wrote to his brother Hans about the date. Hans acknowledged his mixed emotions:

> A couple of hours ago a letter arrived from Paula of November 10th, no particular contents....Paula also recalled November 10, 1938, in her letter. I believe that in my life I will not forget how our Mama told me by telephone of your arrest and at the <u>same instant</u> you rang at my apartment door!! We thank God that we are in a position to be able to remember that! Unfortunately the situation in the entire world today is not very pleasant. One comes always more often to the question of whether it was worth it to survive all this muck?!

Hans's questioning the value of their quite miraculous survival reflected widespread feelings of "powerlessness" and "rootlessness." Hannah Arendt wrote in the introduction to her 1951 study *The Origins of Totalitarianism* that after the war, people felt alienated and helpless:

> Two world wars in one generation, separated by an uninterrupted chain of local wars and revolutions, followed by no peace treaty for the vanquished and no respite for the victor, have ended in the anticipation of a third World War between the two remaining world powers....Under the most

---

43 Price, *Objects of Remembrance*, 28nn10–12.

diverse conditions and disparate circumstances, we watch the development of the same phenomena—homelessness on an unprecedented scale, rootlessness to an unprecedented depth....

It is as though mankind had divided itself between those who believe in human omnipotence (who think that everything is possible if one knows how to organize masses for it) and those for whom powerlessness has become the major experience of their lives.

Although I don't recall his ever mentioning it, Kristallnacht in Vienna could have been the actual locus of the story that my father told me once which he said, or I assumed, took place in Italy. The story is that he had been picked up with a number of others by the Fascist police when one of the policemen looked at him and saw that he was—what? middle class? educated (kultiviert, ausgebildet)? a foreigner (if this story really took place in Italy rather than Vienna)? not a "typical" Jew? not political? In any case, the policeman covertly motioned him to go, to get away from the site of the roundup and not let himself be caught again. This would fit with Hans's account of Kristallnacht in his 1947 letter, that after their mother learned somehow that Walter had been arrested, he suddenly appeared at Hans's apartment and found shelter there.

Recently I came across credible evidence that despite Walter's assurances in November 1938 that the families were all well, Lilly's father, Arthur Neuhaus, had been one of the approximately 7,800 men caught up in the Kristallnacht sweeps, and he had remained imprisoned for more than two months. In August 1953, Adolf Adler, a Viennese retiree who helped Arthur, Arthur's brother Rudolf Neuhaus, and later Walter successfully negotiate the Austrian pension bureaucracy, wrote to Rudolf in connection with Arthur's recently filed pension application. Adler did not understand why Arthur had not claimed compensation for his unjust imprisonment:

> From the enclosed copy I understand that your brother was in custody from Nov. 10, [19]38 until January 18, 1939, and [in response to the question whether] under Section 15/6 "compensation has been or will be applied for" your brother wrote the word <u>No.</u> Why? 1800 schillings, which in my opinion he could receive, is still more than £72.—He could amend this under the related article about compensation for false imprisonment and civil servants.

Adler was correct, the details confirmed by handwritten documents in the Austrian State Archives. Arthur eventually filed a claim for compensation with the Austrian government based on his having been imprisoned for these nine weeks. He also argued that the experience had caused him to become disabled and unable to work afterwards. After much delay, Arthur's basic claim for compensation was approved, though the portion asserting future inability to work was denied. A greater surprise is that nothing in Lilly's contemporaneous letters suggest that she knew that her father had been incarcerated. Correspondence from the Neuhaus and Haim families in Vienna must have been strictly self-censored to hide those events. Decades later, no mention was ever made in my hearing that my grandfather had been victimized this way by the Nazi regime.

1939 Begins

Walter sent Lilly some sort of little New Year's present, perhaps chocolate, that she was pleased to have in the midst of English dietary blandness. On January 2, 1939, she filled Walter in on the details of her daily life and letter-writing situation:

> Your letter of Friday arrived this morning together with the mail, but you know that was not necessary, we don't live in biblical times anymore: an eye for an eye, a tooth for a tooth. Nothing would be delicious after all these paprika and rice

puddings, so warmest thanks. And I have kept two pieces for a "uniting meal" [Vereinigungsmahl] in some small row boat harbor! So I have to answer all the questions quickly otherwise you will send them to me again, so: certainly, I send most of the letters late because I don't have time to write earlier. Say, has your neuralgia or whatever increased? But take care that you are healthy on the 13th [the date of Walter's visa interview]...!

She also reported on the Canfields' continuing financial crisis and Mrs. Canfield's trip on her behalf to the US consulate:

The Canfield thing looks very bleak. I believe it will be really serious around the beginning of February. If I have everything in order, good, if not I believe I will have to change jobs. Today in any case she is at the Consulate, believes that she can get something done with charm, which is quite impossible, but I wasn't able to tell her that, though gave her exact *instructions*. Because finally, God willing, the broom will shoot.[44] And then as the last hope, there is always B[ulova]'s letter *if* and *when* it arrives.

She ended with New Year's wishes:

So, Walter, for the New Year I wish you exactly the same that I wish for myself and reverse. With a bit of luck, sooner or later, we will be in the USA.

The next day's letter was taken up with visa disappointments and slivers of information:

Mrs. C[anfield] was at the consulate yesterday but was not admitted without an appointment. In a very decent manner

---

44   This is an eastern European Jewish proverb counseling faith in a possible miracle: If God wills, the broom will shoot and water will flow from the rock.

Chapter 6: Kristallnacht and Beyond

she went there again today and has brought the following information:

They <u>insist</u> on the *statement* from Bulova. (Should you perhaps telegraph to speed it up, or should I?) But it would be easier if you made a *sworn affidavit*—and <u>immediately</u> [underlined five times]—that you will marry me in America as soon as it is legally possible. Single people receive the visa only for 4 months—I haven't heard anything about that. They said if a *satisfying statement* comes <u>soon</u> from B[ulova], it is <u>possible</u> that I can still make the *Volendam* [the ship where Lilly had reserved a berth to New York]—if they still have a place for me. So please: 1.) by return mail: a *sworn affidavit* that you will marry me as soon as legally possible,

2.) nip at B[ulova's] heels. Do you know that my greatest fear now is that B[ulova] will lose patience and let me go whistle. You <u>must</u> telegraph me on the 13th. God grant that you will get yours [i.e., your US visa].

She ended with an admonition:

Please finally write a couple of lines to Mrs. C[anfield].

There was no news two days later, though Lilly was hopeful about Walter's chances for his visa. The Canfields' financial difficulties seemed to have eased, and the marriage was becoming more of a reality:

Here everything is really at a dead end, I can't do anything and nothing moves, but in my deepest heart I am really not without hope, I believe completely that we will all *eventually* land in *America*, only unfortunately not as soon as I had hoped, although even that is not impossible, only unfortunately not probable. I am terribly excited about the 13th. Walter, you must telegraph me immediately when you know something definite, please. I'll keep fingers crossed in any case, it's a week from tomorrow. The things with the Canfields have calmed down a bit now, if they leave here, which is not yet certain, then it won't be until summer. So there is no immediate danger for me at the moment. I am very glad about that because that would have made me crazy in addition to all the visa problems. Now I am quite glad that I haven't written to the parents about it, since you know Mutti, she would have been frightfully upset. If only things could be cleared up as quickly as this problem. But slowly and surely is better than quickly and nothing, right? I believe it would be better now if we give Bulova a nice amount of time and he makes a detailed affidavit than hurry hurry and it still isn't sufficient again. Will you wait for me at the peace statue and wave!—but I won't buy a [wedding] ring, bring it along with you!!!!

Lilly's finances remained slim, but having her hair done was essential:

Tomorrow I will go to the hairdresser, a deep hole in my wallet, but it is necessary.

Walter's US Visa

In early January 1939, Lilly traveled to London to visit the Mayers and came back with some positive news:

Pay attention now: yesterday I was at my uncle Fritzl M[ayer]'s house and of course recounted to him my whole affidavit story and complained about my sorrows. First he knows the people of Bulova (first-class German, what!) and said that he will certainly answer, only he is afraid that he has prepared <u>very</u> many affidavits, which would of course be disastrous for me. But second, he knows the American general consul <u>personally</u> from Berlin, who currently is the general consul for all of

Germany, and he promised me today to write to him asking him to approve my affidavit. That <u>could</u> certainly be very helpful under the circumstances and accelerate this. But of course I don't hope for too much from it. In any case it seems that Mrs. Canfield's [fortunetelling] cards and her mother are right: we have come to a *hitch* and everything should settle down again. She even claims that we will travel <u>together</u>.

As for the wedding, Lilly wrote that she was prepared to spend sixpence for "a wedding ring from Woolworth," but "only <u>after</u> the receipt of the visa." She closed with a lighthearted riff on the geometry of "toi toi toi squared and cubed."

Walter was doing his part in Vienna, sending copies and originals of the visa documents, though they were still waiting for Bulova's response, while Walter's all-important visa interview was approaching. Lilly wrote on January 11:

Yesterday evening your letter with the two copies came with the regular mail and this morning the airmail letter with the three original documents! MOO MOO MOO, though why airmail takes longer than usual is a bit of a riddle to me. In any case the documents are resting in my portfolio and I am waiting now all the more eagerly for Bulova's answer. WILL he write? I hope so but it isn't a sure thing. You will receive this letter in the morning before the medical examination, and I wish you ferociously to break a leg [the German saying for good luck is literally "break your neck and leg"]! I also will fast on Friday because I couldn't on Sunday, and perhaps that will help you a bit! But it could go wrong. Can one bring the documents later? Hopefully you will get them really soon, so that at least you will be able to leave on the 28th according to the itinerary. How long can you make a stopover in Holland? So, *dear*, lots of luck for Friday, and I will be thinking quite hard about you.

The next day, January 12, brought a large piece of good fortune. Walter had applied for a visitor's visa at the UK consulate in Vienna so that he could spend a few days with Lilly en route to New York. This was a long shot. Back in November, a cousin of Walter's in London had warned Lilly that "it is now out of the question to get a visitor's permit," mentioning that another cousin who had emigrated to America had been unable to obtain a UK visitor's visa and so could not leave the ship when it docked in Southampton. Contrary to all expectations, the UK consulate in Vienna approved Walter's application for a visitor's visa, a near impossibility at that time for intending Jewish emigrants. Lilly was elated and sent him an airmail postcard:

> Walter, *dear*, congratulations. I really hadn't thought that they would give it to you. Starting from the *Home Office*, everyone said "impossible." So you see, if God wills, the broom will shoot. Now I think that each telephone call is from the American consulate, but something like that happens only once. And B[ulova] still doesn't write.
>
> Mrs. C[anfield] said she will give me the three days free when you come. So now only get the American visa and then we are so far along!!!!

In a postscript, she reminded Walter again of the expected politesse: "If you got the visa through the C[anfield]s, then write to them!!!!"

On January 13, a second visa miracle took place. Walter passed the mandatory medical examination and received his visa from the US consulate in Vienna, quota immigrant visa (QIV) number 21240, based on the affidavit of support from Arde Bulova. This was the same affidavit that the US consulate in London rejected for Lilly. He was scheduled to leave Vienna at the end of January, two weeks after the visa was issued, and spend three days in London before boarding the *Queen Mary*.

Walter also had been corresponding with a Morris Rudof, an older Russian émigré in Los Angeles, who had arranged for an affidavit and letter from the Hotel Lafayette in support of his visa application. On January 15, 1939, Walter sent Rudof a heartfelt letter of thanks in English by (expensive) registered airmail:

> I do not find words to thank you for your noble deed. It shows such a splendid generosity—one feels Humanity still alive.
>
> I am happy to inform you that I received, yesterday noon, the American visa....
>
> Please believe me that it is quite impossible for me to express in a letter how very, very thankful I am, and shall remain to you; and I only hope that I shall have an occasion to speak to you personally, some day, be it for a few minutes only....
>
> P.S. If there is an occasion, may I ask you, please, to convey my very best thanks to the Manager of Hotel Lafayette?

This letter must have been of unusual significance to Walter. He made a carbon copy and brought it to America with him.

On the afternoon of January 14, Walter sent a telegram to Lilly in Croydon, and she responded happily by airmail. Walter's passport now contained his US immigrant visa and UK visitor's visa, so he could leave the oppression of Vienna, travel to see her in England, and then forge ahead to America. Lilly was elated:

> Walter, so today has paid off. First in the morning your letter arrived with the Los Angeles things and B[ulova]'s letter about the parents. And you know, now I also think that because he writes about the parents, he will send me the necessary *statement* soon, and then...and then in the afternoon the postman went by, looked at the house—I already jumped up—and went on. Then he turned, came back, and brought your telegram.

So, Walter, I congratulate you. I am really entirely stupid with joy. Mrs. Canfield kissed me, I forgave her, and so on. I could hardly believe it. How is it that you had the documents, I mean in time? And say, will you travel first to Switzerland or will you wait until you can come here? You, that would be wonderful. I am frightfully happy already. I really hadn't thought that you would get the British visa. Now you must arrange it with the Holland America Line [owners of the SS *Volendam*] that you embark in Southampton. Will that work? In any case, you must manage. Do you know, I think that my fasting yesterday helped. And for me it was really a "long day," because I have to get up at 6:45 a.m., fasting or not.

Lilly then burbled on about a pleasant trip to the Winter Cavalcade in London's Earl's Court. It reminded her of the shows at the snow palace in Vienna:

First a floor show, and then ski demonstrations and ski jumping *indoors*. Really great. I would like to have borrowed a pair of boards and raced myself. For the joy of the public [Zum Gaudium des Publikums]!

Ending the letter, she returned to practicalities for Walter's travel and stopover in England:

Please, Walter, see to it that you start your trip as quickly as possible....And please don't forget to bring with you: pharmaceutical things, alarm clock, dress brush, school things, you, and if it is possible, bring me a pair brown shoes, but it isn't necessary. And make a plan for what we should do with the three days, and it is always still possible that I will get my visa between now and then, and that we can travel together. So again congratulations, and until we meet again [literally, auf Wiedersehen]

Your happy Lilly

The Cambridge English Exam

Four days later, there was another piece of good news from Vienna: Lilly had passed the Cambridge English exam. The family back home were the first to find out because the results had mistakenly been mailed to the Neuhaus parents' address in Vienna instead of the Canfields' house in Beddington. She had got a "second," and she took care to explain that this grade was "not bad." On the practical side, Walter must have written that he could not bring any money with him under the new German currency restrictions. Emigration and reunion were becoming realities, and Lilly was thinking it all out down to the shillings and pence:

> So that is really a joke about the Cambridge Exam. They made a mistake and sent it to Vienna instead of Beddington! And you all [pl.—implying the whole family, since the letter would have been addressed to the Neuhaus apartment on Grünentorgasse] knew the result two days before I did!!! Now the same certificate of course will also go to Vienna, so you [pl.] have to keep a careful lookout for it. But understand, 2nd *Grade* is also not bad, especially after I totally misunderstood the précis. They certainly took a long time. That was now two good pieces of news, perhaps the third will come soon: B[ulova]'s *statement*. That also is taking such a long time [sooo lang Zeit]....I don't know about the ships, but you will explain that to me orally [face-to-face, mundlich], right! Will you stay on in London or somewhere here? It would be best if you could stay with your relatives and I could get away from here and stay with my uncle. Then from here to Victoria it is only 1/6 return. Can't you bring any money at all? If it is possible to fly, please do it. I will also write to your people, but I don't have any time today. In the evening we are going to the theater and before that I still have lots to do. So close and <u>until we meet again</u>.

In her next letter on January 18, Lilly copied the important portions of the Cambridge certificate. Walter may have been rethinking a stop in England on the way to America, and Lilly did her best to dissuade him. She was waiting anxiously for an augmented statement from Arde Bulova, though nothing had arrived from him. She happily reported her grades on individual segments of the Cambridge exam, two As (in translation to and from German), two Bs, and one C (pass) grade. The topics hopped around, from her grades to a night out to Walter's travel plans:

> I am so proud of the two A's, it is the most important for me for an office or something like that. Monday evening I was at a *pantomime*. Do you know what that is? If not, shame on you and give Kautetzky [their English instructor in Vienna] back the certificate![45] I had the black little purse from your sister with me.
>
> Walter, you <u>must</u> use the English visa. Even if we can't swim across together. That would be a scandal that everything possible was done, then you got it—which is an <u>enormous</u> piece of good luck—and not to use it! And once you get to Holland, don't worry about it if you travel here and then back again. So please, come. And write to me quickly and exactly what I should do about A[rde] B[ulova].

More Frustration with the US Consulate

That same week, Lilly and Mrs. Canfield returned to the US consulate to see if the visa could be issued for Lilly without Bulova's supplemental statement. The answer continued to be no, though this time, a different consular official explained that the process would be easier

---

45   Walter had been ahead of Lilly in their English studies. The University of Vienna philosophy faculty issued a certificate showing that he had passed an exam in English on March 10, 1938, three days before the Anschluss.

if Lilly were to seek a visa as the fiancée of an immigrant. Then the affidavit would be needed from that immigrant rather than a separate sponsor. Lilly again urged Walter to make a stop in England:

> Today your letter from Wednesday arrived and I can tell you once again that it is <u>very important</u> that you come here. And so for the following reason: Yesterday I was with Mrs. C[anfield] again at the consulate to see if perhaps they would give me the visa without Bulova's *statement*, but with your clarification. (Which of course was impossible, I just realized that.) This time we saw a different *Immigration Officer*—not the one who last time required your explanation—and who said that it's a <u>complicating</u> circumstance that I intend to marry someone who is also an emigrant, and so would also need an affidavit from that person. He wants either that you have a job there and then send me an affidavit, or that B[ulova] specifies very exact plans and also the names and addresses of other people for whom he has submitted affidavits and how he cared for them. You see also that things will continue to become more complicated and hopeless for me here. And it would be much easier to discuss this than write letters. Otherwise the matter will drag on endlessly. So, please, if you cannot <u>fly</u> here, then <u>travel by land</u>, but I believe we must discuss everything, otherwise I must simply give up my plans for America, and also those of my parents. The consulate here is as mean as possible. If I had stayed in Vienna, I would have had my visa already and would be able to travel. So see to it that you do what is possible.

That was how things looked to Lilly at six in the morning on January 20: either-or, everything or nothing. By evening she was calmer and added a postscript to let Walter know without drama that the situation was desperate; she needed him:

> So, after I had cooled off a bit, I would like to tell you again quite calmly. Walter, I understand the difficulties which you

have, but please, if it is possible for you, come here. It is sooo [sic] important, not for you but for me. Because I have already failed because of me. So please, Walter, see if you can help me.

Bulova's supplemental affidavit finally arrived, but the consulate summarily dismissed it. Lilly was becoming worn down with frustration and vented in a letter on January 23 to Walter in Vienna while keeping up a positive front for her parents:

Walter darling, you were right. Bulova's statement arrived today. And these pigs rejected it as cold bloodedly as the first. I am desperate. I could scream every moment. Sometimes I think really, I can't go on any more. About that, please, come! He said in this *statement* that he knows me through *personal friends* [this was not true], that I am very intelligent and hardworking, that he undertakes every *responsibility* and they should give me the visa quickly. At 2 o'clock I had an appointment. I had to wait until 4:30, and after about 2 ½ hours, said that they cannot do anything because he did not answer the items exactly enough before the same list as the other affidavit. Tomorrow I will write to him—today I can't any more, I am dead—to thank him and ask him if he can send me still another statement.... Now a month and more of waiting has gone by, now more weeks will also pass uselessly. But I am already done. Sometimes I feel so alone as if I were in the middle of the Sahara but without an oasis. But I will get through, somehow....

So, don't be angry that I have complained to you one more time, but I have to write home as though I were "der liebe Augustin,"[46] full of hope and optimism.

---

46 This is a reference to a popular ballad about Augustin, a poor street musician in late seventeenth-century Vienna. He got drunk one night during a plague outbreak, fell asleep in a gutter, then was carted away with the bodies of plague victims and thrown into an open mass grave. The following morning, Augustin awoke in the midst of the corpses and played his bagpipes until someone pulled him out of the pit. The song is a gallows humor celebration of having nothing left to lose: "Oh you dear Augustin, everything's gone." See, e.g., "Songs and Rhymes from Austria," Mama Lisa's World, accessed January 20, 2022, https://www.mamalisa.com/?t=es&p=3315.

Before he left, Lilly wrote an undated letter to Walter in Vienna that he kept in the envelope with his parents' letter of January 31, 1939:

> Walter, *dear*, this is hopefully the last letter which I will write to you in the German Reich....When you receive this letter, you will also already—*please god*—have the English visa and be standing with one foot on the airplane.

Walter must have written to Lilly with some emotion about how difficult it was for him to leave his family behind, quite possibly never to see them again, on top of all the other uncertainties of emigration. She responded with a no-nonsense tone and a steady hand:

> Walter, I know how difficult leave-taking is but look, I am only a girl and 19 and have also had to survive it, and the hopes that I had were only hopes and not a bit more. Resolve it internally and you will have it much easier, and come here!

CHAPTER 7

Walter Leaves Home—
A Passport and Visit to England

Walter traveled on a German passport. It was valid for only one year and identified him as a citizen of the German Empire ("Deutsches Reich"). A Nazi eagle and swastika were printed on the inside cover page, next to a rubber stamped large red J for "Jude" (Jew). (See page 20 above.)

There is a story behind the infamous red J markings in German passports. Walter's passport had not included the scarlet letter when it was first issued in September 1938. The following month, Germany changed the rules so that passports for Jews were valid only if they were marked with the identifying J. There is a strong suggestion that this was done at the request of Switzerland so its border guards could readily identify which refugees were Jews and treat them accordingly. Walter had to resubmit his passport so the J stamp could be added, and the new date, October 20, 1938, was written in ink on top of the stamp.

This passport confirms the basic outline of Walter's journey. The stamped entry from the foreign exchange office in Vienna dated January 26, 1939, provided that "exemptions and relief from travel may not be claimed"; in other words, once Walter's exit visa had been issued, his departure was mandatory. No last-minute reconsideration about the decision to emigrate was allowed. A Belgian transit visa was issued on January 28, 1939, which was not used. The passport includes the visa for the UK issued in "Vienna," no country identified, on January 27, 1939, valid "for direct transit only." A pen-and-ink entry on the UK visa notes the essential condition for his admission, "sailing from Southampton on 4/2/39 per SS *Queen Mary* to New York."

On the last day of January 1939, Walter took the morning Lufthansa flight from Vienna to the air and airship port at Frankfurt am Main, where a German exit stamp was entered into his passport. Then he flew on to London.

Walter landed at Croydon airport that same day, January 31. There, more stamps were entered into his passport admitting him contingent upon his imminent departure, the stamp reading: "landed on condition of direct transit through United Kingdom to USA," with the destination country added in pen. The prize that made all this journey possible is on page 31 of the passport: a US immigrant visa dated January 13, 1939, signed by the US Vice Consul in "Vienna, Germany."

In this passport, Walter tucked a note from Dorothy Canfield inside a small envelope marked "to be opened aboard." Dorothy wrote, "Julianne is safe here until such time as we can get her visa one way or the other," and she recommended positive thinking: "Push despair on one side and be always determined to encourage good things to come to you and they will."

Hans's first letter best captures the scene of Walter's departure from Vienna. Hans had intended to see Walter off, but punctuality was not his strong suit. This was the last time that the brothers glimpsed each other:

> So yesterday I was deeply mortified. I really got there only a couple of minutes after the departure of the Lufthansa bus at the Opera Ring. That means that I turned from Schwarzenbergplatz onto the Opera Ring. I saw you drive right by then with an air kiss. I thought to myself only a few friendly thoughts, but gone was gone! And so at about 10 a.m. I looked up from the courtyard at Prince Eugene Street (if you still know what that is) at an airplane. Were you sitting in it?

Chapter 7: Walter Leaves Home—A Passport and Visit to England

One last time, Walter telephoned the family from England. Telephone service between the UK and Austria had existed for over a decade, but it was expensive.[47] For the Haim family, the novelty and cost were worth it. Hans wrote the following day, "Vienna has never been so excited as hearing your voice yesterday evening on the telephone." Hans's brotherly sign-off wished Walter "good luck and many good things" and advised him to "write most often and in detail."

Immediately after Walter's departure, the combined Haim family letters began. Typically Walter's father, Martin, wrote the first section and the others followed in "seniority" order, usually Antoinette next, then whichever of the adult children happened to be in the apartment at the time. Sometimes a visitor added a few words and signature. Group letters meant that all of the core family remained up to date on what Walter reported from his travels, while each letter brought him a bouquet of voices from home. The disadvantage was that the family letters to and from Vienna had to be carefully self-censored to include only news that each writer and recipient could share with the entire family circle; there was no place in them for confidences or overt expressions of anxiety. Everyone's unspoken charge was to maintain morale. After the first couple of months, when Walter's loneliness in New York seemed more than he would be able to bear, his sister Paula set up a system for him to write separate letters to her and send them to a friend's address so they each could be more candid.

The first Haim family letter is dated January 31, 1939, the day that Walter flew to London. Martin began and signed his section with the Romanian equivalent of Aufwiedersehen (until we see each other again)—"La revedere, Papa." Antoinette filled out the sheet of letter paper with a section addressed specifically to Lilly. Antoinette wrote to Lilly informally as "du" and signed it with warm anticipation, "your future mother-in-law."

---

47 For a rough comparison, in 1927, a three-minute telephone call between the UK and New York had cost £9 ("UK Telephone History," BritishTelephones.com, accessed January 20, 2022, https://www.britishtelephones.com/histuk.htm).

Walter and Lilly had three days of reunion in London. They went to the US consulate to see whether something could be done to expedite Lilly's visa so that they could travel together. Nothing. Walter paid a visit at the Canfields' house. Beyond that what they did, where Walter stayed, what Lilly felt about Walter's traveling on first alone, are all unknowns. There are no surviving letters about those three days.

Departure on the Queen Mary

On February 4, Walter sailed alone on the British Cunard liner RMS *Queen Mary*, visa-less Lilly remaining behind. That parting must have been as traumatic for Walter as his departure from Vienna. He recalled in a later letter:

> I arrived there [in Southampton] on the night of Friday, 3 February 1939, and departed on Saturday, February 4th, exactly at noon. Without Lilly. Never in my life will I forget that, and never in my life want to repeat that again. Not for anything in the world.

The *Queen Mary* in 2021, permanently moored in Long Beach, California, her three red smokestacks visible from miles away.

The *Queen Mary* had a fast crossing and docked in New York five days later, on February 9. The family story is that the sea was rough, but Walter was not seasick and so had the tourist class dining room essentially to himself.

The passenger manifest identified Walter as thirty-six and single, with the profession of "hotel director," though this may have been something of an overstatement. On the IKG emigration questionnaire, he had described his last employment as "manager of a large, well-known hotel and café-restaurant in the 1st District." This was the Hotel Wandl on Petersplatz in Vienna's Inner City.[48] Yet on the same questionnaire, Walter described his job specialties as bookkeeper and foreign language correspondent, with no mention of supervising staff. Whatever his exact former position, he had been unemployed since shortly after the Anschluss, when he, along with all other Jews, had been summarily fired. The *Queen Mary*'s manifest said that he could read and write in German, with no other languages identified (the IKG questionnaire listed his "language skills" as French, Italian, and English, with the latter demonstrated by a university exam). His "nationality" was German, his "race or people" Hebrew, and his last place of permanent residence "Vienna, Germany."

Walter had time to write letters on the *Queen Mary*. Hans's response to a letter that Walter had written to their parents during the voyage contains one of the few open acknowledgments of the degrading conditions that prevailed in Vienna. Hans wrote in February 1939:

> I read your first America-letter, which actually is still a water-letter, and was happy that things seem to have gone well for you on the journey and that you have had it well. It must be a sublime feeling to be like an equal, free, and respected

---

48 My father spoke with some affection about the Hotel Wandl, where he began working in November 1932. He said that when it was built in 1850, each room had its own private bathroom, at the time a luxurious novelty. By the late 1930s, it must have been crumbling, as Martin wrote about the hotel's chronic "non-functioning" condition in April 1940. Two generations later, the Hotel Wandl had been revived and was operating as a four-star hotel. On a visit to Vienna in September 2017, I saw a colorful billboard ad for it by the Danube Canal.

human being among humans again?! I believe that this alone is worth an initial loneliness and homesickness that now you will naturally have to endure.

In Vienna the Jews' situation was that of unequal, unfree, and unrespected subhumans. The onerous terms of the Nuremberg "racial" laws had been extended to former Austria in May 1938, and Jews were fired from their jobs. Immediately after the pogrom of November 1938, all Jewish businesses were closed. Then Jews were prohibited from attending public theaters, movie houses, and exhibitions, and Jewish children were banned from German schools.[49] Beginning in January 1939, Jews with names of "non-Jewish origin" had to adopt stigmatizing middle names—Sara for women, Israel for men—and use those names for mail and special identity cards. Jewish doctors were generally forbidden to practice or use their academic titles and could treat only Jewish patients. These dehumanizing events were never, or almost never expressly acknowledged, but they swirled in the background.

Hans's suggested remedy for Walter's inevitable "loneliness and homesickness" was for him to write home, frequently and in full detail:

> In any case, fight your loneliness by communicating with us all in detail by letter, the more often you write to us, the more often you will receive an answer. We are interested in every step that you undertake there and each word that you speak with anyone there.

Walter's sister Paula anticipated from the outset that separation would take an outsized toll on him, writing on February 1, 1939:

> Today things are going well for you. You are still in London with Lilly. But when you have this letter in hand and Lilly really cannot accompany you, it will be sadder for you. Dear

---

49 Matthäus and Roseman, *Jewish Responses*, 448–451.

dear Bobbi, don't break down. I am convinced that we will soon be together again. Everyone, everyone, also with our parents....

Bobbi, servus! We think about you uninterruptedly. Things must go well for you.

As a kid, I recognized "servus" as the greeting and departure phrase used by my father and grandparents. Far removed from its distant etymological origin (in medieval Latin, a "servus" was a servant or slave) and more literal meaning of something like "at your service," it implied warmth, closeness, a whiff of long ago and far away. "Servus" was Hans's invariable letter closing.

Arrival in New York

The great disappointment, mentioned over and over in the letters, was that no one met Walter when he disembarked from the *Queen Mary* in New York, not Mr. Bulova nor any of his employees. On his own, Walter found shelter at the Hebrew Immigrant Aid Society (HIAS) hostel for new immigrants on Lafayette Street in lower Manhattan, a few blocks east of Washington Square with its classic triumphal arch. Walter had much to accomplish as a new immigrant, a greenhorn—find a job, find a place to live, and find a way to get Lilly's visa application approved so she could join him and they could be married. These tasks would have loomed like the labors of Hercules, objectively impossible for mortals. Subjectively they were all the more difficult for Walter because he was alone in New York.

Although it was never talked about in my hearing, my father must have retained strong feelings about the ocean voyage and his arrival in New York. On a cold winter day in 1959, my parents, my brother, and I drove out to a pier in Manhattan on the Hudson River where the *Queen Mary* was docked. In response to some whining, my mother told us that my father wanted to go there because it was twenty years since he had arrived in New York on this ship. There were no follow-up questions. Twenty years is eternity for a ten-year-old, and this was not only ancient history, it also was walled about with a familiar emotional warning: noli me tangere.[50]

Alone in New York

Lilly's first correspondence with Walter in New York was made more frustrating because her father and Paula had sent her inconsistent versions of his address. Lilly was "spitting mad" when she wrote on February 18. She had already written "a meter-long letter" and timed it to be carried on the *Queen Mary* and so arrive with him in New York. Now it would be delayed or lost entirely because of an incorrect address.

Other than this glitch, things sounded on track and reasonably hopeful in London, with civil formalities being maintained. In bullet points, Lilly outlined the contents of her previous letter:

> In case you really don't get my first letter because of the stupid house number, I will repeat the contents in brief:
>
> a) The approval for my trunks arrived. Timid question: can you deposit them somewhere? If not, they will come to my uncle Fritzl Mayer.
>
> b) Mrs. Canfield wrote to you, write and thank her.
>
> c) I think about you an awful lot and I love you very very much.
>
> d) Your cousin Zinne Feder wrote to me asking whether she can be my successor when I travel to the USA (toi toi toi,

---

50 The phrase, meaning "do not touch me," is originally from the Latin Vulgate Bible, John 20:17.

editor's note). Mrs. C[anfield] and I perhaps will meet with her at the beginning of *May* in London.

e) Your mother, also sister, wrote to Mrs. C[anfield] and she was very happy about that.

Lilly wrote a reasonably cheerful letter on February 24, the day before her twentieth birthday:

Walter, *dear*, ring ring at the door and two letters from you arrive. You really are golden, writing as diligently as at the beginning. For that you get an *extra* kiss written on your account.

Lilly had predicted that Walter would have countless problems to worry about when he landed, and she was right. Her tone remained resolutely upbeat, though she could see that Walter was not telling her everything:

I imagined the "first impressions" of America correctly, right? Take a look at my first letter! If, of course, you received it!! But look, what can happen to you? Even if there is (or was), no Bulova, you are quite an ordinary "unemployed" person and can take any job that you find, and if not, you are in the *shelter*. And for the time being you aren't breaking your head about me....So don't worry, anyhow how did you get into that shelter? Was no one at the harbor? You know, although you write so well, it isn't a fraction of what I would like to know.

She returned to the subject of Walter's disappointment that Bulova had refused to see him, remaining confident, practical, seemingly prepared for ups and downs:

Now you will already have spoken to B[ulova], but I am expecting absolutely nothing from that. But you poor dear, I can imagine how broken up you must have been when you went to see him twice and he didn't admit you. It doesn't matter, he isn't the only one who can help. And I also believe that you will find a job in less than two months, and if not, that also is no misfortune. If you are in financial need, would the HIAS people give you money also, or only food and a place to live?

A couple of weeks later, she commiserated again about Bulova's refusal to see him, but thought that making an appointment might help:

I am already curious what sort of impression Bulova has made on you. But I also thought that he would not let you in without an *appointment*. He is really a big beast [a big jerk, ein grosser Vieh]. Write to me always everything entirely exactly, yes? Because curious is no expression for what I am.

CHAPTER 8

Life at the Canfields Continues

Towards the end of February, Lilly received birthday greetings and presents from Vienna. They had suffered some predations en route, but that was another secret. She wrote to Walter:

> Yesterday I received a long birthday letter from your folks, even your father wrote, and Paula has written to me once again asking how I will use the rubber brush, but for the moment the parcel isn't here yet. I received a parcel from my people: 2 dresses, 2 pairs of shoes, and handkerchiefs, ect., and you know that I don't have a trunk, so where will these things go. And imagine, Gustl sent me such a pretty box with candies, and those pigs at the border totally demolished the box and bit into the candies. Filthy ____ [illegible because of water damage]. Of course I haven't written anything about that to Vienna.

The story of the molested birthday parcel was worse yet. In addition to the sweets, she wrote in a letter two days later, the package had contained a bottle of eau de cologne that had simply been pilfered.

At the same time, the Canfields were keeping her busy with housework and some social outings:

> This evening we are going to their [the Canfields] "noble" acquaintances. Graciously, I am also invited!!! Now the season is beginning and with that visiting, so I can wash more dishes!

Lilly's next letter reported on her birthday doings. Her parents had phoned from Vienna. The following day she was to meet a cousin in London. When the cousin did not appear, Lilly treated herself to a visit to the British Museum. She relished her time there and was pleased at not being caught out for inadvertently violating a no-umbrellas rule:

> I finally was traipsing around between mummies and Indian peace pipes for an hour. As I was leaving I noticed a sign that umbrellas must absolutely be checked, and I had already carried mine around the entire time and all the guards did not make me!

One of the dining rooms at Lyons Corner House, Marble Arch. Note tablecloths, modern recessed lighting, and bentwood caned chairs.[51]

Afterwards, she took herself to a Lyons Corner House café for the consolation of "music, hors d'oeuvre, and pastry." Although they are now gone, Lyons Corner Houses were an English fixture for the first two-thirds of the twentieth century, especially in London's West End. Featuring modish art deco design, they provided a shopping cornucopia. The ground floor offered a delicatessen, sweet shops, bakeries, and flower stands, plus hair salons and telephone booths. The floors above had themed restaurants with live music. For all its Anglo-Saxon sounding name, Lyons was founded and owned by Jewish families,

---

[51] "Maisons Lyons in Marble Arch," Marble Arch, London, July 24, 2019, https://marble-arch.london/culture-blog/maisons-lyons-legacy-in-marble-arch/.

Sir Joseph Nathaniel Lyons (a watercolor painter), and members of the Gluckstein and Salmon families (originally tobacconists).[52]

In the same letter, Lilly wrote again about how tired she had become of Mrs. Canfield's gyrating moods:

> At the moment the C[anfield]s get to me, that means on my nerves, so that I could wring their necks hourly. She has a "crazy *period*," is so nervous that in the evening she even hit him—in front of me—and grabbed his hair. What do you say, what sort of little dove I am in comparison!

Lilly remained clear-eyed about practical things. Walter need not write to her every other day; one letter per mail delivery brightened her day:

> And, Walter, I want to tell you something, but don't take it wrongly, ok? You know how every day from morning to evening how I wait for your letters, but if you write every other day that is a waste of postage, because the mail ships are not so frequent. The letters come then together, and you have had to pay twice. So the letters should be should always be sent so that they reach a mail ship directly, I believe that is twice a week and sometimes even more. So don't be cross, I meant well.

In early March Lilly was frustrated with the "muddled" letters her mother sent from Vienna. She also was testy about being at Mrs. Canfield's constant beck and call. A letter from March 8 embodied a well-meaning but insensitive interruption by Mrs. Canfield, who fortunately could not read the body of the letter because it was in German:

> At home there was already the customs inspection of my trunks, and Mutti wrote that the trunks are already under

---

[52] "Joseph Lyons," Wikipedia, accessed January 20, 2022, https://en.wikipedia.org/wiki/Joseph_Lyons_(caterer), and "Salmon & Gluckstein," Wikipedia, accessed January 20, 2022, https://en.wikipedia.org/wiki/Salmon_%26_Gluckstein.

way. All in all her letters are so muddled that I really don't understand, she doesn't even write to where the trunks are addressed. Now I sent her a "questionnaire."

[In English, in a different handwriting:] *Dear Walter, Just a line. Do hope things are not too bad with you; cheer up and God bless you always. For [sic] your sincere friends. A. & D. Canfield*

[Back to Lilly's handwriting] As you can see, she interrupted me yet again!!

Lilly continued to worry that Walter was stretching himself too thin with work and efforts to obtain the necessary immigration papers for her:

Walter, I would like terribly terribly to be with you. Don't let it happen that you work yourself to death to get an affidavit for me, after all it is only a *statement*.

But those darker clouds could blow away, and she wrote enthusiastically about sightseeing trips with the Canfields:

On Sunday we went to Richmond Park and Kew Garden. Can you still remember how we learned all about that in Kautetzkey's [English] class! But it was beautiful, the weather wonderful, and everything so interesting as the people there go riding without cares! But who knows what lies ahead, we have already gone through the most difficult, right, Walter? That's always the distribution! Otherwise there's nothing in particular here. Occasional visits, once we went to Croydon, then again to Wallington [a scenic town in Surrey], ect.

Lilly had gotten wind of a conspiracy theory book that was about to be published in the United States. Issued anonymously, it claimed that Hitler had been secretly assassinated the night before signing the Munich Pact, and that the book's supposed author, a Hitler look-alike, had begun ruling in his place:

> Now I have to ask you something, maybe it is a stupidity. Pay attention: a book is about to be released in America, *"The strange death of Adolf Hitler."* He is supposed to have been poisoned in September and now his *double* rules. Have you heard anything about that?

As nonsensical as the story is, it has staying power. A reprint was still available on Amazon in early 2024.

Walter continued to blame himself for having traveled to New York and leaving Lilly behind in England when her visa did not come through. She disagreed strongly with his self-recriminations:

> Yesterday your letter of the 28th arrived, and I am very sad that you are still blaming yourself. <u>Please</u>, Walter, don't do it, you have done the <u>only right thing</u>, naturally you went to America as quickly as possible. And now there are four ways for me to come to you: a) you buy an affidavit for me, b) you can provide one for me, c) Sigl [Lilly's uncle] provides one for me, and d) you get a good job. So you see, Walter, no reason for despair, things are going well for you for the time being, and take care of yourself. In a foreseeable time, you will find work there and will see that everything will look quite different then.

Marching Towards War

The international news was frightening. In mid-March 1939, Hitler invaded the remaining portions of what had been Czechoslovakia. This action violated the infamous Munich Agreement of September 1938, which had allowed Hitler to take over the Sudetenland, a crescent of land in western Czechoslovakia with a large ethnic German population, in return for what Prime Minister Chamberlain touted as "peace for our time." Six months after Munich, the Western democracies did nothing to stop this next German advance. Lilly read the newspapers and listened to the radio:

> Of course I am now dreadfully worried about Vienna again, what do you say about that miserable dog…But I believe England will _____ [take action? The word is illegible because of water damage], at least that is what Chamberlain said.

Earlier that week, Hitler's latest aggression and Britain's lack of response were front-page news in the *New York Times*:

> The destruction of Czecho-Slovakia tonight was not enough to shake Britain from her recent apathy towards events in Central Europe, although it must have destroyed some of the favorite assumptions on which the British policy has been based in the last twelve months.
>
> …Tonight Hitler crossed his Rubicon; for the first time he had subjugated millions of non-Germans who are considered within the Reich to be the "racial" inferiors of Germans.
>
> Yet there was no sign that the implications of this immense event had been appreciated at 10 Downing Street or in the House of Commons.…
>
> Most of the newspaper placards in the streets today proclaimed in eight-inch letters, "Another Great Stand"—but by the British cricket team. By the British Government there was no suggestion of any "stand" whatever.[53]

---

53 Ferdinand Kuhn Jr., "Invasion No Shock to British Leaders," *New York Times*, March 15, 1939, https://www.nytimes.com/1939/03/15/archives/invasion-no-shock-to-british-leaders-chamberlain-in-house-says-no.html.

Domestically, chez Canfield, there were days when the lady of the house was "normal and agreeable," and Lilly reported that she had "finally washed the last curtains, it was high time, though I could scream if I look at my hands, about the way they look." Roiling the domestic situation were Mrs. Canfield's intermittent fits of hysteria, and a friend had tried to poach Lilly. In response, Mrs. Canfield gushed to Lilly about "how happy I have made her life since I have been here, ect. ect."

Hopes for Lilly's parents being able to get to England were diminishing, and she wrote to Walter about the "heartbreaking letters" that they sent her from Vienna:

> That the parents, or at least papa, can come here is completely illusory and impossible. The *Ex-Service-men* answered in one sentence: *We regret to have to tell you that at present we are unable to do anything for your father*....Yesterday I finally had mail from the parents...but they don't write anything other than that they are nervous. Do you think that the current events can have any effect on them? Write to them, Walter, they write such heartbreaking letters to me that quite do me in.

She earnestly reassured Walter:

> Walter, you write that you go crazy if you are alone, but you are <u>never</u> alone because I am <u>always</u> with you, so there is no reason to lose your nerve, right?

Brave words, though a couple of days later, Lilly acknowledged that when she was alone, she, too, felt "crushed" by the weight of her family's need for an escape from Vienna and the world situation. She dealt with it sensibly by going out to a movie:

> Yesterday the C[anfield]s were at their parents and at first I sat at home and racked my brain because of the parents, war, ect., but at the end it became too much for me, I packed myself up

and went to the movies. I have become so pleasure-seeking because if I am all alone, that is the only way I can distract myself for three or four hours. That is all for today....Walterlein, grit your teeth, we will get to the goal, and until then we must play the "heroes," but perhaps not for too long, agree?

Walter must have written that he was looking for work by making cold calls at hotels in New York. Lilly included practical advice in a letter sent on March 24 about the best way to present himself—dress up rather than down:

You, Walter, don't be cross if I give you a piece of "motherly" advice, as though I had sooo much more experience than you. When you go to various hotels to introduce yourself, wear the <u>best</u> suit that you have there. If they go for it, when you have a position, you can buy a new one, and you will know how much you will be earning....So please follow my advice, no wool vests, ect. *in public*, yes?

Lilly ended this letter with a political note, still possible to include in a letter sent from England in the prewar, pre-censorship days:

What do you say about that pig Hitler? But I recall you once said that the faster he over-gorges himself, the better. And his appetite really leaves nothing to be desired!

Days when Lilly didn't receive any mail from Walter were disappointing. One letter made the day good, and days when three letters came were, she wrote, "very good." For Walter's birthday, Lilly sent him some surprisingly erotic verses in English that she had begun to sketch out:

If we were on top of the hill,
And all the world around is still,
Would you?

> *If we were in a desert place,*
> *Between us just a piece of lace,*
> *Would you?*
> *If we were lying face to face,*
> *Locked in a very deep embrace,*
> *Would you?*

Then she ended with a self-deprecating, "No, I wasn't diligent enough."

Despite her frustrations, Lilly's life with the Canfields was not all curtain- and dish-washing. In late March she accompanied Mrs. Canfield to a fashion show at a London department store—a "Mannequin parade." It was not bad, she judged, though provincial fashions in England could not compare with couture in Vienna. Then she went with Mrs. Canfield to a séance but remained skeptical:

> Yesterday I was with her at a spiritualist *circle*! What do you say to that! Finally I will let myself be convinced!

At this time Lilly was waiting for Paul's arrival in England, but there was a snag: "He still doesn't have his passport." The situation at home in Vienna remained worrisome. She hadn't heard from her father, and there were problems with the amount of his military pension: "The pension matter is still not finished. He is provisionally making 'progress' again, but at least he had something to live on." Having a pension, even one that had been arbitrarily reduced, was a rarity. A year after the Anschluss, most Jews remaining in Vienna were unemployed. With bank and investment accounts frozen and no source of income left to them, they survived on charity handouts from the IKG.

Lilly urged Walter to send her more details—"reports instead of letters":

> And Walter, how are you, I know really sooo little about your current life. Sometimes when I lie in bed in the evening and

think hundreds of things come to me: who is washing your laundry, do you get pocket money? Are you at some organization? Do you still see the people from HIAS whom you befriended? What do you do on Sundays, do you stay at the home or do you go and look around the city? Do you need anything which I can send to you from here? Ect. Ect. So you see, you must write ____ [word illegible because of water damage] reports instead of letters!

In the larger world, Europe continued its slide towards war. The day before this letter was written, on March 22, 1939, Germany bullied Lithuania into ceding the Baltic port city of Memel (Klaipėda in Lithuanian). The rationalization was a familiar one: A majority of Memel's population was German-speaking, as the area had been part of East Prussia before the post-World War I territorial divisions. Britain acceded to Germany's latest unilateral action in Lithuania as a fait accompli, despite a recent treaty that provided for multilateral consultation before any such action. The *New York Times* reported on page 1 that Prime Minister Chamberlain wanted to convene an international conference with the goal of issuing "a four-power declaration pledging resistance to further acts of German aggression," but he could not muster the political backing even for that timid plan. Domestically, Chamberlain made a superficially defiant statement to the House of Commons the day after the Memel annexation, warning that Germany's "steps to dominate Europe...would rouse the successful resistance of this and other countries who prize their freedom," but this was just talk. No action was forthcoming. The *New York Times*'s correspondent in London summarized dryly, "Diplomatically this was a day of successes for Germany and of temporary frustration for Britain and France in their halting efforts to prevent further German expansion eastward."[54]

---

54 Ferdinand Kuhn Jr., "Chamberlain Firm on Reich Threat," *New York Times*, March 24, 1939, https://www.nytimes.com/1939/03/24/archives/chamberlain-firm-on-reich-threat-warns-nazi-domination-will-be.html.

Chapter 8: Life at the Canfields Continues

Lilly included an oblique mention of these events in her letter:

> Now I have listened to the radio and eaten and now I am writing. What do you say about Hitler, Walter, he takes one piece after the other and they hold conferences and send protests.

The following week there was good news even if on a small scale. Walter had a job, though it paid only sixteen dollars a week, and had moved out of Congress House, the HIAS hostel. The news crossed the Atlantic to Vienna by cable and then ricocheted back to England:

> Today the folks in Vienna [Lilly referred to them collectively as "die Wiener," the Viennese] wrote to me that you had telegraphed that you finally got a *"job."* Walter, how happy I am, and I don't at all have to tell you how I am happy for you. The beginning is done. And that is always the hardest. So, Walter, *dear*, congratulations! Now of course, I am already burning for the first letter about it: what, how, where, in what way, ect. I intentionally wrote a *job* and not "the *job*," because I am quite certain that you will have to change, like I did; the first post is generally not a lasting thing. But what does that matter? The first earned *dollars* (or *cents*) are already a good foundation! This letter will probably not reach you any more in *Congress House*, but you will certainly get it or it will be forwarded....
>
> Say, Walter, haven't the streets in New York become much cleaner?! Always write to me exactly where you are living now, what you are doing, entirely exactly, understand?

She ended the letter with a beloved's sweet request:

> Walter, please, take a pencil, hold it tightly in your hand for five minutes, don't let anyone touch it, wrap it up and send it to me.

Walter must have complained that the families in Vienna received more mail from Lilly than he did. Lilly countered in a letter sent on March 29 that she "had no peace to write here" and detailed Mrs. Canfield's criticism of her scribblings:

> Walter, dear, I tell you straight out that I don't write as much to you as to those in Vienna, otherwise only twice a week. But you yourself have seen under what conditions I write here and on Monday, as I wrote to you, she gave me a sermon that I am here to entertain her and how tedious it is for her if I write and she sits there and has to look on.

Lilly's uncle Sigl had written from New York about his views of the pros and cons of America, and she was not impressed:

> As for the Landsmanns, I already told you that they are rarely decent and conscientious but "crazy." And I know whether or not I want to go to America without their "travel descriptions."

When Walter complained some about Americans, Lilly rose to their defense:

> But Walter, dear, don't be sooo ungrateful and don't complain about the Americans. First they are the only ones who do something against Hitler and about us; that is like going to the dentist, it hurts us, but it frees us from a great evil. I have nothing against the Americans because they may have saved you from Dachau.

She closed with a "bag full of kisses" and went off to darn her stockings before dinner.

An Aside about Dachau

Lilly, Hans, and Paul all mention Dachau. It was a real threat, not a metaphor. Dachau was the first Nazi concentration camp. Located only a few miles outside Munich, it was opened in March 1933, less than two months after Hitler's installation as chancellor. The first inmates were political prisoners, primarily Communists and Social Democrats. Surprisingly, the regime allowed British journalist G. E. R. Gedye to visit Dachau in early 1933.[55] Dachau was not an extermination camp per se, but from the beginning the prisoners there were physically and mentally maltreated, and many died. The families found out when an urn with their ashes was sent home. After the Anschluss, a number of senior officials from the former Austrian government, that is, Austrian Fatherland Front nationalists rather than Jews or Socialists, were interned in Dachau. Even former Chancellor Schuschnigg was imprisoned there for a time.

Ordinary members of the Vienna Jewish community, not just the leadership (which kept silent), would have known about Dachau because between May and June 1938, about five thousand Jews were deported there from former Austria.[56] An additional 3,700 Jewish men were sent from Vienna to Dachau following Kristallnacht.[57] Some were released if they could show that they had a visa that would allow them to emigrate from Greater Germany within two weeks.

Even before the war, conditions at Dachau were no secret. In 1938 a German Social-Democratic party journal published an account in English and German written by a former prisoner, focusing on the maltreatment of Jewish inmates there. So much about Dachau appeared in the western press that in March 1939, Gedye reported that the German government ordered Jews in Dachau to be further punished in "retaliation for articles describing concentration camp life which had appeared abroad." Their rations were reduced to half

---

55 G. E. R. Gedye, *Fallen Bastions* (London: Victor Gollanz, 1939), 167–169.

56 Rabinovici, *Eichmann's Jews*, 45.

57 Pauley, *From Prejudice to Persecution*, 287.

or less than those of other prisoners, resulting in slow starvation, and they were subjected to public tortures and executions.[58] Gedye characterized Dachau simply as "hell," "that Bavarian inferno."[59]

Scraps of Normalcy

While the daily news about Germany remained threatening, there were still bits of normalcy. In early April 1939, Lilly's parents were able to send her two parcels from Vienna containing "2 hats, 1 dress, 1 winter coat, 1 pair of shoes, 6 handkerchiefs." It was a promising day, and she had an immediate occasion to wear one of the hats on a visit to London with the Canfields. She closed the letter to Walter with "unfortunately only printed kisses."

In mid-April, things looked a bit less dire. Lilly wrote to Walter that Paul was in line to get his UK visa. On the world stage, in the face of British inaction, President Roosevelt took the lead and cabled letters to Hitler and Mussolini on the night of April 14 asking: "Are you willing to give assurance that your armed forces will not attack or invade the territory or possessions of the following independent nations," followed by a list of thirty countries in Europe and the Middle East.[60]

In exchange, Roosevelt offered US participation in international discussions aimed at reducing the "crushing burden" of Germany's and Italy's rearmament and facilitating international trade so that all nations could "possess assurance of obtaining the materials and products of peaceful economic life."[61] He closed with an oratorical appeal to history and morality:

---

58 Gedye, *Fallen Bastions*, 341–342.

59 *Fallen Bastions*, 14, 83.

60 Franklin D. Roosevelt, Press Conference Online by Gerhard Peters and John T. Woolley, April 15, 1939, The American Presidency Project, https://www.presidency.ucsb.edu/node/209531.

61 Roosevelt press conference.

Heads of great Governments in this hour are literally responsible for the fate of humanity in the coming years. They cannot fail to hear the prayers of their peoples to be protected from the foreseeable chaos of war. History will hold them accountable for the lives and the happiness of all—even unto the least.

Roosevelt's was a dramatic gesture, but it had no effect.

Still, Lilly sounded slightly more hopeful about all-out war being averted, though she remained careful not to write anything alarming to the parents in Vienna and to downplay the seriousness of what she knew from the British press and radio. She wrote to Walter:

The political situation is really very, very bad, but I still don't believe that it will come to a war, particularly now where Roosevelt has taken the things in hand. There will perhaps be a scramble about the Mediterranean Sea, but nothing big official [nichts Grosses Offizielles] now that all the agreements with Russia, Greece, and Romania have been made. In any case I pray for peace and for you. Of course I wrote to home that the situation seems from here to be entirely harmless, perhaps that will comfort them a bit.

She ended optimistically and with practical, answerable questions and requests:

How are you managing with your $16?...And are you sleeping enough?? <u>Please</u> write to *Mrs*. Canfield for my sake. Now close, Walter, it <u>won't</u> come to any war and you will see, in 1, 2 I will be with you and then everything will look different, right?

A week passed with no new letter from Walter. Lilly never doubted that the fault lay with the US postal service, not Walter's failure to write:

> The mail is really outrageous! If I were the president of America, that would be changed radically!

With that off her chest, Lilly wrote about the difficulties of maintaining family communications by letter and telegrams. Some disturbing facts could not be revealed to parents: for example, that Walter was working nights. While some correspondents, like Walter and later Paul, took a stoic position, others, in particular Sigl Landsmann and his family, were masters of strategic complaining:

> Today Mutti wrote to me that you had written to her that she promised you not to complain [lamentieren] to me, so she will keep to that. Very diplomatic, eh? Say, are things really going so bad for the Landsmanns? My people are quite horrified that Lissi, the poor child, has to work 8 hours a day in a factory and has sore hands. What do you say to that? I wish I had an 8-hour day and went home to my parents in the evening. So, and you already know what my hands look like. Some people always understand how to arouse pity, and it is always to their benefit. How you could go on and complain about the night work, but no, you are happy that you at least have it. In any case Irma wrote to Mutti that you now are working on the night shift—your people know <u>nothing</u> about it—and Mutti asked me whether I knew about that. I didn't respond to that, and it seems that it didn't make an impression on her! I tell you, more than one border separates the folks in Vienna and the emigrants!

Lilly was glad that Walter had opened a savings account with his minuscule salary. Although increasingly anxious with the endless waiting for her visa and the pressures of being a sociable "companion" in the Canfield household, her sense of humor could still spark:

> If only I were already there and nothing comes between. I tell you, sometimes I am so anxious that I think I have to run away from here and "swim on foot to New York."

On April 24 Lilly took the audacious step of going to the US consulate without an appointment. She detailed the inconclusive result in a letter two days later:

> I managed to get into the room where we had been together. A young lady who brought along your affidavit and marriage declaration, the affidavit from Henshel with the letter, and the declaration from parents to Maney [a US immigration officer] came back and said he will write to me. God only knows what that means.

Paul Arrives and Lilly Is Stymied

The day after Lilly's visit to the consulate, April 25, 1939, Paul arrived in London. Lilly recounted:

> Yesterday evening I picked up Paul at the airport. The others waited for him in London, so it was quite good that I was there, otherwise the poor guy—he was terribly nervous—wouldn't have had anything for the porter. As stupid as I am already, I had only 7/6 with me, but the Wilheims [Paul's relatives on his mother's side] had sent him a letter with 10 shillings.

Paul had arrived with empty pockets because Germany had increased restrictions on currency being taken out of the country. Lilly told Paul about her visa situation, and he suggested that a friend might be able to help, but Lilly noted, "that fell through."

The Canfields continued to entertain, meaning that there were more dishes for Lilly to wash, while her future depended on heartless bureaucrats:

> Yesterday we had two visits the entire day until 10 p.m., so enough to do. The ladies and gentlemen dine all day

long.—Walter, sometimes I am so afraid for you that I don't know at all what I should begin, I could shriek, and everything depends on a stupid stamp, called a visa, one can hardly believe it, right? But it will happen, right? And then everything will all go well for us!!

On May 1 the telephone rang early with a telegram from New York, and for a moment Lilly thought perhaps there had been a decision by the US consulate. But not so: "Now we must wait yet again…one must give the consul 2 to 3 weeks' time until one can get in the line again."

Lilly tried to reassure Walter with pious optimism and worldly practicality: she would have an assertive, native Englishwoman phone the consulate for her:

But look, Walter, it was God who sent us both to Kautetzky, and he will lead us together again. This morning Mr. Canfield's secretary called the consulate to see if she could get an answer. Because if anyone can, it is she. Three times the consulate disconnected her as she said what she wanted, and the fourth time she was successful in speaking to Maney's secretary. (Can you imagine how quickly she would have brushed me off!) He hasn't yet seen the affidavits, the wretch. After longer and longer conversation, the secretary finally said she will put the papers in front of him today (whether she has done it??) and the consul will answer *in due course*. He can't be pushed, although one can do whatever one wants. Walter, the Canfields are really doing what they can for me, and you haven't yet written to them once from America, please do it, for me.

She promised to telegraph as soon as she received an answer from the consulate, whether good or bad.

The consulate delayed some more. Feeling helpless and frustrated, Lilly spun possible scenarios of leaving England to apply at a

US consulate on the Continent, while cautioning Walter to sit tight with his ill-paid night job in New York:

> I am so sad that I can't tell you anything; I am so sorry about everything and I am so helpless. Say, Walter, do you think it would be better or also a possibility if I tried to go to a different country, where there is a different American consul? I would do everything to finally reach the goal. I ask you only one thing, Walter. <u>Don't</u> leave Klein [S. Klein, a down-market department store on 14th Street in Manhattan] or try to get a job with more pay because otherwise you yourself will sit between two chairs, and so with this $16 you are saved from the worst. Perhaps the Sephardim can intervene—although the consulate hasn't ever informed me that there is an affidavit for me—perhaps *Bloomsbury House* (previously *Woburn House*). Yesterday I wrote and asked for an *appointment*. I don't leave anything untried, but now only an official or semi-official office can help.

Lilly was losing patience again with the Canfields, even as they tried to help her with the visa process:

> The Canfields are as useless as wooden dolls. And you know how hard it is for me here to get away for an afternoon or even to telephone. When I come back she is either "sick" or otherwise something has happened. On the 15, 16, and 17th she will have x-rays and perhaps will need an operation, you can imagine the drama ["Theater"], it makes me sick. I tell you, I don't care about anyone here, as they don't care about me, it's all the same to me. By the way, the Canfields have lost money again and in spring may have to give up the house (including me), but it isn't certain yet. I really don't care so much if I have to look for another position with more work, but also with more free time. But I won't leave yet. As a thank you for everything, the following just happened: a "friend"

of Mrs. C[anfield] wanted to snatch me away, of course I said no, and now she does her best to stir up Mrs. C[anfield]: I work a lot for little, ect. ect. No, and you can imagine that it does not go unnoticed.

Lilly reminded Walter once again that these problems had to remain a secret from her parents. He was her only outlet:

Walter, I know I shouldn't write all this to you because you have your own difficult people [Pinkerl] just as I do, but I can't mention any of this to Vienna, and to whom should I pour out my heart if not to YOU? We are both in the same situation, equally miserable.

Paul, newly arrived from Vienna, took a contrarian attitude, as she wrote in this same letter. In Paul's view, her situation was not so bad:

Paul claims that I am absolutely not to be pitied! But I can't describe to you how alone I am here among these empty people, who have no other worries than clothes and whether or not they should buy a second car. And if I am not merry and a good creature, to put it mildly, I get on their nerves, so I have to have a good cry when I am alone and write to you. Are you cross with me, Walter? I know that today's is no "heroic" letter and that I am only making your heart heavy with it, but I have to express myself to you otherwise my heart would wither away. And you understand me properly, agreed?

Walter's response must have let on yet again that he was continuing to run himself ragged trying to help Lilly and the families in Vienna while dealing with poverty and loneliness in a foreign city. She wrote on May 14:

Walter, <u>please</u>, don't use your nerves like that, *you can't burn the candle on both ends*. Night work alone is already enough and too much for you, and if you always upset yourself so and break your head and torture your brain so, you will have a nervous breakdown or two, and we want to be happy and enjoy the days when I come. Don't believe that I don't understand and cannot sympathize with you, I understand it only too well. I have already been in the same situation as you for <u>8</u> months, and in November I also thought it doesn't help if I make myself half-crazy with worries, cares, and racking my brains until I was told that I was not being a good companion [i.e., not doing the job for which she was being paid]. And you also can't carry out your work if you wear yourself out so. You must pull together your work, and me, and the folks in Vienna and take it much more calmly. <u>I know</u> that this is much harder than worrying. But do it for the love of me, ok? Biggest word of honor! Finally we both are still young and two or three months are very, very long, but don't really matter.

Lilly added that Paul had written to her. Things were not going well for him and his sister Olga, who had arrived in England in August 1938 and was working as a nanny (a "highly over-qualified baby nurse," she told me decades later) for a family in Kidderminster, a historic town near the industrial city of Birmingham. While Olga looked after the family's sickly infant twins, Paul did manual labor:

Otherwise there isn't much going on here, mail came from Paul yesterday, he writes that he works from 6–11 in the garden, garage, and cellar and that is too much for him and Olga.

She closed with a literal, manageable question about New York:

Is your work in a skyscraper, I wanted to ask you that so often.

The following week, Lilly traveled again to the Jewish aid associations at Bloomsbury House in London to see about her visa. The building was a former hotel in Bloomsbury Street that in 1938 became the headquarters for Jewish organizations dealing with refugees' issues. A Mr. Rothschild (a resonant name) there explained that it was a matter of demonstrating, albeit to a skeptical consular official, that one had enough funds to pay one's own way. She was advised to exercise yet more patience:

> Yesterday I was at Bloomsbury House and told Mr. Rothschild—who is over the *oversea department*—my entire life story and he said the following: the American immigration law explicitly forbids anyone to receive an *immigration visa* who cannot pay for his own travel.... He will discuss the case on Friday at the committee meeting and write to me at the beginning of next week. His personal advice is this though, that I should write to the consulate here that since November I have already earned such and such amount and so I can pay for the journey myself. He is convinced that this is the entire snag, but said that in any case I should wait with this until Tuesday, until I know the final decision from the committee. Walter, if that were really the case, one would be ready to tear one's hair out, but still the most favorable, no? So we will see. It won't be over yet for a couple of weeks. And you will be good and patient, right? Must set a good example for me. You know, I really admire the folks in Vienna.

Walter continued to sound "desperate," fearful that war would break out, stranding Lilly in England and the parents in Vienna. In response, she continued to reassure him that the political situation had been on edge for some time already, and there was no reason to think it wouldn't stay that way:

> Today your letter of May 1 arrived and you are still always so desperate. Walter, I repeat it over again, *believe me*, that it won't come to a war where everything will be lost, as already so often in the past two years.

The international game of chicken would continue for four months before another war ignited, though no one knew that at the time.

Dorothy Canfield was feeling better, and both the proposed x-rays and operation had been called off, according to a letter Lilly sent on May 11. Around that time Mrs. Canfield sent Walter a cheery card:

My dear Walter,

Very many thanks for your letter received today. You know of course that we shall do our very best to help Julianne to secure her Visa, but I may as well warn you that unless some other pressure is brought to bear from people on your side of the Atlantic Ocean it is going to be very up-hill work. It is ever increasingly obvious that it is not child's play to influence Mr. Maney [the US consular official], but never fear we will do all in our active power, as well as praying, for her to have it as soon as possible so that you may be together once more which I know to be your ambition and rightly so. Cheer up, for, in spite of present appearances I know and feel that all will be well. Look after yourself and press ever onward. Please believe that we both wish you all luck and health and eventual lasting happiness together with Julianne.

God bless you therefore, always.
Sincerely, Dorothy Canfield

Frustrations continued the following week. Lilly received more inconclusive advice from Bloomsbury House. She also had to deal with the freight forwarders who were supposed to deliver her trunks from Vienna to Fritz Mayer's house in the London suburbs but kept tacking on questionable charges. Then a long letter from Walter arrived but it wasn't for her. A letter to his parents had been put in the wrong envelope:

Yesterday your letter of the 9th arrived. Phooey, was I disappointed when I opened it, I found three full pages and…look, but they were not to me but to the parents. You know, you tell them much more about New York than me, you naughty guy! You don't write anything at all to me about that.…Friday my trunks should be delivered to the Mayers, and today I received a further bill from the forwarding agent for £1 4s, whom I had already paid £3 10s, that means 3s in storage fees for 2 weeks, and 21s for the delivery to Golders Green [where Fritzl Mayer lived]. So his [Mr. Canfield's] secretary phoned again and see here, see here, it was an *"oversight"* and I need pay only the 3s. When this gang detects a *foreigner*, they tackle him from behind, and if I didn't have anyone to take this matter in hand for me, I would have to pay dearly. That's the English decency!!

Lilly assured Walter that she had written to both their mothers for Mother's Day and signed his name as well. Later she had to send a correction. She had mistaken the date of the holiday, which Germany had politicized:

You, we were both wrong about Mother's Day, this time it is a week later, probably a "Tscherman" innovation ['teutsche' Einführung].

In fact, the Nazi government had co-opted Mother's Day (previously a non-denominational American commemoration), holding a ceremony on May 21, 1939, to publicly award a Cross of Honor of the German Mother to "racially pure" German women who had given birth to and raised at least four children.[62] As misguided as it seems in an overpopulated world, this was not an exclusively Nazi idea. After the carnage of the Great War, France began distributing a similar Medal of the French Family in 1920.[63]

---

62 "Cross of Honour of the German Mother," Wikipedia, accessed January 20, 2022, https://en.wikipedia.org/wiki/Cross_of_Honour_of_the_German_Mother.

63 "Cross of Honour," Wikipedia.

Lilly returned to Bloomsbury House again the following week, but there was no comfort there. She received a sensible bit of third-hand advice from Vienna—combine all the requested answers into a single response so as not to make the consular officials do any extra mental work. She wrote to Walter on May 19:

> The Mandlers' landlord went to the American consulate in Vienna, I don't know whether they spoke to the porter or the General Consul, but he was someone, and Aunt Emma told him about my case, and he said if the Consul keeps sending the same *form* with the same three questions, then he wants these three questions answered <u>together</u> in <u>one</u> document (That is his view.)

She fantasized about leaving her position with the Canfields but was held back because that job was part of her immigration case:

> Walter, *dear*, do you know how terribly much I love you. If it weren't so, do you know what I would do? Go to London to a great house as a parlour maid, where I would have a uniform and £1 a week and time off twice a week and tips. I stay here in Beddington <u>only</u> for love of <u>you</u> and the parents.

The actual life of a foreign maid in an English great house was far from her romantic fantasy. A few weeks later, Lilly met up with a friend of her uncle Gustl Landsmann who had just such a job in Dorking, a small market town in Surrey about sixteen miles from Beddington. Lilly reported that the friend "works herself half sick in a great house." Still, she was unreservedly happy about this woman's compliment on her English:

> She told me first how well she knows English, and then when I spoke with the *butler*, she said: "So yes, you speak English English!" I felt tickled!

Later in June Lilly came to a decision. Rather than passively waiting for the consulate's next response, she would engage a lawyer:

And, Walter, I have now put together the following plan: So much is now in progress with the visa, everything needs the last push to secure me the visa, so I will now hand the matter over to a lawyer. I have already written to the parents about that and asked them because I will perhaps need to get more money from them. And so I will go to the lawyer whom Fritzl Mayer directed everything. Last Sunday when I was there he gave me that advice, and I will definitely discuss it with him at Pentecost. He said that in the cheapest case, it will cost me 5 guineas, but if there are complications it will be more. I know I can hardly afford that because I have spent so much in the last three months that I can't spare it, but I believe now is the time for this step.

While continuing the battle for a visa, she was also going on country outings with the Canfields and could wonder at the extravagant English sight of Derby Day, one of England's grandest horse races:

For the past couple of days we have gone for a drive by car in the evenings, and during the day we went to the Downs. We got out on a hill and played there like small children. At the end they put me in a wastebasket! (Funny, ha, ha!) Yesterday was *Derby Day*. Tell me really, best word of honor, did you know that Derby is not held in Derby but in Epsom? In any case, we went there in the evening when everything was over to look at the "remains." So you can hardly imagine, an entire Prater [the large amusement park in Vienna's 2nd District] had been built, ½ a million people were there of all races and colors. Really wonderful but to me—all the same! Only one thing still interests me, when will I get the visa.

Lilly ended the letter with a memory of their courtship in Vienna and a reassurance:

Chapter 8: Life at the Canfields Continues

What are you doing on the holidays, Vienna Woods? It will happen again, understand?

Near the end of May, Walter wrote that he was working a second job, doing some sort of paperwork for a Dr. Miller to augment his income for the immigration application. Lilly was upset and maternal:

Walter, *darling*, I thought that Dr. Miller gave you this confirmation only pro forma, but I am floored that you really work there. Walter, you cannot keep that up, no one can do it. Please, please, please, don't overwork yourself, otherwise you will be worn out at the end, and I will have to put you on a milk *diet* to get you back on your feet!! Please, take care of yourself!!

Pentecost was a long holiday weekend in England, and while the Canfields went away, Lilly got to spend nearly three days at leisure with the Mayer family in London:

The C[anfield]s are at their parents, and I was in London from midday on Saturday until Monday evening.

I tell you, I squealed like a small child with joy that for once I did not have to hurry back in the evening....If you were in London again, I would be really happy....In the evening we went walking in Hampstead Heath, these people, inconceivable. Then in the evening, that means night, because we got home only at 11:30, they put down a mattress for me—who had just arrived—and made up a bed, and I got up at 8:30 on Monday, I felt myself like the Empress of China....We had wonderful weather for the holidays, only our poor folks in Vienna couldn't enjoy it. But you know my Mutti always writes to me that she gets courage from your father, he is so confident. Really admirable.

Walter's next letter traveled from New York to England on the first transatlantic airmail service, the Pan American Yankee Clipper.[64] The letter would have taken a multi-stop route through Bermuda, the Azores, and Marseilles before arriving in London.[65] In her return letter on June 2, Lilly seemed to have absorbed something of the Haim family's philatelic interests:

> Hardly had I sent off the letter to you on Thursday when your Yankee Clipper arrived. You know, I will save it because in a couple of years it will certainly become a rarity: arrived with the first airmail flight from America!!

Turning to the visa saga, Lilly reported that "Paul and the folks in Vienna were also enthusiastic" about her engaging a lawyer. The US consulate's delay remained frustrating, but Lilly was enjoying the English summer and evening excursions to the Downs:

> Walter we've had a few wonderful days here. For the last 15 days no rain, so an *"official drought"* has been proclaimed in Greenwich!! I am already very nicely sun tanned. In the evening we still go often to the Downs to play ball games. This evening the Canfields have finally gone alone to make a visit, and so I have a large mail completion [time], I should write at least 6 letters.

Walter was continuing his regular correspondence with both families in Vienna. Lilly teased him because they were receiving more details than she was about his life in New York, including his new furnished room. Then she signed off sweetly:

---

64 "Airmail: A Brief History," Historian, US Postal Service, March 2018, https://about.usps.com/who-we-are/postal-history/airmail.pdf.

65 See also "1939 in Aviation," Wikipedia, accessed January 20, 2022, https://en.wikipedia.org/wiki/1939_in_aviation#May. Pan American's Yankee Clipper northern route, with mail service from the United States to England via New Brunswick, Newfoundland, and Ireland, began on June 24, 1939.

So good night, Walter, that means you should have a snack first. Is it summer there yet? And many many closest kisses.

The following week Lilly was too preoccupied with domestic details and summer heat to write letters. On June 9 she wrote at last:

This time again I haven't written for a whole week but look, I simply wasn't able to. Not only is there nothing at all new, but also a heat wave (90°) so that we don't do anything at all the whole day long other than say "puuh" and only venture out of the house in the evening. Next week we will go on vacation for 8 days, me too. But blindingly decently, they will pay as much for me as for themselves. We will leave on Saturday the 17th and return a week later....We will go to Brendon, North Devon, 6 miles from the sea, so about 9 minutes in the car, that means every day if we'd like, even twice....He [Mr. Canfield] said I can travel calmly because in case of an emergency I can be in London in 6 hours. That callous [literally, hard boiled—hartgesottene] dog [at the consulate] still has not answered.

Paul and Olga's difficult situation with their employer (and visa sponsor) was an eye opener for Lilly:

So now I see for the first time what a paradise I am in. (If only I were out of it!)....Really all a matter of luck. Perhaps we will also have luck with the visa, so? Only a little bit of luck and I will be seasick! [that is, on the way to New York]....Look, take care that you stay well and it won't last long and we won't have to write any more!!! Until then a paper kiss.

The Landsmanns in New York—Sigl, Irma, and Lissy—remained a subject of ambivalence. Lilly was glad that Walter was seeing them regularly, as otherwise he would have been entirely alone in the city, but on June 13 she warned him not to rely on them too much:

You know, Walter, I understand you very well and how glad you are that they are close at hand, but go, you are now so close but don't run around so much to the extended family [Lilly uses the nonce word "Mispochologie," a combination of a Yiddish/Hebrew root and a Latin ending] because in particular, Irma is not as sweet as she seems or wants to seem!

The following week Lilly was back from the seaside vacation with her employers in Devon and reported on June 29 that "Mrs. Canfield is much more normal. I told her that, only in somewhat selected words!" She mused about the future: "I will be able to bathe again next summer, but at *Coney Island!*," one of New York's most popular beaches. There was more about the endless problems with affidavits, and a new wrinkle about the imposition of £11 in customs duties (a fortune) for some jewelry Arthur Neuhaus's relatives had brought to England for her. When Walter wrote something favorable again about the Landsmann family, Lilly remained polite but skeptical:

Did you notice the meeting [Rendezvous] with Irma? Say, are the Landsmanns really dear and nice, I really can't believe that. No, but I'm not convinced. In any case, very nice greetings, ect. ect. I leave it up to you what to tell them, what you should do and accomplish with them!!

"Lilly Received the Visa"

Lilly finally engaged the lawyer recommended by Fritz Mayer, a Mr. Jacobs, to help with her visa situation, but he could not work magic. In June, Lilly forwarded to Walter the unfortunate news that her lawyer had received from the consulate:

1) Affidavits from third parties cannot be considered at all.

2) I can receive a visa only if you earn enough.

3) The consulate has not received your statement about the $14 from Dr. Miller [Walter's second job on top of his working the night shift at Klein's].

Twenty-year-old Lilly could be "all business" when needed. She set out precise instructions for locating the missing statement on June 21:

> I now need the following from you: You have already registered the letter with the Miller confirmation. Do you still have the *receipt*?? If yes, have the New York main post office investigate what happened to the letter. Further send me the number of the letter <u>immediately</u> so that I can have an investigation from London. Because if we can prove that the Consulate has received the letter, we've gained a lot. In any case still send a confirmation from Miller. To me or Mr. Jacobs, <u>not</u> directly to the Consulate. Today I have written to Jacobs that you will make an investigation about the letter and will send a second *statement*. Please do it.

In the midst of increasing political tensions, Lilly's parents sent her several photos dated July 1939 as reassurances of normalcy in Vienna. One, captioned "Mama considers what to cook today" (in Viennese dialect, "Mama denkt nach was koch ma heit"), shows a residential street scene taken from above, probably out of an apartment window. Pauline stands among a group of women clustered around what could be a horse-drawn vegetable cart. At least three of the women wear tracht (Austrian national costume), so this was a "German" or mixed crowd of customers and probably not a Jewish vendor. Pauline, marked by an inked cross overhead, is wearing a stylish dress with a dark and light geometric print.

Another photo, addressed to "our dear Lili" and signed Gustl and Omama, shows them seated at apparent ease on a park bench.

However ordinary the scene looked, it was tinged with minor rebellion. Since June 1938 Jews in Vienna had been forbidden to enter public parks.⁶⁶

Pauline shopping for dinner, July 6, 1939.

Gustl and Omama on a park bench, July 9, 1939.

Then there was a hiatus in Lilly's letters for nearly a month. But on July 27, 1939, the miracle came through. Lilly must have telephoned her parents, and her father Arthur then sent a terse cable from Vienna to Walter in New York with the news: "Lilly received the visa." The same day,

---

66 Hecht, Raggam-Blesch, and Uhl, *Letzte Orte*, 254; and Gertrude Schneider, *Exile and Destruction: The Fate of Austrian Jews, 1938–45* (Westport, CT: Praeger, 1995), 20.

Chapter 8: Life at the Canfields Continues

Lilly mailed Walter a postcard. Space was limited, so she wrote in a sort of telegraphese:

> Walter! I have had the visa in my pocket for two hours. Can you sympathize with that?
>
> Already have the ship prospectus but don't yet know which ship I will take. Don't want to rush. Am sooo happy and have not had a minute of time (until now!). But soon now, Walter, I will be over there. If I write less now, don't worry, I will have so much to do.
>
> Much much love. Your happy Lilly

Packing

In the spring of 1939, Lilly's parents had sent trunks of her clothing to England. Lilly wondered whether it would be practical to bring this ample wardrobe from her former life in Vienna to what she correctly foresaw would be cramped lodgings in New York, or whether she should raise cash by selling some of the clothing in London. She wrote in May:

> Our apartment will have to be very nice for us to bring all the things over, it is a puzzle to me, if also not my greatest worry! I myself have 7 coats!! The parents told me through Paul that I must leave them here for £10.

Despite that advice Lilly seems not to have sold much, if anything. The red folders included her luggage inventory for the ship. Her trunks contained three winter coats, a spring coat, a tussore silk coat for evening, a fur coat, and ski clothing (a remnant of Albertgasse's annual ski trips to the Alps).

Lilly's Departure for New York

Within a few days of receiving the visa, Lilly had arranged third-class passage on the SS *Manhattan*. (Three years earlier, this large American liner had brought the US Olympic team, including legendary runner Jesse Owens, to the 1936 Berlin Olympics in deluxe first-class style.) She sent Walter a cable date-stamped August 2, 1939, reading: "Have tickets travel on the Manhattan *eleventh August* kisses."

This time, Lilly left England as scheduled, embarking on August 11 and arriving in New York on August 17. A comparison of the entries for Lilly on the manifests of the SS *Volendam*, the ship that she did not sail on in February 1939 because her US visa had not been approved, and the SS *Manhattan* highlights the changes during that intervening half year. On the *Volendam*'s manifest, Lilly had given her nationality as "German/Austrian." She abandoned that futile distinction on the *Manhattan*'s manifest, declaring only that she was "German." Both manifests indicate her ethnicity as "Hebrew." In February, Lilly had listed her profession as "student/teacher," but in August, she had moved beyond a student role and identified herself solely as a "teacher." Perhaps most significant are the entries for language. In February, she had claimed two languages, German and English. In August, the only language she acknowledged on *Manhattan*'s passenger manifest was English.

Walter's last letter to Lilly in England, written on August 2, brims with his anticipated joy and love:

Now the future lies in front of us, Lilly, our joint future.

Glitches

Earlier in August there had been a final blowup between Lilly and the Canfields. She left with no notice ("ran away" according to the Canfields) and then seems to have initiated legal proceedings for back wages. The Canfields threatened to countersue for the amount of health insurance they paid for her in addition to "one week's holiday in North Devon, permanent hair wave charged to our account,...supplying traveling rug, weekend outings, teas, and hotel expenses and theaters," totaling £24.17.7. Immediately after arriving in New York, Lilly wrote a letter to Mr. Jacobs, the solicitor in London who had helped to secure her US visa, setting out her response to these claims. Eighty years later, the details don't matter. What stands out is how well Lilly's mastery of English enabled her to lay out the facts.

This tempest eventually blew itself out. In December 1939 Dorothy Canfield sent Walter a note thanking him for his greeting card and asking him to forward her regards to the mothers in Vienna ("When you write to Frau Haim and Frau Neuhaus please tell them I hope God will bless them, as I cannot write them on account of the war, you see."). She added "kind wishes to Julianne."

Another dispute arose immediately before Lilly sailed for New York, this one with her uncle Sigl. Lilly planned to live on her own for the short time between her arrival and the wedding, but Sigl objected strongly. (Lilly and Walter had briefly thought of avoiding this problem by being married aboard the SS *Manhattan* when it arrived in New York, but the captain lacked authority because they weren't both passengers on the ship.)

Sigl wrote Walter a rather prissy letter in his minuscule, draftsman's handwriting dated August 12 and must have had it hand-delivered, since the envelope lacks both a stamp and Walter's address:

Unfortunately, I did not have the occasion this Saturday to give you my view about Lilly's lodging before the wedding, so I will put it into a few written words.

Lilly is of age and can do and leave what she wishes; her decision that she should live alone before the wedding is, in any case, not in agreement with my view, so I say firmly that this will be done without my agreement and against my will.

Let me note about this, that I would treat this the same even if Paula [Lilly's mother] hadn't written to me: "Look after my child." I understand this sentence to mean that we should stand in the place of her parents as long as Lilly is not married.

Despite the posturing, Sigl may not realistically have expected Lilly to stay with the Landsmanns in their small furnished room, since he backed away from that option at the end of the letter:

If a temporary accommodation in our house comes into question, as we as intended, so you must decide before Lilly's arrival, if then you decide against Lilly's intention, since we definitely have to obtain the consent in advance of Frau Neuhaus (New York!). [That Frau Neuhaus was the Landsmanns' New York landlady, not Lilly's mother.]

Walter, ever the diplomat, had written to Lilly on August 3, before her departure from England, about the Landsmann problem, discussing whether Lilly would stay with them during the inevitable lag between her landing in New York and the earliest date that they could get married. This is one of the very few saved letters that Walter himself wrote:

I believe we both don't want you to stay so long with the Landsmanns. I also don't feel so warmly towards them....Look, dear, from the outset the following is certain: what you don't want, I also don't want. Consequently you must be reassured under all circumstances. Apart from that, Irma was <u>really fabulously</u> [underlined four times] decent to me. On the other hand, Lissy has always behaved like a 12-year-old to me, always got terribly on my nerves. If you can expand her mind a little—and you wrote that you will try it—she will possibly become a halfway human. Under her father's regime, never. Sigl himself is an odd person. I am not quite certain about him, but until now he has not been half as congenial to me as Gustl was from the <u>first</u> word. He is a cynic. I don't like cynics.—These are my notations about the Landsmann family.

CHAPTER 9

Walter in America— Letters from the Haim Family

This chapter backtracks to trace Walter's first few months in New York as they appeared to his family, a parallel perspective to Lilly's letters.

Walter's First Weeks in New York

The youngest of the Haim children and not the hardiest in temperament, Walter became the pioneer by chance because his visa had come through first. His parents and siblings were concerned about how he would fare outside the family circle, all the more since he would be alone in New York until Lilly could get her US visa.

Walter sent a cheery travel report to his parents, but as seen in Lilly's letters, his arrival in New York was a cutting disappointment. Contrary to expectations, no one met him at the pier, and Mr. Bulova did not respond to any of Walter's attempts to contact him.

The Haim family had anticipated some sort of ongoing relationship with Bulova. They sent one of the first family letters and a telegram, complete with a ten-word prepaid response coupon, to Walter in care of Bulova. In February 1939 Hans wrote optimistically, "In particular I am curious about your debut with Mr. Bulova, the impression that he made on you and if you can assess it, the impression that you made on him." The following month,

Paula recognized that the family had put too many of its eggs into the Bulova basket rather than preparing for contingencies. She wrote to Walter in March:

> It's a shame that one was not able to think this through before your departure. But we were all so firmly fixed on Bulova.

Martin agreed, writing in November that "Mr. B[ulova] should go to the devil because of his inaccessibility, but unfortunately one cannot do anything about it."

The New York that Walter arrived in was awash in pro-German and antisemitic sentiments. On February 20, 1939, less than two weeks after Walter disembarked from the *Queen Mary*, the German-American Bund, a pro-Nazi organization of ethnic Germans living in the US, held a "Pro-America Rally" at Madison Square Garden, a large sports arena in Manhattan. The rally featured goose-stepping uniformed marchers and Hitler-style salutes. A large banner of George Washington, identified by the Bund as "the first fascist," hung by a stage that was framed by swastikas and American flags. Later that year, a month after the war had begun in Europe but while the United States remained neutral, the Bund staged a pro-Nazi march in Yorktown, a predominantly German neighborhood on Manhattan's upper east side.[67]

Walter did not write about the Bund at the time, but it remained an active memory. In the early 1960s, long after the Bund had fallen apart and its leader been deported back to a defeated Germany, I overheard him telling our mother that the German couple who owned the bungalow colony in Stony Point, New York, where we stayed for so many summers (our fellow holidayers were the usual NYC mixture of Irish, Italians, and Jews), were the type who would have been members of the Bund.

---

67 Alan Taylor, "American Nazis in the 1930s—The German American Bund," *The Atlantic*, June 5, 2017, https://www.theatlantic.com/photo/2017/06/american-nazis-in-the-1930sthe-german-american-bund/529185/.

Nazi parade in New York City, 1939.

"Badly Hidden Despair"

After the first few weeks, Walter seemed to be barely coping alone in New York. At the end of April 1939, Hans wrote Walter a forceful big brother letter, separate from the joint family letters, urging him to buck up and be patient. Walter should put the New World's trials into perspective—he was no longer under the looming threat of Dachau. Despite a list of hardships that Hans catalogued, including "the brutal ruthlessness of life," he insisted that Walter was fortunate to be in New York. He had found an office job, even if it was a temporary one that paid only a pittance. This saved Walter from having to take to the streets to try to earn pennies as a porter or shoe cleaner. Perhaps Hans made this vivid comparison because they all had seen poor Jewish refugees from the Eastern reaches of the former monarchy working at just such menial tasks to survive in Vienna. Hans wrote:

> It is just that clear and understandable to me that one who is alone in a foreign country becomes very isolated and that homesickness for home becomes strong. That this will grow stronger for you is clear to me also. But despite that your position is not a desperate one! When I take everything into consideration, the foreign country, the foreign language, the new and unfamiliar and unpleasant conditions, the general heartlessness of people, the brutal ruthlessness of life, and

with that the constant insecurity as long as one is not a doer [a Macher, a string-puller], the lack of the family circle and of knackwurst [one of Walter's favorite foods], etc., etc., so I must find that you have had a certain luck, and still have it, and that you still always had reason to be satisfied before and so <u>must exercise patience</u> to deal with this burning question with a little more calmness. Set heaven and hell in motion to fulfill your wishes, do what you possibly can to force and achieve Lilly's travel there, but for God's sake don't lose your sanity doing it. Consider this *epistle* as only an impression of the badly hidden despair that one reads in every word and every tone from your letters. And you have, God willing, no reason yet for an advance desperation! Quite the contrary! You are encouraged there through a nice reception in the country; you have it very difficult, but still, with help have found a position. I know that again it is not yet certain whether this is a secure lifetime position. I know that it is a subsistence wage, but you are working as a *greenhorn* and just for your livelihood. Without that you would have to carry loads or clean shoes in the street. You have a place to live with decent people, Europeans, close countrymen,...and you do not have the slightest possibility there of experiencing things like Dachau or anything similar. So then why so desperate? Because Lilly's arrival is delayed?...You should not lose your nerve but remain totally self-assured about this bride and concentrate your strength and calm for life's difficult battles. It will soon be three months that you have been alone there, but the time is almost over when you won't be alone anymore, and you won't know how it went so fast....So, <u>you must</u> have patience!

The word "European," as Hans used it, can best be understood as shorthand for Austrian Jewish refugees. For a short time after the Great War, Austrian writers Stefan Zweig and Joseph Roth lauded the ideal of escaping narrow nationalism by becoming "quite simply 'a European.'" Unfortunately, rising above nationality into utopian Europeanism was a short-lived pipe dream. Hannah Arendt got it right when she wrote that by the 1930s, "the Jews were very clearly the only inter-European element in a nationalized Europe."[68] Another scholar, born in Vienna and brought to America by her parents as a child, noted that "by 1933...the year Hitler came to power... the dream of a pan-European identity was pretty much dead."[69] Some realists had foreseen the triumph of virulent nationalism. Nineteenth-century Austrian dramatist Franz Grillparzer predicted that mankind would devolve "from humanity through nationality to bestiality." The pendulum swung back towards internationalism to an extent after the war. With no small irony, Otto von Habsburg, the last heir to the Austrian throne and an exile for most of his life, was praised as "a great European" when he died in 2011 at the age of ninety-eight.[70]

Conversely, Walter worried about what he perceived as the family's "desperate" situation in Vienna. Hans dismissed that out of hand. Things were stable, Hans maintained. No one was "desperate," and the biggest problem was the old one of unemployment. Hans wrote in April 1939:

> Further I see in all your letters that you judge our local conditions to be much too difficult. You write to us that we should not be desperate about the local conditions and have patience. I share with you that none of us here is desperate and that we have much more patience than you know. <u>There is absolutely no reason</u> for any of us to be desperate. Absolute calm reigns, and except for unemployment, one could put up with current conditions for years....

---

68   Hannah Arendt, *The Origins of Totalitarianism* (New York: Mariner Books, 1951), 40.

69   Marjorie Perloff, *Edge of Irony: Modernism in the Shadow of the Habsburg Empire* (Chicago: University of Chicago Press, 2016), 52.

70   Michael Shields, "Eldest Son of Last Austrian Emperor Dies at 98," Reuters, July 3, 2011, https://www.reuters.com/article/us-austria-habsburg-idCATRE7630YX20110704.

> Then don't worry unnecessarily about us here in Vienna. At this instant there is nothing that can be done, and until later we still have time.

While Hans was putting on a good face, life in Vienna was becoming more straitened day by day. Another historian, an infant at the time, summarized his family's situation before they were able to emigrate in March 1939: "Each day staying in Vienna was crisis-ridden, anticipation of disaster."[71]

Walter's letters were read very closely by the family in Vienna for completeness, tone, and mood. When Paula felt that Walter was not forthcoming, she would say so. For example, Paula wrote about five weeks after Walter had left Vienna and a month after his arrival in New York:

> You write a lot without saying anything in particular and thus deliberately. Bobbi, dear, always write everything even if not home. Perhaps one can help somehow. One despairs if one cannot see clearly.

"Train Not to Take Things So Tragically"

Even Paul sounded exasperated by Walter's disturbing letters from New York. He wrote from Vienna in early March:

> Finally for once write an orderly letter, for example, got up at __ x hour. I had breakfast at __ at __ then I went, and so forth. Don't let it get you down so much.

This prescription of an orderly routine and stoicism was to sustain Paul through what he called the "blows of fate."

Towards the end of May, Walter must have written to Paul that his last good day was on the *Queen Mary*—that is, after he had left Europe and before he landed in New York—and that he could not continue

---

[71] Price, *Objects of Remembrance*, 34.

to bear separation from his family. Paul counseled resigned fortitude. It had always been that way; children left their homes to start a new life and almost never saw their parents again. Paul advised work and more work, self-mastery, and not thinking about what is past. He wrote from England on June 2:

> My child, for now the last good day was on the ship, now is a worse day, and I don't say this just to comfort you, and also one always must struggle with himself and everyone must master himself until better days will come again. I don't say good days, but bearable. One must cut the ties/break away from the old people. It was always that way. The young son goes to America or somewhere, the daughter marries to _____ [Buxti?]. In the rarest cases, one saw one's parents again. The only difference is that when one is young he is without cares, and also the parents are younger and hope for a reunion. Bobbi, lonesomeness is very hard, I know that, but there is medicine against it. The most necessary thing is to work until you turn green. The least necessary is to drink. I have cousin called Winkler who has sat continuously in Dachau since April 1938. Even today, there are fresh accusations and indictments against him. His wife gave herself up to drink. Bobbi, I know things aren't going well for you, but believe me, don't picture such an endless, deep misery for yourself, and you, you must now see the time through until Lilly's arrival. And then, Bobbi, I don't know if it is feasible, but try not to think about the past, otherwise one is recklessly wrong about oneself and everyone, that everything is past. Done. Look, I was once dictator of 500 workers, today I am a degreed errand boy [Hausknecht] who eats the bread of charity. Can't do anything, it is over, and it will eventually change again.

A degreed errand boy indeed. Paul had earned a doctorate in chemical engineering from Vienna's Technisches Hochschule, now the Vienna Technical University, graduating in 1923 with the title of Ingenieur. That was a particularly threatening time for Jewish students. The new republican Austrian government could not, or chose not to, control ongoing violence by antisemitic, pan-German student groups. At the university, Paul specialized in animal greases and waxes, specifically lanolin, a product derived from sheep's wool, as well as in wood used for pianos, furniture, and fine paneling. That knowledge and his abilities took Paul to the position of plant manager for Central Europe's largest piano manufacturer, Hofmann & Czerny. Paul did not play a musical instrument, but he understood wood, essential for producing concert-quality pianos.[72]

A week later, Paul advised Walter again about how to get through the early, difficult days alone in New York. Paul was able to carry on in exile not just because he could distract himself with woodworking, as Walter had suggested, but also because he was more advanced in the practice of not taking things "too tragically":

> Just yesterday I received your second letter. This can't be an answer to my answer to your first letter. (Well said, isn't it?) As far as I recall, my first letter was very stupid, but it doesn't matter. <u>It was a letter and one shouldn't take it tragically</u> [to heart]. Dear, dear Bobbi (I believe I genuinely love you, funny, isn't it?). If things go better for us in a year or two, I won't be able to confirm even once how things always went badly for us. And that things are better for me than for you is already certainly right, but not because I can use a saw or a plane, but because I am far further along than you, specifically, in not taking anything so horribly tragically [to heart]. We are not at all different from a little shuttlecock that is tossed here and there by anything, knocked around, bumped about, made crazy, set up, blown down, blown up, brought from happiness to unhappiness. No, Bobbi, things unquestionably are not good for you as long as you are so far from all who are dear to you, and you still have such an unhappy nature that

---

72 Paul identified himself as a specialist in wood used for pianos, furniture, wood panels, and the like on the emigration questionnaire that he submitted to the IKG in May 1938. Knowledge of lanolin would have been useful for piano manufacturing too, as wool felt was used to make piano dampers and cushion the hammers.

takes everything tragically. Bobbi, train a little, please, not to take things so tragically.

Three months earlier, Paula (a weekend hiker) had used the same metaphor of "training" for resilience, advising Walter:

> One must train one's soul's muscles so that they become stronger and don't react to everything. And one can do that only if one—despite one's own cares—has counsel.

This was Paul's stoic philosophy. One had to do what one could and at the same time be prepared for it all to come to naught:

> Look, Bobbi, it is tragic but unchangeable and I always put up silently with my own heavy blows of fate (and believe me, dear child, they were not few and not at all gentle). Bobbi, fate….That you are looking towards Canada [as an emigration destination for Paul] is very dear of you, but if you have little time, don't do it at all unless you won't be grieved if nothing comes of my being able to go there.

In July 1939 Walter's aunt Malvine wrote him a four-page letter. Typically less sensitive than the rest of the family to Walter's fragile emotional state, she opened with a melodramatic flourish:

> I almost always read your not-private letters and—also almost always cry over them! Crying is obligatory with us because there is nothing at all to cry about in your letters. You are happy, even if you aren't content at the moment.

Malvine, never the diplomat, let slip details about the mounting insecurities of life in Vienna that the Haim parents and siblings had buried in silence. By this time, both Hans and Walter's uncle Julius Feder had been turned out from their longtime apartments, events that were excluded from the Haim family letters. Malvine wrote:

You can be called fortunate because in the first place you are out of here....and when you get up in the morning, there is still a roof over your head if you can pay for it.—! Julius and Hans unfortunately must envy you. Hopefully your parents will not have to also.

What Malvine was referring to indirectly was that Vienna's long-standing tenant protection laws no longer applied to Jews. Thus none of the family could count on remaining in their apartments even if they diligently paid the rent. Once evicted, the only lodgings open to displaced Jews were rooms in overcrowded communal apartments in "Jewish buildings," mostly in the 2nd District.

Haims and Neuhauses

The Haims continued to behave graciously towards the Neuhaus parents after Lilly left for England. On November 8, 1938, Lilly wrote a very formal letter from London to her future mother-in-law, thanking her for inviting Lilly's "poor, abandoned" parents to visit them. Lilly crafted this letter in her most polite tone and handwriting, addressing the envelope to Hochwohlgeb[oren], or Honorable, Frau Antoinette Haim and using the formal second person "Sie" rather than the familiar "du." She began:

> Mutti wrote to me that you [formal], dear lady, were so dear as to invite my parents several times, and I am truly thankful to you for that, that you worry so much about my "poor, abandoned" parents.

To fill out the page, Lilly then offered a report on the English climate:

> As far as the weather goes, the day before yesterday we could actually take a sun bath, something quite exceptional for November in England.

She signed off with more old-fashioned formality: "…and I remain gladly [Handkussen, literally with hand kisses], Your [formal] Lilly Neuhaus."

Paula took care to write about Lilly. In one of the earliest Haim family letters, from February 1939, she first asked Walter, "How did Lilly look to you?" She added that "Mr. and Mrs. N[euhaus] come often and are very dear." Paula listened carefully to Pauline's conversation and told Walter that "Mrs. N[euhaus] reads Lilly's letter with a mother's eyes." For example, Lilly wrote that at the Canfields, one got a fresh napkin every day. The conclusion that Pauline drew from this detail was not amusement at a bit of comic extravagance, but concern that this meant more work for Lilly, who had to wash and iron the linens.

Despite large differences in Walter's and Lilly's ages and temperaments (the latter almost certainly not as visible then), the Haims were uniformly positive about Lilly and her family. In the first letter to Walter after he had left for England, sent February 1, 1939, Paula compared their situations—each had found a good partner:

> We both always had luck. At least with important things. We each of us has found someone who will stick by us through thick and thin and who is a valuable, decent human being.

A Wedding in New York

As Hans had predicted, Walter did not have that long to wait alone in New York. During the six months that succeeded their three days together in London, Lilly finally overcame the visa obstacles and sailed to America during Europe's last peacetime August. They were married two weeks after Lilly's arrival, on Friday, September 1, 1939, in the study of the assistant rabbi, Jessurun Cardozo, at Shearith Israel, New York's venerable Sephardic synagogue.

Sigl and his family must have attended the wedding, as Sigl sent an account back to the Neuhaus parents that was duly shared with

Lilly and Walter, December 1939.

the Haims. Martin Haim wrote on a postcard in late September:

> Although still no letter from you [pl.], we still received the information from Mama N[euhaus] that they have received a letter from Uncle Sigl in which he sends a detailed report about your wedding, how beautiful Lilly and how elegant Walter was. Shame, shame that we could not be there.

Lilly and Walter detailed the presents they had received, including an electric iron, a fruit juicer, and some sort of organ (the letter is water damaged), all questionably practical but hardly romantic. In October, Martin responded with a story from his and Antoinette's wedding fifty years earlier:

> For our wedding we received three coffee services, a couple of oil and vinegar paintings, and similar nonsense, and so we had the most necessary things, although the donors had asked us before what we need. It seems to be the same internationally. With God's help, you [pl.] will slowly buy yourselves what you need.

"Oil and vinegar" would have been Martin's term for kitschy oil paintings.

In December 1939 the newlyweds had their photograph taken and no doubt sent a copy to Vienna. They noted on the back, "Fortunately we don't really look like this."

Wedding Telegrams

On the last day of August 1939, Walter and Lilly sent a telegram to "Neuhaus Haim" to notify the combined families in Vienna that the wedding had been scheduled. The draft that Walter saved reads: "Wedding Friday first of September 12 noon American time, Library [of the] Spanish synagogue, Cardozo. Kisses Liliwalter." They had concocted a joint signature for telegrams because costs were computed by the word. Martin engaged in some linguistic teasing about their combined name "Lilliwal" on a telegram to the Neuhaus family, which was immediately shared with the Haims. Martin spun similar polyglot wordplay in a letter sent on Christmas day 1939:

> From the N[euhaus] family we received your [pl.]...radiogram. After that I looked in vain for a sea monster that is called "Lilliwal" [Wal in German is a whale]. I have to assume that a good fairy that also signed the telegram under this pseudonym helped in your [pl.] efforts for the affidavit. Or was it perhaps the blond *"Beershopmaid"* [sic] that merged with Waldorf and transformed into the fairy Lillywal??

Walter saved the flurry of congratulatory telegrams. Both sets of parents sent a joint telegram from Vienna that was delivered on the afternoon of Thursday, August 31, 1939, to Walter c/o Stern. It reads in the usual telegraphese: "With you in spirit. Most heartfelt happiness and blessings in unending love. Kisses. Congratulations, your parents Neuhaus and Haim." The same day, Walter's brother Hans and his wife, Lisl, sent a telegram addressed to "Walter and Lilly Haim," offering "congratulations and all the best for your wedding celebration and wishes for happiness and blessings on all your paths."

On the afternoon of September 1, Paula sent a telegram from Vienna on behalf of the Kurz family, both present and scattered, that read, "Most heartfelt wishes also from Paul, Olga, Mathilde. Kisses, Paula." At the time, Paul and his sister, Olga, were in England, while their mother Mathilde was living in the Haim family apartment along with Paula. (For Paul's less conventional acknowledgment of the wedding, see his letter of September 18, 1939, discussed below.)

The extended Neuhaus/Landsmann family at Grünentorgasse 4 sent a joint telegram to Sigl and Irma Landsmann's address. They wished the couple "Congratulations from our whole hearts, untroubled health, God's blessing." It is signed Kindl (the Neuhauses' long-time neighbors), Tante Rosa (a name I don't recognize), Omama (Lilly's grandmother, Regine Landsmann), Rudi Schefranek (perhaps Omama's brother or a nephew), and Gustl (Lilly's uncle).

Nana Kindl on the left, Pauline Neuhaus on the right, October 1937.

The Kindls had lived in the apartment across the hall from the Landsmanns and Neuhauses since December 1919. The family, which was Catholic, consisted of the mother, known as Nana, and her two children, Ada and Rudi, both a few years older than Lilly. As a little girl, Lilly referred to them as a collective, "Rudiada." The story is that Pauline and Nana Kindl were such close friends that every New Year's Day, each formally invited the other into her apartment.

Then during the rest of the year, they would pop in and out without any ceremony. My mother stayed in touch with Ada into at least the 1980s and visited her on the two trips she took back to Vienna, the first in 1969.

September 1, 1939, was the day that Lilly and Walter were married in New York, but it was also the day that Hitler began the second major European war in twenty years. They could not have avoided the news. The *New York Times* proclaimed in a large-type, margin-to-margin headline at the top of the front page, "German Army Attacks Poland; Cities Bombed, Port Blockaded; Danzig Is Accepted into Reich."[73] The *Times* also reported on page one that the USSR had entered into a nonaggression pact with Germany the previous day, a shocking reversal that upended the European powers' previous alignment.[74] The family in Vienna knew that war was imminent, but they sent only hopes for the future in their congratulatory telegrams. See section below, War Begins.

Paul's View of Marriage as a "Private Occasion"

On September 18, 1939, Paul sent Walter his contrarian thoughts about marriage:

> Early today I received your dear letter of September 8th thus seemingly without delay worth calling that. I knew already that you had married; dear child, I won't congratulate you on it. I believe that is a private occasion however one feels about it, that it would be smarter not to marry as to congratulate. In any case, give your wife warm greetings if she will put up with them and wants to remain happy.

---

73   Otto D. Tolischus, "German Army Attacks Poland; Cities Bombed, Port Blockaded; Danzig Is Accepted into Reich," *New York Times*, September 1, 1939, https://archive.nytimes.com/www.nytimes.com/learning/general/onthisday/big/0901.html.

74   Tolischus, "German Army Attacks Poland," *New York Times*.

Paul's unconventional view that a marriage was a "private occasion" rather than a public festivity is reflected in the circumstances of his and Paula's wedding. As recorded in the IKG marriage register, Ing. (Engineer) Paul Kurz was married to Paula Haim on March 10, 1932, a Thursday, at the City Temple at Seitenstettengasse 4 in Vienna's 1st District. The record contains the usual details. Both were single, living at their parents' addresses. Paula had a profession as an auditor. Paula was thirty-five and Paul thirty. It is the witnesses who raise an eyebrow. They were the groom's sister, Dr. Olga Kurz, profession physician, and the bride's younger brother, Walter Haim, occupation office worker (Beamter, an indefinite sort of official or civil servant), also resident at Margaretenstrasse 121 in the 5th District (the bride's address). Contrary to tradition, neither of the bridal couple's fathers, nor even the bride's older brother Hans, signed the register as a witness. This is the only instance I have seen in the IKG records where a woman was allowed to act an official witness to a marriage or birth.

Paula and Paul, 1932.

My deduction from the register is that Paula and Paul eloped, in a way. They were married at the Inner City temple, one that neither of them would have been affiliated with (Paul lived with his family in the 2nd District, while the Haim family belonged to the Sephardic congregation). They asked this unusual pair of siblings to accompany them as witnesses on that Thursday afternoon so they could present both families with a fait accompli and thus avoid traditional wedding festivities and congratulations from extended families.

This may be as close as Paula and Paul came to having a wedding picture made. They are dressed with unusual formality: Paula wears a cloche hat, a coat (perhaps daringly short), gloves, and a fur piece around her neck, while Paul is in a three-piece suit with a rather broad-brimmed hat. They both have something of Mona Lisa smiles, and Paula looks to be Paul's age or younger.

The Ketubah, or Forgotten Names

There were no wedding photos or similar keepsakes in our apartment. I may have been told once, though I don't recall any specific circumstances, that our parents were married at City Hall, which would not have been true. For years, we drove every Sunday afternoon from Jackson Heights to my grandparents' apartment on West End Avenue in Manhattan and then back home in the evening. Each time, we passed the Sephardic synagogue, a striking neoclassical building on the corner where West 70th Street enters Central Park. My father once pointed out the building's architecture, but other than that, it was never mentioned.

In January 2004 the then-current rabbi of Shearith Israel, Marc Angel, emailed me a copy of my parents' marriage record. The page was almost entirely in Hebrew, with a note handwritten at the top in English, "Walter Haim Julianne Neuhaus, Sept. 1, 1939." This was a ketubah, or marriage contract, rather than an entry in a marriage registry like those I had leafed through at the IKG. I recognized my father's signature but none of the others.

Later in 2004, the rabbi of the Orthodox Sephardic congregation in Portland translated the marriage record for me. The names were a revelation. The groom was identified as "Binyamin, son of Moshe, also called Chayim" (a phonetic English transliteration of the Hebrew for Haim), while the bride was "Ruth, daughter of Alter, called Neuhaus." This was my first inkling that my parents had had Hebrew names, and that they were Benjamin and Ruth. "Ruth" was the greater surprise. My younger daughter, born in June 1987, had been named Ruth for her paternal great-grandmother, a descendant of nineteenth-century Swedish immigrants. My mother visited us often in Oregon and, as Ruth grew older, spent hours playing arithmetic games with her. During all those years, she never hinted that her granddaughter Ruth's name had any particular resonance for her. My mother may have simply forgotten that Ruth had once been her name for Jewish ceremonial purposes, or she may have actively repressed that memory. Or she may have known full well but dissembled any sign of recognition. There is no way to know.

Decades earlier, the Haim parents in Vienna certainly knew that their daughter-in-law's Hebrew name was Ruth. Martin wrote affectionately about "Mrs. Ruth," referring to Lilly. He wrote to Walter in April 1940: "Most importantly, you shouldn't write to us so much about Mrs. Ruth's cooking art and about all the wonderfulnesses that she creates, you are making our mouths water." In the same letter he teased, "I would never have dreamt that both you and Lilly are becoming zealous Sephardim. Yes, fate plays ball with little humans." Later he asked, "Are you or Mrs. Ruth Haim still sometimes together with the Sephardim in the temple?"

Lilly and Walter's First Home

Walter and Lilly's first home together was the furnished room where Walter had been living in Washington Heights, a neighborhood in upper Manhattan. That meant a shared bathroom and, at best, limited access to the kitchen for cooking and laundry. A furnished room was near the bottom rung of the new immigrants' housing ladder, though up a step from Walter's initial residence in the HIAS hostel. Into the 1960s the name of their landlord, Mr. Stern, remained a byword for cold-hearted miserliness. I recall hearing two stories about him. One involved a saying of his, "Eisen is immer neu" (iron is always new), which landlord Stern used to brush aside complaints that the old steam radiator in their room was not working properly. The second is an English-language preposition glitch that hadn't been forgotten. Walter and Lilly were commiserating with each other about the awfulness of Mr. Stern when Walter said, "I am even more disgusted with you than him." What he meant, of course, was "I am even more disgusted than you with him." The Haim parents in Vienna, not suspecting what a trial life was in the Sterns' furnished room, routinely included polite greetings to the Stern family in their letters.

After two months in the furnished room, Lilly had had enough. The Sterns had been stealing from them, making off with Lilly's English umbrella and Walter's laundry. In short order, they moved out to somewhat better lodging. Martin wrote on November 15, 1939, in response to what must have been a detailed account, giving Lilly all credit for the move:

> We are all indignant about the baseness of St[ern], one still would not have imagined that was possible. Happy that Lilly got out of that so quickly. The poor beautiful umbrella. Hopefully you aren't missing too much. But Lilly is a second Sherlock Holmes. Walter would not have been on it so quickly. Hopefully that was your [pl.] last loss and the last unpleasant experience.

Antoinette added:

> Now I didn't remember anymore that Walter always needed socks and shirts....Mrs. St[ern] has helped [herself] from a shortage to an abundance.

PART 3

Refugees in England, Then Enemy Aliens

CHAPTER 10

Paul and Paula in Vienna

Leaving the Linke Wienzeile

Paul's sister Olga was the first of the extended family to find refuge in England. She had been there August 1938, working as a baby nurse or nanny for a family named Humphris in Kidderminster. Later that year, the Humphris family agreed to take on Paula and Paul as additional household employees. Paula and Paul had been laying the groundwork for this move. Paula wrote that the previous fall:

> I sent a stuffed camel to Kidderminster to the small two-year-old boy. When someone asked him what the camel was called, he answered: Aunt Paula. You can see he has a spirit related to yours [that is, Walter's].

The plan seemed to be moving forward. Paula wrote in early February 1939:

> I just received a letter from Mrs. Humphris in which she invites me most heartily and can offer only a job as a *Cook-General* with them and that she is already happy about Paul [i.e., that Paul will be coming and working there as well].

Preparing for emigration, Paul and Paula began packing up their apartment at Linke Wienzeile 158 in the 6th District. The building, with a beautiful Jugendstil façade, faced the Wien River canal, across from the city's specialty food market and informal restaurant center known as the Naschmarkt. Paula and Paul had shared an apartment there with Paul's aunt Grete Wilheim since their marriage in 1932. (Shared apartments were the norm, as Vienna suffered from chronic housing shortages.) Grete, the youngest sister of Paul's mother Mathilde Kurz, was only a few years older than Paul and Olga, and so was referred to with mild irony as "Tante Grete."

Paul was energetic, Paula somewhat enervated, by the dismantling of their home and domestic life. She wrote in a letter sent on February 1:

> Soon our fashionable furniture will be picked up and then a commotion and now look out there! Paul slaves away for three, and I do nothing at all.

The relationship between the Kurzes and Tante Grete had become strained before the joint household was broken up. As part of the Haim family letter, Paula wrote on February 14 that she and Paul were doing "very well" back in the Haim parents' apartment at Margaretenstrasse 121, "much better than during the previous time at the Wienzeile." She elaborated more candidly in a separate letter sent to Walter in early April:

> Grete is already in Cardiff. During the past years I have never known so many people to leave, which I don't like, but she is the first person from whom I have recently taken leave and am happy not to see any more. Remarkable, no? Earlier, when things were going badly for her, when she still thought to get by as an opera singer, she was much more enjoyable and natural. Or is it that we just got into the habit; being poor has many benefits. Later, with her brother in the factory [Grete's brother, Rudolf Wilheim, and his wife's family operated a paper manufacturing and printing company], she became an insufferable, snotty, arrogant person whose egoism no longer knew any boundaries. Since I moved from the Linke Wienzeile

in February I have not visited her anymore....[Paul "S"] Weisz, who intends to marry her, will be letting himself in for a lot. By the way, he is not much better. Enough about them.

Things didn't go smoothly at the beginning for Grete in Cardiff. Paula wrote to Walter a month after Grete's departure from Vienna:

> Grete is rather unhappily in Cardiff. Weisz has not been able to take up the position there, and they are hanging completely in the air. She would like eventually to go to Cuba or Australia. But unfortunately the desire alone doesn't get anyone anywhere.

Alice observed, adding a few lines in English to the Haim family letter of February 6, that like Walter, Paul and Paula were starting a new phase of their lives:

> Paul's [sic, i.e., Paula and Paul] are moving to us this week and then one period of their lives is at an end too.

Paul and Paula moved into what had been Walter's small room in the Haim family apartment, leading Paul to write wryly to Walter a few days later:

> Now I have your room to live in and so need not think of you anymore.

The English "Permit" Arrives

The day after Walter departed for England en route to the United States, Hans wrote that Paula and Paul had received a "permit" for England, using the English word. Hans reported in his letter on February 1, 1939, that the couple was vacillating:

Just now at midday Paul called Mama and informed her that he and Paula had received a *permit* for England through Olga's boss, but that they do not want to go there!? I don't know anything more at this instant.

Paula sent the news to Walter on the same day:

There is nothing new since you left. Only that this morning we received a permit for Paul and his *wife*. That would be me! Funny! I haven't yet thought about leaving in my dreams.

Paul scribbled a quick and optimistic note at the bottom of Paula's letter ("in a rush") that "today I received a *permit* for England. You see, one must begin, the others soon will follow."

In February 1939 Paula, Paul, and Hans still wrote with some confidence about the entire family's eventually relocating to some foreign land, whether the United States, Australia, or elsewhere to be determined, but leaving no one behind. "Hopefully," Paul added, "we will be able to go there soon, as agreed, but everyone please, that means not reduced at all." A brittle four-leaf clover is still taped to a corner of this Haim family letter.

On March 8, Paula wrote to Walter, with more unchecked feeling than she usually allowed to seep into the family letters, that she had decided to stay behind with the parents for the time being when Paul left for England. She knew that their reunion was not certain. This selfless decision proved to be life altering for both of them:

Paul doesn't know a date yet for work. I believe that I already wrote to you that I will remain here for now. We don't necessarily have to leave together. It certainly was easier for him, but I will not do it because of all the parents. We can only hope that we (Paul and I) will be able to meet again. And you, dear Bobbi, I tell you, if one of us stays put anywhere, he won't rest until we are all together again. There aren't so many with whom one would like to be reunited. We all must come together then, Olli [i.e., Olga], Hansi [a friend of Alice's], Minka, Nettel [a friend of Paula's, then in Japan working as a dietician in an American girls' school] (the older Neuhauses of course!).

In late April and early May, Paula deflected Walter's concerns about the deteriorating conditions in Vienna. Walter probably read accounts in the New York press that Jews were being displaced and persecuted, but Paula, like Hans, resolutely denied it all, blaming it on sensationalism:

Here everything is really in the best order. If the newspapers there write something different, it is simply fabrication. (Word of honor!) You know that the American newspapers are more interested in the size of the circulation than in the truth. Also at home everyone is healthy and everything is in order.

Paula cited Sigl Landsmann's teary letters back to Vienna as an indulgence to be avoided:

From Mrs. Neuhaus I hear that her brother [i.e., Sigl] writes her such woeful [jammervolle] letters. He is together with his wife and daughter, suffers hardship, but—as far as one can judge from here—he doesn't have to make his mother's and sister's hearts so heavy. But who knows what one would do if one were in the other's situation. Though I still believe he writes too much about his tears.

Several of Paula's acquaintances and relatives were having a difficult time in exile, not only Walter. Paula reported at the end of April 1939 that her friend Benedikt "Fred" Dolbin in New York was not doing so well despite his artistic talent and education, while Grete Wilheim, though safe in Cardiff, was moping (literally, "blasts tribulation"). She relayed a cautionary story about a friend in England who had run into an insoluble immigration problem. He had "a nice position in London (L 5.-.- a week) and the company had applied for his work permit," but that turned out to have been the wrong procedure. The application should have been submitted by the German Jewish community, and as a result, the friend "received immediate expulsion as an answer." Paula ended her letter with a deliberately brighter note, looking close to home rather than overseas: "Papa sits on the balcony," she wrote, and it was becoming spring so they could think about going out to the Müller family's garden in the suburbs. She closed with big-sisterly advice:

> My dear dear brother stay healthy and in any case don't skimp on food. One soon becomes sick. One must keep one's strength.

Bureaucratic Obstacles in Vienna

After the initial hurry of moving out of their apartment in January 1939 and the surprise arrival of the English permit on February 1, progress towards Paul's departure slowed.

In early March Paula still anticipated that Paul would leave shortly. She wrote about his imminent departure in the middle of a letter focused on Walter's disappointing situation in New York. She surmised that Walter must be physically sick because of the difficulties he described and his failure to look up acquaintances from Vienna. Her letter also gave Walter a glimpse into their mother's constricted life. Antoinette spent her days getting Paul's old clothes ready for travel (Jews could not buy new ones) and waiting for the mail:

> Now Paul is leaving soon. He has it better than you, he at least will meet his sister there....Now Mama patches and darns Paul's things. So the poor dear is always busy. She is good and brave and waits most longingly for the letter carrier.

Seven weeks after Paul had received the English permit, on March 21, Hans reported with his typical ironic tone that Paul's departure for England had been stymied by negligent tax bureaucrats in Vienna:

Paul cannot move forwards with his passport, his matter was lost in the tax office and probably will have to begin all over again. That is also pleasant, no?

Paul would have read Hans's addition to this letter before it was mailed, and he added a short line and signed it, "your old Paul."

Paula outlined the same news in her private letter sent that day: "Paul still does not have a passport because his tax return has been lost. So now it could be a couple of weeks until he leaves." At the same time, her letter indicated that emigration to Australia, Paul's preferred destination, remained a live possibility for both of them:

Paul's passport, March 1939, showing water damage.

We don't have anything in hand from Austr[alia]. Only the assurance that a guarantor has been found for us there and has submitted for permits for Paul and me. So everything is well on the way.

Finally on March 29, the police office in Vienna issued Paul a German passport, complete with stigmatizing red "J" on the first page and stamp with the Nazi eagle and swastika. This passport was for Paul only; Paula would need a separate one. (The passport included spaces for the bearer's wife and children, a common procedure well into the 1970s.) The passport photo shows Paul looking off to the side, worried, skeptical. The signature includes his academic title of "Ingeneur," engineer.

On March 31, Paula wrote that since Paul had finally received his passport, he could leave once an unexplained delay at the British consulate was resolved. She did not mention the status of her own passport. Emigration to Australia appeared to remain an option, though she reported that "we still don't have anything in hand yet from Austr[alia]." A week later, Paul's UK visa application remained on hold despite their best efforts. The IKG had submitted a request to the consulate for acceleration four weeks earlier, and Hans followed up with another request, presumably on behalf of the Sephardic community. There's no evidence that any of this helped.

During the days and weeks of waiting, life continued in the crowded Haim apartment. Paula wrote the day before Walter's thirty-seventh birthday, setting the scene:

> It is the eve of your birthday [Paula used the Hebrew word for eve, so the phrase appears as the polyglot "erev Geburtstag"], and I am lying on your bed by your little lamp, everyone is sleeping already and I want to write to you. I will see how long Paul will last before yelling "Sleep!"

Paul Leaves for England

About two weeks later, Paul finally was able to leave Vienna. The passport stamps show that on April 24, 1939, he paid 99 Reichsmarks (RM) for a single-use exit permit that was valid for one month. This meant that even with his German passport, Paul could not return to Vienna, or anywhere within Greater Germany. He flew out the next afternoon, April 25, on a KLM flight. Unlike Walter's solitary departure, both Hans and Paula went to the airport to see Paul off. That evening officials at Croydon airport admitted him to the UK for one year on "the condition that [he] will emigrate from the United Kingdom and will not take any employment or engage in any business, profession, or occupation in the United Kingdom." These conditions were more restrictive than Lilly's visa, which allowed her to work as a domestic servant in the UK for one year and could be extended.[75]

Paula's letter to Walter on the day that Paul left contains a rare instance of her openly questioning her decision:

> Today was a difficult day for us. Paul flew to London at 3:30 in the afternoon. And I sit here and do not know whether I have destroyed my life because I remained here. We will see everything.
>
> And you are in the same situation and despite that are totally alone. Paul is probably now together with Lilly at this instant. She wrote once that she will meet him at the airport, and I have notified her. He was going to remain in London for a couple of days, perhaps until Saturday. Then they will certainly have spoken several times. Father and Mother Neuhaus were also very excited about his departure. Now everyone is already tackling everything. Uncle Gustl [Lilly's uncle] also bid him farewell. Hans was with me outside at the airport. The weather was heavenly and here, everything is well and in order. He flew with the Dutch line via Rotterdam. The morning planes are not flying at the moment. Because of that he unfortunately arrived so late at Croydon. He will perhaps stay with a cousin of Mrs. Humphris [Olga's employer] in

---

75 Aliens Order, "Kurz, Paul," April 25, 1939, National Archives of Australia, A435, 1946/4/2361, https://recordsearch.naa.gov.au/SearchNRetrieve/NAAMedia/ShowImage .aspx?B=6990757&T=PDF.

London. In any case I will try to call him around 11 p.m. at this lady's. Then on Saturday he will travel to Olga. If only there is no war, then everything will become better for us all. My dear dear Walter, don't break down. Paul has various addresses where he can inquire in London to try to bring Lilly to you as quickly as possible. Goal! And then if possible we will want everyone to come together. Here so far everything is in the best order. The parents and Aischi [this was the family name for Alice] are healthy. Only today newly sad again.

Paula telephoned Paul in London on the evening of his arrival. He told her about the stormy flight and that Lilly had met him at the airport as planned. Lilly did not know that Paula would not be traveling with him, and her absence was a surprise. Paula wrote:

Yesterday at exactly 11:30 I spoke with Paul by telephone. Things are outstanding for him. It was the worst flying weather that one can imagine, he said. Grey and snowstorm. They were flying at 4,000 meters. All except him and the stewardess were seasick. But nevertheless they arrived on time. Lilly was at the airport and gave him 6 Sh. for fare money [emigrants were forbidden to take money with them out of Germany]. The lady with whom he lives brought him home. He was received and welcomed in the most charming way. Today he has another rendezvous [Paula's word] with Lilly only for longer. She was astonished that I did not accompany him.

A few days later, Hans reported similar details of Paul's bumpy flight to London in the second part of a chiding letter to Walter. Thus far, Paul's mood seemed to be high:

So on Tuesday Paul flew to London, you will already have been informed of this. He had magnificent flying weather.

Hurricane-like snow storms, they had to go to an altitude of over 4,000 meters, iced-over windows, loud air, he and the *stewardess* and a one-year-old child were the only ones still alive. So far, his two letters are very merry.

CHAPTER 11

Paul in the Midlands

On May 3, 1939, the police in Stourbridge, Worcester, registered Paul as an alien and issued a Certificate of Registration. Paul used the same photograph for this English certificate as the one in his German passport. Like Lilly, he had to report to the police whenever he moved.[76]

Paula's next letter to Walter, on May 10, reported that "so far things certainly are going very well for" Paul in Kidderminster:

> He writes that he does heavy garden work the whole day, cleans out the garage, etc. But he does that all eagerly. The children love him, all three, he writes. Mr. H[umphris] is uncommonly pleasant to him, the wife also seems to be good and dear.

Hopes for Emigration

In later years, no one talked about Paula's remaining in Vienna with the parents rather than accompanying Paul to England. The letters show this was a series of ad hoc, short-term decisions. After Paul had left for England, she continued to pursue the many steps necessary for emigrating. In August 1939 Paula wrote to Walter that she had obtained a passport. Then she faced another problem. Although the UK permit that had arrived at the beginning of February had included them both, Paul had used it to travel

---

76   Aliens Order, "Kurz, Paul," NAA.

there alone in April. The permit apparently was not valid for a wife traveling separately, at a later time, to join a husband who was already in England. Paula thus had to restart the uncertain process of applying for a UK permit. All the while, war threatened, and conditions in Vienna worsened.

During the spring and summer of 1939, Paula wrote as though she believed that it was not impossible for Martin and Antoinette to leave Vienna as well. The elderly Haim parents were preparing themselves, at least mentally, for any destination:

> It is yet to be made clear to me that we can go somewhere. For the time being, I have still no idea how I could bring that about. But: if God gives a job....
>
> Papa and Mama have already adjusted to the departure. I believe that they would prefer to start for New York today rather than tomorrow. But they would also go to Australia. One slowly accustoms oneself to underestimating these distances!

Paul was far less sanguine, and in fact quite realistic, about the lack of options for the parents. No country was admitting European Jewish immigrants who were beyond working age. On May 8, he wrote to Walter from England:

> In Vienna everyone really is well, as long as everything is in order, only the old problem of what one will do with the old people remains crushingly hopeless.

Walter's sister Alice also remained hopeful. She wrote (in a letter that seems to have been sent to Walter along with Paula's letter on May 11) that her three newest English students were their parents and "Mother Kurz." Writing in English, she asked Walter to encourage them:

> Please write in your next letter that everyone, including the old people, should learn English and that it is very important

and very enjoyable for those concerned if they go to America and understand a bit.

Alice also asked about English language teaching materials in the United States:

You can look and see what sort of book emigrants learn from. That would interest me. It is certainly entirely without grammar, so similar to Berlitz I imagine. Write to me about it.

As Paula had requested, Walter sent some letters to her individually in care of a friend, in which he could write more candidly without the letters being seen by their parents. She acknowledged that things were somewhat easier for Paul than Walter because his sister Olga was in England, and Paula in Vienna was physically closer to Paul than Lilly in England was to Walter in New York. In late May, she let Walter know that she had forwarded his letters to Paul:

I have sent Paul both your private letters to me. He is sad about you and would give a lot to be able to help you and Lilly. I don't know whether he has already written to you. He is exhausted from work and I think writes only to me. And still things are much better for him there than for you because he is not so entirely alone and at least is on the same continent as I. But you know, one should never mourn if one doesn't have to; as our dear Dr. Rudolf said, you shouldn't take any advance on troubles.

In May 1939 Paul responded to one of Walter's private letters to Paula, writing in some detail about isolation and exhausting work as a method for keeping loneliness at bay. He also relayed news that Jews in Vienna had begun receiving eviction notices, a disturbing development not mentioned in the Haim family letters. Paul continued to acknowledge more openly than Paula or the Haim parents that emigration possibilities for the parents' generation did not exist, while options for himself and Paula were narrowing. Paul was emphatic that he would not go to Australia, or anywhere, if it meant leaving behind his sister Olga (in England) and mother (in Vienna):

> Today I received a letter from Paula in which she told me that the Jews who live in apartments in the Aryan districts were given notice to leave. Perhaps the Neuhaus family has gotten one of them, but I do not know for sure. Your parents have not yet received one. Dear Walter, I also received your letter to Paula, really you are very good so I will not undervalue it, that is why you have it the hardest, because you have never trained for lonesomeness, but believe me, and believe also that it is miserable for all of us, and evenings I know that I must clutch the cushions and bite them in half. I heard already from Lilly that you have night work. Bobbi, one becomes accustomed to anything if one gets used to it.…Write to me once if you have a little time. I wish above all that you have little, as I know from experience that it is better if one has none so that one cannot think so much. When I work so hard in the garden, and it is really hard work because the garden is uncared for and has gone wild, then it is better for me because I can't reflect so much. All that thinking is of no use. It is very questionable whether we prefer to go to Australia. I can't leave my sister and my mother behind, and because of this I refused Australia. Maybe we will be together again in America, though it is absolutely not the land of my dreams.

Paul ended this letter with this: "But we are already too old to remain alone, so it would be good if we reunited."

War Begins

In late August 1939, newspapers on both sides of the Atlantic anticipated an imminent outbreak of war. On August 23 the foreign ministers of the USSR and Germany signed a ten-year mutual nonaggression treaty. It included a secret addendum in which they agreed to divide Poland and other parts of Eastern Europe between German and Soviet spheres of influence. The following week, on August 29, the *Guardian* revealed that German tanks were positioned on the Polish border.[77] The *New York Times*'s lead headline on the same date read, "Europe Remains Poised for War," although tensions had "eased" a bit after an exchange of diplomatic notes between Germany and the UK.[78] On August 31 Poland began mobilizing its men of military age, an astounding 2,500,000, in preparation for an anticipated German assault.[79]

In Vienna the Haim family was aware of the bellicose preparations and that mail could stop once fighting began. Martin wrote to Walter on August 28, repeating what he had written in an earlier letter sent via Amsterdam, that all was calm and hopeful. At the same time, if everything came to a sudden close, this letter could serve as a paternal valedictory:

> We all find ourselves well and quiet and look to the future with confidence. But if, as God forbid, the conflict is not resolved and the mail is discontinued, then only further courage and continue calmly on your [pl.] way. Don't break down, everything will be better again....Hopefully in a couple of days everything will be quiet again and the black clouds will disperse without doing any harm. So courage, hope, and confidence. Be very well and happy.

The next day, August 29, the Haims sent a postcard filled with lines written by Martin, Paula, Antoinette, and Alice. They

---

77   Margalit Fox, "Clare Hollingworth, Reporter Who Broke News of World War II, Dies at 105," *New York Times*, January 10, 2017, https://www.nytimes.com/2017/01/10/business/media/clare-hollingworth-reporter-who-broke-news-of-world-war-ii-dies-at-105.html.

78   *New York Times*, August 29, 1939, https://timesmachine.nytimes.com/timesmachine/1939/08/29/issue.html.

79   Jerzy Szapiro, "Poles Mobilizing Army of 2,500,000," *New York Times*, August 31, 1939, https://www.nytimes.com/1939/08/31/archives/poles-mobilizing-army-of-2500000-all-men-between-ages-of-21-and-40.html.

confirmed again that "everything is in best order," that "a lot of mail from America has just come in." Added signs of normalcy were that the Neuhaus parents had visited the previous evening and stayed until ten at night, and Paula, Mathilde Kurz, and Olga's good friend Dr. Martha Müller had spoken by phone with Olga and Paul in England.

Germany invaded Poland at dawn on September 1, the day of Walter and Lilly's wedding in New York. Two days later Britain and France formally declared war. Then in the middle of the month, the Soviet Union cashed in on its recent nonaggression pact with Germany, invading and occupying eastern Poland.

For the first few days after the beginning of the war, the Haim family continued to send daily reassuring postcards to the newlyweds in New York. They could not be certain which mail channels were open, so they sent the cards via different routes. A postcard from Paula dated September 3 was addressed to "Mr. Dr. Kurt Müller" at the Hotel Sappho in Antwerp, who must have successfully forwarded it from Belgium to New York. Paula wrote:

> Because we don't know if you [pl.] receive them, we are trying today via Belgium. Here everything is quiet and in order and we all in Grünentorgasse [the Neuhaus parents] and Margaretenstrasse [the Haims] are healthy. Also we have regular news from Paul.

This card, like the others, included greetings from Martin and Antoinette. None of the cards or letters mentions even indirectly that on September 1, an eight o'clock curfew for Jews went into effect in Greater Germany (extended to nine o'clock in summer), and Jews were no longer allowed to own radios.[80]

Two weeks after the war began, and in the midst of only indirect communications from England and a dearth of mail from the United States, Paula acknowledged Walter's "foresight" in being the first to leave:

---

80 Hecht, Raggam-Blesch, and Uhl, *Letzte Orte*, 255.

It has come to pass that you are the smartest and most foresighted. Hopefully we will all come together once again. Don't you [pl.] worry too much.

Once Germany was officially at war, it halted mail to and from enemy countries. This meant the end of direct contact between the families in Vienna and Paul and Olga in England. News could be conveyed and received only indirectly, via family or acquaintances in still-neutral territories. Even then, those communications needed to be limited and circumspect. Sending letters from Vienna to recipients in neutral locations that contained messages for persons in enemy countries was forbidden. The IKG's *Jewish Newsletter*, to which all Jews (and persons considered Jews under the Nazi "racial" laws) in Vienna were obligated to subscribe, printed the official notice on September 22:

No Postal Traffic with Enemy Foreign Countries

All postal traffic with enemy foreign countries is discontinued. It has now been observed that letters for neutral foreign countries are being sent to recipients who live in hostile foreign countries. Sending such letters with such inclusions will be punished.

In a letter from September 18, the same letter where he explained his non-congratulations to Walter on his marriage to Lilly, Paul wrote as openly as he had to date about the separation from Paula. He tried to minimize the emotional effect on him of her decision to wait and (a recurrent theme) to deflect Walter's attempts at consolation. Paul acknowledged that despite all the stupidities that life in England posed for refugees, it was still "a free country," another recurrent theme:

And then please you really shouldn't be consoling me. I am not at all in need of consolation, I live in a free country, unimaginable that there is something like that after our life in Vienna. That Paula is not with me, dear child, is her affair. She had possibilities on top of possibilities before war broke out to come here but she drew it out so long until it was not possible any more. If we come together again, it is good; if not it's also OK. Everyone will be blessed in his own way, and I am not the sort of husband to exercise any sort of compulsion over his wife. Otherwise one plays a role that way. My mother is still in Vienna and that is really a comfort for me to know that she does not have to deal with the savages all alone, especially since Paula also is sometimes with her. Bobbi, please don't pity me. OK? Sad? I don't know what sad is anymore because I certainly don't know any more what happy is, or if we say something is not sad. Everything has become unimaginably incomprehensible for me, and one takes it and carries it as long as one can. Certainly, one day this carrying will all be over. But I am not sad about it, at most one can call it *stupid* [Paul wrote that word in English to emphasize its absurdity].

Their aunt Helene expressed a more flattened view of Paula's choice to remain behind when Paul left Vienna. She wrote in March 1940 to Walter from Manila:

Now in this unlimited misery poor Paula is still with her parents to take care of them, how good she is, that she did not leave them.

Paul Moves to Bradford

In early October 1939, Paul left Olga and the middle-class Humphris family, with their large household and unruly garden, to move about 140 miles north to the industrial city of Bradford for a job in his field of lanolin chemistry. There, he boarded with a Miriam Hopkinson and her husband in a tiny, narrow row house at 9 Westfield Terrace, a working class area.

On October 17, Paul warned Walter even more strongly not to try to "console" him and advised him to fill his letters with facts rather than "sentimental rubbish":

> Surely you have received my previous letter for some time and know, if you again would like to write to me, that your next letters should no longer compose consolations, OK, please? You would like to say this is because "I'm shy," I can only say that I don't like letters like that. So you are well, that makes me honestly happy, and you don't write anything about how much you are earning already. Maybe you are afraid that I will ask you for a loan; that's out of the question but I am still curious. Are you still with your first company or have you already become so Americanized that you change your job every month? Next time write to me something in detail about yourself and leave out the sentimental rubbish; if you still must fill it up with ballast, nicely packed into a good parcel, and if you are 100 years old or older (I believe that you have the talent to live that long), then you may again unpack your sentiments and tell your great grandchildren about this time. I will certainly be completely dead already, and maybe so decomposed by then that your sentimental outpouring won't bother me anymore.
>
> Dear Bobbi, please don't take it amiss, but if the next letter seems like this again, I will send it back to you unanswered.

Lilly was reading Paul's letters as well as Walter. She scribbled a note to Walter in pencil on a scrap of graph paper asking, "So what do you say about Paul???" He kept Lilly's note in the envelope with Paul's letter. Of course, Walter did not live to one hundred, but he never told his children, or anyone else, about that time.

Britain Classifies Its Resident "Enemy Aliens"

During the late summer of 1939, the British Home Office set up ad hoc civilian tribunals to classify "enemy aliens" who were living in Britain to determine whether they should be interned.[81] Initially, the rules applied to persons from Germany and former Austria. Italy was added later after it joined the war on the side of the Axis.

The system had three options: Category A individuals were considered immediate threats who should be interned immediately; Category B aliens were not interned but were subject to restrictions (e.g., on travel and owning cars, cameras, and large-scale maps); and Category C aliens were those who did not appear to pose a threat and could remain at liberty, at least for the present. The tribunals' guidelines instructed that Category C was intended to include refugees who had been "subject to oppression by the Nazi regime upon racial, religious or political grounds," as well as those who had lived in Britain for a significant time if they could produce "evidence of character, associations and loyal intent."[82] In all, some 64,000 "enemy aliens" were classified as Category C, about 90 percent of them Jewish.[83]

The classification guidelines manifested British ambivalence towards non-refugee Germans. The most dangerous group, Category A, was reserved for Germans and Austrians "who were to be expected, given the opportunity, to help their own countrymen or hinder the war efforts of [Britain]." At the same time, the guidelines took care not to stigmatize them as people of bad or hostile intent. They advised that Category A could comprise "men or women of good character who, if they acted in a manner

---

81 See Peter and Leni Gillman, *Collar the Lot: How Britain Interned and Expelled Its Wartime Refugees* (London: Quartet Books, 1981), 42–46.

82 Gillman, *Collar the Lot*, 43; Cyril Pearl, *The Dunera Scandal* (Sydney: Angus & Robertson, 1983), 4.

83 "Fact File: Civilian Internment 1939–1945," BBC.com, accessed January 20, 2022, http://www.bbc.co.uk/history/ww2peopleswar/timeline/factfiles/nonflash/a6651858.shtml; see also Connery Chappell, *Island of Barbed Wire: The Remarkable Story of World War Two Internment on the Isle of Man* (London: Robert Hale, 2004), 21.

prejudicial to [Britain], would do so from a sense of loyalty or duty to their own country."[84] Class A also included "past or present army officers and civil servants"—that would have included Arthur, had he been able to get to England—and anyone "with special knowledge of aircraft, marine or transport services, or of chemistry, mechanics, engineering and the various munition services."[85]

In October 1939, the month after the war began, both Olga and Paul appeared before local classification tribunals. The tribunal in Herefordshire determined that Olga was exempt from internment as a Category C refugee. A form the size of an index card recorded her "normal occupation" as "children's doctor" and her "present occupation" as "nurse." The tribunal noted as grounds for its decision: "Is a refugee from the regime against which this country is fighting and anxious to help this country. Is anxious to do National Service."[86]

In Bradford, the local tribunal placed Paul in Category B, though no order for internment was issued at the time. His "normal occupation" was given as "Chemist—Grease and fats," and his "present occupation" simply "chemist." His employer was Messrs. Crawford Smith and Co., Ltd, in Bowling Old Lane, Bradford.[87] As a specialized industrial chemist, Paul would have met the criteria for Category A. Perhaps as an act of leniency, the tribunal placed him in the more favorable Category B.

Once the UK was formally at war with Germany, letters from Britain were subject to censorship. Beginning with his letter of October 17, Paul began each letter by typing in the upper left corner, in red ink and all capitals: "This Letter is written in German."

---

84 Pearl, *The Dunera Scandal*.

85 Gillman, *Collar the Lot*, 43.

86 Enemy Alien, "Olga Kurz," October 1939, National Archives, ref. HO 396/50; https://search.findmypast.com/record?id=GBM%2FHO396%2F50%2F00523&parentid=GBM%2FENEMY%2FALIEN%2FWWI2%2F0940624.

87 Enemy Alien, "Paul Kurz," National Archives, accessed March 31, 2022, https://search.findmypast.com/record/browse?id=gbm%2fho396%2f142%2f00275.

Dimming Hopes for Emigration

Paula continued to look for possible ways to rejoin Paul after the war began. The United States remained a possible destination if Walter and Lilly could make the essential affidavit come through. An alternative escape route went via Antwerp, where a cousin of Paul's was located, though Paula recognized that this could result in her becoming stuck in the Netherlands. She wrote in December 1939:

> Before everything I would like to thank you [pl.] for having taken trouble about our affidavit despite all the rest. You don't need to be afraid at all to report to me any eventual failure. I am unfortunately no optimist and would be more surprised by success than by failure. I have inquired here and also learned that if I just receive an affidavit, I could travel alone [i.e., not with Paul] if I were part of the [US] Romanian quota [Paula could be counted under the smaller but less popular Romanian quota since she had been born there, or alternatively, based on her marriage to Paul, under the heavily over-subscribed German/Austrian quota]....It is all rather sad with my chances for emigration. I believe that I wrote already that Paul's cousin Winkler [the son of one of Paul's father's two sisters] is in Antwerp and would arrange for my entry there. But I don't know if that makes any sense. I cannot find out here whether I could go on further to Paul.

Paula was finding her energy sapped by endless immigration issues, errands for all sorts of "family matters," and assisting friends in difficult situations. For example, she devoted time to helping the mother of a family friend, Hansi W., whose father committed suicide, hanging himself in the dining room of the family apartment. She wrote in early December that Hansi's father was "a good, highly gifted man, only unfortunately his frame of mind in recent years let him consider such a violent end." She responded to Walter and Lilly, "Your [pl.] detailed letter made me very happy. Unfortunately,

I myself can't write a letter. I have only powidl [plum purée] in my head." She asked whether Walter could forward Paul's letters to her and sent her return greetings to Paul via New York:

> Are Paul's letters not such that you can send them to me to read? In any case, my very dear greetings to him. It would be nice if I could see him once again. Look you [pl.], these are decidedly powidl thoughts.

Finally at the end of 1939, there was a breakthrough in Walter's efforts to obtain affidavits for Paula and Paul through the Sephardic Refugee Committee in New York. Paul sent an exuberant letter on January 5, 1940:

> Dearest Bobbi and Dearest Lilly!
>
> Only rarely have I been as happy about a letter as with yours of the 9th. Not because of the announced affi[davit] (I am not at all happy about that as it regards myself) but that you [pl.] have not entirely forgotten me.
>
> Then the two thank you letters [to contacts at the Sephardic Refugee Committee] will absolutely be sent out with the next post. They will be written in English. I only pray that Bulli [his pet name for Paula] can start something with your [pl.] affidavit. Maybe she can go to Holland with it...and from there to here, or otherwise somewhere.

Though glad that Paula now had a glimmer of hope for a way to the United States, Paul rejected it for himself. He cited first objective-sounding, professional reasons that kept him in the UK and after that his unconditional need to remain with his sister Olga:

> Then dear child I am so thankful to you (I mean that sincerely) for this affidavit, for myself it is certainly out of the question.

I am a chemist not only through studies but also in my soul. I have found work here in my specialty and believe I can be useful to this country (whose guest I am) with it. Otherwise I earn my living with it and maybe also for one or two people. To go to you disregarding the difficulties, which I cannot or may not explain to you further, only no reason concerning having found work possibilities, otherwise there is a point and a "TABU" [sic], I will not leave my sister again, even if (don't say a word about it) we both perish as a result.[88] However it is said, the last possible effort must be made for Bulli if it hasn't been already, so at least she can go to you. Anticipating I will only say that I believe that Sydney will be the city where we will all see each other. (Perhaps, I certainly don't know for sure.) If I stay in correspondence with a lanolin factory being built (there are enough sheep there (I mean only four-legged ones)) and hope that I will have the ability to go so far, that all of us will meet again there (you also know how uncomfortable it is for you that you must take your chances).

Now I will ask you not to take what I have said about my not going with Bulli as thoughtlessness. Only I know how dear she is to me and how I suffer under this separation (I was always a decent guy and will remain one, fate has not stopped recognizing that). I cannot leave my sister alone (it would be choking on it a bit but I must write further), and I cannot give up a halfway-secure position for something else over by you, and I have no interest in starting again from the beginning, if perhaps such a possibility were to be had. The USA does not need any lanolin specialists.

Paul had visited Olga in Kidderminster over the holidays, but things were going badly:

---

88   Olga's situation was less of a secret than Paul seems to have believed. Paula wrote in December 1939, "This week I spoke with Olga again. She is very weakened and completely crushed by unhappiness."

I was with Olga during Christmas week (express train time from here). It was very nice and, as one says, I traveled back here with a bleeding heart. Incidentally, Olga's work also is oppressive.

He was also under financial pressure, barely carrying the heavy load of relatives who depended on him:

Also my uncle Rudolf [Wilheim, living near Grete in Cardiff] is not well, not business-wise either. They all sit on me as though this horse (I) can carry that much; yes, if we only had had more time. I will soon have been here for a year and have not yet come a long way. Grete is doing the best. She is and remains one who makes the best of things [Lebenskünstler].

Paul asked Walter to write more about their daily lives, and hinted that he had some contact, no doubt indirect, with the families in Vienna. Their situation, he admitted, was a "horror":

But Bobbi I have noticed reading through your letter again that you have not written anything about yourselves. What kind of income do you [pl.] have? Where do you [pl.] work? And above all, I ask that in your next letter you write more about you [pl.]. Bobbi, you are very dear to me. Hang in there. I hear a bit from our people. I don't want to get accustomed to the horror, although I should already be used to it....I don't know any more, I am already all hollowed out, already have a beautiful bald head.

Paul's spirits rebounded somewhat after the Christmas holiday. In a letter dated March 10, he confirmed that he had written the two thank-you letters, complete with the expected civil niceties, to the Sephardi contacts in New York who had provided an affidavit for him and Paula:

If the postal ship is not sunk, then Mr. Katzner [the man who signed the affidavit] and Mr. Tarry [an official of the Sephardic congregation and its refugee assistance committee] certainly have received my thank-you letters, with otherwise nothing from me other than what would be done by a genuine Englishman, that is the stylistic requirements have been complied with, which one cannot claim at all about my letters.

Paul followed with some banter about Walter's having been sick:

You were ill, you poor bunny, but if one has his wife by him, then sickness must be a pleasure. I take care in spasms not to become sick, but I am not 100% successful, otherwise my landlady would also take good care of me, but I prefer my wife every which way before everyone, and so I wait virtuous and well behaved until I meet mine again, even if it be in heaven, and without hesitation I would hurry to hell if I didn't find your lovely countenance in paradise.

Paul responded warmly to Lilly's account of their day-to-day life:

Then your daily schedule is very interesting, but going home is always your most important occupation; no Lilly, you know that I expect a lot from you, but if you cannot disabuse your wedded half from this disgrace, then I won't expect anything from you anymore.

A theme of alcohol wound through the letter:

It is still morning, I have still not had any whiskey under my belt, but I am so happy already looking forward to the one I will have around 9 p.m. (a triple), that I am already elated. Yes, children, I still hope to become a dignified alcoholic....

> Now enough for today, write again soon to your drunken [signature] Paul

Next to his signature on a letter that otherwise is typed, Paul added in pen, "Already an alcoholic's handwriting?"

A couple of weeks later, on April 19, Paul responded in the negative and with a bit of a joke to Walter's question about whether he had given up his drinking habit:

> My dear Bobbi, I have not yet broken the habit of drinking whiskey. First, I already tolerate it somewhat, and second, drinking is much too nice to leave off. Further I have still another excuse, now I also drink to your health.

Whatever Paul's earlier taste in whiskey had been, it dissipated. Many years later, he drank barely an occasional sherry. Paul said that one's ability to taste fades with age, so he put sugar and milk in his coffee (unlike in earlier times) and no longer drank wine.

Olga's Situation Worsens

Paul's next letter, of March 15, 1940, was far more agitated. He typed it as an unbroken, page-long paragraph. To increase the chances that it would be received, Paul took the unusual step of making a carbon copy and mailing the two separately to Walter. Both copies arrived and were saved. Here, Paul disclosed to Walter for the first time details of Olga's position. Her job with the Humphris family, the sponsor of her UK visa, had become untenable. There had been a quarrel, and Mrs. Humphris said she no longer needed her. Olga's health was impaired from her endless work nursing the Humphris' premature twins. Paul believed that Olga's being reunited with Paula, wherever that might be, was her best hope. He again staked out his position that he would not emigrate and leave Olga behind. None of this, Paul emphasized, should be communicated to the family in

Vienna because they could not do anything to alleviate the situation, and it would only distress them further:

> Bobby, the contents of this letter contains a thing which I have not disclosed to any of our people until today, a sort of confession, and if you have read through to the end, so you will understand the terrible inhibitions which I have overcome to disclose this request....Listen: in my various letters I have often shared with you allusively that things are not well ordered for my sister. Now the truth is that she has become a wreck, unrecognizably exhausted, tired, tired, tired. Previously I was not in a situation to make her see reason and let go of this *immense* work and duty that she has undertaken, to look for easier work without choking responsibility, or to move here and live modestly with me. Now the thing has come to a head in the last days so that she simply can't continue. Her boss who has always said how she values her and she is indebted to her—because she has, quite objectively speaking, made genuinely viable children out of a pair of twins who were in very bad shape at birth—I think I can evaluate this objectively, it was to be expected, today when she [Mrs. Humphris] does not need her any longer, she is dissatisfied so there was a heated argument—yes, my God, first one squeezes out the apple's juice and then just throws the husk away—so it is, she will come to me soon, and we will somehow live for the time being. Now I am not the man—as idolatrously as I love my sister—who can again upend her and bring her again halfway to a suitable life (let's call it life, the vocabulary of each language is too small). The only salvation that I see, and that probably she sees, is to reunite again with Paula, who is not only very very wise, but who also has a good real-life influence on my sister....Anticipated I have your word, manly honor, that you will not say anything to any of our people about Olga's situation. They cannot help it, and it can only harm the others....Bobbi the dance lurches on. Bobbi I have

told you only the naked facts, I am no longer in a condition to untangle them.

In his next letter on March 28, Paul noted to Walter, "Your letters now sound steadier than they sounded at the beginning, and I try also not to let mine become too soft." As for Olga, Paul had visited her over Easter, but things had not improved for her:

She looks pitiful, completely unrecognizable; her management has already requested a substitute for her from somewhere, and as soon as she is there she will come to me....Bobbi, I remain strong still and wish only that you remain as strong as I, only Olli's situation takes me a bit off, but otherwise I really could bear it. If my letters also sometimes seem soft, Bobbi, I will endure it, I have already had to endure so many things that you don't know anything about, only don't worry at all about me, if only our others will get through.

Paul also responded to Lilly, thanking her for her separate letter: "You know sometimes I wish I were as young as you are, and sometimes I am happy that I am already so old." Recognizing her increasing English competence, he asked her to look up factories in the United States that process lanolin from raw wool grease and then draft inquiry letters, signs that Paul for the first time was seriously considering possible emigration to the United States:

And if you have forked up such addresses, then write me a lovely letter in which all my capacities as a lanolin specialist are set out and send it to me; I will sign it and send it out. I ask this of you because I assume that you now know English the best among our family members.

In April 1940, with the war seemingly on hold, Paul summed up his own status: "Things are going well for me, unchanged and industrious." In response to Walter's question, he described his life as a boarder with Mrs. Hopkinson in Bradford with characteristic irony:

> Bobbi you ask who keeps my things in order, and that this was such a problem for you, hmm, I wish most sincerely that this would be my greatest care. First then, my landlady[89] is an angel, I have full pension [that is, all meals] with her, and this is also included: Wash laundry, darn socks, mending, sew buttons, etc., although I can sew and darn quite well myself, and if it were not included I would just do it myself.

In his next letter, Paul added an unusually colorful description of Mrs. Hopkinson:

> I will tell you about my landlady. She is my main prize. A dear nice decent type. [Paul uses the Austrian colloquial word "Kerl," a guy, chap, or fellow, which can refer to a male or female.] I feel completely at ease with her. She is 50 years old, small, rather fat, and has a completely great voice. In the club that I frequent here, someone told me that 20–25 years ago she had a completely grandiose voice but never could go (or be taken) on the stage because of her squat shape and her poverty. She cooks like a fairy tale, almost as well as Paula or my mother.

The following week, Paul wrote in anticipation of the arrival in New York of Lilly's uncle Gustl and sent warm greetings to him. The only other news was that Walter's birthday letters to his parents would have arrived at the right time, and Paul still anticipated Olga's moving in with him in Bradford, though it had not yet happened.

The US consulate in London now turned the obstructionist tactics that it had exercised with Lilly against Paul, rejecting affidavits of support and demanding ever more documentation from his

---

89 Paul uses the word "Hausfrau," which usually denotes a housewife, less commonly a hostess or, more remotely, landlady.

would-be sponsors. Paul disgustedly transcribed and sent Walter a copy of the consulate's ten additional requests concerning the affidavits for him and Paula. For the moment, Paul was out of patience with this latest turn of the bureaucratic screw:

> P.S. If I were my guarantor, I would throw this questionnaire into the wastebasket, yes, throw!! And take back my guarantorship. Now I am happy that I never was my own guarantor but always someone else's, and maybe they won't throw this in the wastepaper basket.

The Possibility of Italy

As long as Mussolini's Italy remained neutral, it was available as a jumping-off point for emigration. Lilly's uncle Gustl was able to sail from Genoa to New York in March 1940. At about the same time, Paul's friend Kurt Müller wrote to him from Vienna that he and his family had "decided to travel to Italy," but later that month, Paul seconded Walter's conclusion that this plan was futile: "I agree entirely with your exposition and will do my best possible to turn them away from that." In his next letter, Walter must have written on the subject of Vienna versus Italy, advising that remaining in the eye of the storm was best. Paul concurred, writing on April 19: "Bobbi I agree with your idea that without question, it is calmest in the center of a whirlwind, completely agreed."

Paula, desperately trying to find an exit route from Vienna, also considered traveling to Italy, where the family had relatives, as a stepping-stone to the UK. She wrote to Walter in a family letter from March 1940, during the lull in hostilities known as the "phony war":

> I have already filed an application for a 6 month residence in Italy. What do you think of that?

Paul remained skeptical and thought that such a move would be "more madness these days that it was maybe two months ago." He wrote to Walter:

> My wife tries everything possible to go to Alfred and then from him to come here. First I consider that unattainable, and who can tell me what the political situation will be tomorrow. I believe that private travel will stop.

This Alfred was Martin's nephew and Paula's cousin, Alfred de Majo. Earlier, Alfred had been a substantial businessman, the managing director of an international tractor manufacturing company called Hoffherr Schranz, where Walter had his first job after graduating from business school.

Alfred de Majo and family in May 1935, before the deluge, posed to embody a family circle. In the front row from the left are the patriarch Alfred, looking distinguished in a dark suit and tie, his grandson Robert Schischa (later anglicized to Shaw), and his wife Regine (née Guttmann) de Majo. Standing in the back row from the left are younger daughter Bianca de Majo, son-in-law Siegmund Schischa (later Shaw), and Siegmund's wife Alice (née de Majo).

In retrospect, Paul's premonition was proved correct. Paula's joining Alfred in Italy would have been useless. Alfred and his wife Regine (née Guttmann) had been living in Milan since 1937. Once Italy entered the war in June 1940 on the side of the Axis (opportunistically waiting until it was clear that France had been defeated), it stopped extending residence permits for foreign Jews. When Alfred and Regine's residence permits expired in March 1941, they had no option other than returning to Vienna. Their two adult daughters somehow got visas and eventually escaped to the United States, but once back in Vienna, the parents were trapped. Paula recognized when she wrote in March 1941, soon after their return, that Alfred and Regine had no possibility of emigrating. That autumn, on October 15, 1941, Alfred and Regine de Majo were deported from Vienna to the ghetto in Lodz, Poland (renamed Litzmannstadt in 1939 after a German general), where they died in "about 1942" (per Yad Vashem, the World Holocaust Remembrance Center). The approximate date suggests that even the diligently bureaucratic German occupiers of Lodz didn't bother recording their deaths.

The German Blitzkrieg Moves Westward

In the spring of 1940, the "phony war" (in German, "sitzkrieg," or sitting war, in implicit contrast to the blitzkrieg, or lightning war) turned real. That April, Germany invaded Norway and Denmark. On May 10, the German armies turned south and carried out successful blitzkrieg attacks against the Low Countries and France. The same day, Neville Chamberlain resigned and Winston Churchill became prime minister. The position of the British Expeditionary Force (BEF) in France and the Netherlands turned into a disaster. Famously, something over 200,000 British forces and another circa 130,000 French and other troops were evacuated from Dunkirk between May 27 and June 4, 1940, though many soldiers and massive amounts of British war materiel were left behind.[90] The French

---

90 See, e.g., Gillman and Gillman, *Collar the Lot*, 141.

government fled Paris on June 10 and two days later declared Paris an open city, concluding that any attempted defense would be futile. On June 14, a month before Bastille Day, German troops marched unopposed into Paris. France formally surrendered on June 25.

Aggression was not confined to the western front. In June 1940 the Soviet Union invaded and occupied the Baltic states of Latvia, Lithuania, and Estonia. It then demanded and got land concessions from Romania.

At the end of June, Germany bombed, invaded, and in short order occupied the Channel Islands with no resistance from Britain. Everyone anticipated, quite reasonably, that Hitler's next target would be mainland Britain.

Suspicion Falls on "Enemy Aliens"

After its unstoppable series of victories along Europe's Atlantic coast, Germany demanded that the UK surrender or face the consequences. This stirred up frantic suspicion about the thousands of "enemy aliens" who were living in the UK, primarily German and Austrian Jewish and political refugees. Some in the British intelligence community believed that a fifth column[91] of infiltrators had significantly aided Germany's successful invasion of Norway, and warned that the same could happen in the UK. Anticipating an imminent German invasion, the UK government expressly identified "the presence of 73,000 non-interned enemy aliens" in Britain, almost all of whom had previously been classified as B or C, as a possible source of subversive activity.[92] The tabloid press played on

---

91 The phrase "fifth column," referring to an enemy within that undermines the main group, generally in favor of an external adversary or invader, was a relatively recent coinage. It originated during the Spanish Civil War when a Nationalist (i.e., pro-Franco) general boasted that he had four columns of troops advancing on Madrid and a "fifth column" of supporters inside the city. It was quite the popular term at the time. Ernest Hemingway titled his only play *The Fifth Column* (1938), while in June 1940, *Life* magazine published a photo essay of events in the United States titled "Signs of Nazi Fifth Column Everywhere."

92 Gillman and Gillman, *Collar the Lot*, 84–89.

popular mistrust of refugees and attendant hysteria: "Week after week, the *Sunday Express* and the *Daily Sketch* published inflammatory and wholly unsubstantiated stories of refugees acting as spies and saboteurs."[93] A local historian of internment on the Isle of Man summarized the situation: "The popular press was not on the side of the aliens. They were an easy target. It made good copy."[94]

Once Churchill took charge, internment of foreigners in Britain began quickly. On May 12, two days after the change in government, local police were ordered to arrest and detain "enemy alien" (German, Austrian, and later Italian) males over age sixteen and under sixty who lived in any of thirty-one eastern and southeastern coastal counties in England and Scotland, where it was thought a German invasion would first take place.[95] About two thousand were arrested and initially held in makeshift sites like local schools.[96]

The first wave of internments was followed on May 27 by arrests of "enemy alien" women as well as men in Category B. The news on that date readily supported a sense of impending catastrophe. The Dunkirk evacuation was ongoing, and the king of Belgium sought an armistice with Germany, having concluded that "the cause of the Allies is lost."[97] On that same date, the British chiefs of staff fed the hysterical xenophobia with a cabinet paper that characterized "alien refugees" as "a most dangerous source of subversive activity" and advised that "the most ruthless action should be taken to eliminate any chances of fifth column activities."[98]

The scope of arrests broadened and became more arbitrary. On May 31, the Home Office expanded local constables' discretionary authority to intern "any German and Austrian men or women of Category 'C', 'where there are grounds for doubting the reliability

---

93 Pearl, *The Dunera Scandal*, 6.

94 Chappell, *Island of Barbed Wire*, 25.

95 Gillman and Gillman, *Collar the Lot*, 94–98; Pearl, *The Dunera Scandal*, 5.

96 Gillman and Gillman, *Collar the Lot*, 97.

97 William L. Shirer, *The Rise and Fall of the Third Reich* (1960, 1990), 729.

98 Gillman and Gillman, *Collar the Lot*, 141.

of an individual.'"[99] "Mass arrests" of Category C aliens (i.e., Jewish and political refugees) began on June 24.[100] The following day, which happened to coincide with the French surrender, an expanded order was issued to intern all Category C men under the age of seventy, with a few minor exceptions. By mid-July, about thirteen thousand Category C refugees had been arrested and locked up.[101]

Britain was ill-prepared to cope with those numbers, even though the government had begun discussing the possible internment of "enemy aliens" before the war began, and memories of Britain's problems dealing with internees during the Great War were only twenty years old. There was inadequate housing, food, and other necessary services for those detained. Only seven months after the round ups began, in January 1941, the Home Office admitted to the US Embassy that "no proper arrangements had been planned by the Home or War Office to care immediately for a large number of internees."[102]

---

[99] Gillman and Gillman, *Collar the Lot*, 145.

[100] Gillman and Gillman, *Collar the Lot*, 173.

[101] Pearl, *Dunera Scandal*, 8.

[102] Gillman and Gillman, *Collar the Lot*, 97.

CHAPTER 12

Internment in England

Paul Is Arrested

The local police arrested Paul, a Category B "enemy alien," on May 12, 1940. He was held initially at an improvised alien internment camp at Uniacke Barracks in Harrogate, Yorkshire, about twenty miles from Bradford.[103]

A letter sent on June 5 from Uniacke Barracks was Paul's first communication to Walter since early May. Unlike Paul's letters from Bradford, his letter from the internment camp was handwritten in English rather than typed in German. Initially Paul had thought that he might be able to return quickly to his job in Bradford, but by June he expected that he and the other internees would be moved to another site. He did not know what had happened to Olga since he had been arrested, and he had not heard recently from Paula in Vienna. Letters from internees were subject to censorship, so Paul adopted a thin protective code, referring to Paula as "Paul" and asking whether Walter had "met" rather than received correspondence from the parents (Martin, Antoinette, and Mathilde) without disclosing that the people he was asking about were in Vienna, enemy territory. He wrote:

> It's about one month that I want to write to you. Since 3 weeks I am in this camp and as I thought I will be soon back in Bradford

---

103 Report on Prisoner of War, "Paul Kurz," 15 Sept. 1940, National Archives of Australia, MP1103/2, E40006, https://recordsearch.naa.gov.au/SearchNRetrieve/Interface/ViewImage .aspx?B=9906510. This timeline is confirmed by the internee report that Paul completed on September 15, 1940, after being disembarked from the *Dunera* in Sydney.

I did not write. Now I see that I have to change my mind. When you will answer this letter please put under the above written address the words "please forward" because it is nearly for certain that we shall be moved from here. As far as I remember I wrote in my last letter that Olga came to me so about 2 months ago in a very bad state of health. I had to leave her and from this time I have no idea of her whereabouts. There is not much to report. I am very well, plenty and good food. Only my brain is already a little bit broken. Yes dear Bobby it is sometimes difficult to keep smiling but we have to carry on till to the last. Beside this problem what will happen with Olga, I have no letter from Paul and Kurt. On the 26th May was Paul's birthday, again without me, I think so a fortnight ago there was Greta's wedding with Sam. And the world goes on. Do you sometimes meet Mathilde or Toni or Martin? Please write me as soon as possible, only a few words on a post-card. Remember me to Lilly.

Olga anticipated that she would be arrested as well during the initial internment frenzy. This was quite a reasonable expectation. In May 1940 Britain interned close to four thousand women, a significant number of whom were Category C refugees like her.[104] In early June, Olga wrote to Walter in a tone of defiant resolution:

I believe that we all will be interned, it doesn't bother me, except that contact with you will probably cease, and that I would rather be able to work even under whatever kind of difficulties. But head high & courage! The Nazis will lose the war and then the world will be freed from their horror.

A month after Paul's first letter from Harrogate, on July 5, Walter and Lilly sent Paul a postcard addressed to the internment camp at Uniacke Barracks in Yorkshire bearing the requested words "Please Forward" in large capital letters. Frustratingly, the card was returned to them in New York with the post office notation "Not traceable,"

---

104 Chappell, *Island of Barbed Wire*, 45.

and a rubber stamp reading, "Undelivered for Reason Stated, Return to Sender." This postcard, which Paul never received, included a reassuring litany of names:

> You cannot imagine how glad we were to receive your card. All of us, Mathilde, Paula, Toni, Martin, etc., are all right. Olga too. She said that it is possible that she will see Grete for a short time. Do write again, as often as possible.

Undelivered postcard from Walter to Paul, July 1940.

Internment on the Isle of Man

From Uniacke Barracks in Harrogate, Paul was transferred to the Isle of Man. This island, off the coast of Liverpool in the Irish Sea, was chosen because it was as far as possible from British military sites and the German presence in France and the Low Countries. Conditions there were primitive and inconsistent, as the Home Office hadn't begun developing plans to use the Isle of Man as an internment site until May 1940. Many of the internees were housed in what had been holiday boarding houses, seasonal hotels, and private homes that had been encircled with rounds of barbed wire. About eight hundred male "enemy aliens" were sent there initially, along with a number of women and children.[105] The numbers then increased.

Robert Friedler's Internment Memories

I have no letters or cards that Paul wrote while he was interned on the Isle of Man. What I do have is a firsthand account from the journal that another Austrian internee, Edith Liebenthal's father Robert Friedler, kept between June and October 1940, and which Edith most generously made available to me.[106]

When I was a child, the Friedlers were part of our circle of daily acquaintances. They lived in a ground-floor apartment on the other side of our apartment building in Jackson Heights. To my friend Judy Liebenthal, he was Opa Robert and his wife, Margit, was Oma Grete. Memorable facts to us as grade-schoolers were that Mrs. Friedler owned a shop on Lexington Avenue in Manhattan where she made custom corsets, while my grandmother had a dress store on Broadway. Mr. Friedler was proud of his large collection of classical music LP records that children were not allowed to touch. The Friedlers' first language was German, but they spoke English to us children and sounded just like my grandparents.

Unlike letters, Robert Friedler's private internment diary would not have been immediately read by a censor, so it contains intimate ruminations about missing his wife and their then-teenaged daughter, Edith. Despite the substantial differences in audience and temperaments, many of Robert Friedler's vignettes of Austrian refugees' situation in English internment camps illuminate Paul's probable situation as well.

---

105 Gillman and Gillman, *Collar the Lot*, 135–136, 140. See also Chappell, *Island of Barbed Wire*, 19–22; and Robert Friedler's internment journal.

106 Robert Friedler, typescript of his memoir, with translation into English by Edith Liebenthal. Author's personal copy.

Chapter 12: Internment in England 191

Sketch of buildings behind barbed wire on the Isle of Man by Austrian internee Ernst Eisenmeyer.[107]

On July 3, 1940, the second day of his diary, Robert Friedler wrote a brief description of the conditions in the former holiday camp at Paignton in South Devon where he was initially interned. Barbed wire and armed guards surrounded the camp's forced inhabitants, mostly Jewish refugees, whom he believed posed no realistic threat to even a very shaky Britain. Robert viewed the situation as an absurdity:

> I'll continue to report about the camp. A large hall with a piano on a stage and a bar-like niche in the background, now used as a counter for the canteen, shows that this room was once used for better purposes. Small wonder, for this area was only a short while ago a summer weekend camp where clever Englishmen rented cabins to savor the joys of the seaside. But then the ugly, high, very high double fence made of barbed wire did not exist yet, and between the two fences there were no marching soldiers; surely no unattractive barricades stood on the corners then, made of sandbags, with two heavily armed guards behind them, playing war games with us civilians....

> There are mostly Jews here, at least ninety percent, and apparently all are "Refugees from Nazi Oppression" [the definition of Category C aliens] who are now being oppressed by Englishmen. Jewish destiny. Almost five hundred internees, most of them intellectuals. Innumerable former professors who taught at the universities of Oxford, Bristol and other cities...and now find themselves interned. Attorneys and physicians, half of them from Vienna, and known to me....Simple English peasant faces, whose good-natured expressions in no way fit the fixed bayonets, carefully guard the camp.

---

107 "World War II Intern's Artwork Returns to Isle of Man," BBC.com, March 30, 2012, https://www.bbc.com/news/world-europe-isle-of-man-17535580.

He closed this section with a flourish, like a carnival barker:

> The world is turned inside out, ladies and gentlemen! Inside, here inside, is the outside and not the other way 'round.

Robert Friedler was more interested in religious observances than Paul. He recorded how the hall was set up as a synagogue on Friday nights and Saturdays and noted that he "was happy to see an enormous turnout."[108]

> In our devotion, we forgot that we had lost our fortunes, our homes and our livelihoods, that our families were chased into exile, we were scattered all over the world, and now even our hosts, who gave us refuge and promised us shelter, are robbing us of our freedom....Then not so much has changed, after all. Jews are praying and outside the guards are watching. "I don't understand the world any more," so wrote Hebbel.[109]

Outside the hall, Robert Friedler wrote, internees played chess among themselves while "civilians walk by, men women and children, and they look up at us—free people, respectable citizens, looking at us who live behind bars like circus animals."

This view was echoed in an account written many years later by an Isle of Man local historian, Connery Chappell:

> The camps were, of course, wired-in compounds mostly made up of boarding-houses and occasionally hotels. Like fish in bowls, the inmates could be seen from outside but had no escape except indoors.[110]

---

[108] See also Chappell, *Island of Barbed Wire*, 77: "Jewish services [were held] in the ballroom of the Lido, a large dance-hall only a few yards along the front from the camp."

[109] Christian Friedrich Hebbel (1813, Holstein–1863, Vienna), a poet and playwright of historical tragedies.

[110] Chappell, *Island of Barbed Wire*, 64.

From Paignton, Robert Friedler and his fellow internees were marched about an hour to a railroad station and taken to a transit camp at Prees Heath, a former military training camp southeast of Liverpool, where they were greeted with some bare tents on an open ground, "no offices, no barracks, not even a dilapidated shack."[111] Amenities for the first night were a supper of "only black coffee (perhaps it was not even that black, but who could tell in the dark of the night)," and tents with "three blankets and an empty straw mattress per man. We hear that straw will only become available tomorrow."[112] Food was in short supply, washing facilities inadequate (tin washtubs and cold water only; "no baths, but endless occasions to get dirty"), and toilets "the most degrading of all...portable tin buckets with lids that one has to use in public."[113]

The English weather affected all the internees. Astronomical summer though it may have been, Friedler emphasized the ill effects of the cold and rain: "our mood depends on the weather: don't think that this is a sign of poor intellect, but the weather conditions are directly responsible for our living conditions." He recorded the details:

> When it comes down in buckets we sit in the tent, in the dark, listen to the rain as it pelts against the canvas, as the ditch that we dug around the tent fills up with water, sometimes in an instant, watch out that there is no flooding inside. It pours all the time...then our heath turns into a swamp and water stands on the meadow....The cold is biting here.[114]

In the midst of the physical muck, there were sparks of intellectual life. The camp commandant "gave permission for lectures etc. to be held" outdoors, though this became a problem during the frequent English rains. The first lecture, on Baruch Spinoza, was presented

---

111 Friedler, 20. See also Chappell, *Island of Barbed Wire*, 36–37.

112 Friedler, 20.

113 Friedler, 23.

114 Friedler, 20–21.

without notes by a "Professor Liebert from Germany, who last held seminars at Oxford."[115] It came to a premature end when the commandant sent a messenger to implement a new rule: "where more than five people are assembled, English must be spoken."[116] Friedler recorded that the professor "immediately changes over to English, but points out that he does not master it so completely as to do justice to a difficult topic" like Spinoza's ethics. Shortly after, the lecture series ended "because of the unrelenting rain."

Friedler found the daily camp routine arbitrary and demoralizing. The internees' "lives are reduced to certain prescribed routines: the internee must, above all, appear at roll call; he may show up for food distribution and finally, he is allowed to use the loo, but not at night. That is all."[117]

All incoming mail for camp inmates on the Isle of Man first had to pass through the censors stationed in Liverpool. The process was slow, and sometimes mailbags piled up in hundreds waiting for the censors' review. In contrast, outgoing mail from the Isle of Man camps was read by on-site intelligence officers with comparatively little delay.[118] At one point, Friedler recorded, a rumor went around that mail had arrived from the former camp, but the "commandant returned them all to Liverpool to be censored," so no one received letters from their families for eighteen-plus days, though at times telegrams and parcels were received and distributed, probably because they were easier to censor than letters.

Fifty-eight years after the fact, Paul's friend and fellow internee Peter Tikotin recalled that internees on the Isle of Man had to exist on what he termed a "starvation diet." He attributed it to the British internment system's being overwhelmed by numbers rather than actual malice.[119] Peter recounted in an oral history video for

---

115 Friedler, 24–25.

116 Friedler, 25.

117 Friedler, 32.

118 Chappell, *Island of Barbed Wire*, 61.

119 Peter Tikotin typed memoirs, December 12, 2000.

the USC Shoah Foundation that the primary drawback for him during internment in Britain was that there was "never enough to eat wherever you went." The officials in charge "expected 500 and got 1,000, they expected 1,000 and got 2,000." Still, internees lucky enough to have cash could buy supplemental food at the camp canteen. After being issued a metal plate to eat on that was a bit greasy, Peter volunteered for washing-up duty in the kitchen and "found that if you volunteered for the kitchen, you always got enough to eat." Peter carried that lesson with him to subsequent internment camps.[120]

Morale on the Isle of Man was low and "tension between the captain and the camp" festered over the dismal physical conditions, inadequate food, and lack of mail. Peter Tikotin recalled that the relatively few prisoners of war (POWs) in the camp—actual Nazi soldiers—were allowed to send and receive letters long before the refugees because that right was guaranteed to the POWs by the Geneva Convention. "Enemy aliens" had no such protection. Robert Friedler indulged in an unfavorable comparison of the conditions he was subjected to in England with Austria's treatment of Russian POWs during the previous war:

> I think of the time in 1916 when I served as inspections officer in the prisoner-of-war camp in Freistadt....I learned about the life of prisoners then, as seen from the outside, outside the barbed wire. There were Russian prisoners of war there, and I can tell you, they were better treated by the old Monarchy than we are here.[121]

Paul had advised Walter that "one becomes accustomed to anything if one gets used to it." Robert Friedler also realized that his initial indignation was giving way to acceptance one afternoon while he watched young soccer players in the internment camp:

---

120 Peter Tikotin, interview code 47969, interview by USC Shoah Foundation Institute in Melbourne, Australia, October 22, 1998.

121 Friedler, 39.

Alas, one slowly gets used to it all, and gives up one's resistance. Anger dissipates, as the realization sets in that nothing can be changed, and, for better or worse, we make the best of it. So, they are playing soccer, many in bathing trunks, and the older ones, the ones with rheumatism, watch them expertly.

In July 1940 Friedler noted that "rumors are flying about plans to ship us off to the colonies." Those rumors proved to be accurate, though he realized that both "news and nonsense travel at speed behind barbed wire." On July 27 he recorded that 120 survivors of the torpedoed British ship *Arandora Star*, the majority interned "enemy aliens," had been placed in a neighboring camp. A number of German POWs were assigned there as well, which roiled the relationship between the two camps:

The people are mostly Nazis and there is immediate tension between our camp and theirs. The curse word 'Saujud,' dirty Jew, is heard again.[122]

Robert Friedler was one of the more fortunate internees. In the fall of 1940, his wife, Grete, managed not only to obtain US visas for the family but also to locate Robert who, according to Edith, was in a "secret" camp whose location could not be publicly disclosed. After eighty-eight days of internment, Robert Friedler was released and sailed optimistically with his family to New York:

I was called to the gate, and you [Grete] were there, I saw you and spoke to you...while you, my love, spoke about the troubled days in London...Show me the longed-for fulfillment. Consul, visa, freedom, the beautiful wife and clever daughter, the ocean crossing to the promised land.[123]

---

122 Friedler, 71–72.

123 Friedler, 90.

"Troubled days in London" meant the start of the blitz, which raged for eight months, from September 1940 into May 1941. Luftwaffe raids were not limited to London and the Home Counties. Coventry in the Midlands and Liverpool on England's west coast were bombed in 1940, and air raids reached as far north as Glasgow in Scotland and across the Irish Sea to Belfast.[124] In contrast, when the Friedlers set sail, the United States was still a "country where no sirens sounded."[125]

---

124 Chappell, *Island of Barbed Wire*, 81–82.

125 Chappell, *Island of Barbed Wire*, 95.

CHAPTER 13

Britain Attempts to Export Its Internees

At a cabinet meeting on May 24, 1940, Winston Churchill as new prime minister stated that he not only supported interning "enemy aliens" but also was "strongly in favour of removing all internees out of the United Kingdom."[126] Under pressure from the UK, Canada agreed to take seven thousand internees.[127] A first ship laden with Category A (dangerous) German internees and POWs left Liverpool for Canada on June 21. It arrived without incident. A week later a second ship sailed, the now largely forgotten SS *Arandora Star*.[128]

The *Arandora Star*

In late June 1940, 734 interned Italian men, 479 interned German and Austrian men, 86 German POWs, 200 military guards, and some 174 British officers and men embarked on the *Arandora Star* in Liverpool. Though built as a luxury liner (the ship originally was so posh that it catered to first-class passengers only, with no second or tourist class accommodations),[129] the vessel was described

---

126 Gillman and Gillman, *Collar the Lot*, 133.

127 Gillman and Gillman, *Collar the Lot*, 161–164.

128 Chappell, *Island of Barbed Wire*, 28.

129 Gillman and Gillman, *Collar the Lot*, 185.

in dispatches from London to the *New York Times* as a "prison ship." Its destination was St. John's, Newfoundland, and Canadian internment camps. Despite unrelenting German submarine warfare, the *Arandora Star* sailed with no escort. Early on July 2 she was torpedoed by a German U-boat off Malin Head on the north coast of Ireland. A few lifeboats and life rafts were launched, but the ship sank in about half an hour with a loss of 805 lives, including the captain and some 90 British crew and guards. Later that day, a Canadian destroyer rescued 868 survivors.[130]

Many of the internees who survived the sinking of the *Arandora Star* were re-interned in South Devonshire, near the camp where Robert Friedler was held. About a week after they had been pulled from the sea, the *Arandora Star* survivors, and internees from the Isle of Man who had been seemingly selected at random, were herded onto another ship, His Majesty's Transport (HMT) *Dunera*.[131] Paul was among them.

The *Dunera*

The *Dunera* sailed from Liverpool on July 11, 1940. The ship was badly overcrowded. Although its capacity as a troop carrier was only 1,600, about 2,500 "enemy alien" internees were crammed on board with several hundred German POWs.[132] About 2,100 of the

---

130   Some confusion still remains about the number and exact identity of those on the *Arandora Star*: "The fact was that there was no really accurate record of the ship's complement." Chappell, *Island of Barbed Wire*, 29. See also "SS *Arandora Star*," Wikipedia, accessed January 21, 2022; Gillman and Gillman, *Collar the Lot*, 185–201.

131   Gillman and Gillman, *Collar the Lot*, 212–213; see also "Survivors Depict Prison Ship Rescue," *New York Times*, July 5, 1940, https://www.nytimes.com/1940/07/05/archives/survivors-depict-prison-ship-rescue-raf-plane-guided-warships-to.html.

132   "HMT *Dunera*," Wikipedia, accessed January 21, 2022, https://en.wikipedia.org/wiki/HMT_Dunera.

internees had been classified as Category C, refugees who were not security threats.[133]

The "rough search" of *Dunera Prisoners*, painting by Hans Jackson, from the *Dunera*.[134]

The troops staffing the *Dunera* were dregs of the British military. Badly trained and poorly supervised, they openly abused and stole from the internees while officers turned a blind eye. A report written in 1940 by some of the victims and submitted to the British High Commissioner in Australia, known as the Dunera Statement, detailed how the internees were "subjected to an 'exceedingly rough search'" as they boarded the *Dunera*:

> Items without value were thrown on to the quayside, but: Valuables were stuffed into sacks or disappeared openly into the pockets of the searching soldiers. Soon rows of empty wallets were lying on the floor.... No receipts were given except by one single searching group. Appeals to the officers standing by were fruitless. Attempts of protest were quickly suppressed....

---

133 Gillman and Gillman, *Collar the Lot*, 244; Pearl, *The Dunera Scandal*, 19, 22; see also "HMT *Dunera*," Wikipedia, accessed January 21, 2022, https://en.wikipedia.org/wiki/HMT_Dunera.

134 "The Art of Hans Hermann Josephy," Kitchener Camp, accessed January 21, 2022, http://www.kitchenercamp.co.uk/the-art-of-hans-hermann-josephy/.

All these searches were carried out without any discrimination, accompanied by acts of violence, and resulted in the loss of an enormous amount of money, valuable articles, toilet necessities and important documents which have never been recovered.[135]

Images of Paul's German passport and UK Certificate of Registration housed in the Australian National Archives show water damage, possible relics of these documents' mistreatment on the *Dunera*. Ink entries are smudged and bleed through the pages, while staples have rusted.

Decades later, Peter Tikotin recalled that the *Dunera* was guarded by British ex-convicts who had been released from prison to join the army. These petty criminals "robbed us left, right, and center, and what they didn't want they just threw overboard."[136]

Conditions aboard the *Dunera* during its two-month journey were horrific. The inmates' Dunera Statement recounts:

> The congestion was such that people slept at night on mess tables, and on the floor during the whole voyage…during the day when no hammocks were allowed, suitcases and every inch of floor space was constantly packed…for weeks the hatches were kept battened down. Neither daylight nor natural air ever reached the decks. The portholes remained closed the whole time.[137]

Lavatories were memorably filthy, toilet paper insufficient, and washing supplies limited to a weekly piece of soap and a single towel shared by ten men.[138] Despite the ongoing threat of U-boats, no lifeboat drills were held on the *Dunera*, and "exercise" was a farce:

---

135 Gillman and Gillman, *Collar the Lot*, 245, quoting from the Dunera Statement, a document compiled by a group of internees shortly after they were landed in Australia. See also Pearl, *The Dunera Scandal*, 20: "Valuable documents, identity and emigration papers, testimonials of all kinds, were taken away, thrown on the ground or even ostentatiously torn up before the eyes of their owner."

136 Tikotin interview.

137 Pearl, *The Dunera Scandal*, 20.

138 Gillman and Gillman, *Collar the Lot*, 246.

There was one exercise period on deck of fifteen to twenty minutes per day, with internees of all ages walking or running on instructions, often accompanied by a string of oaths and sometimes by blows from rifle-butts as well....And all the time the thefts continued.[139]

On the second day out of Liverpool, a German U-boat fired on the *Dunera*. The torpedo did not explode when it passed by the ship, or perhaps underneath, detonating about five hundred to one thousand yards beyond and causing no damage.[140] There was a widespread story among the *Dunera* internees, including Peter Tikotin, that they were providentially saved because the U-boat captain sent a few men to take a closer look at the flotsam and jetsam that had been thrown overboard from the *Dunera*. The German sailors thought they saw some letters that were written in German, so they concluded that there were German POWs on board. The U-boat captain then supposedly radioed the German admiralty, "On no account to hit the *Dunera*."[141] This is an affecting tale, though current scholarship has downgraded it to mythology.

After the torpedo attack, the *Dunera* continued its journey unmolested externally, sailing along the west coast of Africa from Freetown in Sierra Leone to Takoradi in the Gold Coast (now Ghana), south to Cape Town, then east across the Indian Ocean. Peter Tikotin recalled that when some of their number realized that the ship was sailing too far south along the African coast to be evading German U-boats, speculation about their destination turned to Australia. That lifted the mood. Peter recounted: "One fellow said, 'I believe they have trams in Sydney,' so they all breathed a sigh of relief, it couldn't be that uncivilized."[142]

---

139 Gillman and Gillman, *Collar the Lot*, 246.

140 Pearl, *The Dunera Scandal*, 23–25.

141 Tikotin interview.

142 Tikotin interview.

1940—Efforts to Locate Paul

When the prisoners were loaded onto the *Dunera* they were told, or it was implied to them, that they were going to Canada, a plausible destination. By mid-July 1940, three shiploads of "enemy alien" internees and German POWs had been sent to Canada, as well as the ill-fated *Arandora Star*.[143] As yet, the UK had not sent prisoners anywhere else. On July 10, the date he embarked, Paul sent Olga a telegram saying, "Leaving today, destination Canada." This alarming—and false—information was followed by weeks of racking silence.

After a month with no word from Paul, Olga wrote to Walter on August 9, "If you hear by any chance from Paul, please wire to me. It's almost more than I can bear." A couple of weeks later, nothing had changed. On August 22, Olga sent a postcard to Walter saying:

> I am well, my greatest sorrow is Paul. I haven't heard from him since he left this country. May God...help us.

The following week Olga sent Walter a similar postcard from Bradford dated August 30, reporting, "No line from Paul. Couldn't you inquire."

Once Walter learned from Olga that Paul had been transported out of England, presumably bound for Canada, he undertook an international letter writing campaign to try to locate him. He first wrote to officials in Canada asking whether Paul had been transferred there, even sending a prepaid return postal coupon. Walter received a terse letter dated September 20 from the Canadian Department of the Secretary of State, Internment Operations, though they returned the (useful) postal coupon:

> Dear Sir:
>
> We are in receipt of your inquiry of September 15th in regard to the whereabouts of Paul KURZ, who it is thought

---

[143] Chappell, *Island of Barbed Wire*, 28.

was transferred from the United Kingdom to Canada for internment.

Our records do not show that a person by this name was sent to Canada. We, therefore, regret that we are not in a position to give you any information regarding him.

Walter also wrote to officials in the UK. Months later, he received a preprinted form postcard dated October 28 saying only:

The Secretary of the Admiralty has to acknowledge your letter re Paul Kurz [the name added in ink], which will receive attention.

Shortly after, Walter received a letter dated October 29 from an officer at Headquarters, Alien Internment Camps, Douglas, Isle of Man, which contained a key correction. Paul had not been sent to Canada but to Australia:

In reply to your letter of 28/9/40, I have to inform you that Mr. Paul Kurz left for Australia on the 10th of September. [The letter was wrong about the date, though that was a secondary issue. The *Dunera* had sailed in June and arrived in Sydney on September 10.]

The Admiralty duly forwarded Walter's letter of inquiry to the War Office in London. The office of the Director of Prisoners of War sent Walter a letter dated November 23 that further confirmed that Paul had not been on the *Arandora Star* but had been transported to Australia:

I am directed to acknowledge your undated letter addressed to the Admiralty, with reference to Mr. Paul Kurz.

In reply I am to inform you, that we have no trace of Mr. Paul Kurz having embarked on the S.S. "Arandora Star."

Records, however, show a Mr. Paul Kurtz [sic], No. 57492, as having gone to Australia, and it is presumed he is the internee you are referring to.

Letters may be addressed to him as follows:
(Name of Internee and No.)
C/o Prisoner of War Inspection Bureau,
Melbourne,
Australia.

The War Office also returned Walter's prepaid international correspondence coupon (9 cents).

On September 24, two weeks after the *Dunera* landed in Sydney, a cable from Paul with his Australian internment address and prisoner number reached Olga in Bradford. She relayed these details to Walter and added at the end of her letter:

Today is Yom Kippur—can you imagine how I feel? Absolutely lonely, no friends, as a servant nobody I can talk to.[144] But nevertheless I keep smiling and expect a little better future.

Mail between England and the US was slow and erratic, but Olga was receiving even less news from Vienna. In a letter to Walter dated October 26, Olga first reiterated Paul's internment address and then asked, "Do you hear from Paula?"

At this point, the United States was still neutral so information could filter through between New York and Vienna. Walter received a postcard dated December 10, written in rather formal German, from a man in New York, transmitting an indirect request from Paula in Vienna. The man's return address was F. O. Rotter, Home Cleaning Service (a not untypical refugee business, which then as now required only limited capital and basic English), on 201 East 180th Street in New York City:

---

144   Olga was working then as a cook, so by class, a servant.

Dear Mr. Haim:

My sister Mrs. Anny Schablin[145] wrote me today that at the request of Mrs. Paula Kurz, I should ask you for Paul's exact address.

I thank you in advance for your notification and sign

Your devoted [illegible signature]

In the lower left corner of the card, Walter wrote Paul's address in pencil, which he presumably passed on to this brother of Paula's friend:

P.K., No. 57492
Comp. I., Hut II, Camp 7,
Eastern Command, Sydney,
Australia

While this information did not enable Paula or Walter to locate Paul on a map, at least they had an address to which mail could be sent.

---

145 A friend of Paula's in Vienna.

CHAPTER 14

Internment in Australia

Legal Formalities

Australia observed punctilious legal formalities regarding the internees. Upon the *Dunera*'s arrival in Sydney, an Order for Detention of Enemy Alien form was completed for each internee (the individual's name was typed onto a printed form that had been created for the occasion), reciting the legal authority for the detention. The order for Paul's detention proclaims:

> Those persons on board His Majesty's Transport "Dunera," who have been sent from the United Kingdom to Australia for internment in Australia in accordance with arrangements entered into by the Government of the Commonwealth and the Government of the United Kingdom:
>
> AND WHEREAS I am of the opinion that it is expedient in the interest of public safety, the defence of the Commonwealth, or the efficient prosecution of the war that Paul KURZ, being an enemy alien on board His Majesty's Transport "Dunera," who has been sent from the United Kingdom to Australia for internment should be detained.[146]

---

146 Report on Prisoner of War, "Paul Kurz," NAA.

Report on Prisoner of War—Paul Kurz.

On September 15, 1940, the *Dunera* internees filled out a blue paper Australian Military Forces form headed "Report on Prisoner of War" with the latter phrase crossed out and "INTERNEE" penciled in in its place. Paul gave his nationality as "Austrian (German)," his place of birth as "Vienna, Austria" (a token sign of resistance; Austria had not existed for the past two and a half years), occupation "Industrial Chemist," religion "Jewish." The form's categories had been designed for POWs rather than civilian alien internees, so for "Place of Capture" Paul entered "London," and for "Date of Capture," "May 12, 1940." The "Date of Internment" was the same. On the line for "Place of Internment," he entered "Harrogate,

Yorks," and "From Whom Received," he responded, "Police." This information about Paul's arrest and internment in the UK was not what the Australian form-reviewer wished to see; those entries were crossed out and another hand entered the date of internment as September 6, 1940, the place "Hay," and "From Whom Received" as "British Guard."[147] In the block for "personal effects," Paul wrote "nil." Paul noted that he was married and entered the name of his wife, but identified "Miss Olga Kurz" (not using her professional title) as next of kin with her address in Bradford. Like many other internees, Paul signed a card directing that his "name and personal particulars...be not communicated" to the German government and the International Red Cross. (Authorizing the government to send notice of an internee's whereabouts to the International Red Cross but not the German government was not an option that the form offered.)[148]

On the "Prison Train"

Australian officialdom and the public were expecting a ship load of hardened enemies. The *Sydney Daily Telegraph* ran an article on September 7, 1940, about the *Dunera* under headline, "Enemy Prisoners Here from Abroad." The article included photos of a "prison train on a Sydney wharf, waiting to take aboard German and Italian internees and prisoners of war."[149] After the paperwork had been competed, they were loaded onto passenger cars and headed west to Hay, a tiny desert town about 450 miles from Sydney.

Peter Tikotin recalled that the Australian troops who guarded the internees on the journey from the Sydney docks to Hay (where the camp was still under construction) were "much more relaxed" than their British counterparts. Peter told a version of the

---

147 Report on Prisoner of War, "Paul Kurz," NAA.

148 Report on Prisoner of War, "Paul Kurz," NAA.

149 "Enemy Prisoners Here from Abroad," *Sydney Daily Telegraph*, September 7, 1940. See, e.g., https://www.jugendzentrumb58.de/dunera-boys-rolf-joseph-preis-sie-zerstoerten-alles/.

now-folkloric story that an Australian guard he had been talking to on the train asked Peter to hold his gun and bayonet while he went to the lavatory.[150]

The guards did not understand the politics that had landed this shipload of scrawny foreigners in Australia. Peter recounted a conversation with one of them on the train to Hay:

Soldier: A lot of you blokes look Jewish.

Peter: Yes, about 80 percent of us are Jewish, the rest are political.

Soldier: I thought the Jews and Hitler didn't get on.

Peter: I know, but that's—

Soldier: Ah then, the bloody Poms [Englishmen] again.[151]

Here was a comprehensible solution for an Aussie soldier: interning Jews who opposed Hitler made no sense, so blame the Brits, "the bloody Poms."[152]

Another key difference between internment in England, where soldiers were stern and rations scarce, was the abundance of food in Australia, beginning with the rail journey to Hay. Peter recalled that before the train set off, he was issued a box of sandwiches with a Mars bar and a Violet Crumble (an Australian candy bar) packed beneath them.[153]

---

150 See the account on the Dunera Association's website: "There was even one story of a soldier asking one of the internees to hold his rifle while he lit his cigarette" ("Dunera Boys," Dunera Association, accessed July 31, 2022, https://www.duneraassociation.com/dunera-boys/).

151 Tikotin interview.

152 Tikotin interview.

153 Tikotin interview.

The Internment Camp at Hay

Fifty years afterwards one internee, who in 1940 had been a teenager from Vienna, recalled the arrival at Hay with some retrospective fondness. When the "Jewish (and semi-Jewish)" internees arrived, they were:

> ...divided into two equal lots of about 750 each and placed in two barbed wire circles, in shouting distance of each other, in the desert, with a distant view of the eucalyptus trees along the Murrumbidgee river. Each camp with some 25 huts of about 30 bunks, dining halls, kitchens, admin huts, watch-towers (usually un-manned)....
>
> Temperature up to 100° during the day, down to freezing at night. Self-administration inside the camp....No compulsory work of any kind—only occasional roll calls, plenty of food, always sunshine. Read more books than ever before or since....Wonderful desert landscape, sand storms, purple and green sunsets, occasional flocks of sheep filling the view to the horizon.[154]

Less bucolic in actuality than in this gilded memory, Hay was prone to choking dust storms, unlike anything seen in Europe. Such a dust storm was in progress when the internees arrived at Hay railroad station.[155]

At the station, Peter Tikotin followed his usual procedure, hurrying to be among the first off so that he could volunteer to work in the kitchen. Contrary to all previous experience, the problem was

---

154 Walter J. Foster (originally Fast), *All for the Best, or the History of Young Walter*, self-published, 1993, http://www.archive.org/stream/walterjfoster001/walterjfoster001_djvu.txt. Foster summarized his time behind wire at Hay: "Apart from the *Dunera* experience, nothing particularly unpleasant happened to me through internment. My main complaint was inactivity, boredom, waste of time and the frustration of not being able to do anything about the war."

155 Ken Inglis, Seamus Spark, and Jay Winter, *Dunera Lives: A Visual History* (Melbourne, Australia: Monash University Publishing, 2018), 116.

not that the camp at Hay lacked supplies to feed the influx of prisoners, but that there was too much food to cope with. Decades later, Peter recounted this initial exchange with the sergeant in charge:

> Quartermaster sergeant: Thank Christ you bastards have come.
>
> Peter: What's the matter, Sarge?
>
> Sergeant: You should see the so-and-so cool store [refrigerators], the food has been coming in for the last ten days or so.[156]

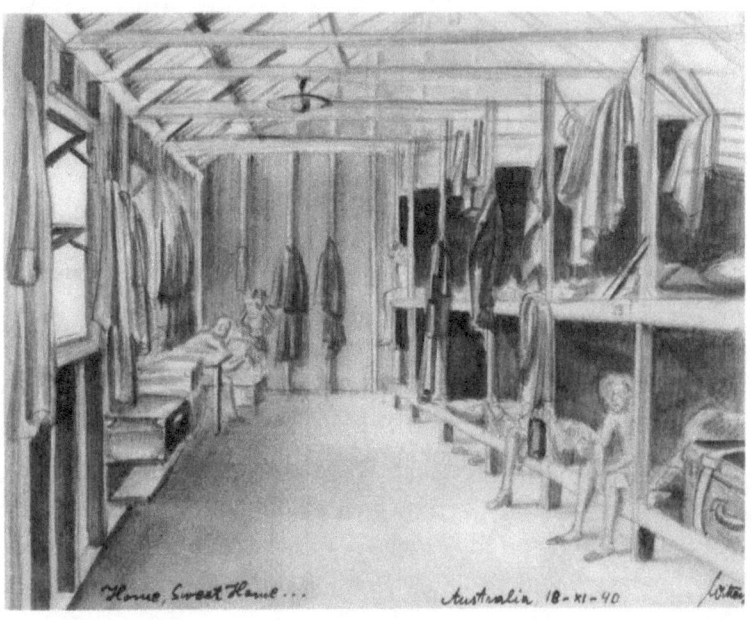

Sketch by internee Emil Wittenberg of a hut at Hay ironically titled *Home, Sweet Home*, November 1940.

Even in 1940, Peter would have spoken fluent, colloquial English as he had taken matric exams and held a job in England before being interned.

---

156 Tikotin interview.

Once in the kitchen, Peter started slicing and buttering bread for the internees' first meal but then thought, "What am I doing, everyone gets a loaf of bread and half a pound of butter, there's plenty for everybody."[157]

The huts at Hay had been hastily thrown together. While primitive, they generally look clean and orderly in internees' drawings. Small tables were built in under the windows for reading, writing, drawing, and studying.[158] A sketch from November 1940 titled *Home, Sweet Home* shows the inside of a hut. Amid the austere order, one man is seated on the bunk, wearing only shorts, staring dazedly into nowhere.

As an internee, Wittenberg also drew the Australian landscape. This scene looks in towards the camp from outside through the inevitable ribbons and coils of barbed wire.

Watercolor scene by Emil Wittenberg, Hay, December 1940, titled *Barbed Wire*.

---

157 Tikotin interview.

158 Inglis, Spark, and Winter, *Dunera Lives*, 148.

Memories of the *Dunera* and Internment

Paul said very little to me about his voyage to Australia on the *Dunera*. Though generally philosophical, he mentioned with some passion that the machine guns on the *Dunera*'s deck were turned inward toward the internees, and not outward toward waters that hid German submarines. He told me that he saw an albatross flying above the *Dunera* somewhere in the Indian Ocean. It was magnificent, he recalled. He also mentioned that they passed wreckage from another unidentified ship that had been torpedoed.[159] Paul did not talk about internment in Australia or England but kept some sketches from the camps at Hay and Tatura in a cabinet in his living room. One showed a very young Peter Tikotin seated by an outhouse next to a drainage trough, holding a book in one hand and a stick in the other ("shit stirring").

Years later, Paul told this story from the *Dunera* passage to my university friend Tim McNamara: "Someone had got seasick and had thrown up on the deck. One of the Tommies told me, 'You, fucking Jew, clean it up.' And for me that represented freedom." Paul's clear-sighted attitude reflected Olga's assessment: "It is thousand times better to be interned in England than to live in 'freedom' in Germany—but it is hard anyhow."

Peter Tikotin told me that when they arrived at the internment camp in Hay, Paul preemptively installed himself in a hut with the "youngsters." They were not happy to have an old guy among them (Paul was thirty-nine and Peter twenty), but Paul said he wouldn't get in their way, he would just do things to be helpful. He began by picking up a broom and sweeping sand out of the hut.

Many years after these events, another of Paul's friends since the *Dunera* days, Bob (anglicized from the original Kurt) Vogel included these recollections of Paul in the section of his autobiographical sketch titled *Arrival in Australia*.[160] Bob Vogel regarded Paul as a mentor and wise father figure:

---

159 See Pearl, *The Dunera Scandal*, 33.

160 Bob Vogel dictated the memoir to his son Peter, which would explain the consistent misspelling in the original of Paul's surname. Spelling and punctuation have been regularized here.

Chapter 14: Internment in Australia   217

After our arrival in Hay…I was fortunate to get into a hut with a bunch of academics; some very nice people, one of whom turned out to be Paul Kurz. I was the youngest in camp [actually Bob, at sixteen, wasn't quite the youngest]….

In my hut there was a chemist by the name of Paul Kurz, and he befriended me, and more or less, became my second father. We walked around the barbed wire every night, and talked and discussed things, and he was an enormous moral support.[161]

Sketch captioned "on the edge of the world," showing two men walking by the wire at the Hay camp.[162]

---

161 "Bob's Story," VogelFamily.net, accessed July 2023, http://www.vogelfamily.net/bobstory.

162 Inglis, Spark, and Winter, *Dunera Lives*, 120.

First Letters from Internment in Australia

The first extant communication from Paul in Australia is a form postcard printed by the Australian military for POWs, postmarked in Sydney on September 24, 1940 (coincidentally Paul's thirty-ninth birthday), and stamped "Defense Forces Mail. No Postage Required." Although the internees had no choice but to use these postcards, they were adamant that they were not POWs (i.e., enemy combatants) but refugees who were loyal to the UK and the Allied cause. On the front, the card gave instructions in three languages: English, German, and Italian. It advised that the only allowable information was the recipient's address and included a warning: "<u>If anything else is added the postcard will be destroyed.</u>"

The back of the postcard, in the same three languages, contained lines for the POW (or in this case, internee) to add a signature and the date. Paul wrote in his name and "13th September 1940." The card repeated the warning that "<u>if anything else is added the postcard will be destroyed.</u>" The preprinted section of the card included the useful information: "My address now is—Care of Prisoners of War Bureau, Melbourne, Australia."

The card offered two options from which the writer could choose to report his status. They were (1) "I am quite well," or (2) "I have been admitted to hospital and am going on well and hope to be discharged soon." The card instructed that "sentences not required may be struck out," and Paul crossed out the second one. A final preprinted sentence stated, "Letter follows at first opportunity," and Paul did not line it out. This postcard, a first sign of life from Paul in over six months, reached Walter some six weeks after Paul had signed it. It was postmarked on arrival in New York on November 8, 1940.

Paul's first regular letter from Australia to reach Walter was dated September 22, 1940. Its course was painfully slow. The letter had to be reviewed by the military censor (no. S133), who rubber-stamped both the letter and the envelope, sending them on via "Defense Forces Mail, no postage required." The letter was eventually postmarked in Sydney on October 30, nearly six weeks after it had been written. The letter is short and printed rather than written in Paul's usual cursive, probably to make it easier for the censor to read and pass it.

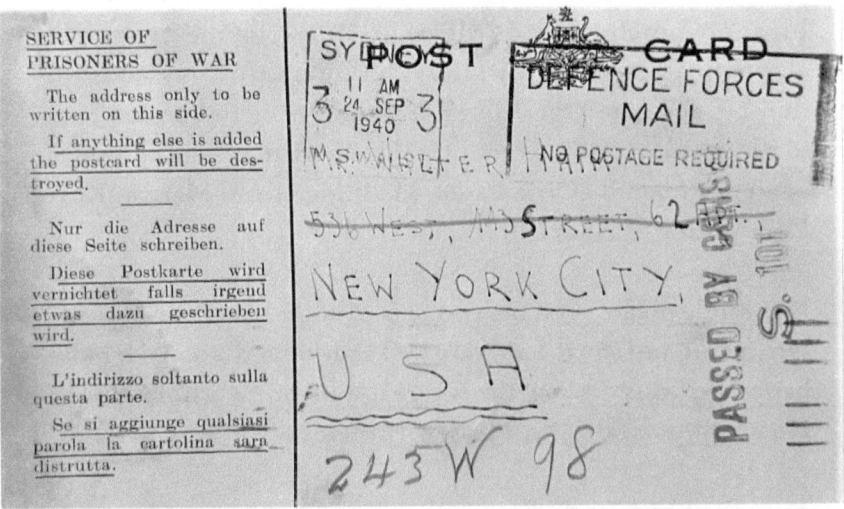

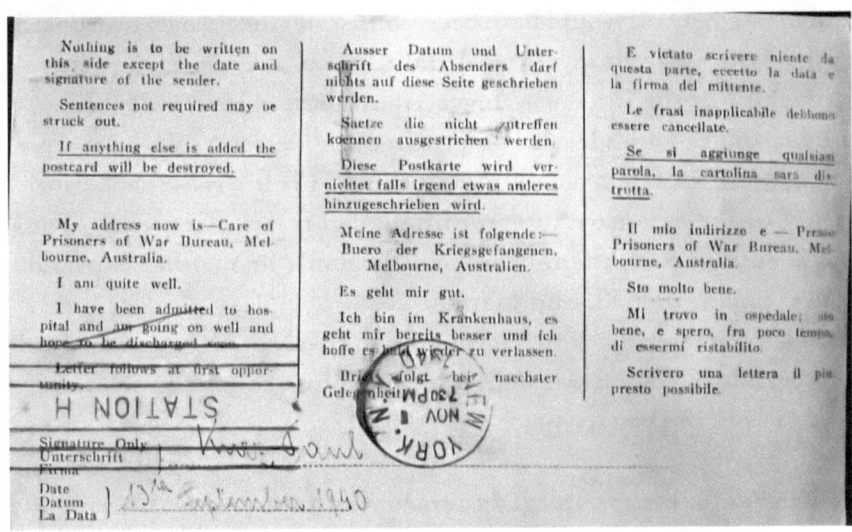

Form postcard for prisoners of war, September 1940.

This was a highly controlled, practical letter. Paul asked for addresses and some clothing essentials. He gave no space to emotion, speculation, or abstract thought:

I wrote already a card. Am here in Australia as internee since 10th September. As it seems impossible to remain here I have to go to your country but it will take some time. On my voyage I lost my notebook and will ask you to write me by airmail all particulars about my affidavit (Guarantor, registration number and date? Etc.) The documents lying in London have to be transferred to this country. Please write me the addresses of all our friends (Olga, Paula, Mathilde, Toni, Martin, Kurt Paul Müller,[163] Nettel etc.).

If possible please send me two pair of socks, one pair of trousers, pants and shirt. I am very well indeed and would be quite happy if I would know the whereabouts of my whole family. How are you and Lilly. Please write soon.

That Paul had "lost" his notebook with addresses was a politic understatement. It would have been confiscated or thrown overboard by the British guards as he boarded the *Dunera*, a victim of the general ransacking of the internees' luggage and theft of their valuables. At the bottom of Paul's letter Walter listed, in German, eleven people whose addresses he needed to send Paul. This is a reasonable indication of the extensive intercontinental correspondence that Paul was keeping up with family and close friends in Vienna, England, Wales, Japan, the US, and Manila.

Walter relayed back to Vienna the long-awaited news that Paul had been located and was well, along with his requests for clothing. Paula wrote in January 1941:

Are Paul's things damaged [havariert, a particularly Austrian term], or didn't he bring anything with him? However it is, I am happy that he is well. Everything else is incidental.

Paul's next letter was written on October 5, in English, on a sheet of now-yellowed lined paper. Like the previous one, this letter was

---

163 The brother of Dr. Martha Müller, a close friend of Olga's and her former medical supervisee.

not postmarked until five weeks later in Sydney, after it had been reviewed by the censor. A stamp on the envelope reads "Service Prisoners of War, C. S. Thane, Lt. Col. Cmdt. Hay." This is the first indication to Walter of the actual location where Paul was being held, in Hay.

Again, Paul wrote about practicalities. He asked for names, addresses, information about his application for a US visa, and questions about family:

> The mail I wrote to you already is one card, one letter and one airmail letter. As it would be possible to have already a reply from you I have none till now and therefore I will write you again and to repeat I wrote in my former letters. I am here since Sept 8th after a 10 weeks voyage.[164] Perhaps I have to go to your country although I would not like to do it because—you know it already—I always think that Australia is the country where I could work in my special line as lanolin maker. But I have to prepare all the papers (documents) for the American visa. On my voyage I lost my notebook and will ask you to send me by airmail all particulars about my affidavit. (Guarantor, registration number and date etc.). The documents—lying in London, partly at the American Consulate General, partly at the lawyer (of which I can't neither remember the name nor the address but you will know it and therefore I ask you to be so kind as to write it)—have to be transferred to this country. Please write me also the addresses of all our friends. Where are your parents-in-law? Do you know the whereabouts of my sister Olga, of Paula? How is my mother and how are your parents? Many questions but perhaps you can answer them.

From the beginning Australia had been Paul's preferred destination for emigration, though not Paula's, because it was the

---

164 This was an estimate. The *Dunera*'s voyage lasted fifty-seven days. See, e.g., Kate Connolly, "Britons Finally Learn the Dark *Dunera* Secret," *Sydney Morning Herald*, May 19, 2006, https://www.smh.com.au/entertainment/movies/britons-finally-learn-the-dark-dunera-secret-20060519-gdnknt.html.

likeliest place to find work in his narrow field of lanolin chemistry. However, Paul was being simply realistic when he wrote that "it seems impossible to stay here." Britain began releasing its refugee-internees as early as July 1940 and acknowledged soon after that interning and deporting them had been a "regrettable mistake." In contrast, the Australian government refused to consider allowing any of the internees to resettle there. Throughout the war, the Australian government stayed firmly committed to its "White Australia" policy, as disconcerting as that term is to current sensibilities. Australia's restrictive immigration laws, which dated to the country's founding as an independent federation in 1901, gave preference to people from the British Isles while excluding people of other "races," a broad term that encompassed anyone who was not British.

In 1940, Australia had a recent history of rebuffing European refugees. At the international conference held in Evian, France, in July 1938 to address the "refugee crisis" spurred by Nazi Germany's antisemitic policies, Australia refused to accept any refugees.[165] Its chief delegate infamously explained, "As we have no real racial problem, we are not desirous of importing one by encouraging any scheme of large-scale foreign migration."[166] Even after the war had begun, Australia's Prime Minister John Curtin clung fast to the exclusionary policy, maintaining: "This country shall remain forever the home of the descendants of those people who came here in peace in order to establish in the South Seas an outpost of the British race."[167] Jews, by implication, could never become part of the "British race." Thus Australia's refusal to allow the *Dunera*

---

[165] Although the US had called for this conference, it did not raise its own immigration quota. "Emigration and the Evian Conference," Holocaust Encyclopedia, United States Holocaust Memorial Museum, updated April 28, 2022, https://encyclopedia.ushmm.org/content/en/article/emigration-and-the-evian-conference.

[166] "Statements from Representatives at the Evian Conference, July 1938," Facing History & Ourselves, accessed May 22, 2022, https://www.facinghistory.org/resource-library/text/statements-representatives-evian-conference-july-1938.

[167] "Abolition of the 'White Australia' Policy," European Parliament, reviewed November, 2010, https://www.europarl.europa.eu/meetdocs/2009_2014/documents/danz/dv/0220_13_1/0220_13_1en.pdf.

internees to settle there, while disappointing, was all of a piece with the country's history and then-current attitudes.

In 1940 Australia had a small Jewish community. They helped to provide books and kosher food for the internees but did not press the government in the internees' favor. The community felt itself constantly embattled and took elaborate pains to avoid any activity that it feared might incite local antisemitism.

Paul's next letter was written on October 26, 1940, on half a sheet of lined paper. An incongruously jolly Santa Claus sticker is pasted in the left margin. The letter again had to pass through the censorship process, but the outgoing mail seems to have begun moving a bit faster, and it was postmarked in Sydney on November 5, only about ten days after it was written. Paul had not yet received any mail. His tone was more distant, suggesting a reined-in desperation. This is the first letter where Paul addressed my father by his formal name, Walter, rather than as Bobby (or Bobbi, Paul's spelling varied):

> There is not much to report from me. The situation is unchanged and the time passes in waiting for news from Olga and from you. Till now I have no letter from anyone. Also the case of my USA visa is unchanged mainly because I need all the dates I asked for in my former letters. Please write me very soon and if possible by air mail via New Zealand. Give my love to Lilly and to all our friends.

At about the same time, Paul sent an undated postcard from the camp at Hay as "a sign of life." His mood appears to have lifted a bit, though he had not yet received any mail:

> Really I have to give you once again a sign of life. I am still quite well. I found very nice comrades here.[168]

---

168 This third sentence is written in smaller letters as though Paul fitted it into the available space after he had written the rest of the card.

Perhaps it is possible for you, if the postage is not too high, to send me some fiction-books, a small dictionary and perhaps also a chemistry-book. If possible direct from the publisher because of the censor.

Please give my love to Paula, Mathilde, Antony [sic], Martin and Lilly. Always your Paul

Paul sent another postcard in November 1940. This one is not dated either but was postmarked in Sydney on November 28. Again, the correspondence was one way only; he had no response. Paul would have sent this card as a periodic "sign of life," though he was no longer explicit about that purpose. He began in medias res with a follow-up to his previous card:

Perhaps you can find out whether the following book is available in New York. Its German title is: "Chemisch Technisches Reseptenbuch" [Chemical Technical Formula Book] by Lange, or perhaps there is a book corresponding to it published in New York in English. If there is, please send me some details, including its price. Perhaps you can obtain the advice of somebody who knows something about these books. I am quite well but still without any letter from you. Give my kindest regards to Mrs. Haim.

Paul continued to send letters into the blue with no responses. The same rigidly controlled tone characterized another letter from the same period, suggesting increasing desperation. Paul reeled out unlikely fantasies about reasons that Walter may not have responded to his correspondence; maybe he was angry with Paul or did not have enough spare change to send an airmail postcard:

Nothing new to report. I am still here and am quite well, only I have no letters either from you or from anyone else. There may be a reason why I do not receive any letters from Bradford but I cannot understand why I have not heard from you yet. There are some comrades who received answers on letters to New York within 10 days. I don't think that you are cross with me. Or if you should be a bit short of money, surely, one post card by clipper can't be so expensive. Please write, you will get this money back one day. The next week I will try again to send air mail cards to you and to Olga. Give my regards to your wife.

While there is no way to verify it, I believe that Walter continued to write regularly to Paul, probably a weekly letter or postcard. That correspondence may not have arrived or may have been delayed because sorting, censoring, and delivering mail to internees would have been a low priority use of Australia's military manpower.

Paul's next letter, dated December 5, again written in English on lined paper, reported the same: no news from Walter, nothing new at the camp, "no work of any value to do," but at least Paul had finally received two letters from England:

I think that all my letters are beginning with the same sentence: I have no letter from you since I am here and this is I am sure rather a long time. I would be only too glad to receive a few lines from you. From Olga and from Bela [Martha Müller's brother, in Sydney] I have already two letters. I have nothing new to report. One day passes like the other, dull, no work of any value to do and the worst of all no letters and no books. But never mind in 50 years it's all the same and nobody will then know anything about our troubles. Please write soon and as much as possible. Give my kindest regards to Lilly.

It is now more than eighty years since Paul wrote this letter, and that generation is gone. What remains are the letters and life-shaping impressions that Paul made on the next generation.

On December 10, Paul received solid good news: a card from Walter had arrived at last. By that time, Walter and Lilly had left New York for Newport News, Virginia:

Thank heavens yesterday I received your card from October 25th. Perhaps you did not get my letters because you moved. At the same time I had a letter from Olga and one from Bela. I am perfectly all right. Don't think that I am down hearted. I don't mind at all this little trip around the world in order to see you all again. The transmigrants of this camp, including me, made an application to the American Consulate General, London, for the transfer of our documents to Sydney. Please write me all the details about my affidavit and also my registration number. Why did Lilly not write a line. Please write more about yourself. What are you doing? What kind of a job have you now? Give my love to all our friends. Ever your Paul. Please send me any book to read.

As with Paul's letters from England, "friends" was a thin code for "family."

On December 16 Paul wrote a separate letter to Lilly, again in English. He sounded positive; things were manageable despite his having been transported literally to the other side of the globe:

As you are the writer of the letter from Nov. 26th, which I received on Dec. 13th, I have to address the answer to you. I can not explain how glad I was to receive this letter because I learned of it that all of you are well. I have also already some letters from Olga who also cabled me some money so that I can write sometimes by air mail. I am awfully sorry that you have such troubles with me as I asked you in my first letter to send me some clothes. All the more as I received already some and as we have here a rather hot climate and I shall not need them. Please forgive me this and please take my heartiest thanks for these things. Further I thank you ever so much for the addresses....Dear Lilly why do not write more about yourself and about Walter? How are you? Why did you move? Are you short in money? What about your parents? Please tell me all in your next letter. Do not think that I am down. I am all right here. I wrote you a fortnight ago by airmail asking you to make inquiries about some chemical technical books. Perhaps you could obtain a catalogue of technical chemistry books especially with regard to fats and waxes. Please write soon and as much as possible. Do not put any reply coupon in your letters.

Paul added the last comment because sending prepaid postage reply coupons was common practice. However, Paul and his fellow internees could send and receive surface mail free of postage. Airmail still had to be paid for.

Not fully trusting the mail, two days later Paul sent Lilly a postcard on which he repeated the substance of his letter of December 16.

1941 Begins

Paul continued to write regularly as 1940 gave way to 1941, though there were still long stretches when no correspondence arrived. He also continued to pursue a possible US visa, though without much enthusiasm. An airmail postcard that Paul wrote on January 3, 1941, was postmarked five days later in Sydney, marking a definite increase in postal and censorship efficiency. The parcel of necessities that Paul had initially asked for to replace items that had been "lost" on the *Dunera* had not arrived, but he was making do without them. Warm clothes weren't needed in Hay, particularly during the southern hemisphere's summer:

> Today I will be a little prodigal and will send this card by air mail, although I had no letter from you since your airmail letter from November 26th. I am all right. Time passes by reading and learning and waiting for post, this waiting is the hardest work because one never gets accustomed to it. I will ask you again as I did in my former letters to be so kind as to write to me the following dates: birthdate of Paula and yours, the date of my

marriage, the date of your landing in USA.[169] My immigration papers have to be transferred from London to Sydney. I fear that the Consulate General in Sydney will ask for a new affidavit because in the meantime the old one has certainly expired and therefore I dare to ask you if it will be possible for you to provide at that time, when I shall ask for it, a new one. Till today I have not received your parcel but please do not send me anymore. I am now equipped with the main things and do not want to carry too much on my next journey. How are you all? Please write soon and much. Give my love to Lilly. Your Paul

Continuing Emigration Frustrations

Paul's US visa application continued to rollercoaster in 1941. The previous year, one Louis Katzner had signed an affidavit of support for Paul through the New York Sephardic Refugee Committee, but the US Embassy in London continued to delay and request more information. Then Mr. Katzner died in February 1941, and his affidavit became worthless. The secretary of the Sephardic Refugee Committee sent Walter a letter dated February 17 with the unfortunate news:

> With reference to obtaining a renewal of the affidavit for your brother-in-law I regret to inform you that Mr. Katzner died the day after Mrs. Haim came to see me regarding the matter. It is therefore impossible to obtain a renewal of Mr. Katzner's affidavit.

In the envelope with this letter, Walter saved an "In Memoriam" column clipped from a Shearith Israel newsletter. He penciled Xs

---

169 Except for the date of Walter's arrival in the United States, it is inconceivable that Paul did not know these dates. Perhaps he wanted to be certain there wouldn't be any avoidable discrepancies on official immigration papers.

next to the laconic entry, "Louis Katzner, loyal and devoted Jew, faithful to his people and his God."

Louis Katzner remains a cipher. Everyone wrote about him formally as "Mr. Katzner." Hans confirmed in a letter written around this time that there had been no connection with him other than his charitably having signed an affidavit of support: "The death of Mr. Katzner leaves everything cold, more so because one could not know anything of him and of his life." Not a prominent man, Mr. Katzner can be remembered as someone who tried to do some good. He was born in Russia, lived in the middle-class area of Prospect Avenue in the Bronx, worked as a furrier, and died young in Manhattan, only fifty years old.

News of Mr. Katzner's death and attendant voiding of his affidavit of support was relayed immediately to the family in Vienna and Paul in the Australian internment camp. Paul responded in a letter dated April 24, urging Walter not to be concerned about its effect on him: "Do not worry about me and about Mr. Katzner," Paul wrote, "I am perfectly all right." He quickly moved on to practicalities and a resonant understatement (one that would both pass the Australian military censor and not unduly upset Walter's equilibrium) about the family's situation in Vienna:

> Please tell me: is there no possibility to do anything for Paula, Lilly's parents, Toni, Martin and Mathilde? As far as I know things do not seem to be pleasant for them. Somehow I feel that this question is a stupid one because this task is beyond your power, but I have to ask it.

With Mr. Katzner gone, Walter reached out to other organizations for help with Paul's emigration to the United States. On July 8, 1941, he wrote to the Board of National Missions of the Presbyterian Church in the USA asking about a possible affidavit of support for Paul. The Board responded quickly and negatively in a letter dated July 10:

I note what you write with regard to the need of an affidavit for him, but am afraid that even with an affidavit there is no prospect at present for him to secure the necessary immigration quota visa to come to the States.

You, of course, know of the new regulations with regard to immigration to America. These are rather drastic and make it well-nigh impossible for any interned individual to come to the States, at least not while the war is on. I am sorry that the situation is thus and that as a result we can hold out little hope to help you in facilitating your brother-in-law's immigration.

The Presbyterian group was correct that US immigration rules had become yet more restrictive. In June 1941 the recently enacted Bloom-Van Nuys Immigration Act, and implementing US State Department regulations, prohibited consulates from issuing visas to any applicant who had a close relative in Axis-occupied territory, making US visas essentially unavailable for would-be Jewish emigrants in Europe and the Commonwealth countries.[170] The impetus for these restrictions included stereotyped security concerns (Jews were likely to be either Bolsheviks or subject to Nazi manipulation through threats to family members who remained in Greater Germany or occupied countries) and fear of an "infiltration of spies and saboteurs among the refugees."[171] Another consideration was old-fashioned antisemitism. The State Department saw itself as protecting the United States from an influx of people who were widely perceived as "ethnically and politically undesirable" (i.e., Jews).[172] The Bloom-Van Nuys Act gave US consuls broad discre-

---

170 "Jewish Refugees from the German Reich," United States Holocaust Memorial Museum, accessed 2022, https://www.ushmm.org/exhibition/st-louis/teach/spread2.htm. See also United States Immigration and Refugee Law, 1921–1980, accessed July 2023, https://encyclopedia.ushmm.org/content/en/article/united-states-immigration-and-refugee-law-1921-1980?parent=en%2F2419.

171 "Jewish Refugees," United States Holocaust Memorial Museum.

172 "Jewish Refugees," United States Holocaust Memorial Museum.

tionary authority to withhold visas from anyone whom they actually knew or "had reason to believe" might "endanger the public safety."[173] There was no review from a consul's negative decision, however arbitrary or wrong-headed it may have been. In short, by the middle of 1941, Congress and the State Department had made emigration to the United States from occupied Europe and elsewhere impossible.

From Hay to Tatura

Hay was notorious as "one of the hottest places in Australia."[174] Australian "bush poet" A. B. (Banjo) Paterson had immortalized the town in the phrase, "'Hay and Hell and Booligal." In April 1941 a visiting liaison officer from Britain's Home Office inspected the camp at Hay and concluded, with the casual racism of the time, that the climate was too hot and dry for Europeans. He recommended that the *Dunera* internees be moved to a camp near Tatura, in the Waranga Basin. This was an artificial lake in northern Victoria that dated back to Australia's gold rush, where the climate was somewhat less "hot, dry, and unforgiving."[175]

The following month, in May 1941, Paul was moved south from the camp at Hay, across the Murray River, which marked the border between New South Wales and Victoria, to Tatura. He wrote about the change with superficial blandness, unimpeachable by any censor, and asked again for some technical chemistry books:

> As you will see on the new address we have moved to a new camp. It is very nice here. I am perfectly all right. Nothing to

---

173 S. 913, Pub. Law 113, approved June 20, 1941. https://www.govinfo.gov/content/pkg/GOVPUB-GP3-723064f5f76bf8557a4e868a41b8b438/pdf/GOVPUB-GP3-723064f5f76bf8557a4e868a41b8b438.pdf1. See also "Jewish Refugees," United States Holocaust Memorial Museum.

174 "Enemy Prisoners," *Sydney Daily Telegraph*.

175 Inglis, Spark, and Winter, *Dunera Lives*, 229.

worry about me. If you are still in touch with Mrs. Glaubach[176] please be so kind as to ask her to provide you with a catalogue of recently issued books on chemical technology of oils, fats and waxes and please send it to me....How are you? Have you already a job? How is Lilly and all our other friends.[177] Please give my love to them. Ever your Paul

Bob Vogel, one of Paul's hut-mates, summarized his experience at Tatura:

In Tatura, life went on much the same as it did in Hay, but being a fruit picking area, we had working parties going out fruit picking. One guard to every fifty or so internees that went out on working parties. And life was generally easier.... We had all sorts of classes, lectures, and actually got papers from the universities [that is, internees could receive credit for university courses].

Another of Paul's young Viennese camp-mates, Walter Foster, recalled Paul from their time at Tatura:

[I] made several good friends with whom I walked endlessly around the perimeter wire probing our many personal problems and worries, discussing the course of the war as reflected in the newspapers, rehearsing our hopes for the future, and trying to recall the ever more receding world outside the wire....There was Paul Kurz, 20 years my senior and a doctor of chemistry; he taught me carpentry in the workshop he had established for himself in Tatura Camp, he also tried to teach me—much less successfully—his philosophy (or was it that of

---

176 This would be Dr. Susi Glaubach, a friend of Paula's who obtained her doctorate from the University of Vienna's Pharmacological Institute. She had arrived in the US in September 1938 and resumed her scientific career at Beth Israel Hospital in Newark, a singular achievement at that time for a woman and a refugee.

177 Once again, "friends" is a rather transparent code for "family."

Pangloss?): to take life as it comes and to make the best of things one is not able to change.[178]

A seven-month gap followed. There are no letters from Paul from May 1941 until one dated January 12, 1942. During those months, Germany invaded Russia, ending the 1939 nonaggression pact between Hitler and Stalin and bringing the USSR into the war, and Japan bombed Pearl Harbor, bringing the United States into the war.

1942—Reading, Learning, Waiting

When letters from Paul resumed in January 1942, he wrote that he had received two postcards that Walter had sent in November 1941 but no mail from Vienna. He did not need food, underwear, or shoes but asked for a new chemistry book on animal and vegetable waxes whose publication had been announced in 1940:

> I received your cards of 26th and of 30th November. I was very glad to learn that you had some mail from Olga. I had none from her since a very long time. I wrote Tonerl[179] already twice and I will write her again but I would like to first receive _____ [the letter is water damaged] an answer from her. I acknowledged already _____ the book-catalog and the parcel...I thank you once more for them...We have plenty to eat...I am perfectly all right. Please give my love to Lilly and to all your friends.

The flimsy code continued. "All your friends" meant "all of our families," unreachable in Greater Germany.

---

178 Walter Foster must have internalized those lessons. In 2013, a book of his memoirs was published with the Candide-ean title, "*All for the Best,*" http://www.archive.org/stream/walterjfoster001 /walterjfoster001_djvu.txt.

179 An affectionate diminutive for Paul's mother-in-law, Antoinette "Antonie" or "Tonie" Haim.

On February 15 Paul wrote again. Little was new. He had received another letter from Olga in England, but there was no mention of any news from Vienna. Camp life was monotonous, alleviated some by studying and reading. A number of the internees, including Bob Vogel, took the opportunity to work outside the Tatura camp in the surrounding fruit orchards, but there is no sign that Paul did:

> I thank you ever so much for your letter of December 21st — I received on 6th Inst....Yesterday I got a letter from [Olga]. She is all right too. She is still working as a matron in a children's hospital. From Irma[180] I had a parcel with a nice cake and from Bela I received a letter. You see I am well looked after by our friends. But on the whole I have nothing new to report. One day passes like the other, learning, reading and so on. If it is possible please do not stop writing, at least do write once a month. Give my love to Lilly.

At the end of March, Paul sent Lilly a postcard responding to her long-delayed New Year's Day card. There was a bit of chat about the climate, counterbalancing the weightier news that Paul's last four letters to Paula remained unanswered. He wrote in a measured understatement that "things don't look very bright" for the family, carefully avoiding identifying their location to avoid arousing a censor's attention, as Vienna was enemy territory:

> At last I received last week your card of January 1st. I was quite happy to read for a change your writing instead of Walter's! Although I had some cards of him of a later date (which I confirmed already a fortnight ago), I would very much like to receive more mail from you or from him. The main task is patience, and hope, for seeing you all again. I wrote already four times to Paula but till now I got no answer. Things don't look very bright for them. I am quite o.k. Learning, reading,

---

180 Irma Müller, Dr. Martha Müller's mother, who was living in Sydney at the time with her son Bela and his family.

waiting. As to your question: The climate here isn't bad at all. Hot days occur everywhere and when I work I don't feel it. But now winter starts here and we get also quite cold days. Please write soon to your Paul

Paul's next postcard, sent in April 1942, was even shorter, going through the wearisome motions:

Although I have no mail from you since five weeks I write you, only to let you know that I am all right. Nothing has changed for me. Time passes by in reading and learning and now and then a little bit of working. Yesterday I had a card from Olga. She is all right too. Still working in a children's hospital. From Toni I have no news since a very long time. Keep well dear. Give my love to Lilly. Your Paul

Then in late May, Paul wrote a letter to both Lilly and Walter. There had been news from Olga and a letter from Lilly, and Paul's response was far more animated than the previous postcards. Once again, he asked for a chemistry book, this time *The Industrial Chemistry of the Fats and Waxes*, a 1927 book by a UK chemical engineer that was still available on Amazon in 2024:

Last week I received your card of March 9th. I wrote you already in my last letter that I got a cable from Olga in which she told me her new address: Belgrave Children's Hospital, Clapham Road, London, SW9.[181] I think that you received already in the meantime a letter from her. Lilly! Right you are in commanding Walter to do some housework, too. Firstly you must keep an eye on his tummy so that he won't get too fat and

---

181 Olga's new employer, the Belgrave Hospital for Children, was a voluntary hospital founded in 1866. While this job got Olga out of the provinces and into London, her employment was still restricted to far below her abilities and training. Olga stayed at Belgrave Hospital for about a year and then in April 1943 began working at Plaistow Hospital in East London. That would have posed additional challenges, as Plaistow Hospital and its surroundings had been damaged in the 1941 blitz.

beside of that one never knows how such a husband needs to know something about needlework and about cooking. The more he works the better for him....

Please for heaven's sake don't send any fiction or detective story. Have you had any news from Toni. I learned from Bela [Martha Müller's brother in Sydney] that he had a letter from Martha who is living with Toni. They are all right. I am perfectly all right only a bit lazy. Keep well both of you and keep on writing to me. Your Paul

Paul's postcard of June 17 from Tatura again had a brighter tone: a sudden flood of mail had arrived. Paul also admitted to being less averse, at least for the moment, to the thought of the family being reunited in the United States. He sounded resigned to being "condemned to stay here idle and to rust because of a little mistake." A "little mistake" indeed. More than a year earlier, Churchill acknowledged in Parliament that deporting Austrian and German Jewish refugees on the *Dunera* had been "a deplorable and regrettable mistake."[182] Peter Tikotin recalled in his 2000 memoir that after Churchill's speech, the internees "called ourselves 'The Mistakes.'" More darkly, there was still no mail from Vienna:

On 14th inst. I received 8 postcards. Three were from you of March 9th, April 26th. The others were from Olga, and today I got two postcards from you of March 22nd and May 10th. You can imagine how proud I feel to have so much mail. Lilly, I thank you especially for your card of April 26th. Walter writes that you are brave and—when he has to leave you—you will have to be more than brave. Dear Walter, as to you, I have to make you a confession. I too would like to see all the members of our family in the U.S. And still more, I would like to be with you now and do something no matter what to give my little share in an honest way. But instead I am condemned to

---

182 Pearl, *The Dunera Scandal*, 137.

stay here idle and to rust because of a little mistake....On the whole I am all-right. I do a bit of reading and learning but it is not much and nevertheless somehow time goes by. Till to now I have no reply from Toni. One thing more to wait for. Keep well both of you. Your Paul

Paul's writing that Lilly may have to be "more than brave" probably alluded to the possibility that Walter might be called upon for military service. In 1942 Walter had registered for the US draft, along with his father-in-law Arthur Neuhaus and Lilly's uncle Gustl Landsmann. Realistically, it was unlikely that any of them would ever be called up, much less pass a qualifying medical exam. Walter was forty, married, with pronounced myopia, while Gustl and Arthur were in their fifties.

The next extant communication from Paul is a letter written three months later, on September 4, 1942. By then, Paul had been interned in Australia for two years, and there had been no word from Paula in over a year. His philosophical stance was taking the long view, and mail was a mood lifter. He assured Walter and Lilly that he was writing to them at least twice a month, and by the dates of their cards, they seem to have been doing the same. Despite the confinement and sameness, one can sense the stirrings of a return towards life. Paul's tone is less rigidly controlled, less like a symptom of shock:

At last I received yesterday some mail from you, i.e., your post-cards of June 7th, 23rd and July 2nd. As I got this week also two post-cards from Olga, I am in a better mood. I am glad to learn from your mail that you are keeping well and that you received at least some of my post-cards. Be assured I write you at least once a fortnight. I also can't get any reply on my different letters to Paula. This month I will try to write through the Red Cross. It is now more than one year I last heard from her, and that is not very easy to bear. But in fifty years' time it is all the same.

I thank you for the trouble you are taking in providing the book I asked for....

I am all right. Don't think that I am bone lazy. I always find some work in our camp and I do not grow too fat.

He closed with the observation: "I always start to write a letter and then I see a post-card would have done it, as there is nothing new to tell."

1943—Release from Internment but No News from Vienna

As 1943 began, the world looked dark to Paul in Australia and Walter in New York. There had been no letters, no sign of life from the family in Vienna since late 1941 and no possibility of communicating via aid organizations once the US was officially at war. In 1942 and 1943, news reached the Allied countries that large numbers of Jews in Greater Germany and the German-occupied lands were being deported to the East, to Poland, but none of them took any action to intervene.

The next letter from Paul is dated five months later, February 25, 1943, which was Lilly's twenty-fourth birthday. Paul asked again for chemical engineering journals, which may have been useful in finding work in his field. He was still interned, though beginning in 1942, Australia finally permitted *Dunera* internees, including Paul's friend Bob Vogel, to leave their camps if they could find jobs or volunteered for military service.[183] Paul wrote to both Lilly and Walter:

One of you has a birthday today, I do not know who of you. Anyhow I wish you all the best, all your wishes may come true

---

183 The regular Australian army did not admit "enemy aliens," so former internees who enlisted had to serve in non-combatant labor groups like the 8th Australian Employment Company. See https://www.nla.gov.au/digital-classroom/year-10/internment-world-war-ii-1939-45/themes/dunera.

and all the rest. Last week I wrote you as to be so kind and to send me a list of the main chemical periodicals published in the U.S., as there are: on industrial and engineering chemistry, fats and soap, electro-physical-colloid chemistry etc. Today I have to add something to my request. Could you make it possible as to send 2–4 of the last published journals on 'industrial and engineering chemistry' probably published in Liverpool, Ohio, and some on 'fats and soap' to my young friend Kurt Vogel,[184] 5 Langham Place, Hawthorne E3, Melbourne. As to me I have not much to tell. I am still working at our vegetable garden. This keeps me quite occupied and fit too....That is all for today. Keep well.

In March 1943 Paul at last found work with a company that extracted lanolin or "wool grease" from the dirty water left over from washing sheep fleeces, so he was released from the internment camp in Tatura. Olga sent Walter a postcard from England on April 15 with the news that "Paul has changed his address too, he has got a job in Melbourne, thank god."

Paul's next extant letter was sent in July 1943 with a Melbourne return address. Paul mentioned that he had written to Walter previously from Melbourne, but I have not found any such card or letter. However, one can partially reconstruct the exchanges that preceded this letter. After more than a year of silence from Vienna and growing fears about mass deportations to Poland, Paul suggested that Walter make inquiries about the family through the Swedish Red Cross and the Society of Friends. Walter wrote a desperate letter dated April 21, 1943, to the Red Cross in Stockholm asking in formal (if imperfect) English:

> Will you, please, have the great kindness to inform me whether

---

184 This is Bob Vogel, who had been released in about June 1942. He recounted in his dictated memoir that when "slowly people started to be released" from Tatura, he pulled a bit of a fast one. Although he had no such credentials, young Bob gave his "occupation as an engineer, as a fitter and turner, and I was called up, one year and ten months after my internment in Australia, to go to a factory in Melbourne. And off I went."

there is any possibility to contact my family, formerly in Vienna, Austria, now most probably brought to Poland. I did not hear from them since November 1941.

He listed four family members:

(1) Antoinette Haim née Feder, born 1869 [the correct year was 1868] Vienna, widow, Jewish/my mother/

(2) Johann Haim, born 1889 Vienna, married, Jewish/my brother/

(3) Paula Kurz née Haim, born 1896 Bucuresti, Romania, married, Jewish/my sister/

(4) Mathilde Kurz née Wilheim, born 1870(?), Veliki Mezerici, C.S.R., widow, Jewish/my sister's mother-in-law/

This letter never left the United States. It was opened and sent back marked "Returned to Sender by Censor." In his letter to Paul of May 16, Walter probably recounted the fate of his letter to the Swedish Red Cross. He counseled that Paul should not give up hope that the family were still alive until they had "definite proof."

Paul responded on July 8 in a factual but deeply dark letter. While he rigidly excluded any expression of emotion, it was the first letter in well over a year where Paul returned to addressing Walter by his family name, Bobbi:

On June 28th I received your letter of May 16th. I appreciate it the more as it is written in plain language, facts without circumscription. I have nothing to add. You are absolutely right in saying I must wait till to a definite proof. I do not think you will get any information either through the Red Cross nor through the Society of Friends. In my first letter I wrote to you from this town [Melbourne] I still was somehow more hopeful and therefore I suggested the Swedish Red Cross but in the meantime all has changed.

I thank you ever so much for the catalogues. The big one I received yesterday. Excuse these troubles I made you just for naught. I do not need any book or any journal.

Please write now and then but not too often to your old Paul

Ten days later Paul wrote another letter filling only two-thirds of the sheet, this one also written from beneath a carapace of fatalism. Paul attempted to forestall any "fairy-castle" speculations from Walter about who might still be alive:

I have both of your letters one of May 24th and one of June 7th. Yesterday I received also the book catalogue "Look It Up." Thanks ever so much for it. Please do not get any head-ache because of me. Believe me it is absolutely useless to make any plans for the future. It always comes otherwise than one thinks.[185] All events happen as they are forced to happen and it is good luck that we never know how they are forced to happen. Please do me a favour: do not worry anymore about my future because there won't be any. Thank heavens you did not make those experiences I did, but I have to ask you not to build your fairy-castles too high. It does not hurt so much if one falls only from a modest height. I am really all-right as far as this is possible. The last letter I had from Olga was of May 24th. Keep well both of you.

Paul's next letter on August 1 was shorter, taking up barely half the sheet of paper. He mechanically reported facts about letters received and a lack of mail, fulfilling a duty to transmit a sign of life but no more:

---

185 This phrase echoes an adage attributed to Wilhelm Busch, one of Walter's favorite writers, "Erstens kommt es anders, und zweitens als man denkt," meaning "first things come out differently, and secondly as one thinks."

This week I received a postcard and a letter from you and a letter from Jetty [Paula's friend who escaped first to Japan and then the US]. I hope she will know by now my new address. I have not much to tell. It is just only a routine letter in order to let you know that I am alive and all-right. From Olga I had no mail since a fortnight but this is not too long nowadays. I think I wrote you already that I got all the book catalogues you mentioned in your last letter. I thank you ever so much for them. That is all for today. Keep well both of you.

1945 and 1946—"Waiting for Miracles Is My Pastime"

After Paul's letter to Walter from August 1943, there is a nearly two-year blank, with no surviving correspondence from him until June 1945, a month after the war in Europe had officially ended on May 8, Victory in Europe (VE) Day. During this time Walter and Lilly appear to have continued to exchange regular letters with Paul, probably with long delays in delivery as the war in the Pacific intensified. From both sides of the world, they attempted without success to obtain information from the Red Cross about the fates of family who were, or had been, in Vienna. Fighting in Vienna had ended in March when the city was taken by the Red Army, but there was no news yet about survivors.

Paul's letter of June 5, 1945, consists of just a few lines. Its tone is severely restrained, almost mechanical:

I have your letter of April 7th in which you informed me about your trying to contact Vienna through your Red Cross. Already in my last letter I told you that I did the same and I'll do it again this month. There is nothing I could report. Give my greetings to Lilly.

Paul appeared to be psychologically close to the edge after so many years of uncertainty, as can be seen from his next letter three weeks later, another short one that again filled less than half the page. He reprimanded Walter for not writing and was uncharacteristically willing to verbalize his feelings of being in limbo:

> The last letter I received from you so about 5 weeks ago was dated April 17th. I answered it already 3 weeks ago. What is the matter with you? Is there something wrong with you? I am not used to such a long letterless period. Please be a good boy and write. There is nothing I could tell about me. One day like the other. Waiting for miracles is my pastime. Give my love to Lilly.

The following year, in early July 1946, Paul sent another half-page letter that included a bit of sharp teasing about both their countries' housing shortage (a welcome sign of life) but no news. Walter had received some sort of communication from Vienna the previous December but nothing since:

> At last some mail from you. I got your letters of April 30th and May 22nd. Then you had a message from Vienna of December 5th. That is seven months ago….Just waiting, that is all I can do. Then you will have to move. Nice aspect that, if accommodation-getting is as bad as here then I can figure out you will have to live under a bridge. From my part there is nothing to report. I just keep going. Give my love to Lilly and write regularly.

The next week, Paul's letter covered only three lines and was his shortest yet, shorter than even the early postcards. Walter and Lilly had returned from Virginia to New York and found an apartment in Jackson Heights, the neighborhood in New York where I grew up and where my family remained until 1980:

> Today I received your letter of May 10 although I had one of May 22nd already last week. I really have nothing to report. Just as you say…waiting is my pastime. Give my love to Lilly.

PART 4

Parallel Threads— The Families in Vienna 1939–1941

This part follows the letters from Vienna to Walter in New York from 1939 until they stopped in October 1941.

CHAPTER 15

The Extended Haim Family

Hans and Playing by the Rules

In February 1939, only days after Walter's departure, Hans wrote an unusually detailed account about his supervisor at the Vienna Jewish Community (IKG) who had tried to cross the border from Germany into France at Saarbrucken without a permit. The supervisor was caught, kept in custody for a day, and then sent back. Not one to give up, the supervisor pulled out all the stops as soon as he returned to Vienna. He sent a petition to King George VI himself and let it be known that he had received a response from a cabinet official, assuring him that "his request to the king will be forwarded to a Jewish Committee in London for processing." Undeterred, the supervisor continued to "write three times a day to the Committee and telegraph every second day." Hans was having none of that. He looked down on the supervisor's "tough pushiness" and wrote, "I condemn these illegal attempts and would never make them, although thousands leave that way...." He then added as a sop, "If I really wanted to go somewhere, then I would only want to go to the USA."

Several qualities seem notable. Hans continued to be ambivalent about leaving Austria nearly year after the Anschluss, while showing unambivalent disdain for the "pushiness" of his boss, who pestered the English government and Jewish organizations with his appeals. Then there is the resilience of Hans's self-identity as a man of honor. Despite the degradations imposed by the new order, Hans continued to pride himself on being upstanding or honorable (aufrichtig). He played by the rules even as he recognized their irrationality and injustice.

The IKG, which Adolf Eichmann used as a puppet organization to administer the Nazis' confiscatory emigration system, adopted a pragmatic rather than a moral position. It disapproved of illegal emigration out of fear that it would undermine the Nazi regime's official emigration program and lead to destination countries imposing yet more stringent limits on legal immigration.[186] The IKG publicly announced that it would not help anyone who had been sent back to Vienna after being caught trying to emigrate illegally.[187] Official disapproval, though, was ineffective: "appeals and threats did nothing to stop illegal escape but at most made it necessary to find different routes."[188]

Tante Helene and the Frieder Family Emigrate to Manila

Hans, like his parents, kept Walter up to date on the whereabouts of former colleagues at Mercury Bank and various relatives who were attempting to escape. Among them were Tante Helene, Antoinette Haim's youngest sister; her husband, Ignacz "Geza" Frieder; and their adult children, Robert and Margit.

In March 1939 Hans reported that the Frieders were located uneasily in northern Italy because "until now [they] have received no extension of stay and are very worried and despondent there because all emigrated Jews must leave the country on March 12th," and they "certainly do not want to stay in a country where [they have] no permit." The Frieders' son Robert traveled to Milan to apply for visas there with no success, while his parents continued to "sit in Como and tremble that they will be thrown out." Finally Paula wrote that the Frieders were able to sail from Italy to Manila

---

186 Rabinovici, *Eichmann's Jews*, 53.

187 Ilana Fritz Offenberger, The Jews of Nazi Vienna 1938–1945 (Palgrave McMillan, 2017), 134.

188 Rabinovici, *Eichmann's Jews*, 53.

in May 1939. They were among the lucky fraction of applicants who received visas for the Philippines.

Jewish emigration to the Philippines is a small diaspora sidestory. The American Frieder brothers, who had owned a profitable cigar company there since the end of World War I, famously persuaded Philippines president Manuel Quezon to take in about 1,200 "qualified" Jews from Germany and Austria between 1938 and 1941.[189] Hungarian-born Geza may have been a distant relative of these American Frieders, but more importantly, he had useful skills. He had owned a successful lumber business in Austria before it was "Aryanized," that is, confiscated under color of unjust laws.

In Manila Helene and her family had to reconstruct their lives in an exotic tropical exile. One emigrant from Germany, who had arrived in Manila with his parents as a boy of eight, recalled that "the oppressive heat and humidity and the bloodthirsty mosquitos were the first experiences the refugees had to cope with."[190]

The Frieder family located an apartment on Taft Avenue, a main street in Manila. Geza and Robert soon found work and Margit became engaged to an Englishman, but Helene seems to have had a more difficult time. She wrote to Walter in March 1941, after nearly two years in Manila, "I have not been happy here for a single minute." Still, the Philippines proved to be a safe enough haven. Helene and her family all survived the war, including three years of Japanese occupation beginning in January 1942 and the bloody reconquest of Manila in February and March 1945 by American and Filipino forces.

New Skills for Hopeful Emigrants—Pauline Learns Millinery

The Jewish Community in Vienna organized a range of classes to provide intending emigrants with portable skills. Paula, an experienced auditor and accountant, reported in September 1939 that

---

189 Frank Ephraim, *Escape to Manila: From Nazi Tyranny to Japanese Terror* (Champaign, IL: University of Illinois Press, 2003), 11–19.

190 Ephraim, *Escape to Manila*, 10.

she had completed a course in purse making. At the same time, she and her friend Martha Müller, a credentialed pediatrician, were looking into taking a sewing course.

Earlier that year, Pauline Neuhaus, Lilly's mother, had enrolled in a millinery class. About a month after Walter's departure, Paula wrote about Pauline's stellar progress:

> Mrs. Neuhaus is taking a fashion course and has made two charming hats for me. The hats are the only ones I've had. She is very lovely and very gifted.

Walter's sister Alice agreed. In March 1939 she and Pauline began bartering English lessons for hats. Alice wrote: "On Friday your mother-in-law begins the first English lesson. For that she makes beautiful hats for the nearer and more distant family."

On April 7 (the day before Walter's thirty-seventh birthday), Paula wrote under the heading "Neuhaus":

> Mr. and Mrs. go diligently to Aischi for lessons. The wife becomes younger and prettier every day. A dear mother-in-law, whom we recently got to know and have fallen very in love with. But she is really charming. She wears a little ladybug that you once gave her on her spring coat.

Alice confirmed that despite Pauline's trepidation, she was continuing to exchange hats for English lessons. Alice wrote:

> Your mother-in-law has already made me 3 beautiful hats and Hansi [a Haim family friend] already 2; she is an artist....She is...afraid of learning English. But it will already happen.

Martin Haim was a fan as well, writing that August:

> Mama N[euhaus] will come next on Friday. She has now very little time because of a new millinery course and for that

reason comes to Alice only once a week, which we regret very much.

And in November:

Mama N[euhaus] is so proficient and diligent and is quite an artist in millinery. She will certainly succeed there [i.e., in the United States].

One of the things that I was sometimes allowed to play with in my grandparents' apartment was a tiny suitcase, the size of a handbag, that contained a set of graduated metal balls set into stalks on wooden handles. They were tools for making silk flowers, brought from Vienna. As far as I know, my grandmother never made hats in New York. Early on she got a job doing alterations for a dress shop on Vesey Street in lower Manhattan (a neighborhood that was razed in the early 1970s to build the World Trade Center). Then in the later 1950s, she opened her own dress store, Pauline Originals, on Broadway between West 73rd and 74th Streets. A store on Broadway seems to have been her dream from the first arrival in New York. Already in June 1941, Martin Haim wrote to Pauline:

You will become a millionaire, whether you intend to or not, and your salon, even if it isn't on Broadway, will still be known and renowned throughout the USA for your brilliant creations.

My grandmother's store specialized in stylish dresses and suits for women whose clothes needed extensive alterations to fit their wearers' unusual proportions, e.g., a size 8 bodice above a size 14 skirt, or vice versa. My childhood recollection is that nearly all the customers spoke German. Whenever a customer came in, I had to stay very quiet in the back of the store among the sewing machines and ironing board and keep away from the fitting rooms.

Affidavits of Support from the New York Sephardim

Since early 1939, Hans, as secretary of the Vienna Sephardic community, had been corresponding with the Sephardic Refugee Committee, a group associated with Congregation Shearith Israel, Manhattan's venerable Spanish-Portuguese orthodox synagogue, urging them to issue affidavits of support. Once Walter arrived in New York, Hans coached him in how to cultivate contacts with the committee and congregation leaders, actions that would have been very difficult given Walter's retiring, nonassertive nature. Hans expected Walter to provide detailed accounts of his contacts and did not hesitate to chide Walter when the reports fell short. Here's a letter from March 13, for example:

> You write that you reviewed my list [of Vienna Sephardic families] with Dr. Cardozo [one of the rabbis of the Sephardic congregation in Manhattan]. But you don't write what he did with it, what he said about it, what you said to him in response. Be more detailed in such a communication!

The campaign of pleading and currying favor with the New York Sephardic Refugee Committee actually bore fruit. Hans wrote the good news to Walter on April 19:

> Yesterday afternoon I wrote to you and in the evening I found at home a letter from Mr. Dr. Sola Pool [the senior rabbi at Shearith Israel] in which he informed me that 17 affidavits have been promised for the Viennese Spaniolen [i.e., Sephardim], which will be sent to us immediately after completion. Think of my great surprise and joy and the joy of the other affected families.

One affidavit from the Refugee Committee covered three Haims—Hans and his wife, Lisl, plus his sister Alice Haim. This affidavit was signed by a Henry S. Hendricks and his wife, Rosalie Nathan

Hendricks. They lived in Westchester County, a posh suburban area just north of New York City. By signing the statement, they affirmed that they were willing to assume responsibility for these three foreign strangers. The affidavit addressed in bland terms the fact that the Hendriks couple were not related to the Haims while strategically omitting any reference to the actual source of their connection, their religious/ethnic identity as Sephardic Jews. The affidavit stated:

> —That in spite of the fact that deponents are not relatives of Mr. and Mrs. Haim and Miss Haim, they are deeply concerned about their welfare and are prepared to receive them upon admission into the United States of America and to see that they do not become public charges in any community therein.

> —That deponents believe that Mr. and Mrs. Haim and Miss Haim to be intelligent, industrious people who should prove to be good citizens of the United States of America.

The affidavit and supplements disclosed that Rosalie and Henry S. Hendricks received income from trusts and investments in excess of eight thousand dollars per year. With these resources, the Hendrickses would have been very comfortably off. A historian of the congregation recognized the Hendrickses and their extended families, which included a network of Nathans and Cardozos, as wealthy mainstays of New York's old and insular Sephardic community. Rosalie Nathan Hendricks in particular was "very much a grand dame" among them.[191]

Nisko: The First Nazi "Resettlement" Program

The first hint of the Nazi campaign to "resettle" large Jewish populations in Poland appeared in a letter from Paula in late October

---

191 Stephen Birmingham, "Who Are They?," ch. 2 in *The Grandees: America's Sephardic Elite* (New York: Open Road Media, 2015).

1939. She did not name the destination other than "Poland" and at this point was hopeful that it might offer a realistic exit from Vienna:

> Here there are relocation projects which have also been started. Retirees, etc., are not highly valued for now. There are only two emigration goals: USA or Poland. So it looks like the both of them [Lilly's parents] can go there to you.

Paula mentioned in passing that "we and all our joint relatives may move in a few months. The rest of them [unidentified] did not want to."

About a week later, Paula wrote some more about the pending resettlement:

> The matter about Pol[and] is still judged relatively favorably by all the [IKG] leaders.

Then in early November 1939, Paul warned Walter about a Nazi campaign to remove the remaining Jews from Vienna and elsewhere in Greater Germany to Poland. There was some hope that people of working age who had relatives abroad could still emigrate, he wrote, but none for the older generation. Paul recognized this as an ominous development:

> As you will immediately gather from the letterhead, I have changed my address [to Bradford]. That means that I have temporarily found work in my specialty. But that is not what brings me to write, old friend, but I have news which is everything other than pleasant, and which I must, despite everything, immediately share with you. If your wife still wants her parents to come to you, she must absolutely immediately hurry to arrange it, because an action [campaign] is being prepared for the collective removal of the German Jews to Poland. The K.G. [Kultus Gemeinde, the Jewish Community] must undertake the administration and its files and must furnish transportation to the east. First the

young people are taken there, then the old people. Old people and pensioners have a few more months ahead of them. Based on the thoroughness and speed with which these things are happening, I believe that your younger sister [that is, Paula,] will soon be taken. I am telling you that I can do absolutely nothing from here, so leave nothing undone to obtain affidavits. As for my mother, unfortunately, I don't know of any possible escape.

As for me, everything is outstandingly well, for the body, it is cared for sufficiently, while everything else depends for the time being on the moon.

This letter isn't long, because it is very heavy.

Paul did not disclose the source of the information underlying his warning. It may have come, however indirectly, from the family in Vienna. Hans, as the secretary of the Viennese Sephardic community, may have had advance information because Adolf Eichmann's organization had co-opted Vienna's Jewish Community (the IKG) to administer the Vienna-based aspects of the Nisko relocation project. On the other hand, Hans's own letters do not mention Nisko. Nor did the Austrian newspapers mention anything about an impending relocation of Vienna's Jews to Nisko.[192]

Whatever the source of Paul's news about Nisko and however it had traveled from Vienna to England, it was accurate. In late September 1939, shortly after the German invasion and Poland's division between Germany and the USSR, Eichmann and his Central Office for Jewish Emigration undertook what historian Doron Rabinovici described as a "badly planned and hastily organized" program to move large numbers of the Jews remaining in Vienna (about one-third of the pre-Anschluss population) and the "Protectorate" (formerly the western part of Czechoslovakia) to a so-called "Jewish reservation" to be established

---

192 See Austrian National Library, "ANNO, Historical Newspapers and Magazines," http://anno.onb.ac.at/.

in German-occupied Poland. This would be the first step in a "territorial solution to the Jewish question."[193] Nisko was selected because it was "a small town in southeast Poland with a railroad station."[194]

Eichmann's group tasked the IKG with filling the thousand-person rail transports, with a special preference for skilled craftsmen. Jews who were retired or not healthy were excluded. At this early stage there were actual volunteers for the transport to Poland, as "many Jews thought that an autonomous Jewish settlement south of Lublin would enable them to survive the war safely." The vaunted "resettlement" scheme became a disaster that ended in the death of most of those transported. Still, from the Nazis' perspective, it wasn't a complete waste of resources. They learned how to organize and manage mass population removals. Rabinovici titled his discussion of the Nisko project "the dress rehearsal for deportation."[195]

The first trains packed with fifteen hundred Austrian Jews left Vienna for Nisko in October 1939 and were followed by two more thousand-person transports.[196] Perhaps to make the Nisko option seem more attractive, during the same period the Nazi government deported about a thousand of the remaining elderly and young Jews from Vienna to Buchenwald.[197]

An official report by Eichmann's Central Office for Jewish Emigration dated October 18, 1939, regarding "Jews being sent to Nisko," confirms Paul's warnings. The Jewish Community (IKG)

---

[193] Rabinovici, *Eichmann's Jews*, 88, 94.

[194] "History of the Austrian Jewish Community," Conference on Jewish Material Claims Against Germany, accessed September 3, 2022, http://www.claimscon.org/what-we-do/negotiations/austria/history-of-the-austrian-jewish-community/#section_2.

[195] Rabinovici, *Eichmann's Jews*, 87–95.

[196] "History of the Austrian Jewish Community," Conference on Jewish Material Claims Against Germany.

[197] See also "Anschluss and Extermination: The Fate of the Austrian Jews," Holocaust Education and Archive Research Team, accessed January 21, 2022, http://www.holocaustresearchproject.org/nazioccupation/anschluss.html.

was made responsible for organizing this first mass relocation to the East. The Nazi goal was to "resettle" two thousand Jews per week in Nisko using rail transports from Vienna. Each transport was to be guarded by twenty-five armed police who were authorized to shoot deportees trying to escape.[198]

In November 1939 Paul repeated his warning about the impending deportation of Jews from Vienna. He also asked Walter for a small favor: to act as an intermediary transmitting a "sign of life" for a fellow refugee and worker in the Humphris household to her sister in Germany. Mail could be sent to Germany from the United States, still officially neutral, though not from the UK:

> Don't be surprised that you get one letter from me so quickly one after the other. First I'll repeat what I said in my last letter, that one cannot tell anything from today's postal circumstances, then I have a little request for you that I will gladly tell you about.
>
> At the house of my former host, Mrs. Humphris,...in addition to my sister, a Miss Else Weilheimer is also on the staff there (as a cook, etc.). Please write as soon as possible to her sister Wally Weilheimer, Mannheim, Hebelstrasse 11, that things are OK with her, and the sister can write to you how she is. She is a very dear and good person and has absolutely no other possibility for exchanging signs of life with her people.
>
> Now I have to repeat again what I already wrote you. Your wife must hurry if she wants her parents to come over to her. Specifically, a campaign is being set in motion whose final goal is the entire resettling of the Jews in Poland. Old people, pensioners, etc., have only a few months left. The young people are now already going one after the other; it

---

198 "Vienna," United States Holocaust Memorial Museum, accessed January 21, 2022, https://www.ushmm.org/wlc/en/article.php?ModuleId=10005452; see also Schneider, *Exile and Destruction*, 41–42, summarizing Eichmann's Nisko "resettlement" project as a "fiasco."

is taking place under the direction of the religious association[199] and also under their orders. This won't be any work service, but rather a preliminary resettlement for all the Jews. How one can ever emigrate from there (if that ever comes into consideration again), will be seen; naturally no one has any idea.

The 1939 removals to Nisko took place more than two years before the advent of extermination camps to implement the Nazis' "final solution." Thus at the time, it was still reasonable to consider the availability of emigration processes for deportees who had been "resettled" in the East. Eichmann's office, with its usual duplicity, told the IKG that emigration from German-occupied Poland would be possible after the war, though not before that.[200]

Paul continued with his warning:

> Your whole family, including your younger sister [Paula], is certainly affected by that, and your brother [Hans] busies himself trying to obtain affidavits by all available means. It is hardly believable that he will succeed before the catastrophe.

> Unfortunately, I was not able to bring Paula and my mother here before the outbreak of war, because I obtained my work permit in my specialty—lanolin production (about which, I believe, hardly 100 chemists in the whole world have mastered this area as well as I)—only shortly before the war broke out. Please this is said only for you and make no mention of it anywhere. [That sentence is typed in red.] What will happen with my mother is naturally grim. That means, stop carrying all the blows of fate, just carry before the junior court the ones that you can bear witness to.

---

[199] That is the IKG, the Jewish Community of Vienna.

[200] Rabinovici, *Eichmann's Jews*, 91.

Olga added a short, handwritten postscript allowing more direct emotion to show through than Paul usually did:

> Greetings, Walter. It is genuinely grim—but we must still believe and hope that after the war the Nazis will be done for—that everything will be different. Those devils!

1939—End-of-the-Year Holidays in Vienna and New York

In December 1939 the Haims in Vienna wrote cheerfully about the holidays. Affidavits for the Neuhauses were in the works, so there was present joy and some hope for the future. There was no more mention of Nisko or deportations. Walter and Lilly seem to have attended some holiday events at Shearith Israel, Manhattan's Sephardic congregation. Martin wrote:

> When Lilly has her parents there, she will be entirely happy. We give them up very reluctantly, but what can be done? Hopefully your [pl.] Hanukah celebration was very nice and you had a good time.

Life had led the young couple in unpredictable directions:

> Walter, did you ever think you would have your wife with you at a Sephardic Hanukah celebration in the USA? And you Lilly, how do you imagine yourself as a Turkish Jewess? And still more as Mrs. Haim in N.Y.?

The core of the Sephardic community in New York consisted of old families like the Hendrickses, Nathans, and Cardozos. They were proud that their Spanish and Portuguese forebears had arrived in the American colonies before the revolution, and at least a century before the late nineteenth-century surge of Jewish migration from Germany, Russia, and Eastern Europe. With this pedigree, these

Sephardim considered themselves "the elite of American Jewry."[201] Walter and Lilly, newly arrived refugees and German speakers, would have been thoroughly out of place in that society.

---

201 Birmingham, *The Grandees*, ch. 2.

CHAPTER 16

1940—Moves and Loss

After the upheavals of late 1939 and the departure of about two-thirds of Vienna's pre-war Jewish population, 1940 began as a relatively quieter year for the remaining community.[202]

Alice

For the Haim family, 1940 began with an unimaginable loss. Walter's older sister Alice, the language teacher, died unexpectedly on January 13 in the Jewish hospital in the 18th District. She was only forty-eight. Walter and Lilly had airmailed a birthday letter to Alice from New York on January 22, nine days after her death. This suggests that the family in Vienna sent them a letter with the news, rather than a telegram, since nothing more could be done for Alice.

The birthday letter from New York arrived in Vienna nearly two months later, on March 16. Hans answered on March 31:

> Before I address your letter, I must go back to our dear, good Alice who will not receive your birthday wishes anymore! The poor dear is relieved of the question, "to East Asia or to America"! She suffered for barely a week, Monday evening she took to her bed, Saturday evening she passed away. As you already know she was laid low by a terrible flu, her weak

---

202 Schneider, *Exile and Destruction*, 49, 54: "For the greater part of 1940, it seemed that conditions for Vienna's Jews had become more stable."

heart and her poor weakened body could not overcome it. If there can be any comfort, if one were to look for it, it is that as far as can be determined, she had no idea about the severity and hopelessness of her illness and passed away peacefully and without pain. Earlier she certainly had suffered greatly. So in this mood we celebrated the [parents'] birthdays this year!

There are few letters from Paula, Hans, and the Haim parents during the winter and spring of 1940. Among them is one from Martin about Alice's funeral. He wrote on April 1:

We had of course notified her students and earlier acquaintances about the death of our poor, dear Alice and also placed a notice in the Jewish newspaper [distributed through the IKG to members of the community]. Whoever was still here was at her burial. Only I could not and was not able to pay my last respects. Can you imagine what sort of feelings I had staying home, and I still think about her hourly. But unfortunately she is lost forever for us.

Although Martin did not explain why he remained at home, the causes would have been the inclement weather and chronic heart disease that had kept him indoors all winter.

On February 9 Martin wrote that Mathilde Kurz, Paul and Olga's mother, had moved in with them, settling into what had been Alice's room:

Since Monday evening Mrs. Kurz has lived with us and in the room of our poor, dear Alice. She moved from the apartment in Leichtensteinstrasse. This is a great comfort for Paul and Paula, and Paula won't have to go running there anymore. She will certainly feel comfortable with us, and we will not be alone. So unforeseen changes take place.

The fact that Mathilde Kurz moved in with the Haim family from an address in Leichtensteinstrasse, a main street in the 9th District, meant that she had previously been evicted from the Kurz's long-time family apartment at Novaragasse 39 in the 2nd District and forced into some sort of communal housing.

On April 4 Antoinette wrote about the family's morale. They were soldiering on, keeping up with visits and news from relatives and acquaintances who were increasingly dispersed around the globe, while anticipating more departures daily:

> Things are so far going well with us. The inconceivable ability of people to become accustomed to such sad, unchangeable conditions helps us a bit to put this sadness behind us. One sleeps, one eats and drinks, and one goes firmly onwards, only one cannot be cheerful any more, we are already too old for that. But whatever God wills!

Martin had abandoned hopes of leaving Vienna. Paula wrote at the beginning of April:

> Papa now does not want to leave any more. He wants to remain by Alice. Despite that he is especially attached to you, always speaks of you [pl.] with longing, waits for your [pl.] letters—he remains with Alice. And after Alice's death, he said that [he] preferred staying in Vienna with her to leaving.

Alice's unexpected death suggested a possible immigration opening to Paul. In March, he asked Walter whether the affidavit from the Sephardim in New York could be modified to substitute Olga's name for Alice's. He posed this question with some trepidation, assuring Walter, and by extension the rest of the Haim family, "I am no grave robber." If this change could be made, Paul wrote, he would consider going to the United States with Olga, but not otherwise:

Bobbi, now the matter....your sister Alice is dead....You had previously procured an affidavit for her....Is it possible to have this affidavit rewritten for my sister? I give you the data in any case. Bobbi this is it. With her I would travel to you, not alone. And with you we can perhaps, or perhaps not, wait for Paula. Bobbi if it doesn't work, write me immediately and completely openly without adornment, then I will have to undertake something else. And still something else.

On a separate quarter sheet of paper, Paul typed Olga's essential data:

Olga Kurz, Dr. Med. Born in Vienna, Nov. 29, 1898; was a citizen/resident of [zuständig] Vienna; received her doctoral diploma from the University of Vienna in March, 1928.

Paula visited Alice's grave in the Central Cemetery fairly frequently despite restrictions on Jews' use of public transportation and the danger of venturing out into the streets. She wrote to Walter in late April, "I always bring flowers for you." Later that spring, they were able to order a headstone. Paula wrote in some detail about it and how she missed Alice:

Today I have chosen a beautiful stone for our Alice. It is rose veined marble, like a chimney back, do you remember, Bibolein? And very beautiful in shape. Instead of a mound, there will be a flat piece on the grave so that it does not look so uncared for, like so many other graves which must be left behind. And behind the stone there will be a climbing rose. It will all be finished in a few weeks, and then I will send you a photo.

Paula's noting the neglected, left-behind graves suggests that at least subjectively, she had not entirely given up all hope of the family's leaving Vienna.

Paula made a special pilgrimage to Alice's grave on her wedding anniversary in March and wrote to Walter about it:

> She was always with me on that day, unfortunately, this time I had to go to her. It is noteworthy that when I stand at her grave, I have to recount to her everything that has happened, what you write, what the parents are doing. Things come to my mind which I otherwise don't think about, as if she would ask me about them. And I hear her almost as though she comforts me and sends me home.

Lilly had had only a few limited meetings with Walter's family, but she wrote a sensitive letter of condolence to the elder Haims after Alice's unexpected death. Paula reported positively to Walter on April 29:

> Walter, your Lilly has won all our love! She is a real good fellow, just like you. That she found such beautiful words for our parents shows how she is for you also. I am enormously happy about that and God keep you both in your happiness. How most marriages are still messed up [askew, Verhatscht]. But neither you nor I could live in such a marriage.

The following year, as living conditions in Vienna became ever more oppressive for the remaining Jews, Paula wrote that she still brought flowers for Walter on every visit to Alice's grave. On the first anniversary of Alice's death, Martin reported that "Paula and Hansi went to her grave in the morning and Mama and Hans in the afternoon even though the entire cemetery lay deep in snow." As the weather was "cold and very windy," Martin had to stay in the apartment.

In February 1940 Antoinette wrote that the family continued to have regular visitors and enjoyed Mathilde Kurz's presence with them:

Everything is continuing, only unfortunately without our poor Alice. But it is good for her, she has her peace, only the sorrow for her remains for us. It seems to me always as though she must come in the door; I have not yet totally grasped it, otherwise I could not stop crying or divert myself. And for Papa it is the same. We are very glad that Paul's mother is with us, also a diversion from our thoughts, especially for Papa who otherwise would sit all alone in the room the whole morning. We have a visit just about every day. Malvine and Otto [one of Antoinette's younger sisters and her husband] also often come in the evening.

Looking for Ways to Leave

In February 1940 Paul learned in a roundabout way that the US consulate in Vienna had received only one of the two affidavits for Lilly's parents. The Neuhaus parents had been preparing to leave Vienna, but their plans now would have to be delayed. Paul wrote from Bradford:

> The affidavits for Lilly's parents have not entirely come, that means only the one for the father has been submitted to the consulate, while the one for her mother in some mysterious way has been lost. Although they have already broken up the apartment, it will take longer to put this matter in order and speed is needed....
>
> Otherwise I actually have nothing else to report, things continue to go well for us [i.e., Paul and Olga], unchanged, only the problems about wife and mother are still unresolved as before.

Even Hans was finally considering emigration. Antoinette wrote on March 11, 1940, after a Sunday afternoon visit from Hans,

Lisl, and their dog, that "Hans is now thinking more intensively about emigrating," though he continued to vacillate. A week later, Antoinette wrote that despite Aunt Helene's complaints about the heat in the Philippines ("She writes that they are all healthy, working, and—sweat!"), "Hans would rather go to M[anila] than to NY because he sees an earlier possibility of employment there....But it hasn't gone that far yet. He would prefer to remain here." Later in April Hans continued to lean towards Manila, though Antoinette thought "it would be more congenial for me if he went to NY because of the climate. But we will see what God has ordained." Later that month, according to Paula, Hans received a final denial from the Frieder brothers' committee in Manila, ending hopes for his emigration to the Philippines.

In a letter written on Walter's birthday, April 8, Antoinette wrote that Hans had been ill without identifying the problem and left it to Uncle Gustl (due to arrive shortly in New York on the SS *Manhattan*) to give Walter and Lilly the details. She acknowledged indirectly that inadequate food rations, as well as illness, were taking a general toll on all the family. Hans had lost weight while he was ill, Antoinette wrote, and "Lisl lost about 12 kilos during his sickness, but <u>she</u> looks better for that. Paula and I have not yet determined the number that we have lost."

Typically, Hans had mentioned nothing about being sick in his letter of March 31, which is filled with details about tangled interpersonal politics and the unreasonable demands of visa sponsors. As for his own emigration, Hans wrote dismissively, "I have as little desire to emigrate to the USA as to Manila," and "I consider America is too difficult a ground for people of my age. [Hans was 51.] But we will see." Visas and affidavits aside, Hans alluded to the terrible situation their parents would be in if he or Paula were to be able to escape: "The parents, thank God, are healthy, they have really suffered a heavy blow, one sees it much less in Papa than in Mama. It is hardly to be considered, that one should leave the parents behind alone here!"

In April 1940 Martin wrote again about missing Alice:

> I miss our dear, good, poor Alice in all ends and corners. As often as I go into her room, I see her in front of me, but unfortunately only in the mind. But what can I do. Nothing, other than mourn for her. God should give you [pl.] all happiness that remains that was denied to her.

In the midst of this loss and straightened physical circumstances, the Haim family maintained a version of their former domestic life. Antoinette kept busy with practicalities, while Martin's days had contracted to reading, sleeping, and sometimes chatting with visitors. Martin recounted in response to Walter's question:

> What Mama and I do here is quickly told—she cooks, cleans, sews, mends, keeps house, and goes to [her sister] Malvine while I, I wait during the day until it is evening, and at night until it is day again, so highly eventful, otherwise I read novels and once in a while get visitors.

Later that evening, while Martin slept, Antoinette added some news about relatives in Milan, Helene and her family in Manila, and family and acquaintances in Vienna, writing on the sewing machine table by the fading spring light.

The Problem of Omama

Lilly's parents hoped to leave Vienna, but the question of what to do about Omama, Pauline's mother Regine Landsmann, had become a source of constant tension in the Landsmann-Neuhaus household. In February 1940 Fritzl Mayer, the uncle whom Lilly visited in London, wrote candidly from Zurich to Lilly in New York:

> Grossmama [that is, Omama] stays in her room all the time!!! Certainly disagreements don't improve the general situation. I certainly am not telling you anything new if I tell you that Papa

[Arthur Neuhaus] wants only to emigrate, even if alone with Mutti [Pauline]. Mutti, however, cannot find it in her heart to leave the old lady to her fate, even though she partly acknowledges the justification of his desire. It is hard to advise, because both sides are correct. Thank God there are no major debates, only inner discontent.

In April 1940 Omama was moved to the IKG's old age home at Seegasse 9 in the 9th District, three blocks from the family apartment. This could have been part of Pauline and Arthur's preparation for their eventual emigration to the United States, or Omama may have begun to need more care or become unable to climb the stairs to the family's fourth-floor apartment. Antoinette visited Omama shortly after the move. Without alluding to any reason for the change, she wrote positively on April 22 about Omama's new situation:

Last Thursday I visited Mrs. Landsmann in Seegasse. She was altogether very well and had a visit from three ladies other than me. Mutti [Pauline Neuhaus] took care of Mrs. L[andsmann]'s move into a beautiful parterre room with a view of the garden, and I went away from there with a very reassured feeling for Omama's wellbeing.

Two-thirds of the Jewish community had emigrated from Vienna at this point, but Antoinette still ran into acquaintances and distant relatives at every turn, including at the old age home. She wrote that "there in the courtyard I met Mrs. Steffi Schüller (Café Habsburg) who was the head of the kitchen at Seegasse" and who happened to be a sister of Pauline Neuhaus's brother Gustl's late wife's mother.

That August the Neuhaus parents were forced to move out of their apartment at Grünentorgasse 4 into lodgings a few blocks away in Rögergasse, still in easy walking distance of Seegasse.

The Second Year of War Begins

As the second year of the war began, life in Vienna seemed on the surface to be stable. On October 3, 1940, Martin sent greetings to Walter and Lilly for the Jewish New Year:

> Today is the first day of the Jewish New Year and we wish you also on this occasion everything dear, good, and beautiful. Hopefully the New Year will bring you the fulfillment of all your wishes. Yesterday afternoon Lilly's parents and Hans were here to congratulate us on New Year's Eve.

In characteristically Austrian fashion, Martin referred to the festivities on the eve of Rosh Hashanah as "Sylvestergratulation," greetings for St. Sylvester, whose feast day in the Gregorian calendar is celebrated on December 31, New Year's Eve. Martin also offered specific reassurance that the Neuhaus parents "are healthy and have long become accustomed to their new apartment."

In her September letter, Paula wrote about a range of worries: the Neuhauses' visa applications seemed to have stalled; Paul had not been located, they knew only that he was an internee en route to an unknown destination; and how difficult being "left behind alone" in England was for Olga. Walter had noted in his letter that Paul's birthday was coming up. This was the second year that Paula would be separated from him on that day:

> Yes, next week is P[aul]'s birthday! One can't do anything about it. In previous years I wanted to be with him already for his birthday. It's still good that I am with the parents, most importantly now when Hans and Lisl will soon emigrate. But sometimes one thinks that one will go crazy. And there I was already crazy, isn't it true, Bibolein? At least you always claimed that.

This letter suggests that the possibility of Manila was still alive for Hans and Lisl, though communication with Tante Helene was not always clear. Antoinette wrote in this same letter that "Hans has received the approval for M[anila]," though this seems not to have been the final step. Ultimately their application was denied.

In October Martin brought Walter and Lilly up on the news that Mathilde Kurz, Paul and Olga's mother, had received a letter from her niece Trude Wilheim in Brazil. The letter had been en route for eleven months, since November 1939. Trude had married a German refugee, Peter Scheier, who worked for an advertising agency in Sao Paolo, and things were going well for them. Trude cooks, Martin reported (perhaps unusual in Brazil where domestic help was cheap), and "they are very content."

Paula added to the letter, noting that "this week we received lots of interesting ancient mail" that had been sent in November 1939. She was "already curious about how things are going for you in your new apartment" and wondered whether Walter and Lilly had heard from Paul. There was some speculation that he had arrived in Canada from internment in England, though Paula interpreted the hints and scraps of information less sanguinely.

There was little domestic news during the fall of 1940. One international mail day in October, Martin wrote at length about how there was nothing new for the family to report. Paula filled in the bottom quarter of that page with a cake recipe that substituted sieved boiled potatoes for flour and sandwiched a thin layer of marmalade between a base of dough and a woven, gridded top, something like a Linzertorte. The following week, Martin noted that "today it is already 9 months that our dear, good Alice left us, and she remains so alive to me." Paula wrote only that she had recently written a separate letter and had nothing new to add to it.

In that private letter sent on October 11, Paula showed unusually frank anxiety about her husband Paul's location since he had been transported away from England and his narrowing emigration possibilities. Walter seemed to be changing the dates by when he hoped to have news of Paul's whereabouts. So far, efforts to obtain an affidavit for a US visa for Paul had come to nothing. Paula was concerned about Olga, who was isolated in the UK after Paul had been interned that June, particularly now that direct communication with Vienna was interdicted:

> Now to your letter to me. This unfortunately shook me in several directions. First, you shifted the fixed date at which you can have news from Paul from the middle of October (your last letter) to the end of November and then say that Olga can have news at this time. I would very much like to know how you calculated that since you do not know in fact where he is. Also the situation with the affidavit is terribly sad. He has practically nothing. The affidavit for him was my single hope for him. He is a poor devil. God knows what sort of a state he is in. Unfortunately he was never all that strong. These cares are insanely heavy to bear. I can vividly imagine Olga's state....
>
> Ollie's birthday will be on Nov. 29th. Please tell her that she must remain healthy for Paul, for her mother, and for me, and that I love her endlessly.

The following week there was still no definite news about Paul. Antoinette wrote that Tante Lotte (another of her sisters, Charlotte [née Feder] Degner), "diligently sends cards" from Berlin. They also had received a letter, only five or six weeks en route, from Tante Helene in Manila, where "everything is in order," or so Antoinette wrote. She continued to visit Omama regularly on Sundays and had met up with Pauline Neuhaus at the Seegasse old age home. The Haims continued to have visitors, sometimes Flora Haim (Martin's niece), often Hans with his dog. Paula was enjoying a pattern-making and tailoring class organized by the Jewish Community. In short, they portrayed a surface of recognizably normal life.

By early November 1940, there was some solid information about Paul. When Paula received Walter's letter that Paul had finally been located, she responded in a rush of joy, her handwriting three times as large as usual, filling half the page of a family letter:

> I am happy about your news. I don't have time to write more. Send Paul's new address eventually to Hans or also to me in a separate letter. Have you written to him already? More next time. All healthy. Many kisses.

The Family Is Forced to Move

On December 1, 1940, the family dropped something of a bombshell. Martin wrote:

> A piece of news. Tomorrow morning we will move, but you must not be frightened because we already, thank God, have another apartment, namely a room and a small room [Kabinett] and use of a kitchen. Our new address is: III/40 Sechskrügelgasse 2, 2nd stairs, 1st floor, door 9. We were informed about 3 weeks ago, but after a long walk and many many visits, Paula unearthed the new quarters.

Much was left unsaid in this letter. The family had known for the previous three weeks that they would have to leave their apartment at Margaretenstrasse 121 but kept it hidden from Lilly and Walter until the last minute, continuing to write blandly that there was no news and all was well. Also unsaid was that leaving Margaretenstrasse, where the Haims had lived since the early 1920s, meant the loss of most if not all of their remaining furniture, china, silver, rugs, books, and mementos assembled over a lifetime.

There was more sad news. The mother of Hugo Kühnl, Walter's close friend, had died. Martin wrote:

Yesterday afternoon Hugo was here to let us know that his poor mother died on November 28th after a few days in the hospital. He was of course quite broken up, sends Walter greetings and noted our new address. The burial is on December 2nd, and Paula will go to the cemetery and lay a wreath on the grave for us without an inscription and a second with the name "Walter" for you.

The cemetery wreath from the family was anonymous because "Haim" was recognizably Jewish and so would raise a risk of vandalism or worse. The name "Walter," in contrast, was neutral.

The following week the family wrote from their new rooms in Sechskrügelgasse, with Martin leading off:

Yesterday it was a week since we moved to our new quarters, and we already begin to accustom ourselves to it. It will be ok.

Antoinette continued the practical tone. She had been working to get things settled in their reduced new space and was "still not finished, but hopefully soon."

Paula, too, wrote reassuringly in bits and pieces between December 6 and 10, when the family letter was mailed:

We have already moved! Everything went flawlessly, we really are content. Papa and Mama slept for one night at the Brösslers [family friends, whose adult son was in the US]. Now we are already fully in order. The lady with whom we live is very dear and everything will go well. Next, when we have more time, a detailed description will follow. Everyone is in outstanding health and mood. Word of honor!

The owner or primary tenant of the apartment, "the lady with whom we live," is never identified. The reality is that five adults with all their remaining possessions—Martin and Antoinette Haim, Mathilde Kurz, Paula Kurz, and Martha Müller—were crammed into one room and a small "Kabinett" in what perforce had become a communal apartment. Harmony and good spirits in these situations were far from the norm. One oral historian, a child of a mixed couple who had moved into a single room in an apartment that was shared with six other people, recalled many years later: "Cooking took place in a small kitchen. There were daily arguments and bickering, everyone's nerves were on edge, living together became an ordeal."[203]

Paula resolutely conveyed only positives about the move:

> We are already well adjusted. The best of it: the stove heats dazzlingly. [Although they hadn't mentioned it at the time, there had been no heat in the Margaretenstrasse apartment during the family's last cold season there.] I haven't been so warm in a long time. Today it looks as though a snow storm may come.
>
> We are all really in the best well-being.... Martha Müller continues to live with us as before. She is a very dear person.

In letters to Walter, the family consistently minimized what must have been the trauma of this relocation. Shortly after the move, Antoinette's sister Malvine wrote on January 2, 1941, that "the parents, thank God, are doing well in Sechskrügelgasse. They have already quite resigned themselves to everything and are content if everything stays the same." Paula took issue with Malvine's characterization in the family letter and insisted on a more reassuring version:

> The parents are not "resigned," as our dear aunt wrote above. There is absolutely no *resignation* in it. Things are really and truly good for us. Papa has all his accustomed comfort, his

---

203 Quoted in Michaela Raggam-Blesch, "Survival of a Peculiar Remnant: The Jewish Population of Vienna During the Last Years of the War," *DAPIM: Studies on the Holocaust* 29, no. 3 (November 4, 2015), 11, https://www.tandfonline.com/doi/full/10.1080/23256249.2015.1106789?scroll=top&needAccess=true.

warm stove, his accustomed thick armchair, and he is of good courage and thank God in good health.

Then only six weeks after having been evicted from Margaretenstrasse, in early February 1941, Martin calmly reported that there had been another move. As of "the afternoon of Friday Jan. 17th we live in the 4th District, Favoritenstrasse 12, door 4." Paula put the best spin on the situation, telling Walter in a family letter, one that was opened and read by both Wehrmacht and US censors, that "we are now together with very dear people in our apartment community and we feel really well." The number of rooms in the apartment on Favoritenstrasse, how many people lived there, what sort of cooking, heating, and plumbing amenities they had, can't be discerned. Antoinette and Martin continued to reassure Walter in New York that they were content and things were all right without disclosing any of the physical details.

In the same letter, Martin commiserated with Walter that he had not received a holiday bonus:

> We regret that Walter received only a warm handshake for Sylvester [New Year's]. He has already had such bad luck with the esteemed *bosses*. Well, hopefully this also will take a turn for the better. Gustav Brösslers wrote from Michigan that he received a silk shirt for Christmas but otherwise his people only donated food parcels or invited them to eat. Noblesse thus generally seems not to be *modern*.

A few days later, Antoinette was the first one to claim the letter paper, and she set the scene in the new quarters. She was continuing the daily routine of preparing food, sometimes even an elaborate cake. In a resolute way, without sentimentality, she acknowledged that she no longer expected to meet up with Paul again or the rest of the scattering family:

Chapter 16: 1940—Moves and Loss   277

Dear children,

Today I begin the letter because I still have some time before I go to the kitchen. Menu: fake [falsche] soup, roasted potatoes and a shortbread cake, here we call it fan cake[204] if you remember it, Walter. But in the meantime Mrs. Kurz is fabricating it, and the rest I will make later. I am happy that Lilly is such an excellent cook [Kochkünstlerin, literally cooking artist]....So the potato cake [probably the one for which Paula had sent the recipe] also is successful and tasted good....We are very content in every respect [at the new lodging], if it would always stay this way! Tomorrow Hans will come, it is his 52nd birthday. Also it is Trude's birthday [this was probably Gertrud Oliven, the daughter of Antoinette's sister Josefine (née Feder) Mayer, then living in Amsterdam], but I forgot to write to her this year. Good news has come from the folks in Amsterdam, also from Helene and A[unt] Lotte. I have passed on your greetings to Malollo [Hans and Lisl's dog[205]]....and [she] reciprocates warmest greetings to you both.

In the next paragraph, Antoinette turned from cataloguing what they had to recalling losses:

---

204 What Antoinette called Fächertorte, which translates literally as fan cake, is an elaborate pastry constructed of three layers of filling (apple, walnut, and poppy seeds) inside a shortbread casing. Recently, a blogger pieced together a history of Fächertorte as a Jewish holiday specialty: Liam Hoare, "A Sweet Slice of Jewish History," *Tablet*, March 10, 2019, https://www.tabletmag.com/sections/food/articles/a-sweet-slice-of-jewish-history. Antoinette and Mathilde Kurz appear to have teamed up to make a version of this complicated recipe for Hans's birthday, doing the best they could in 1941, given the strictures of universal food rationing (with even smaller rations for Jews) and cooking space limited to a shared kitchen in a communal apartment.

Demel's patisserie shop in Vienna currently serves Fächertorte, but it seems not to have been widely known in earlier decades. Grete Friedler's comprehensive cookbook, *Wiener Küche*, whose twenty-sixth edition was published in 1906, presents detailed instructions for Sachertorte (acknowledging the assistance of Frau Anna Sacher's hotel cooking school) but has no entry for Fächertorte. Olga Hess and Adolf Hess, *Wiener Kuche*, 26th ed. (Leipzig and Vienna: Franz Deuticke, 1906).

205 In February 1942 Jews would be forbidden to keep pets (Hecht, Raggam-Blesch, and Uhl, *Letzte Orte*, 255). It's not clear whether Lisl would have been exempt as a "German."

You have quoted Paul incorrectly, he never said à la Toni, but à la Ton*erl*! It hurts me a great deal that I will never hear that any more, but at least I would like to read his letters. Yes, the time flies by, it is hardly to be believed that Alice has no longer been with us for a year; it seems like yesterday and is still so painful. The thought that she died peacefully and is released from all suffering makes the unchangeable bearable, though I would have liked it if we all had another year together and that it was a happy one. Now my free time is over, Many greetings, Mama

Two days later Antoinette again began the family letter and added some more details about their new living situation in Favoritenstrasse to help Walter visualize it. As always, she avoided complaint or negativity. The Haim parents, Paula, Mathilde Kurz, and Martha Müller all occupied a single room, the size of the dining room in the family's former apartment in Margaretenstrasse:

Dear children,

After afternoon snack [Jause] at 4 o'clock, I have a little time again and so I will sketch things out a little. Now the first letter from you [pl.] is certainly en route to our new address and then to our newest [that is, first to Sechskrügelgasse 2, and from there to Favoritenstrasse 12]. Dear Walter, you can imagine our room precisely like the one in Margaretenstrasse because is set up and divided exactly like there with our furniture, the beds like there, in the middle Alice's 4-cornered table, your green checkered oilcloth on top, Papa's armchair in front of it, and the rest of the armchairs around. We have temporarily discontinued your green armchair. The room is as big as the Margaretenstrasse dining room only with a large 4-part high window, curiously also ventilation above, but light and sunny and nothing opposite. So we are quite satisfied with the exchange, particularly Papa because he again has a little nook for his bed. Next to the bed he has the polished drawer cabinet which you had, on it is the polished little pharmacy box. Otherwise exactly Margaretenstrasse! The kitchen is larger and better than there, my gas stove again by the window and everything else from the kitchen. Our greatest satisfaction is the fellow occupants, quiet, calm, and accommodating. Thus never annoyance.

The "fellow occupants" of this apartment are never identified.

A month later in March, Antoinette responded reassuringly to what appears to have been Lilly's questions about their latest accommodation:

Dear Lilly, the house is not next to the Skala [a large theater originally built in 1921] but only a couple of houses further.... Our room has a view onto Floragasse and across it a very old, low house so that we have nothing opposite, which I know how to value when I think about Margaretenstrasse....Papa sits in the armchair in the sun and reads hefty pot-boilers.

As positive as Antoinette's letters were, current scholarship recognizes how physically and psychologically debilitating these forced moves were to Vienna's remaining Jews: "The dispossessed and evicted Jews lived in extremely cramped conditions. The housing situation changed the mental state and outward appearance of the victim, who began to resemble the stereotype of the abject ghetto Jew."[206]

---

206 Rabinovici, *Eichmann's Jews*, 96.

CHAPTER 17

The Neuhaus Parents' Emigration Saga

The Neuhaus parents' quest for US visas lasted from 1939 into 1941 and was a saga of ups and downs, high hopes and arbitrary reversals.

December 1939—An Affidavit is Sent

On December 11, 1939, Walter and Lilly sent a telegram to the Neuhauses telling them that an affidavit of support for them was on the way. Martin Haim wrote to congratulate Walter and Lilly on their efforts and triumph: "That was a masterpiece, and the day on which your [pl.] telegram arrived was a day of joy for us also."

However, the Neuhauses' mood remained low when faced with the actual possibility of leaving. Paula took them to task for conjuring up unjustified worries. She wrote to Walter in the same letter:

> Today I must complain a bit about your parents-in-law! They have in an astonishing manner not shown any happiness about the affidavit but are more depressed than ever. They will starve, they will be a burden to you [pl.], etc., etc. Today, when I got the letter from them, I gave them a long talking-to. But it won't have much effect. They are both unfortunately inclined to see many shadow lines rather than to appreciate the good that they

always have. Why am I writing this to you [pl.]? So that you can see clearly and not be paralyzed in encouraging both of them. Perhaps it is only like this at the beginning, until they have gotten used to the thought of folding their tents.

As the war expanded, potential emigration routes closed down. In late March 1940, Lilly's uncle Gustl Landsmann was able to sail to New York from Genoa in still-neutral Italy after receiving his US immigrant visa in Vienna. But on May 30, a telegram from Zurich, probably from a Jewish emigration assistance agency, informed Lilly that this option was barred:

Hopeless currently transit through Italy closed = Goldberg

The telegram had been delivered to Lilly's uncle Sigl Landsmann. His wife, Irma, then phoned Lilly to tell her the news, and the telegram itself ended up in Walter's de facto archive. The emigration route through Italy closed permanently with Mussolini's declaration of war against the UK and France on June 10.

September 1940—Renewed Emigration Hopes and Disappointments

In September 1940 the Neuhaus parents' visa approvals seemed to be coming together after long delays. On September 16 Antoinette wrote that Arthur and Pauline's medical examinations for their US visas were scheduled for the next day. Antoinette planned to visit Omama at the Seegasse old age home to learn the results in person.

Two days after the medical examinations, Paula followed up with what looked to be good news about the Neuhauses' visas, though the outcome was not yet certain:

Mutti [Pauline] just phoned. She was at the examination and then took the oath. They don't know if they will receive the visa. Mutti believes soon, Papa [Arthur] believes not. They will receive the notification in writing.

The numbers were discouraging. The US consulate in Vienna had approved only about one hundred visas in August, and there were plans at the upper levels of the State Department to limit visas for refugees even further.[207] With the heightened emphasis on supposed security risks posed by refugees, visa applicants were subjected to an intimidating final interview before a "board of consuls," while their answers were recorded by a German stenographer. A representative of the American Friends Service Committee stationed in Vienna sent a "confidential report" to the committee's executive secretary in the summer of 1940 detailing the applicants' no-win predicament:

> Now very few non-Aryans in Germany entirely trust the German members of the U.S. Consular staff, and to reply to questioning in a way which would damn the Nazi government, and to know that those replies are being taken down by a German, naturally terrified the applicant. On the other hand, if he doesn't say what he thinks about the Nazi gov't, he feels that the U.S. Consuls will judge him potential 5th Column material and refuse the visa accordingly.[208]

---

207 "Breckinridge Long," Holocaust Encyclopedia, United States Holocaust Memorial Museum, accessed September 3, 2022, https://encyclopedia.ushmm.org/content/en/article/breckinridge-long. See also the letter from Margaret E. Jones, a representative of American Quaker groups assisting with immigration, protesting a memorandum issued by Breckenridge Long, Assistant Secretary of State, in which Long advised that even if Congress did not vote to limit or end immigration, the Department had the power to reach that result through bureaucratic stonewalling: "We can delay and effectively stop for a temporary period or indefinite length of the number of immigrants into the United States…by simply advising our consuls to put every obstacle in the way and to require additional evidence and to resort to various administrative devices which would postpone and postpone and postpone the granting of the visas" ("Letter from Margaret E. Jones, an American Quaker Working with European Jews Hoping to Emigrate to the U.S., Expressing Her Distress at the Impact of Breckinridge Long's Memo," America and the Holocaust, PBS, accessed September 2, 2022, http://www.shoppbs.pbs.org/wgbh/amex/holocaust/filmmore/reference/primary/barletter.html.)

208 "Letter from Margaret E. Jones," PBS. See also "Quakers," Holocaust Encyclopedia, United States Holocausts Memorial Museum, accessed September 3, 2022, https://encyclopedia.ushmm.org/content/en/article/quakers.

Arthur's pessimism about their US visas proved to be well founded. Ten days later, at the end of September, Antoinette wrote:

> Unfortunately today they received a rejection decision from the cons[ulate]. They expected it, since no one receives a visa now, but it is still depressing for the moment. Hopefully something better will come as a substitute for that!

December 1940—No Help from the Landsmanns

Since Walter and Lilly's affidavit did not satisfy the US consulate, the Neuhaus parents needed more documentation for their visa applications. Lilly asked Sigl for an affidavit, and he "flatly refused." A Viennese friend living in the Bronx named Mary Fanta, in whom Lilly had been confiding, wrote to Pauline about Sigl's behavior in December 1940 and sent Lilly a carbon copy of her typed letter. Mary Fanta advised Pauline:

> Begin by writing a quite desperate letter to Sigl to bring him around. I can tell you that the three of them [Sigl, Irma, and Lissy] are working without interruption, so really one would have to search for better luck with a lantern [that is, they don't know how good they have it]....You want to go to your child, so you cannot have any further consideration for anyone else. You sacrificed all your young years to your family, now for once think about your husband and your child.

Mary Fanta noted that Gustl was caught in the middle. He shared rooms with Sigl and did not want to rock the boat, a pragmatic but not admirable stance:

> Gustl of course, because he lives there, dares to say nothing and is silent on this point. It would be over and done with for him if he said that he is sorry about Paula but is glad about

his mother [that is, glad that Pauline was still in Vienna with their elderly mother].

Mary Fanta also reassured the Neuhaus parents that despite Lilly's having lost some weight and Walter's intending to become slim, "one cannot starve in America." Sigl's refusing to help his sister may have contributed to the existing coldness between Lilly and her uncle.

March 1941—Success at Last

The following spring, the situation for the Neuhauses reversed again. Hoping against hope, in February 1941 Walter deposited $150, several months' wages, with the Joint Distribution Committee (JDC) in New York towards the Neuhaus parents' travel expenses. Then the miracle came through: they received their immigrant visas from the US consulate in Vienna on March 5. Putting that into numerical perspective, during the first half of 1941, the US Consulate in Vienna approved visa applications for only 429 Jews, though tens of thousands remained on the visa waiting list.[209] Even that trickle was cut off three months later in June 1941, when Hitler calculated that he no longer needed to observe the Molotov-von Ribbentrop Pact and invaded the USSR. With that, the emigration route through Russia and Siberia was closed. In July the US shuttered its consulates in Greater Germany and German-occupied Europe, ending all legal emigration to the States from those areas.[210]

The Neuhauses left quickly, within two weeks after their visas had been issued. On March 14 Antoinette wrote to Lilly that her parents "will leave already on Monday." The first stop on their route was Berlin, so Antoinette gave them the address of her younger sister, Tante Lotte, and hoped that they would have time to visit

---

[209] Rabinovici, *Eichmann's Jews*, 136.

[210] "Chronology of U.S. Diplomacy in the Holocaust," Rescue in the Holocaust, accessed August 2, 2022, https://www.holocaustrescue.org/chronology-of-us-diplomacy.

her there.[211] In the same letter announcing the Neuhauses' pending departure, Antoinette thanked Walter and Lilly for their birthday wishes (Walter's calculation was off by two years; his mother had turned seventy-three, not seventy-one), and told them that Paula had brought her flowers in both their names.

A Move to Virginia

In March 1941 Lilly and Walter sent a telegram with the surprising news that they had moved again, this time out of New York City to Richmond, Virginia. They did not stay long in Richmond but quickly relocated to Newport News, a Navy shipbuilding town where jobs were more readily available than in landlocked Richmond.

Since the late 1930s, Jewish charities had encouraged immigrants to leave New York for more dispersed areas, although there is no evidence that this directly influenced Walter and Lilly. Job opportunities for newcomers were very limited in New York, where waves of new arrivals competed with each other for the same few entry-level jobs. The charities also wanted to lessen the concentrations of Jews in the bigger cities for fear that "further massing of immigrants would enhance American antisemitism or inflame disruptive and divisive tendencies."[212]

The telegram raised an avalanche of unanswered questions, such as these from Martin in a letter dated March 21, his eighty-second birthday:

What is the reason that you so suddenly left New York? Was Walter let go by Klein [the department store where he had

---

[211] Later that spring, in May 1941, Tante Lotte floated the possibility of returning to Vienna from Berlin after her son Paul had died in some sort of sanatorium or institution. Antoinette thought that this move would have been a "relief" for Lotte but wrote in a typical understatement that this was impossible because of the "difficult housing conditions" in Vienna. That is, Jews were restricted to "Jewish housing," in their case, five adults crammed into one room in an overcrowded communal apartment.

[212] Price, *Objects of Remembrance*, 40.

been working nights in the accounting or billing department]? Why did you go to Richmond? Did Walter get a job there (hopefully better and more agreeable) and through whom? Will you be able to live there? Does Lilly have any prospect of work? How and with whom are you living there? What did you do with your boxes and other things? Are they still in New York? How and when did you leave? Do you have any recommendation or otherwise some lead in Richmond? Is there a Jewish Committee there? Did you take leave of Dr. Cardozo and Mr. Tarry [officials at the Sephardic synagogue], or did you notify them some other way of your move? Don't be angry with me about the many questions, but I would actually have a lot more.

Paula, too, was puzzled by their move:

Yesterday morning we received your radiogram with the news of your move. We see it for now as a riddle, why this sudden decision came about. Or perhaps it was not at all your decision.

The timing also was odd. News of Walter and Lilly's move to Virginia arrived the same day that the Neuhaus parents left for the US.

If Lilly and Walter explained to the family in Vienna why they left New York for Virginia, at the exact time when Lilly's parents were beginning their journey through Russia and across the Pacific Ocean, that explanation was lost. On June 10 Antoinette wrote:

It was nice on Friday the 6th and Sunday the 8th when we received a letter from you [pl.], No. 20 and 21. Only letter No. 11 may not arrive any more. It probably contained the underlying information why you left N.Y., which would have greatly interested us. But now we are very happy to see your [pl.] contentment from your letters.

Sidestepping psychological speculation, the impetus for the move seems to have been financial. Walter had been earning barely subsistence wages at his nighttime job at Klein. Antoinette hoped that in Virginia he might be able to get a job at a hotel, preferably with daytime hours, or give up an external job search all together and, tacitly following Alice's lead, earn a living teaching languages:

> Or couldn't he give lessons. It would be best if the students came to you [pl.] and couldn't you both open a language school, I mean as much as Walter is earning now he could earn by giving lessons. It wouldn't have to be more at the beginning, if the people get cheap lessons and make progress through them, they will tell about it and the number of students will rise. Think it over carefully.

Completely in character, and despite all his questions, Martin was supportive of the young couple's out-of-the-blue exodus from New York to Virginia. His handwriting in April 1941 was a little shakier than it had been two years earlier but not terribly so:

> Dear children! Thank God that you two are again healthy and also do not have to suffer the hardships of New York any more. Certainly it was Lilly's initiative because Walter certainly would not have risked his livelihood. May God help you [pl.] now in Richmond and may things go well for you.
>
> More next time, thousand kisses, Papa

Martin groused that Antoinette had begun the letter and filled up most of the page, though she ended her section, "Doesn't matter. [Machs nichts.] He will write more next time." She also noted that "unfortunately we do not have a map of Virginia but will soon obtain one."

My parents talked a bit about their time in Newport News. One story is that my father managed to get rid of the bedbugs that infested an apartment they rented by diligently taking the bed apart each day and washing the pieces down with kerosene. In the hot and humid climate, weevils attacked a white Persian carpet they had received as a wedding present, and my mother did not know what to do about them and so threw the rug away. Answering a wartime call for rubber, they donated their European set of graduated hot water bottles but slit them open first so that they would not be pilfered. Although they had seen films about champion runner Jesse Owens and cheered for his victories at the 1936 Berlin Olympics, they came face-to-face with Southern racial realities in Virginia and their own place on the favored side of the racial divide. For example, they said that the stringent blackout rules in Newport News seemed not to apply to the Black ("colored") part of town, which remained brightly lit at night. They were disillusioned when a Black cleaner apparently stole from them even though, contrary to Virginia usage, they had made a point of addressing her politely as "Mrs." and by her family name.

In May 1941 the first regular mail from Newport News reached Vienna. Martin congratulated Lilly on finally having a place to live that was not a shared apartment or furnished room, and a "job" (he used the English word). He wrote his characteristic braided stream of encouragement and questions:

> Then I congratulate you [pl.], particularly you, dear Lilly, on your own first apartment in the USA, small but sweet. With God's help it will always become larger, nicer and more comfortable. That after 2 years Walter no longer has to sit in the office at Klein…in my opinion is not only a physical recovery for him but also less monotonous employment, from which he can acquire knowledge that often comes in very handy. On the other hand, you, poor Lilly, just started office work. You must eat more, sleep well, and go walking as much as possible. What sort of goods does your [pl.] store trade in? What sort of business office hours do you [pl.?] have? How far is Newport News from Richmond? What have you [pl.] done with your crates? Are they still with the Sterns in the basement in New York?

Both Lilly and Walter worked at Nachman's department store in the center of Newport News, which she sometimes talked about fondly. In 1993 a local newspaper reported, "Downtown Washington Avenue in Newport News is Deadsville today, but for the first half of this century it was the Peninsula's Main Street. And the center of its booming commerce was a locally owned department store called Nachman's. Everybody shopped at Nachman's."[213] A family business, the store had been founded by European immigrant Sol Nachman in 1894; after he died it was run by his wife Ida and later by their daughter.[214]

The Eastern Route from Vienna to America

On March 17, 1941, the Neuhaus parents left Vienna. Antoinette wrote:

> This evening Lilly's parents leave at about 9:30 p.m. from the east train station to Berlin and beyond. Mother [Pauline] already took her leave from us yesterday afternoon. Father [Arthur] always has all sorts of purchases and things, but possibly during the afternoon will be able to take a break to see us.

The next day, according to a letter from Paula, the Neuhauses telephoned from Berlin to say that they had arrived and were scheduled to travel further later that day. Their ultimate land destination in Asia was Kobe, Japan.

On March 21 Antoinette wrote that they had received a postcard from the Neuhauses in Berlin, and "things are going well." Antoinette acknowledged her mixed feelings about their departure

---

213 Parke Rouse, "Nachman's Was the Life of NN's Downtown," *Daily Press*, May 29, 1993, accessed March 24, 2022, https://www.dailypress.com/news/dp-xpm-19930530-1993-05-30-9305300171-story.html.

214 "Encyclopedia of Jewish Communities—Newport News/Hampton, Virginia," Goldring/Woldenburg Institute of Southern Jewish Life, accessed January 19, 2022, http://www.isjl.org/virginia-newport-news-encyclopedia.html.

Chapter 17: The Neuhaus Parents' Emigration Saga

and its effect on Omama, Pauline's mother. Characteristically, after a cry she pulled herself together, and so did Omama:

> I am again very sick and very sad that they aren't here any longer, and I always believed until the last moment that I would be very happy that they were traveling to you, and that you would be glad and happy about that, and now I sit here and cry. But once, with God's help, they are really with you, I will be amazed and will be able to be happy about it with you. Yesterday I also found Omama very sad and we cried together, nothing else is possible. Then we were a little bit happier, and when I left we had already discussed and talked about our own trip to you.

The older generation's ever obtaining visas for the United States was the stuff of dreams, but being able to fantasize together seemed to have offered some present comfort. (Antoinette, Martin, and Omama did not even file applications for emigration assistance with the IKG.)

The Haims continued to track the Neuhauses' journey using maps and itineraries provided by the IKG. Antoinette wrote a week and a half after their departure:

> The Neuhaus parents are already very far away; we follow their journey on the map that the emigrants receive and that we have also. Tomorrow Paula or I will go to Omama...maybe she has news.

Two evenings later Paula added more details to Antoinette's account while she was at work:

> It is 10 p.m., I am sitting on night duty and will finally write to you in detail. First of all, Lilly, concerning your parents, we have already received five letters from their trip. One from Berlin, three from Russia, the last from Moscow. The trip

is going according to schedule for them, and they are doing quite well.

While tracing the Neuhauses' journey, Paula continued to look for visa opportunities for "both my mothers" (i.e., Antoinette and Mathilde Kurz). She wrote to Lilly, "I would like to experience your happiness with you" when her parents arrive, and in the next sentence recognized that the reunion would be different for Walter. He had no realistic chance of seeing his parents again: "For you, my dear, dear Bibo, there will always be a lot of melancholy mixed in with happiness."

Antoinette wrote more about the voyage few days later: "Now your parents have already been gone for 16 days and, as I see on the itinerary that the IKG put together for their trip, they should already be in Shanghai today." In another letter written while the Neuhauses were still on their trek, Antoinette addressed the fact that there would be fewer letters coming from Walter and Lilly because there was only one set of parents left in Vienna for them to write to:

> Now I will make only one request of you, dear Lilly, keep sending your detailed letters to us despite your parents not being here any longer, because we are now doubly orphaned, and even more detailed and good news can comfort us.

On April 1 the Neuhauses sent a postcard from Manchouli (now Manzhouli), a railroad and land point of entry between the USSR and what was then Manchuria (now Inner Mongolia), where their journey seemed to have stalled. Manchouli, under Japanese control since 1931, was the site of a modernist building boom, much of it carried out by Chinese forced labor. The postcard reached the Haims in Vienna about four weeks later, on April 27. Paula wrote specifically to Lilly about the postcard:

> They write that they have been waiting for 5 days to travel further. Things otherwise are going very well for them.

She continued to assure Lilly about her grandmother: "We visit Omama once a week (at least!), she is doing really well and she looks good" and has numerous visitors. Using the most direct route through the central city, it is about a fifty-minute brisk walk (a bit under 4 kilometers) from Favoritenstrasse 12 in the 4th District to Seegasse 9 in the 9th. In May 1941 Paula wrote that she was "still taking courses in Seegasse, and so visit[ed] Omama 2–3 times a week, also not counting visiting time," and Antoinette also visited there once a week. Each visit would have required a deliberate, courageous effort.

The Neuhaus parents eventually were allowed to proceed from Manchouli to Japan, where they boarded a Japanese passenger liner, MS *Hikawa Maru* (named for a Shinto shrine on Honshu), for passage to the United States. It was a luxurious ship, with "a reputation for service that combined splendid food and beautiful art deco interiors, and she was nicknamed 'The Queen of the Pacific.'"[215] The *Hikawa Maru*'s manifest recorded that Pauline and Arthur had embarked from Kobe, Japan, on April 14, 1941. A souvenir remained from those days. When I was a grade-schooler, I was sometimes allowed to play dress up with a black silk kimono embroidered with a sinuous red dragon and pink flowers that my grandmother told me she had got in Japan. Beyond that, my grandparents never said anything to me about their journey from Vienna to the United States, and I never asked.

Arrival

Pauline and Arthur landed in Seattle fourteen days later, on April 28, 1941, having passed the formalities of a medical inspection and admission by an immigration officer. The manifest information about them was quite straightforward, no job history exaggerated or facts hidden. Arthur was identified as age fifty-two, married;

---

215 Reuben Goossens, *ssMaritime*, accessed July 3, 2023, http://ssmaritime.com/hikawamaru.htm; "*Hikawa Maru*," Wikipedia, accessed January 19, 2022, https://en.wikipedia.org/wiki/Hikawa_Maru#cite_note-SSM1-3.

his profession was originally typed on the manifest as "none," but that was crossed out and "retired major" written in. Pauline was identified as age forty-five, a housewife. "German" is the language they both could read and write. Like all nineteen passengers on that page of the manifest, their "race or people" was identified as "Hebrew." Their nationality was recorded as "German"; their place of birth "Vienna, Germany"; their last permanent residence "Vienna, Germany." They were traveling in Class B.

From Seattle Pauline and Arthur would have taken a train east and then south to Newport News, Virginia. Lilly and Walter sent a telegram to Vienna on May 5 when the Neuhaus parents arrived. Everyone was overjoyed. Antoinette wrote:

> My dears, all together, yesterday was a hugely happy surprise with your [pl.] telegram. I said to myself one "Thank God" after the other the whole day, and so in spirit imagined you all together. It was a lovely picture, but despite that hardly corresponding to the reality.

Paula, who was just about to begin a twenty-four-hour nursing shift, took the telegram with her to read it by telephone to a "Dr. F." This Dr. F. then informed someone else, who arranged for a note with the news to be sent to Omama through the Seegasse porter. The following day, Antoinette visited Omama and conveyed the news in person. Antoinette reported on May 6:

> I was there today myself; Omama laughed and cried, but she also said one thank God after the other....Omama is well, she is healthy and has the best appetite. Omama handed the letter over to me, dear Paula [i.e., Pauline Neuhaus], it was of the greatest interest and each one shook their head on reading it. So now everyone is happy! Understood, and from now on we anticipate only happy and favorable news from and about you all, before everything about your mutual reunion, about which you [pl.] can't write to us too much detail.

The first optimistic plan was for the Neuhaus parents to stay with Walter and Lilly. Antoinette wrote:

> I am very glad to know that the parents can live there in your new apartment, at least temporarily, since you are now the possessor of a large apartment. The apartment drawing, dear Lilly, satisfied me very well, in my thoughts I see you [pl.] go from one room to the other, sit on the veranda, and go up and down the steps. Hopefully that all will be permanent and will satisfy all of you.

Martin addressed a separate section of his regular letter to Pauline and Arthur Neuhaus, complementing Pauline on her hat-making and writing skills (unfortunately, none of Pauline's travel letters survive) and anticipating a bright future for the reunited family:

> Dear Mr. and Mrs. Neuhaus! I bid you [pl.] heartfelt happiness and am very glad that you finally have arrived well and are finally safely with the children. We read several travel letters which Mama Paula [i.e., Pauline Neuhaus] sent to her mother [Omama], and read with nothing other than deep regret about the colossal strains which you had to suffer in addition to Kobe and the cold, but I also admired the art of giving a lifelike and impressive picture of the journey and your experiences with relatively few words. So the old ugly mother-in-law is not only a milliner and clothing maker but also a writer-genius. She will certainly, according to my prophecy, become a dollar-millionaire....We wish you both everything dear and good. The old Father.

As always, Antoinette was practical and positive, not fazed by reports of bedbugs or other vermin in the apartment. Unlike Hans, she did not criticize their relying so much on canned food in America:

> Hopefully you will find an apartment to your liking. It is a shame that there are these big mistakes at the present because

it was just right for you, I know Papa and Mama [Neuhaus] would like to have their own apartment, and they are correct because it is better if young and old, pardon, older, don't live together. Perhaps one can fumigate the apartment or treat it with gas to make it clean? With the plan from Lilly I can imagine it very clearly, with veranda, etc. Though perhaps there are many apartments with verandas and little gardens. Dear Lilly, I can imagine how good you feel in your own apartment, it is something else, and how happy you are with the unpacked, well-known things! Walter's description about cooking, eating, canned food, etc. etc., this sort of housekeeping is certainly very practical; we only aren't accustomed to it, but one quickly gets used to the practical, particularly when so there are so many kinds of canned foods and they all are good.

Among their "unpacked, well-known things" were Walter's old bathrobe (Antoinette was glad that "it has held up so well") and the vials of tea and sugar that Antoinette had given him when he left home. She advised Walter to hold on to them because they might prove useful and even fantasized that perhaps she would be the one to use them. Another item from home that Lilly and Walter were able to unpack in Newport News was a red wool table cover. Antoinette explained that it had been embroidered by a team consisting of Antoinette herself, Alice, "Teresa in Bucharest," and "whoever just had the time." There were also bedside rugs that Lisl had made.

Antoinette then addressed Pauline Neuhaus, "Mama II," happy that she was constructing a household for herself bit by bit with new purchases. She was also pleased that they had received a surprise visit from Uncle Gustl, for whom a trip from New York to Newport News and back must have been quite an enterprise. She included a reassuring report about Omama:

Your lines, dear Mama II, gave us a lot of joy, but why didn't Papa II write anything this time, we missed his collaboration. Paula will report about Omama because she is there almost every day. She went there today at noon. In any case I will tell you that yesterday Paula found her fresh and lively and left her that way as well. I am very pleased that you make such a big purchase every week. Hopefully curtain rods and a potato peeler will be incorporated into your new household this week. Even such little things make one happy, and I grant you many joys. How did Lilly find your appearance? You were really very run down. That Uncle Gustl surprised you [pl.] with his visit pleased us all very much, how all of you one can imagine! We thank him for his greetings and return them most heartily.

Martin added a section to this happy letter, thanking Lilly and Walter for their Father's Day wishes and responding enthusiastically to the news about their new jobs at Nachman's: "an enormous difference from Klein," even if "only a small step." He, too, anticipated that with Lilly's parents there, "you [pl.] can lead a much better and more comfortable life."

CHAPTER 18

1941

Martin

As 1941 progressed, Martin's contributions to the Haim family letters became shorter and more formulaic: an enumeration of the latest letters received, a brief weather report, and sometimes a bit of news. He made gentle, comic references to his affinity for warmer weather. On February 28, the middle of winter, he wrote, "Here is the sun it is 14–17 R[eamur] [about 64–70 deg. Fahrenheit]. I play crocodile and warm myself." Then a week later, "We have spring-like weather which is especially pleasant for the Padre." In March, while the Neuhaus parents were on their epic journey from Vienna across Russia, Siberia, and the Pacific Ocean, Paula wrote candidly about Martin's declining health:

> A sea crossing doesn't come into consideration any more for our dear, good father, Bibolein. He is completely undiminished in mental vigor but physically is quite changed, and his heart will not always go on.

Shortly after, she wrote again: "Speaking very plainly, such a journey to you is hardly to be considered any longer for him [our father] except in summer, but it also would be questionable whether he could handle the trip." At the same time, Paula recognized that it would be "extremely important" for her and Antoinette to be able to join Walter and Lilly in the United States.

March was the Haim parents' birthday month. Even in their reduced circumstances, token celebrations were still possible. Paula wrote, "We will put some flowers on the table from you both."

On April 8, 1941, Walter's thirty-ninth birthday and his third away from home and family, Paula sent birthday congratulations and reported on their father's uneven health:

> Papa was not quite together for a couple of days, but this morning he was so fresh and lively and for the first time ate breakfast with an appetite, and I told him that this is the right birthday present for you. His heart was not in order, but now, thank God, things are going upward again.

Hans conveyed the same picture, though less rosy and with a characteristic twist at the end:

> Last time I wrote to you about Papa's situation. He is still bedridden, today significantly better, but this changes three times a day. It seems to stem from vascular cramps, very painful, afterwards always inevitably great weakness, with a very serious wait. Although the doctor is very satisfied, the patient is not helped.

The following week Hans wrote again about their father's health in a separate letter to Walter:

> Today I can gladly tell you that Papa, thank God, is significantly better. There was a decisive improvement that took place in the last days, the attacks fortunately have stopped, his general state of health is much better, he has an appetite and eats normally and is already out of bed for more hours both in the morning and afternoon. Hopefully the improvement will continue! It was very serious this time and has never lasted this long! Mama was very busy with his care, and it was a monstrous plague and labor for her. To convey this once pleasing news I am using a separate airmail letter. Still something!

On June 15 Paula sent a separate letter consisting of half an onionskin sheet addressed to Walter and a whole one to Lilly. Paula emphasized that the parents at the moment were healthy, although Martin rarely, if ever, left the apartment. (In May, Paula had written that "Papa is again doing outstandingly, as he hasn't for a long time. When it becomes a bit warmer, he will go for a walk.") The implication was that Martin had been housebound for another winter. Now that it was spring, Paula expressed a ritual hope that they could all be together again, but without relying on any impossibilities:

> The most important: Papa is doing perfectly well thank God, and Mama is as smart and nimble as a hare, as always. They will certainly go on an outing today. How eagerly we would like to be with you [pl.]. With God's and your help perhaps that may happen.

To Lilly, Paula wrote in some more detail about Omama:

> Now I will tell a bit about Omama. She is healthy and looks well and has already become very attached to me. She greets and leaves me always with a very dear kiss. We make plans that one day we will suddenly appear by you [pl.], and then the two of us both laugh together. I wanted us to have a very small but justified spark of hope.

Paula, like Antoinette, urged Lilly to keep writing to them now that her parents were in the United States, and then she took a bit of a dig at the Neuhauses:

> Lilly dear, urging doesn't help, you promised that you would also write a lot again. Please do it! We all like your funny and dear way of writing and describing so much that you must write a lot for the parents' sake. Bibo will tell you that I am not one for giving out compliments. Also not *fishing for compliments* like your dear Mama, who sends greetings to all whom she

has not yet forgotten!! Well so what! I say absolutely nothing. By the way, Mrs. Käthe Fuchs always sends your Mama warm greetings. She says she has especially taken her into her heart. "So, and not me?" your Papa then will ask.

Two months later, on the evening of August 10, 1941, Martin died in the shared room that had become the family's home. He was eighty-two years old. Paula was out working a night shift. None of the contemporaneous letters were kept, so I do not know any other details, who else may have been there with Antoinette and Mrs. Kurz, whether Martin had had cardiac symptoms that day, or whether a doctor had been called. No matter. The facts are that Martin was buried in the Jewish section of the Vienna Central Cemetery two days later, in the same grave plot where his older daughter, Alice, had been buried in January 1940. The family in Vienna knew that Walter and Lilly had gone on a short vacation for their second anniversary. To avoid ruining those days for them, instead of a telegram, they sent a letter that they knew would not arrive until after their return.

On September 15, five weeks after Martin's death, Antoinette wrote to Walter and Lilly about how she kept her life going with practical domestic activities, cooking, having guests over for a meal. She was able to write about her deep sense of loss without drama:

> I now have just a little time, and I don't know of anything better to do than to converse with you [pl.] in my thoughts. I must carry it out on paper because unfortunately it is not possible in person. It is 11 a.m. Paula came home at 9 a.m. from night duty and is sleeping now. Mother Kurz is at Löwinger, Therese has gone to Hansi. I have prepared the food, and so I always write a couple of lines to pass the time in between stirring and watching the yeast. Mrs. Dr. Müller comes today and will eat with us. I am happy whenever someone comes, it always distracts one somewhat from one's troubles, one can't really say troubles but thoughts, so no, the wound is still very fresh when one looks around the room and he is not here

anymore, but everything reminds me of him, and through that he still lives with us, but it is a sad substitute for him. So, it can't be changed and so one must stay with as good as it gets.

Antoinette's philosophical view of their fate was similar to what Paul had written to Walter the previous year. The world turns, the older generation must pass away. She continued:

I am glad to have your [pl.] letter already and see from it that you, Walter, don't rebel against the business but otherwise say to yourself that parents must die some time. That this point in time always comes too early is understandable but can't be changed....I am very happy and reassured that you, my dear Walter, have your good, brave little wife beside you, and she will soon help you to bear your pain. That was always Papa's comfort and pleasure to read your letters, and to know that she is your good comrade. Now my free time is over.

A few days later Antoinette wrote again, thanking Lilly for her letter of condolence and looking forward to Lilly and Walter's having a brighter future. Hopefully the next year, they would return from their anniversary trip to happier news:

You, my dear Lilly, be thanked for your friendly thoughts about Papa, and for your dear words to us and for your loving assistance to Walter. God will reward you a thousand times in happy, cheerful hours, days, and years that you live together with my Walter. So you [pl.] found the sad news at your arrival home. Your next wedding anniversary should be a great day of happiness for you, and with everyone with whom we belong able to take part in it together. May God fulfill this my heart's wish!

During the summer of 1941, Paula had been studying to become qualified as a "Pflegerin," a caregiver or practical nurse, working in institutions that had been created to care for the ill and elderly

Jews remaining in Vienna, including those "considered" Jewish, regardless of their individual religious affiliation. Paula wasn't worried about the exam, and she welcomed this draw on her energies:

> There isn't much to say about the test, it was child's play. And most of the poor candidates were at a bit of a disadvantage because of their homey milieu and otherwise a bit behind, so that it really was no feat to be among the best. For me, I was already familiar with so many medical things from the yearlong rotation with Brügerl [a family friend] and Olli....I am happy about my profession and it suits me, and it is a true blessing for me that it is demanding.

Paula, like Antoinette, wrote that September about Martin's absence and his continuing presence for her. The physical objects around her resonated with his former presence:

> I sit in the room in which he felt so comfortable, his fat, brown armchair sits in the sun—but empty. It is very very frightful, how we miss him. I write with his fountain pen, I have taken over his section (in your former little chest of drawers) and I know that he would only be happy about that. He would also have been happy about my test, which I passed "with honors." He wouldn't have expected anything else from me. He always had a good opinion of me. That has always done well, that aspect of him. If one were disheartened and faint-hearted, he understood how to strengthen one's backbone through a dear comment. All of his words are unforgettable to me. And he loved you both a good deal and had a great respect for "little Lilly." He always liked upright clear people who, in his opinion, also knew how to bear difficulties.

Paula noted that Paul's birthday was approaching: "In three days it will be Padli's birthday. The third without me. How many more?"

Later that week Antoinette wrote again that she and Paula would "continue to do [their] duty, which distracts and makes one satisfied." Life was going on; there was still "good news" from relatives abroad—Helene and family in Manila, Tante Lotte in Berlin, the Mayer family in Amsterdam—and visits from Aunt Malvine and others in Vienna. Paula was working on night shift and sleeping during the day. Walter's friend Hugo Kühnl had sent them a picture postcard, and "tomorrow Thursday afternoon Paula or I will go to See[gasse]" to visit Lilly's grandmother. The remaining family were carrying on despite the huge loss. Antoinette described her mix of hope and fatalistic acceptance:

> Dear Walter, I go with what is for me a creed, "whoever lets the dear Lord rule, things are ordered for the best." And that is what I believe and hope that we will see each other again. The Lord will choose the time and place, and the occasion will be joyful that brings us together. I am very happy that you two have used your free days to go on an excursion. Certainly the news that awaited you was devastating, but now we are comforted and thank the Lord that He made it so easy for him.

Antoinette responded to Walter's question about her health. It was good: "No cough, no sniffle, as you always asked about for Papa. Paula and I sleep at night by an open window; she has bad air both day and night in the sickrooms, and I also like fresh air as you know."

The Yellow Star and Further Restrictions

While the letters do not mention it, the family's leaving their cramped lodging for any reason became increasingly dangerous. Jews were allowed to shop only during limited times and in designated Jewish stores. Restrictions on Jews' use of public transportation also increased inexorably. The situation had worsened in November 1940, when a new Gestapo rule required ration cards for Jews in Vienna to have the word "Jude" stamped on them in red, so every shopping trip became even more fraught.[216] Circumstances became worse in September 1941, when a new order required Jews over age six in Greater Germany and some of the occupied territories to wear a yellow six-pointed star with the word "Jude" (Jew) on it on their outer clothing anytime they were in public.[217] An exception was allowed for the Jewish wives of Aryan husbands, like Malvine, but not for Jewish husbands in a mixed but childless marriage, like Hans.[218] Jews venturing into the streets wearing the star were harassed, hit, spit on, pushed down staircases. A nurse at the Rothschild Hospital was attacked while waiting for a tram near the opera house.[219] Overall, "due to the increased number of attacks, many [of the remaining Jews] hardly got out of their apartments," while Jews who were found outside without the star risked arrest and deportation.[220]

Ironically, the newer Jewish section of Vienna's Central Cemetery, Gate 4, became a place of limited freedom as it was one of the very few outdoor areas where Jews could gather without the stigmatizing yellow star. Some IKG groups were able to grow "urgently needed" fruit and vegetables in the open land there. One survivor, a teenager at the time, recalled that the "grave land" of Gate 4 was "our country house, our summer freshness":

> Here it was green, there were trees and right by the entrance, before the rows of graves, a large meadow. We could lie in the

---

216 Rabinovici, *Eichmann's Jews*, 96, 98, 112, 156. The IKG's ration card lists were later put to the fatal use of organizing deportation transports from Vienna.

217 Evan Burr Bukey, *Jews and Intermarriage in Nazi Austria* (Cambridge, UK: Cambridge University Press, 2010), 30. "Jewish Badge: During the Nazi Era," United States Holocaust Memorial Museum, accessed January 19, 2022, https://www.ushmm.org/wlc/en/article.php?ModuleId=10008211. (The text of the police decree, translated into English, can be viewed at https://www.vaholocaust.org/police-decree-on-identification-of-jews/.)

218 Rabinovici, *Eichmann's Jews*, 11.

219 See, e.g., Evan Burr Bukey, *Hitler's Austria: Popular Sentiment in the Nazi Era, 1938–1945* (Chapel Hill, NC: University of North Carolina Press, 2018), 164, and sources cited by him: "Ever since the Anschluss, Jews had been regularly beaten in trolley cars, or kicked in the streets by passersby."

220 Hecht, Raggam-Blesch, and Uhl, *Letzte Orte*, 35.

sun here and play ball. And there was no warning or prohibition: Gate 4 meant all Jews were welcome, the living and the dead.[221]

Gate 4, entrance to the newer Jewish section of the Vienna Central Cemetery.

Through it all, Antoinette continued to cross the city to visit Lilly's grandmother in the 9th District. She wrote about these visits with an air of normalcy, never hinting that using public transportation or simply walking in the street was a dangerous gauntlet for her. In a letter of September 18, 1941, Antoinette encouraged Lilly to write to Omama:

> Your promise, dear Lilly, to write to Grossmama pleases me, and it will certainly also please her greatly. Everyone seems to have forgotten her birthday because she didn't get a letter from anyone, and this hurt her a lot.

The war resulted in shortages of ordinary consumer goods, with clothing, shoes, and staple foods rationed. These limitations were imposed more severely on the remaining Jews than

---

221 Hecht, Raggam-Blesch, and Uhl, *Letzte Orte*, 40, quoting Elisabeth W. Trahan, *Geisterbeschwörung: Eine jüdische Jugend in Wien der Kriegsjahre* (*Exorcism: A Jewish Youth in Vienna during the War Years*), (Vienna: Picus Verlag, 1996), 157.

Vienna's general population.[222] Antoinette wrote in September 1941, looking forward from fall to winter, "So today I just covered a straw hat with black fabric and have made myself a winter hat." On the surface, this could have been a bit of thrifty home economics. Underneath, the fact was that there was no means for her to buy a warm hat.

For Paula, Walter's response to their father's death signaled that he had come of age, assuming the responsibilities of manhood, in a way like a bar mitzvah. She wrote to him with genuine admiration:

> Your letter no. 37, of Sept. 7th, came yesterday. The mail goes very quickly now. I was on duty and was suddenly called that there was a visitor for me. It was Mama, who wanted to take a little walk and brought me your letter. I am as happy about the visit as about the letter. Bibolein, do you know what your lovely letter means? That you internally, by yourself, have taken over from Papa the responsibility and care for Mama and me. You, the youngest, our Bibo.

In her next letter that September, Antoinette wrote that life was continuing. There were visitors, cooking, Paula's work, and cross-city visits to Lilly's grandmother. Paula added a paragraph to fill out the sheet. She noted that "tomorrow is Yom Kippur" and wrote, "Today I was at Meseritsch for the first time in 20 years," probably referring to a dream or daydream. (Gross Meseritsch, now Velke Mezirici in the Czech Republic, was the hometown of Mathilde and the extended Wilheim family. Paul had worked there for a time in the 1920s as a chemist at an uncle's glue factory after getting his university degree.) She mused about missing Paul:

> Every day when I come off shift, I tell Paul in spirit everything that the day brought me. Unfortunately only in spirit, and if I am sometimes at a loss, no one answers me. A good *training* to cope with everything alone.

---

222 See Bukey, *Hitler's Austria*, 155–57.

Not yet publicly known was that on the eve of Yom Kippur 1941, Eichmann informed the IKG leadership that thousands of the remaining Jews in Vienna would be sent to the ghetto in the Polish city of Lodz (renamed Litzmannstadt), and that the IKG would be required to manage the deportations.[223]

Antoinette's last extant communication to Walter is a postcard dated October 6, 1941. She assured Walter that "everything is in order" in Vienna, reported on visits and messages from scattered relatives, and continued to be concerned about Lilly's grandmother, who seemed to be declining:

> I am therefore writing this card so that you will have news and learn that we are all well and also that everything is in order. Hopefully, it's the same for you. From you there is already again a lack of news, we expect it today or tomorrow. We told you everything that has gone on in our latest letter, No. 26, September 30th. Hans was here on Saturday, he and Lisl are well and also Malollo [their dog]. Last Tuesday I was with Oma and she is ok, although it seems to me privately that this time she was a little bit less all together. She had a letter from Sigl and Gustl [her two sons, by then in the US]....Notably, Oma has not had a letter from her daughter for months, the 82-year-old woman naturally suffers greatly from that. That is inexplicable to me.

---

223 Rabinovici, *Eichmann's Jews*, 103–104.

PART 5

After the Letters from Vienna Ended

The wartime correspondence from Vienna ended in early October 1941 with Antoinette's postcard. Walter kept an airmail envelope from Paula postmarked October 25, 1941, but I have not found a letter corresponding to that date. Hans's saved letters stopped even earlier, in April 1941. This means that there are no firsthand accounts from Antoinette, Paula, Hans, or their circle in Vienna about their lives during the following four years. Instead, to follow them through that period, I have relied on public records, contemporaneous journalism, subsequent scholarship, and other survivors' memoirs and oral histories.

CHAPTER 19

Restrictions Upon Restrictions

As Germany amassed conquests in the west and expanded the war to an eastern front by invading the USSR in June 1941, Jews in Vienna became ever more isolated and their daily lives more constricted. Their food rations shrank, they were subjected to proliferating antisemitic legal restrictions, and the daily environment became ever more hostile.

This is a partial list of legal restrictions that were imposed on Jews in Vienna during this period:

- October 1941: Jews, both male and female, were compelled to do forced labor.

- October 23, 1941: Jews were generally prohibited from emigrating.

- October 24, 1941: "Friendly contacts" between Aryans and Jews were prohibited.

- November 13, 1941: Jews were required to surrender their typewriters, adding machines, bicycles, cameras, and telescopes.

- December 12, 1941: Jews could no longer use public telephones. (Private telephone lines for Jews had been prohibited since July 1939.)

- January 1942: Jews could no longer own walking shoes, ski boots, or furs.

- February 17, 1942: Jews could no longer subscribe to newspapers and periodicals. The only exception was a publication called the *Jewish Newsletter* that was issued by the IKG until it was dissolved in November 1942, and then by the successor Council of Elders. It was used to inform Vienna's dwindling Jewish population of ever-multiplying Nazi rules, prohibitions, and requirements. With typical Nazi cupidity, recipients were compelled to pay a subscription fee for this newsletter.

- March 24, 1942: Jews could no longer use any public transportation without express police approval.

- April 10, 1942: A yellow star had to be posted on the entry door to apartments with Jewish residents. While no physical ghetto was set up in Vienna, Jews had been systematically evicted from their residences beginning in 1939 and forced into overcrowded collective lodging in "Jewish" areas, primarily the 2nd and 9th Districts.

- June 11, 1942: Jews were no longer allowed to buy tobacco products.

- June 22, 1942: Jews were no longer allowed by buy eggs.

- July 10, 1942: Jews were no longer allowed to buy milk.

- September 18, 1942: Jews were no longer allowed to buy meat and wheat flour.

Violations of any of these rules, whether intentional or inadvertent, could lead to severe punishment, including deportation to the East.[224]

---

[224] Hecht, Raggam-Blesch, and Uhl, *Letzte Orte*, 254–256.

In addition to the physical privations, the remaining Jews lived amid constant terror and intimidation. H. G. Adler, one of the first historians of Theresienstadt, summarized the trajectory: "Life became more and more difficult" as the war continued.[225] Adler's study focused on the "Protectorate," that is, German-occupied Bohemia and Moravia, but Jews in Vienna lived under a comparable reign of terror:

> House-to-house searches could happen every hour, and Jews feared the loss of apartments, raids, and conscious or unconscious violations of the thicket of prohibitions and regulations, which could lead to blackmail and reports to the police. There was hardly a Jew who did not violate a rule here or there—it was impossible not to....Things generally went badly for those who were caught; often it meant death in a concentration camp. People were arrested on the most flimsy pretexts.[226]

Following the Family through Housing Records

Through all the dislocations, the City of Vienna kept up its long-term practice of diligently registering changes of residence. For thirty-five Euros, the City Archives will search the housing records for a particular name. Their records for Paula during the war years are consistent with the addresses on existing family correspondence.

Beginning in December 1940, Paula was officially registered as a resident of Sechskrügelgasse 2, where she and the family stayed only for about six weeks. Her next official address, effective January 17, 1941, was Favoritenstrasse 12, apartment 4, in the 4th District, a few blocks behind Karlskirche. This was the last address that Walter had for Paula and his parents until after the war ended, and it is the

---

225 H. G. Adler, *Theresienstadt 1941–1945: The Face of a Coerced Community* (Cambridge, UK: Cambridge University Press, 2017), 11. (Originally published in German in 1955.)

226 Adler, *Theresienstadt 1941–1945*, 11.

return address on Antoinette's last postcard, sent in October 1941. In this shared apartment, Martin, Antoinette, Paula, and Mathilde Kurz, and sometimes Dr. Martha Müller, occupied a single room, and Martin died there in August 1941. It was not a quiet area. The building housed a cinema, and beginning in 1942 a construction company used the neighboring building at Favoritenstrasse 10 for its Croatian forced laborers. Living next to a forced labor camp was no rarity. Dozens of such sites pockmarked the city between 1942 and 1945.[227] Currently, Favoritenstrasse 12 is a well-kept Jugenstil building that houses the Hotel Johann Strauss. There is no external no hint of its past. When asked whether the building had been used as "Jewish housing" during the war, an older man at the front desk shrugged and implied well could have been. But that was all.

Hotel Johann Strauss at Favoritenstrasse 12, 2023.

---

227 "Zwangsarbeiterlager Favoritenstrasse," Wien Geschichte Wiki, accessed January 24, 2022, https://www.geschichtewiki.wien.gv.at/Zwangsarbeiterlager_Favoritenstra%C3%9Fe.

Chapter 19: Restrictions Upon Restrictions   317

After thirteen months at Favoritenstrasse, the records show that Paula moved again, this time into the 2nd District, where most of Vienna's "Jewish housing" was concentrated. Her official address from February 28, 1942, until March 3, 1943, was Novaragasse 40, apartment 28. A House List (preserved among IKG/Council of Elders records in Jerusalem) confirms that Paula, Antoinette, and Mathilde Kurz lived in this communal apartment along with three unrelated people, a married couple and the husband's mother.

Stolperstein at Novaragasse 40, 2023.

Novaragasse 40 is across the street from Novaragasse 39, the building where the Kurz parents had lived for decades, raised their children, and operated a grocery store. Perhaps Mathilde still had acquaintances in the area who helped them find this lodging when they had to leave Favoritenstrasse. When I last visited Novaragasse in 2023, the Prater Ferris wheel, a Vienna landmark which had been owned by a Jewish businessman before the Anschluss then "Aryanized," still loomed as a ghostly presence at the end of the street. A small brass plaque set in the sidewalk by the front door of number 40 commemorates the "144 Jewish women and men and seven children who were crammed into collective housing in this building and afterwards were deported and murdered."

Lazenhof Then and Now

After Novaragasse, Paula's residence was registered at Lazenhof 2, apartment 10, in the 1st District. This building belonged to the Council of Elders, the successor to the IKG, which used it to house some Council employees and as a clothing and furniture depot for families that had been bombed out. Lazenhof was located in what had been Vienna's ancient Jewish area, close to the City Temple on Seitenstettengasse.

Paula was a registered tenant at Lazenhof 2 from March 11, 1943, to May 9, 1945. On June 7, 1946, over a year after the war had ended, New York's German émigré newspaper *Aufbau* published list of "surviving Jews in Vienna." Among them are Paula Kurz, born on May 26, 1896, in Bucharest (that information is accurate), with the address Lazenhof 2 in the 1st District. While the address was outdated, it had been correct thirteen months earlier.

The streets around Lazenhof lay in the thick of the fighting during the battle for Vienna. In the first half of April 1945, artillery exchanges between the advancing Red Army and retreating SS tank troops leveled swathes of the Inner City and 2nd District. All but one of the bridges over the Danube Canal were destroyed. Where Paula and Antoinette sheltered during the Soviet offensive and the chaotic aftermath of rape and looting is not the stuff of official records.

On my first trip to Vienna in December 1968, Paul pointed to a window in the back of a fairly anonymous building above an outside staircase deep in the Inner City somewhere near Judengasse (literally, Jew lane) and said that this is where Paula had spent the war in hiding. It was clearly an emotional subject for Paul, so I did not ask any questions. On subsequent trips I returned to Judengasse and tried unsuccessfully to find the building again.

Then in September 2017, after receiving Paula's addresses from the City Archives and locating the *Aufbau* record online, I searched for Lazenhof 2 along with Tim McNamara, a friend of Paul and myself since my university days in Melbourne. Lazenhof 1 existed, but there was no doorway or building entryway marked Lazenhof 2. We were able to get into the back courtyard of Lazenhof 1. This part of the Inner City had become trendy, and the courtyard was filled with hydrangeas and other well-tended greenery.

Two sides of the courtyard at Lazenhof 1 are bounded by new construction, and the buildings further down the street where Lazenhof 2 logically would be are also newer, from about the 1960s by their look. The old building at Lazenhof 2 may have been damaged during the war or torn down during the city's extensive post-war modernization projects. In either case, it is now gone. In retrospect, I am certain that this is the area that Paul pointed to in 1968.

In 1990 the City of Vienna named a bare, graffitied little plaza off Judengasse and a block from Lazenhof for Desider Friedman, a lawyer, Zionist, and last president of the IKG.[228] A plaque on Desider Friedman Square announces that the city had previously named the staircase leading upward from Judengasse for Jerusalem as a sign of solidarity upon the latter's three thousandth anniversary. Not untypically, the commemoration is thoroughly disconnected from any consideration of Desider Friedman himself[229] or Vienna's own history.

---

228 Adler, *Theresienstadt 1941–1945*, 214. See also "Desider Friedman," Wikipedia, accessed January 25, 2022, https://de.wikipedia.org/wiki/Desider_Friedmann; "Desider-Friedman-Platz (Jerusalem-Steige), from Fleischmarkt, Wikimedia Commons, accessed January 25, 2022, https://commons.wikimedia.org/wiki/Category:Jerusalem-Stiege,_Vienna#/media/File:Desider-Friedmann-Platz.JPG.

229 Friedman, with thousands of Jews who remained in Vienna, was deported to Theresienstadt in 1942 and then murdered in Auschwitz in fall 1944. After the war, Friedman was seen as something of an ambivalent figure. He had not opposed the IKG's "strategy of cooperation" with the Gestapo's mass deportations from Vienna because he held the (ultimately illusory) belief that acceding to the Gestapo's demands would save more Jews than attempting active (and manifestly futile) opposition. Rabinovici, *Eichmann's Jews*, 159.

The Jerusalem Staircase leading off Desider-Friedmann-Platz in September 2017.[230]

Zeltgasse 1

After the war ended, Paula and Antoinette moved once more. According to the Vienna City Archives, Paula's residence from May 9, 1945 (the day after VE Day), through July 10, 1947, was Zeltgasse 1, apartment 2, in the 8th District. This record suggests that a mere four weeks after the Soviet conquest of Vienna, the city administration was functioning sufficiently to continue registering addresses. During the post-war occupation, Zeltgasse had the advantage of

---

230 Digitalpress, *Vienna, Austria – February 6, 2020: Jerusalem Stiege is a stairway between Fleischmarkt and Desider-Friedmann-Platz in central Vienna*, February 6, 2020, photograph, https://www.123rf.com/photo_142402871_vienna-austria-february-6-2020-jerusalem-stiege-is-a-stairway-between-fleischmarkt-and-desider-fried.html; ©digitalpress/123RF.COM.

being located in the US zone. Zeltgasse 1 remained Paula's official residence. She used this address for correspondence with Walter and to receive relief parcels, though in fact she lived with Paul's sister, Olga, after the latter's return from England in 1946. Olga's apartment was at Neustiftgasse 55 in the 7th District, also in the American zone.

Zeltgasse 1, front doorway, 2020.

In February 2020 I visited the building at Zeltgasse 1, a few blocks behind the Parliament. It was well kept and elegant, with decorative wrought iron front doors, mosaic tile floors in the halls, and the ironic touch of a Che Guevara doormat outside the polished entry to a first-floor apartment. No signs remain of what the building would have been like in 1945 and 1946.

Hans and Lisl—War Years in the 2nd District

The Marian Bridge in 1910 and the southern end of Lilienbrunngasse.

The City of Vienna also sent me the address registration history for Hans. It echoes the return addresses on his correspondence. Hans and Lisl lived at Salmgasse 3 in the 3rd District (in what had been the Feder grandparents' apartment since 1913) when Walter left in January 1939 and during his first few months in New York. Then on April 16, with no explanation given, they moved across the Danube Canal into the 2nd District, to Lilienbrunngasse 5, apartment 10, a half block north of the Marian Bridge. (This was a modern bridge, designed by Otto Wagner in the early twentieth century and named for its statue of the Virgin Mary.) In May 1939 Malvine hinted in a letter that Hans's move had not been voluntary. Then in September, Antoinette wrote that Hans was "very satisfied with the new apartment," likely a reassuring fiction.

In April 1945 heavy fighting along both sides of the Danube Canal destroyed the showy buildings on southern end of Lilienbrunngasse and the Marian Bridge at the end of their street. Currently, the entire first block of Lilienbrunngasse consists of postwar construction anchored by a modern IBM office building on the corner. No structures remain from the time when Hans and Lisl lived there.

The Marian Bridge lying in the Danube Canal and destroyed buildings at the southern end of Lilienbrunngasse, 1945 or 1946.[231]

Unusually, Hans and Lisl stayed in the apartment in Lilienbrunngasse for the duration of the war instead of being shuffled around. This may have been a benefit of Lisl's being considered "German," even though their marriage offered less "protection" than those where the husband was "Aryan" or where there were children. Still, they were in some sort of collective Jewish housing. A House List from 1942 names Hans as a resident of apartment 10 at Lilienbrunngasse 5, along with a woman named Marta Sara Fischer, born in 1888, so about Hans's age. Hans is identified as an employee of the IKG, though no employer is listed for this apartment-mate. Lisl is not on the list, possibly because as a "German," she did not fall under the IKG's mandate to track the residence addresses of anyone considered a Jew under the Nazi "racial" laws.

---

231 Jurgen Klatzer, "Im Dienst der zertrummerten Republik," ORF.at, April 28, 2020, accessed March 24, 2022, https://orf.at/stories/3162693/.

At the end of April 1945, two weeks after the Red Army conquered Vienna, Hans was registered at a new address, Lederergasse 4 in the 8th District. This building was only a two-block walk from Zeltgasse 1, where Paula was registered. Hans and Lisl did not stay there long. On June 16, 1945, they were registered at Iglaseegasse 51, apartment 3, in the outer 19th District. This was a neighborhood of modestly sized apartment blocks that had been built in the 1930s during the "black Vienna" period, that is, under the rule of the right-wing Fatherland Front that succeeded the socialist era of "Red Vienna." "Quite a nice apartment," Paula wrote of it in her letter of December 15, 1946. This remained their residence for several decades. Lisl lived in the Iglaseegasse apartment after Hans's death, and I visited her there with Paul in the winter of 1968 and again in 1971.

Work Records

Insight into the work that Paula, Hans, and others in their circle did to sustain themselves after the letters ended must also come from secondary sources. For Hans, the answer is straightforward. He continued to work for the IKG at its offices in the 1st District on Seitenstettengasse, and for its successor, the Council of Elders. Famously, the central city synagogue at Seitenstettengasse was the only one in Vienna that survived Kristallnacht. The structure had been built behind a façade of townhouses—Emperor Joseph II had allowed non-Catholic religious buildings to be erected, but they could not be visible from the street—and there was concern that neighboring buildings inhabited by "Germans" would be burned down. Thus while the interior of the synagogue was vandalized, the building itself continued to stand.[232] After the war, Hans continued to work for the revived IKG as its cashier. Lisl probably worked as well, though I have not found any record of what she did.

---

232 Michaela Feurstein-Prasser and Milchram Gerhard, *Jewish Vienna*, 3rd revised ed. (Vienna: Mandelbaum Verlag, 2017), 44.

Paula, like Hans, was employed by the IKG, and subsequently the Council of Elders, as a Pflegerin (a caregiver, comparable to a practical nurse). In 1941 she trained at the IKG's old age home at Seegasse 9 in the 9th District, then worked at the facility in the 2nd District at Malzgasse 7, which was used as an old age home for women from February 1940 to late June 1942. After that, the building served as a collection site for deportees until April 1943. When the large-scale deportations ended, the building returned to its former use as a Jewish old age home, with most of the residents protected from deportation by non-Jewish family members. Towards the end of the war, Malzgasse 7 became an emergency hospital for Hungarian forced laborers. The City of Vienna demolished the old building in the mid-1950s and erected a featureless apartment house, naming it Theodor Herzl Court as a gesture towards the site's history.[233]

Vienna and its oil refining and industrial facilities were targets of repeated Allied bombing raids beginning in mid-1944. They ended only with the Soviet capture of the city in April 1945. During the air raids, the cellars in Malzgasse 7 and the nearby building at Malzgasse 16 were used as bomb shelters for Jews, who were not allowed to use shelters provided for the general, non-Jewish population.[234]

Dr. Martha Müller, Paula and Olga's friend and Paula's sometime apartment-mate, also was employed by the IKG as a pediatrician at a Jewish children's home in the 2nd District. She continued there until September 1942, when she was deported to Theresienstadt.[235]

---

[233] Hecht, Raggam-Blesch, and Uhl, *Letzte Orte*, 247; "Rothschild-Spital," Wikipedia, accessed January 24, 2022, https://de.wikipedia.org/wiki/Rothschild-Spital.

[234] Malzgasse 16 had been used as a Jewish old age home from November 1939 until June 1942. Then it, too, became a collection site for deportees until the end of October 1943, and most of the home's residents were deported through there. After that, the building served as a Jewish hospital when the venerable Rothschild Hospital, formerly in a magnificent building out on the Währinger Gürtel, was forced to move to the 2nd District. Hecht, Raggam-Blesch, and Uhl, *Letzte Orte*, 248.

[235] Anna Hajkova, "Medicine in Theresienstadt," *Social History of Medicine* 33, no. 1 (February 2020), 79, 90n64, https://doi.org/10.1093/shm/hky066.

CHAPTER 20

Into the Maw of Theresienstadt

Deportations of family members to the ghetto at Theresienstadt figure large in the reconstructed years when there were no Haim or Kurz letters from Vienna. My main sources were the objective facts that can be mined from Czech, Austrian, and Israeli online databases, supplemented by books written by two men who survived imprisonment in Theresienstadt, Norbert Troller (1896, Brno–1984, New York) and Hans G. Adler (1910, Prague–1988, London). They both had the immense advantages of being German-speaking Czech males in the prime of their lives when they were deported from the "Protectorate" (the western portions of former Czechoslovakia that Germany had annexed early in 1939) to Theresienstadt. Their books are quite different: Troller's a personal memoir, Adler's a scholarly study. Yet both books return again and again to the terrible suffering of the old people at Theresienstadt that the authors witnessed.

Origins as a Habsburg Fortress

Theresienstadt began as a military site. It was built as a fortress in what was then the province of Bohemia by Holy Roman Emperor Joseph II, who named it for his mother, the Empress Maria Theresa, a pious and virulent Jew-hater even by the standards of her time and place. The fortress was finished in 1780, the year Maria Theresa died.[236]

---

236 Adler, *Theresienstadt 1941–1945*, 24.

Theresienstadt was laid out as a twelve-pointed star with six entry gates and space inside for a town as well as the military camp. Its outer walls were high, about twenty-five feet or more, so that from outside the grass-covered ramparts, only the tops of tallest structures were visible, "the church tower, the water tower, and the chimneys of a small brewery."[237]

For all its design features, Theresienstadt had no military importance. Adler summarized, "The fortress was never besieged, and after being ignored by the Prussians in 1866 [during the short Austro-Prussian war], it was abandoned in 1882, but...remained a small military city."[238]

Selection as a Ghetto and Transit Camp

In 1940 the SS in Berlin chose Theresienstadt for use as a ghetto and transit camp, initially intended for Jews from the "Protectorate." The site was so unimportant that it did not even have a railroad siding. The closest station was two miles away at the town of Bohusovice (Bauschowitz in German). The Czech village within the fortress had about three thousand residents, but it was poor and economically insignificant, so that limited resistance could be expected to orders for removing its inhabitants.[239]

When prisoners began arriving by the tens of thousands in 1941, Theresienstadt had no infrastructure to absorb them. The existing civilian houses were "generally uncomfortable and were more than one hundred years old....They typically lacked any modern sanitary facilities."[240] Worse, the fortress had been built on a flood plain between the Ohre (Eger in German) and Elbe Rivers, so the area was damp and uninviting. In Adler's words,

---

237 Adler, *Theresienstadt 1941–1945*, 24.

238 Adler, *Theresienstadt 1941–1945*, 24.

239 Adler, *Theresienstadt 1941–1945*, 22–25.

240 Adler, *Theresienstadt 1941–1945*, 25.

"Dust swirled on dry days, and after rainfalls everything turned into a quagmire."[241]

Some large barracks remained from Joseph II's day. Adler described them as "handsome buildings in a late baroque style typical of Austrian military buildings, with open arcades and broad courtyards on the inside."[242] Whatever their exterior aesthetic value, they were in no condition to house crowds of transplanted civilians:

> The...barracks, massive red brick structures, [were] hardly suitable as quarters, due to their darkness and cold damp. Only one...was remodeled and made livable after World War I.[243]

First Transports

The first two transports were sent to Theresienstadt in November 1941. They were filled with about three thousand younger Czech artisans and professionals, with their families, who had "volunteered" to be relocated there. Their role was "to organize, in the role of pioneers, a ghetto with the intention of increasing the population of the [small Czech] town [of Terezin] tenfold."[244] The Gestapo promised these firstcomers, designated AK1 and AK2 for "Aufbaukommando" (construction detail), that they and their immediate families (a maximum of five people per worker) would be protected from subsequent transports to the East. This promise, Adler wrote dryly, "was not always kept."[245]

These first two groups of transportees became the most favored and "protected" inmates of the ghetto, on a par with the camp's

---

241 Adler, *Theresienstadt 1941–1945*, 25.

242 Adler, *Theresienstadt 1941–1945*, 24.

243 Adler, *Theresienstadt 1941–1945*, 25.

244 Norbert Troller, *Theresienstadt: Hitler's Gift to the Jews* (Chapel Hill, NC: University of North Carolina Press, 2004), 26.

245 Adler, *Theresienstadt 1941–1945*, 26–27.

primarily Czech Jewish Council of Elders, the Ältestenrat. As early arrivals and Czechs, the AK1 and AK2 prisoners held "all the key positions in all departments," including "all food and water distribution, waterworks, gasworks, agriculture, [and the] hospital kitchens." These positions provided opportunities to scavenge food above the allocated starvation rations.[246] Troller recalled:

> Cook, baker, food distributor, and warehousing manager were among the most privileged, sought-after jobs. They provided enough food to eat one's fill and to have some left over for illegal barter for cigarettes.[247]

Troller, who had studied architecture, wangled extra rations and "protection" for himself and his family by designing modernistic furniture and interiors, constructed from scavenged scraps of wood, for Theresienstadt's most "privileged" prisoners. Later arrivals from Germany and former Austria had significantly lower status and less "protection."

"Protection" and Corruption

The quest for "protection," that is, protection from selection for transports to the East, was the moving force behind the prisoners' lives in Theresienstadt. The ruling SS gave the orders to the puppet Council of Elders to select the required number of inmates to fill each transport.[248] The "devilish baseness and cunning" of this process, Troller recalled, resulted in "ever-increasing corruption

---

[246] Troller, *Theresienstadt*, 26, 37, 39.

[247] Troller, *Theresienstadt*, 39

[248] Adler, *Theresienstadt 1941–1945*, 243. To avoid being implicated in this system, Adler did only manual labor at Theresienstadt and refused any work connected with the ghetto's administration.

in the ghetto; its single solitary goal was life and 'protection' from transports."[249]

Looking back as a survivor of Theresienstadt (and later Auschwitz), Troller found that his "most difficult problem after the war" was to come to terms with the effects of having pursued his own survival at all costs: "The psychological corruption affect[ed] all of us, including me." Fifty years later, Troller was clear that there was nothing heroic in the camp regime. It destroyed character rather than creating it:

> ...human beings cling to life, and fighting against death seems to be a law of nature, to do anything and everything for as long as possible to assure oneself of another sunrise....Who could blame us, condemned to ghettos and other concentration camps, if ethical maxims were slowly displaced by the instinct for self-preservation, and we all became corrupted in the desperate flight towards "protection"? Our ship is sinking. It is each man for himself.[250]

Troller recounted the rhythm of existence in Theresienstadt. First came the "terror-laden atmosphere in times of transport," which was followed by "short periods in which we could take a hopeful breath. Perhaps, we thought, this was the last transport." But it was never the last time, and the cycle repeated. The result for prisoners was "increasing demoralization, the gradual loss of our humanity, our ethical principles, our compassion."[251]

---

249 Troller, *Theresienstadt*, 40.

250 Troller, *Theresienstadt*, 44.

251 Troller, *Theresienstadt*, 50 (with modifications to internal punctuation).

Large Deportations Begin

Adler, who was deported to Theresienstadt in February 1942, witnessed firsthand the camp's explosion in numbers and its overcrowded, chaotic conditions. Large-scale deportations to Theresienstadt began in mid-1942, when 73,065 Jews from the Protectorate were shipped there. Starting in June 1942, Jews from the "Old Reich" (Germany, nearly 33,000 in 1942) and the "Ostmark" (former Austria, 13,922) began to be deported to Theresienstadt. August 1942 saw the arrival of 13,469 prisoners on 36 transports. About 55 percent of the total number of prisoners were considered elderly, over age 65. More than 6,000 prisoners, nearly half the new arrivals, were assigned to the unfinished, uninsulated attic spaces above the ancient barracks.[252]

Theresienstadt's prisoner population fluctuated, although it was always overcrowded. About 141,000 Jews were deported to Theresienstadt between late 1941 and 1944, crammed into an area that had held a prewar civilian population of only 3,000. The net number of prisoners at Theresienstadt grew each time transports arrived from the Reich, and then contracted as subsequent transports departed for the East. Between January 1942 and October 1944, transports left Theresienstadt regularly, taking about 88,000 inmates East to annihilation in Auschwitz, Minsk, Lodz, Birkenau. Of those transported out of Theresienstadt, only about 3,500 (less than 4 percent) survived. Another 33,500 prisoners remained in Theresienstadt, many of whom, particularly the older ones, died of disease and starvation.[253]

---

252 Adler, *Theresienstadt 1941–1945*, 33, 608, 647–648.

253 Adler, *Theresienstadt 1941–1945*, 48–50, 466–468, 749.

The Particular Destruction of the Elderly

There is a fair amount of postwar writing about cultural life in Theresienstadt and the children who were imprisoned there (only very few of whom survived the eventual transports to extermination camps in the East). Far less has been written about the old people, though that is where the visceral connection lies. My great-grandmother Regine Landsmann (Omama) and Paul and Olga's mother, Mathilde Kurz, were wrenched out of their lives in Vienna, however contracted those lives may have become, and taken away in mass transports to imprisonment and death in Theresienstadt.

Among Theresienstadt's prisoners, the elderly were the least "protected" and most expendable. The top tier of "ghetto aristocracy" consisted of prisoners who had the most protection from transports, or so it seemed: the Council of Elders and the Czech AK1 and AK2 workers. Second were the "officialdom of workers who were absolutely indispensable for the functioning of the ghetto: waterworks, power station, hospital, sewage, the smithy, agriculture, and their 'spongers.'" Below them came the children. Troller recounts that the adults "tried every which way to keep the children [alive] until peace would finally arrive," though he admits, "we did not succeed."[254] There was no such hope and attendant marshaling of resources for the elderly. They were on the bottom, allotted the least food and worst housing and sanitary facilities. The result was predictable. Troller observed firsthand:

> The old people, critically undernourished, died like flies of gastroenteritis and decrepitude and starved by the hundreds.[255]

---

254 Troller, *Theresienstadt*, 93, 112.

255 Troller, *Theresienstadt*, 93.

Enteritis, or "infectious diarrhea," was by far the most common disease in Theresienstadt, with 35,000 cases recorded during the second half of 1942 and about 5,000 deaths.[256] Adler identified the causes as "vitamin and protein deficiencies," as well as "the inadequate amount and poor quality of often spoiled food and the dismal sanitary situation."[257] Enteritis of this sort is a painful, off-putting condition typically caused by an *E. coli* infection. Its symptoms are fever, abdominal cramps, bloody diarrhea, and nausea. Caring for even one enteritis patient in a normal healthcare setting would strain sanitary, janitorial, laundry, and care staffs. The situation of hundreds of elderly enteritis sufferers, many with dementia, in overcrowded and filthy ghetto conditions, is beyond imagining.

Later, some survivors of Auschwitz purported to recall "how 'good' Theresienstadt had been" in comparison to the extermination camps.[258] Adler rejected this conclusion. He recognized that "what was endured by these elderly people in Theresienstadt brooks no intensification." Even without gas chambers and other machinery of intentional mass murder, Adler argued, the old people at Theresienstadt were subjected to ultimate dehumanization and loss of dignity:

> As long as there is still life left in a body,...the intensification of suffering is not death but the degree of degradation and indignity inflicted on a living human being.[259]

Adler also rejected a popular mitigating argument that the death rate at Theresienstadt was high because so many of the prisoners were old when they arrived. Elderly prisoners died sooner from the terrible conditions that the camp's overseers deliberately maintained

---

256 Adler, *Theresienstadt 1941–1945*, 454–455, 619.

257 Adler, *Theresienstadt 1941–1945*, 454–455.

258 Adler, *Theresienstadt 1941–1945*, 91.

259 Adler, *Theresienstadt 1941–1945*, 91.

than they would have in their former situations. This maltreatment, Adler maintained, should count as murder:

> It is true that the average age of the deceased was high; however, this only adds to the guilt of those responsible for the deportation of the aged...because quite a number of these elderly people had enjoyed undiminished, or at least decent, health before deportation, and it was only the "journey" and their stay at the camp that caused their rapid demise. We include the shortening of the life of the elderly in our definition of murder.[260]

The "Triage Mentality"

The fact that the large population of elderly prisoners suffered the worst conditions at Theresienstadt was not due to happenstance but rather deliberate policy. What one recent writer calls a "triage mentality" among Theresienstadt's Jewish administrators and healthcare systems prioritized "protected" and "notable" individuals, able-bodied workers, and children at the expense of the elderly. Consistent with this hierarchy, the old people were allocated less food, worse housing, and less healthcare than the more favored prisoner groups. She summarized:

> The conditions of Theresienstadt, created by the Nazis, were ideal to foster disease and, accordingly, the physicians [camp inmates themselves] faced a large percentage of the population being ill. In this situation, the Health Services applied a triage mentality in which the most frequent disease, enteritis, which was usually dangerous only for the elderly, was seen as unimportant. This triage mentality in medical care echoed that of the [ghetto's Jewish] self-administration in food distribution. Following incarceration, hunger and dirt, this categorization

---

260 Adler, *Theresienstadt 1941–1945*, 469.

contributed to an extremely high mortality rate among the older patients.[261]

For example, during typhoid outbreaks in the first quarter of 1943, the inmate physicians "reiterated the triage mentality" by focusing on the number of children who died in each of these three months (twenty, twenty-eight, and twelve respectively), while they "barely registered the 6,000 deceased elderly people in the same period."[262] Adler, like Hajkova, acknowledged that "the overall quality of medical care was very high" in Theresienstadt, but at the same time, "among the sorriest chapters in the camp's history was the neglect of elderly, helpless patients." He documented:

> Services were not provided, were performed negligently, or were made dependent on gifts. The [elderly] sick were not cared for, fed, or washed. Often their food was taken from them or denied them, and what they received frequently was inedible or cold....Many patients perished as a direct result of this deplorable state of affairs.[263]

The food rationing system was devised broadly by the German SS but administered in fine detail, like the transport selections, by the Jewish Council of Elders. The elderly received smaller rations than any other group, and as a result older prisoners endured more individual suffering and debilitating hunger than the more favored classes of inmates. Troller recalled:

> The SS...doled out our daily rations of calories according to a head count; we therefore had to give larger portions to the workers, smaller portions to the children and the sick, and

---

[261] Hajkova, "Medicine in Theresienstadt," 79, 84.

[262] Hajkova, "Medicine in Theresienstadt," 86.

[263] Adler, *Theresienstadt 1941–1945*, 442.

minimal rations to the poor old people. The old ones were in a desperate situation; they starved.[264]

Troller observed elderly prisoners who were so desperate for food that they even sought out the camp's so-called lentil soup, "made from dried ground lentil pods, gray, tasteless, unappealing, stinking water without any nutritional value." This swill was so inedible that even the chronically undernourished inmates who were capable of work "would throw it out disgustedly until we found regular takers for it: old people." Elderly prisoners scavenged among the discarded potato peelings behind the camp kitchens: "Clusters of old people would crowd around these heaps and would pull out the thickest peels to put into their bowls. They would gnaw off any potato left in the peel or would try to make soup from the peels."[265]

During the ghetto's typhoid epidemic, some of the stronger and more fortunate among the elderly, perhaps also those with better connections, got work as "privy guards."[266] Their job, for which they received a somewhat increased bread ration, was to sit by the table holding a basin of chlorinated water that was placed outside every indoor toilet and remind each user, "Please wash your hands."[267]

Housing, always in short supply, was distributed according to the same triage hierarchy. The "unprotected" among the elderly were assigned to the unfinished attics of the two-story barracks buildings. Those cavernous spaces had no insulation against winter cold and summer heat, "no lighting fixtures, no toilets, and no water pipes." They also were infested with lice and could be reached only by "trudging up long flights of stairs." Adler described the attics as "catastrophic."[268] Troller made a sketch in 1943 of an "elderly person

---

264 Troller, *Theresienstadt*, 53.

265 Troller, *Theresienstadt*, 52–53.

266 Adler, *Theresienstadt 1941–1945*, 286.

267 Troller, *Theresienstadt*, 84.

268 Adler, *Theresienstadt 1941–1945*, 98, 281.

climbing to attic quarters." A caption, added later in English, reads: "42 steps in one flight and two of these flights and the old people live in the hot attic & die there."[269]

Sketch by Norbert Troller, 1943. Used with the kind permission of the Leo Baeck Institute.

Disposing of the Dead

The number of deaths in Theresienstadt peaked in September 1942: 3,941 people, averaging 131 a day, disproportionately concentrated

---

[269] Troller, *Theresienstadt*, 54.

in the old people's quarters.[270] By October 1942 the total number of dead among prisoners aged sixty-five and older exceeded 10,000. Most had succumbed to enteritis and other illnesses predictably exacerbated by overcrowding, poor sanitation, and inadequate food. Disposing of bodies thus became a major undertaking. For the first year or so, prisoners who died at Theresienstadt were placed in crude wooden coffins "nailed together from six rough boards" and "buried in a cemetery dug out of the entrenchment." Troller recounted that the cemetery was set up "first in a hodgepodge manner, without any visible order, later in regular rows. Everything was in shades of dull brown, with little wooden slats as headstones, indicating the name, place of origin, and date of death of the deceased. In time the dates were washed away by rain and snow."[271] At first individual graves were dug, later mass graves. The cemetery was located in a high-water table area: "The earth was moist when dug to one meter, and upon further digging the graves would fill with water."[272] Adler described the macabre scene: "The corpses were tossed into these water-filled graves so that water splashed in all directions."[273]

Funerals were held, at least for a time. Catholic and Protestant funerals (to accommodate the sizable number of inmates who had been baptized but were considered Jews under the Nazi "racial" laws) took place daily at 8:30 a.m., Jewish funerals at 9:00 a.m. Adler recalled that "the services were very sober and as brief as possible."[274] Troller observed:

> The attending family members would repeat the rabbi's prayers dry-eyed. Death was a daily occurrence. In spite of the grief, the immediate family members, if there were any, would breathe a sigh of relief. They were rid of the worry of

---

270 Adler, *Theresienstadt 1941–1945*, 98, 469.

271 Troller, *Theresienstadt*, 84.

272 Adler, *Theresienstadt 1941–1945*, 471.

273 Adler, *Theresienstadt 1941–1945*, 471.

274 Adler, *Theresienstadt 1941–1945*, 470.

seeing their dear old ones sent to the East to their death and knew they had been spared unbearable suffering.[275]

Burying so many corpses was inefficient, so a crematorium with four electric ovens was built and began operating in September 1942.[276] (Troller speculated that the crematorium was intended to save the expense of wooden coffins.) Ashes from the crematorium were stored in cardboard containers, each about the size of a shoebox, marked with the name and dates of the deceased.[277] In October or November 1944, as the end of the war and the Red Army approached, some seventeen thousand of these boxes of ashes were thrown into the neighboring Eger River. A bucket brigade of inmates at the children's home passed the boxes from hand to hand, out of the crematorium storage area and to the river.[278]

Selection of Jews in Vienna for Deportation

The SS co-opted the IKG in Vienna to act as its agent first for selecting the number of Jews demanded to fill each transport (about one thousand per train) and then for rounding up, assembling, and hauling them to the railroad station. Initially the IKG mailed notices ordering the designated victims to appear at collection points, but that was insufficiently effective for the SS. Adler summarized:

> In Austria—which was basically synonymous with Vienna [as all the Jews who lived in the provinces had been forced to relocate to Vienna]—the assembly of transports was left to the [IKG].... As some of those targeted did not appear in the collection

---

275 Troller, *Theresienstadt*, 28–29.

276 Adler, *Theresienstadt 1941–1945*, 471, 709.

277 Troller, *Theresienstadt*, 29; Adler, *Theresienstadt 1941–1945*, 471.

278 Troller, *Theresienstadt*, 29–30, 166n24; Ruth Thomson, *Terezin: Voices from the Holocaust* (Candlewick Press 2013), 57, 62.

camp, the authorities soon switched to brutal methods: SS men or a group of thugs—in the form of the Jewish police, or "Jupo," who hardly lagged behind the Gestapo in inhuman harshness—dragged people out of their houses. The victims were set upon unprepared; they had to hastily pack a few possessions and were brought to the collection camp, which was full of lice and where scandalous conditions prevailed.[279]

The IKG personnel who acted as the front lines for the SS included, in addition to the notorious Jupo mentioned by Adler, teams of "Ausheber," literally "excavators," who "raided homes and took the victims" to the collection sites, and "Kripos," who "found hidden Jews."[280] These were all employees of the IKG. They wore colored armbands to identify their duties—yellow for excavators/Ausheber, blue for luggage storage, green for packing service. The excavators even wore tin badges in a grotesque emulation of police insignia.[281]

There is no record of the particular method by which Regine Landsmann, Mathilde Kurz, or Martha Müller were selected and rounded up for deportation, of their responses, or of the impact on family and communities left behind. What survives are typed lists of deportees and Theresienstadt death certificates.

Anteroom to Deportation—The Vienna Assembly Sites

Once individuals on a transport list had been "excavated" from their residences, they were brought to an assembly point and held there in terrible conditions for an unpredictable length of time, anywhere from a day or two to a week or more. Until recently, little historical attention had been directed towards these assembly sites. The reason in part was limited material; prisoners in the assembly sites were not allowed to

---

279 Adler, *Theresienstadt 1941–1945*, 52–53.

280 Adler, *Theresienstadt 1941–1945*, 754n243f, citing J. Singer, "Erinnerungen aus Wien und Theresienstadt," MS, 1955.

281 Hecht, Raggam-Blesch, and Uhl, *Letzte Orte*, 43.

send or receive mail or have any outside contact. In addition, almost none of the people who had been held there ever returned, and for the few who did, memories of their relatively short time at the assembly sites would have been overwhelmed by those of their later camp imprisonment. Only in 2019 was a study published called *The Last Places before Deportation: The Vienna Assembly Camps 1941/42* (not yet translated into English, the book is cited here by its German title, *Letzte Orte*).

The largest and longest-used of the assembly sites in Vienna was the school at Kleine Sperlgasse 2a in the 2nd District. Looking at a map and walking around the area, I found it striking that this building was just a block away and around the corner from Hans and Lisl's communal apartment at Lilienbrunngasse 5. They cannot have escaped the noises of trucks and buses unloading and then reloading their human cargo.

Kleine Sperlgasse school in 2023.

The building at Kleine Sperlgasse 2a, originally erected by the City of Vienna as a public school, was used as an assembly site for deportees in February and March 1941 and then again from October 1941 until the end of October 1942. Most of the estimated 45,451 people who were deported from Vienna passed through Kleine Sperlgasse before they were trucked to the Aspang railroad station and crammed into trains.[282] The building was returned to the City of Vienna in August 1943 and, despite its awful history, continues to be used as a public elementary school.[283] A plaque at the entrance commemorates the "40,000 fellow citizens who were under gestapo arrest in this school and were deported from here to extermination camps. Never Forget."

Shortly after Vienna was conquered by the Red Army, a survivor and former Jewish official at Kleine Sperlgasse named Otto Kalwo[284] wrote this verse entitled "The Sperl School Is Buzzing." Particularly poignant is his focus on the futile last hopes of the old people who were dragged there. They hoped to see their children who had escaped abroad once more, but that was only fantasy. The actuality was that the prisoners "will go East":

Thousands of Jews have been made available for a transport to the East.

Movement fills the house. Up and down stairs, that's how the restless wander.

Old sick people are dragged into the rooms and dropped onto buggy, gutted mattresses.

There they lie, helpless, their dull eyes directed to a world they no longer understand.

---

282 Hecht, Raggam-Blesch, and Uhl, *Letzte Orte*, 239.

283 Hecht, Raggam-Blesch, and Uhl, *Letzte Orte*, 239; "Sammellager Kleine Sperlgasse 2a," Wien Geschichte Wiki, accessed January 24, 2022, https://www.geschichtewiki.wien.gv.at/Sammellager_Kleine_Sperlgasse_2a.

284 1918, Vienna–2012 (2008?) USA, name changed to Lawrence Otto Calvo; "Lawrence Otto Calvo," Geni.com, accessed January 24, 2022, https://www.geni.com/people/Lawrence-Calvert/6000000042695795025.

They still want to come to their children abroad, see them and kiss them and smile with the joy of seeing them again....

Nothing comes of it. They will go East. To a ghetto....

This is how they spin their thoughts away. Abroad, children, East....[285]

The assembly campsites were overcrowded and filthy, breeding grounds for lice, despair, and suicide. One later writer summarized the "disastrous situation":

> All furniture was removed from the flats or school rooms and many people were crammed into these spaces on mattresses or straw sacks or on the bare floor. The rooms were not heated and there were no covers. Everyone was limited to the space of his or her mattress or straw sack. There were only very few toilets and wash basins, vermin was rampant; there was little medical support and the food rations were meagre because the IKG had to pay for medical and food supply from its scarce resources.[286] Furthermore the violence and aggression of the SS personnel was unsupportable....In Gestapo reports in the first three weeks of the large deportations 84 suicides and 87 suicide attempts of Jews were recorded. All in all, until October 1942 390 Jewish suicides and 277 suicide attempts [in the assembly sites] were registered by the Gestapo.[287]

---

285 "Sammellager Kleine Sperlgasse 2a," Wien Geschichte Wiki; see also Hecht, Raggam-Blesch, and Uhl, *Letzte Orte*, 239–310.

286 As the IKG's cashier, Hans may even have even known that the IKG was paying the Gestapo for "upkeep" of the assembly camps' inmates.

287 Susanne Wurm, "Nazi Collective Camps ('Sammelager') and Life in Hiding as a So-Called 'U-Boot' ('Submarine') in Vienna 1938–1945 and the Survival Strategies of the Persecuted," Central European Economic and Social History, September 2, 2020, http://centraleuropeaneconomicandsocialhistory.com/nazi-collective-camps-sammellager-and-life-in-hiding-as-a-so-called-u-boot-submarine-in-vienna-1938-1945-and-the-survival-strategies-of-the-p.

Another survivor recalled that at the assembly camp, "SS personnel... confiscated our birth certificates and left us only with our identity cards after imprinting them with the stamp 'Relocated to Theresienstadt.'" Adding to the program of dehumanization, "before being taken away, all the women and men were forced to have their hair cut."[288]

The Aspang Railroad Station

From October 1939 through the end of 1942, all the trains crammed with Jews being deported from Vienna left from one spot, the Aspang railroad station in the 3rd District. The station had been built in 1880 for a regional railroad, and it was smaller, with less traffic, than the grander stations that served national and international rail lines. In normal, pre-war times, trains from the Aspang station had taken skiers up to the Schneeberg, one of Vienna's local "house mountains." When Austrian writer Hilde Spiel returned to Vienna in February 1946 for a first visit after eight years of exile in England, the station reminded her of scenes from her student days:

> Every Sunday at five in the morning the first train left from Vienna's Aspang station for the Schneeberg. From all the districts of the city came young people, students, officials, workers, wandering through the cold and dark, many of whom had got up one or two hours earlier to be there in time. Under a cover of skiers and skis, which formed a second roof from luggage rack to luggage rack, we traveled for a long time, dozing and whispering, in unlit carriages, until the valley station was reached. Then, alone or in groups, while winds raged around the solitary peak, we made the ascent in the bitingly cold dawn.[289]

---

288 Joy Singer, testimony, quoted in "Transport 42, Train Da 519 from Wien, Vienna, Austria to Theresienstadt, Ghetto, Czechoslovakia on 24/09/1942," Yad Vashem, https://deportation.yadvashem.org/index.html?language=en&itemId=6962219.

289 Hilde Spiel, *Return to Vienna: A Journal* (Ariadne Press, Riverside, California, 2011), 104–105.

Here, Spiel seems to have recorded her memories with innocent nostalgia. There is no sign that she knew of the Aspang station's role in the mass deportations.

The Aspang station was demolished in 1977, and the site became a local park. The first visible acknowledgment of its infamous history was erected nearly forty years after the war's end. In 1983 a private group of Holocaust survivors placed a memorial stone there with an inscription in German only:

> During the years 1939–1942, tens of thousands of Austrian Jews were transported from the Aspang train station to extermination camps and never returned.
>
> Never forget.[290]

In 2017, seventy-two years after the war ended, the City of Vienna erected a sculptural monument in the park where the Aspang station had stood. It consists of two concrete rails with the inscription "47,035 deportees" etched on one track and "1,073 survivors" on the other. (Arithmetically, this is a survival rate of less than 2.3 percent.) The rails become smaller over a length of around one hundred feet and "lead into a dark, hollow concrete block, a symbol of death, nothingness, forgetting."[291] The numbers of victims and survivors, plus another statistic, "47 transports in 1939 and 1941/42," are inscribed at the far end of the installation with a quotation from Primo Levi in German, English, and Hebrew:

> It is not permissible to forget, it is not permissible to be silent. If we are silent, who will speak?[292]

---

[290] "Gedenkstein fur ermordete Osterreichische Juden," Wien Geschichte Wiki, accessed January 24, 2022, https://www.geschichtewiki.wien.gv.at/Gedenkstein_f%C3%BCr_ermordete_%C3%B6sterreichische_Juden.

[291] "Mahnmal Aspangbanhof," Wien Geschichte Wiki, accessed March 24, 2022, https://www.geschichtewiki.wien.gv.at/Mahnmal_Aspangbahnhof.

[292] "Mahnmal Aspangbanhof," Wien Geschichte Wiki.

Austrian-Israeli historian Doron Rabinovici suggests that official recognition of Aspang as "Vienna's train station for the murdered" took so long because its existence implied that the Viennese knew what was being done right there in their city, not in some faraway camp: "The train station was actually in the middle of the city...these transports were something that everyone could know."[293] Other writers made the point that the deportations were not a secret. Passersby lined the streets and jeered whenever trucks left the 2nd District for the Aspang station.[294] An elderly survivor who was deported to Theresienstadt through the Aspang station spoke at the memorial's dedication in 2017. He commented on the "scorn and mockery" with which people in the streets observed truckloads of Jews being carried to the station: "'The tragedy was a triumph for the Viennese at that time,' he said, there was 'no sign of compassion and humanity.'"[295]

Prisoners' Arrival at Theresienstadt

Arrival at Theresienstadt was chaotic, further dehumanizing the already weakened and demoralized prisoners. One of them recalled, "One didn't 'arrive'" in Theresienstadt, "one was delivered and handed over" like an object.[296] Adler, possibly recalling his own arrival at Theresienstadt, concluded that "perhaps a picture might convey an idea of the state" of the arriving prisoners, "but language hardly can":

> Finally they arrived at the train station [at Bohusovice] exhausted and destroyed—with the SS, gendarmes, and other Jews yelling at

---

[293] Marie-Theres Egyed and Peter Mayr, "Aspangbanhof: Wiens Banhof der Ermordeten," *Der Standard*, September 2, 2017, https://www.derstandard.at/story/2000063481317/aspangbahnhof-wiens-bahnhof-der-ermordeten.

[294] Egyed and Mayr, "Aspangbanhof."

[295] "Aspangbanhof: Deportationsmahnmal eröffnet," *Der Standard*, September 7, 2017, https://www.derstandard.at/story/2000063751365/aspangbahnhofdeportationsmahnmal-am-frueheren-wiener-eroeffnet.

[296] Adler, *Theresienstadt 1941–1945*, 233.

them—with confused expressions, uncomprehending desperate looks, and anxious gestures....These debilitated people were then expected to begin the arduous march to the camp, unrefreshed and burdened with their miserable possessions; often they were no longer able to go on. In that case, they were loaded onto trucks or tractor trailers like cattle, packed together so tightly that they could neither lie down nor sit. Therefore, they had to stand—ill, exhausted, thirsty, apathetic or screaming, women with tangled hair, invalids on crutches, blind people with trembling limbs, to be driven into town. Once, one of the drivers, a young SS novice known as "SS Children's Home," catapulted twenty-seven people from the wagon while recklessly taking a curve. Ten died on the spot; the others died in the hospital or were crippled.[297]

Once the trucks reached the old fortress, the "horrible" process began of "unloading of the sick and elderly." Adler wrote:

[Emptying the trucks] had to be done quickly, in order to avoid exciting the rage of the SS drivers. A wooden crate was dragged to the truck—it looked like a conductor's or speaker's stand—and the helpless people attempted to climb out. Many did not succeed, and they were unloaded in a manner worse than that used for livestock.[298]

On arrival at the fortress, the elderly prisoners in particular exhibited "psychological shock" and "confusion...accompanied by loss of memory, amnesia, and other disturbances. Many people fell into neurotic or manic and depressive states or suffered hysterical outbreaks or screaming and crying fits." Others simply "seemed apathetic." Adler concluded, "Almost everyone who was subjected to a transport suffered an inextinguishable trauma."[299]

---

297 Adler, *Theresienstadt 1941–1945*, 90.

298 Adler, *Theresienstadt 1941–1945*, 119.

299 Adler, *Theresienstadt 1941–1945*, 117.

Conditions in the Ghetto

Adler detailed the miserable conditions that the prisoners who arrived at Theresienstadt during the summer of 1942 were thrown into after the debilitating deportation process. Housing was in ruins, sanitation and healthcare glaringly inadequate, and only the vermin seemed to flourish:

> Many arrivals from Vienna and Cologne were afflicted with clothing lice and head lice [mostly acquired during the prisoners' enforced confinement in assembly points]. No provisions had been made for effective disinfection. The civilian houses, which had stood empty for a few days [after their Czech inhabitants were evacuated], became living quarters on July 7 and were soon overcrowded as never before.... Mountains of garbage lay in the rooms and in the courtyards; rats and vermin had made their homes there, creating problems that could not be remedied in days or weeks. [Initially] there were no hospitals or infirmaries. The sick were placed onto the bare floor; often they remained uncovered, as did the people in the other rooms. People died without peace, untended, without a word of comfort or a friendly glance.[300]

Hospitals in Theresienstadt—Limited Oases

Theresienstadt eventually developed an elaborate hospital and clinic system staffed by inmates who had been medical professionals before their lives were upended. Although crowding and hunger could not be eliminated, patients there experienced a limited respite from the everyday privations of the ghetto, and some lived to record favorable memories of their stays. Norbert Troller described his surgery in Theresienstadt for ileitis. (He explained that this was the result of "the radical weight loss due to which

---

300 Adler, *Theresienstadt 1941–1945*, 91.

the intestines, previously surrounded by layers of fat, were dangling around freely, and had gotten twisted into the scar tissue of previous operations."[301]) He recalled that the hospital had actual beds, instead of sacks stuffed with straw or wood shavings, and cloth sheets:

> Waking up in a white hospital bed with fresh linens, I was deathly ill from the anesthetic. I was weaker than usual, miserable, the hospital smell making me want to vomit....
>
> I was lying in a large hospital room with high vaulted ceilings, one of the wards of the former garrison hospital originating from the eighteenth century. Forty or fifty other patients recently operated on shared the room with me. Having been weakened by undernourishment and the results of the surgery, I recuperated very slowly.[302]

Adler agreed, some of the hospital rooms "even had real beds" and linens, though the wards were so crowded that "it was difficult for nurses to get to their patients' beds."[303]

A former teacher deported from Berlin had similar positive memories of her stay in one of the ghetto's hospitals. She recalled after the war:

> Those six weeks that I spent in the hospital were the nicest time of my stay in Theresienstadt: Clean beds, kind nurses, better food, far from the misery of the accommodation.[304]

However, these hospital respites were generally available only to the relatively younger camp prisoners:

---

301 Troller, *Theresienstadt*, 128.

302 Troller, *Theresienstadt*, 128.

303 Adler, *Theresienstadt 1941–1945*, 445.

304 Hajkova, "Medicine in Theresienstadt," 87n40.

For the elderly, whose friends could only infrequently bring extra food or bribe for reliable medical help, the first disease often became fatal.[305]

Although Theresienstadt had a separate clinic for the elderly, medical positions there were considered second rate, "neither prestigious nor interesting."[306] Doctors had to make rounds of old, sick patients in their dark, vermin-infested living quarters. One doctor who was assigned to the old people's clinic reported with disgust:

> It's a bad job. I have to climb into all kinds of caves, crowded, dark, and often full of lice. I have to work by candlelight and I can only put watch glasses and flasks [for taking samples] on foot stools.[307]

Regine Landsmann, Transport No. 38

Firsthand reports about Regine Landsmann stop with Antoinette Haim's last postcard of October 6, 1941, but the story does not end well. The Seegasse old age home became increasingly overcrowded. In 1941 the IKG reported that the home had 611 residents despite having been designed for only 430.[308] How much Omama continued to decline in her final year at Seegasse, how aware she was of the deteriorating conditions, and the extent to which Paula, Antoinette, and others were able to continue their regular visits to her cannot be known.

Less than a year after that last glimpse in Antoinette's postcard, Omama was selected for deportation to Theresienstadt. A former nurse described the horrific process when residents of the Jewish

---

305 Hajkova, "Medicine in Theresienstadt," 88.

306 Hajkova, "Medicine in Theresienstadt," 91.

307 Hajkova, "Medicine in Theresienstadt," 91n68.

308 Rabinovici, *Eichmann's Jews*, 139.

old age home at Malzgasse 6 in the 2nd District were evacuated for deportation in 1942:

> The people struggled, of course fighting for their lives. They were thrown roughshod into this truck without checking whether they had somewhere to sit or not. One wheelchair-bound patient was hauled from his wheelchair by two men, one at the shoulders and the other at the feet, and thrown in, without feeling, needless to say. They never had any feelings.[309]

There is no reason to think that the eviction of Omama and others from the old age home on Seegasse was much different.

A typed list of the deportees selected for transport no. 38 to Theresienstadt survives.[310] It contains a thousand names in alphabetical order, about thirty per page, each with the obligatory addition of "Israel" or "Sara," and each deportee's residence address, date of birth, and number within the transport. The addresses are predominantly in the 2nd District with some from the 9th District, the areas in Vienna in which Jews had been concentrated. One hundred fifty-five, some 15 percent, of the deportees on this transport no. 38 were from the old age home at Seegasse 9. Forty-four of them had been born in the 1850s, putting them well into their eighties in the summer of 1942. The oldest was about ninety-two. A very few individuals on the list have only a year of birth by their names, suggesting not only present dementia, but that they had no longer been able to recall or communicate their own dates of birth when they were moved into Seegasse. The average age of prisoners on this transport was seventy-two, including among them a sister of Sigmund Freud, Rosa Graf, age eighty-two or eighty-three.[311] "Regina Sara

---

309 Rabinovici, *Eichmann's Jews*, 132, quoting DÖW, Judische Schicksale (Jewish Fates), 503.

310 "Transport 38 nach Theresienstadt, 27.8.1942," Arolsen Archives, https://collections.arolsen-archives.org/en/archive/1-2-1-1_82273049/?p=1&doc_id=11203840.

311 "Transport 38, Train Da 507 from Wien, Vienna, Austria to Theresienstadt, Ghetto, Czechoslovakia on 27/8/1942," Yad Vashem, https://deportation.yadvashem.org/index.html?language=en&itemId=6962069.

Landsmann" of Seegasse 9 is listed as deportee number 679 in this transport. At age eighty-two, she was one of the older ones.

After being evacuated from the old age home, Omama would have been hauled to an assembly site somewhere in the 2nd District, kept there in degrading conditions for an indeterminate length of time, and then trucked to the Aspang railroad station and crammed onto a train destined for Theresienstadt. The date that transport no. 38 left Vienna is recorded—August 27, 1942.

Omama died in Theresienstadt on September 11, about three weeks after being pulled out from her life at Seegasse. The Council of Elders at Theresienstadt had death certificate forms printed in German, and one was completed for her, signed by two or three camp medical officials.[312] On the surface, it all seems very orderly. The cause of death was entered as instructed in block letters, in both German and Latin, as "old age weakness" or "marasmus senilis," progressive wasting of the aged without any identified infection or other acute cause. The time of death was 5:55 a.m., the place of death was the quarters to which she had been assigned, building E a III, room 192. This was part of the Genie Barracks, which in 1942 included a hospital and old age home.[313] Omama appears to have been assigned to the old age section of the Genie Barracks rather than the general quarters for the elderly, possibly because she was in such visibly fragile condition when she arrived at Theresienstadt. Based on the recorded time of death, she was probably found dead in the morning. Verses written in 1943 by a Theresienstadt inmate named Ilse Weber titled "Genie Kaserne" (Genie Barracks) capture the scene:

> Death passes through the Genie Kaserne in silent steps, taking in its clutching grasp the sleeping elderly.[314]

---

312 "Landsmann Regine: Death Certificate, Ghetto Terezin," Holocaust.cz, last modified January 12, 2016, https://www.holocaust.cz/en/database-of-digitised-documents/document/82345-landsmann-regine-death-certificate-ghetto-terezin/.

313 Adler, *Theresienstadt 1941–1945*, 278.

314 "Moritz Müller," Yad Vashem, https://www.yadvashem.org/yv/en/exhibitions/last_portrait/muller.asp.

A "mortuary examination" was conducted the same day, the death certificate completed and signed, and that was that. One fewer elderly Jew. This was the week after Theresienstadt's crematorium began operating, so Omama probably did not get even a perfunctory funeral or soggy grave.

In 2002, after my mother died, I asked her cousin Lissy if she recalled anything about their grandmother, Regine Landsmann. Lissy responded that her father Sigl and uncle Gustl were two wonderful men who loved their mother so much that if they could have carried her across the street instead of letting let her walk, they would have done it. The subtext, which could not be spoken, was that all three of Regine's children of necessity left her behind in Vienna when they escaped one by one in 1939, 1940, and 1941, respectively.

Mathilde Kurz, Transport No. 45

Mathilde Kurz was deported from Vienna about six weeks after Omama, on October 9, 1942, in transport no. 45. This, too, was an "elders" transport; 411 of the 1,300 deportees were sixty-one or older, with an average age of fifty-one.[315]

There is no record of when and how Mathilde was summoned or taken away from the communal apartment at Novaragasse 40 that she shared with Paula and Antoinette, or the reactions of those left behind. Looking back one can imagine terror and helplessness but not begin to approach the depth of those feelings. A diary entry from an unidentified prisoner who was also deported on transport no. 45 captures the physical situation and feeling of dehumanization:

> I was allowed to take with me a backpack weighing 25 kilograms. What can one pack when one doesn't know what one

---

315 "Transport 45, Train Da 525 from Wien, Vienna, Austria, to Theresienstadt, Ghetto, Czechoslovakia on 9/10/1942," Yad Vashem, https://deportation.yadvashem.org/index.html?language=en&itemId=6996322.

will need? We traveled by train to Prague and then on to Bauschowitz in a cattle car. To Theresienstadt we were forced to walk. Twenty corpses were left lying by the roadside....My yellow Star of David shone on my chest and my number swung as if on a cow's neck. From now on, this is my name. From now on this number is me. My name and my past have been eradicated. I am moving toward darkness.[316]

The prisoners selected for transport no. 45 were deposited first at Sperlgasse in the 2nd District. Another prisoner on this transport later recalled being hauled from Sperlgasse to the train station through jeering crowds and then the rail journey, comparing treatment of the Jewish prisoners to that of animals:

From Sperlgasse, the assembly site for deportees destined for Theresienstadt, we were taken by bus to the train station, where were made to stand like animals. [On our way] to the station, we were accompanied by rabble that gradually filled every street corner in Vienna with loud cries of "Die, Jew."

At ten o'clock at night we were loaded on to horse trucks and arrived the following morning at 10 a.m. at Bauschowitz.[317]

According to Theresienstadt's surviving records, Mathilde Kurz was assigned to quarters near her widowed younger sister, Anna Schwarzwaldova. They both were in building H V, the Dresden Barracks, room 173, housing for elderly women.[318] Mathilde was sixty-seven years old and Anna sixty-two. The Dresden Barracks, like each of the others, was supposed to be "a self-contained whole," housing branch offices for the Council of Elders' various departments, including building management, provisions and food

---

316 "Transport 45, Train Da 525," Yad Vashem.

317 Frances Tritt, *Diary 1942–1945*, quoted in "Transport 45, Train Da 525," Yad Vashem.

318 Adler, *Theresienstadt 1941–1945*, 77.

preparation, medical clinics, work assigners, and cleaning and maintenance services.[319] The medical care there was unexpectedly sophisticated. Adler recorded that early on, an operating room was set up in the Dresden Barracks where "some difficult operations were carried out using the most primitive means."[320]

Mathilde's sister Anna had been living in the family's hometown of Gross Meseritsch, in Czech Velke Mezirici, when she was deported to Theresienstadt on May 18, 1942, about four months before Mathilde's arrival.[321] Whether Anna had been able to let Mathilde know that she was in Theresienstadt, and whether Mathilde had been able to send her sister any correspondence or assistance from Vienna, can't be known. In Theresienstadt Anna would have had the marginal advantage of being conversant in Czech, the language of the camp's ruling inmates, while Mathilde may have retained some Czech from her childhood.

An unusual amount of official, impersonal detail survives about Mathilde's death. The Theresienstadt death certificate records that she died at 4:10 p.m. on February 24, 1943, from "cardiac insufficiency" during or just after surgery to remove an enlarged right kidney. The location where she died is identified as building E VI, room 36, surgery. E VI was the Hohenelber Barracks, where the camp's central hospital was located.[322] Her personal details were diligently entered on the death certificate: name Mathilde Sara Kurz, née Wilheim, born in Gross Meseritsch. She was a widow whose profession was "homemaker." Her religion was Jewish ("mos." for "Mosaich"), and her citizenship "DR" (Deutsches Reich). Anna Schwarzwaldova was identified as a relative in Theresienstadt.[323]

---

319   Adler, *Theresienstadt 1941–1945*, 68.

320   Adler, *Theresienstadt 1941–1945*, 69.

321   "Anna Schwarzwaldova," Holocaust.cz, last modified January 12, 2016, https://www.holocaust.cz/en/database-of-victims/victim/123359-anna-schwarzwaldova/.

322   Adler, *Theresienstadt 1941–1945*, 277.

323   "Kurz Mathilde: Death Certificate, Ghetto Terezin," Holocaust.cz, last modified January 12, 2016, https://www.holocaust.cz/en/database-of-digitised-documents/document/95567-kurz-mathilde-death-certificate-ghetto-terezin/.

When and how Paula in Vienna learned of Mathilde's death is another unknown.

Anna must have been strong and resourceful to survive in Theresienstadt for a year and a half. Then she was deported a second time on December 18, 1943, to Auschwitz, one in a huge transport of 2,503 prisoners. There she died an unrecorded death. Anna was sixty-four years old. When I visited Velke Mezirici in 2008, a handwritten poster in the former synagogue, now used as an exhibit space, included Anna Schwarzwaldova's name among victims from the town.

Deportations to Theresienstadt Beyond the Immediate Family

In 1942 the extended family circle continued to contract. The cause no longer was emigration—everyone had left who could—but large-scale deportations of the remaining Jews.

Martha Müller—Transport No. 42

Olga and Paula's close friend Dr. Martha Müller was deported on September 24, 1942, with transport no. 42, the eleventh transport from Vienna to Theresienstadt. Of the 1,300 prisoners on this transport, 673 were older than sixty-one, so it was considered an Alterstransport (old people's transport.) Seventy-eight of the prisoners had been taken from the Jewish old age home at Seegasse 9.[324] With the Gestapo's continuous demands to fill the transports, employment by the IKG provided diminishing protection against deportation. Martha Müller worked as a pediatrician at an IKG's children's home, and several prisoners in transport no. 42 were registered as residents of the IKG's building at Lazenhof 2.[325]

---

324 "Transport 42 nach Theresienstadt, 24.9.1942," Arolsen Archives, https://collections.arolsen-archives.org/en/archive/1-2-1-1_82273053/?p=1&doc_id=11204036.

325 "Transport 42," Arolsen Archives.

Martha was prisoner number 1,251 on the transport list. Her residence in Vienna was recorded as Mohapelgasse 3 (now Tempelgasse 3) in the 2nd District, a Jewish children's home. The last fourteen children who had been cared for at the home were deported on that transport as well.[326] The facility at Mohapelgasse survived to the end of the war, caring mostly for children who were considered Jewish under the Nazi "racial" laws but were protected from deportation by having a "German" parent.

The surviving records include the usual punctilious detail. Transport no. 42 left Vienna's Aspang station at 7:25 p.m. It was routed through the Vienna Nordbahnhof (north train station), then continued north through the city's suburbs and on to Prague, and finally reached Bohusovice, the old railroad station about two miles from Theresienstadt.[327]

Accounts by survivors of transport no. 42 shed some light on what must have been widely shared experiences of these victims. One survivor recalled in later oral testimony that two days before their deportation date, the Jews who had been selected for this transport were rounded up at their apartments, taken to a collection point in the 2nd District, and held there until the afternoon of September 24. She recalled in particular the humiliating drive across the Danube Canal and through the city to the Aspang railroad station in the back of an open truck through hostile crowds:

> On the night of September 22, a Jewish man arrived at my apartment from the "Kripo" (criminal police force), in order to take me away....Despite my protests, I was taken to the assembly camp....The first trucks arrived at nine in the morning to collect us from the transit camp and the last ones arrived at 2:30 in the afternoon. We were forced to stand upright in

---

326 Anna Hajkova, "Medicine in Theresienstadt," *Social History of Medicine* 33, no. 1 (February 2020), 79, 90n64, https://doi.org/10.1093/shm/hky066.

327 "Transport 42, Train Da 519 from Wien, Vienna, Austria to Theresienstadt, Ghetto, Czechoslovakia on 24/09/1942," Yad Vashem, https://deportation.yadvashem.org/index.html?language=en&itemId=6962219.

the open trucks, while people in the crowded streets jeered at us as we were driven past. We were taken to Aspangbahnhof... where we received the paper bag with our food for the journey. But there was nothing to drink. The SS men locked the doors and some of them traveled on the engine. The windows had to be kept closed and we were forbidden to look outside. Our transport, the eleventh from Vienna to Theresienstadt, departed at about five in the afternoon on Tuesday....The train traveled all night. When I looked out of the window at ten thirty in the morning, despite being forbidden from doing so, I recognized Prague. We continued to travel at great speed and arrived in the afternoon at Bohusovice, where we had to alight. The transport consisted of old people and a medical team.[328]

Another survivor recalled that transport no. 42 included some "prominent" people and their families (among them the president of the Vienna Jewish Community Desider Friedman and a former member of parliament) and "many professors from the Rothschild Hospital."[329] Long after the fact, this survivor also remembered the dehumanizing roundup of those selected for the transport, the limbo of the transit site, and their finally being hauled through the city in the back of open trucks "like transportation of beef to the abattoir":

On September 20...as usual the roundup [Aushebungen] of the [Jews] was carried out late at night...when I was brought to the assembly point in the Second Quarter, the building was already packed full....When the order came to prepare for evacuation on September 24, each of us was forced to pass before the Gestapo with his or her backpack or suitcase....We were then loaded onto trucks; to me—as a meat trader—this image of the evacuation resembled the transportation of beef to the abattoir in Vienna.

---

328 Joy Singer, testimony, quoted in "Transport 42, Train Da 519," Yad Vashem.

329 Munish Menashe Mautner, testimony, quoted in "Transport 42, Train Da 519," Yad Vashem.

The people of Vienna couldn't care less what happened to the Jews....We arrived in Theresienstadt the following day at about noon. As we alighted from the train, we already had the first dead...who hadn't survived the transport.[330]

For some, the sight of relatives being herded onto trucks and then hauled away towards the Aspang station created indelible mental scars. Austrian writer Ilse Aischinger was born in 1922 and survived the war in Vienna. She was considered a Mischling Grade I (of mixed background) and thus was not obligated to wear the stigmatizing yellow star, even though she lived with her Jewish grandmother and aunt. Decades later Aischinger wrote about the traumatic final view of her grandmother being carted away in the back of a truck over the Danube Canal:

> The camp in which everyone was assembled first was over the bridge in what had earlier been the ghetto, in a former school [in the 2nd District]. And then they were finally transported away over a bridge in trucks. I stood there and saw her, with a kerchief on her head. And someone yelled, look, here is Ilse. But she did not turn....I remember how my Grandmother in a truck was deported over the Sweden Bridge.[331]

In September 1942 Martha Müller would have found an extensive medical establishment amid the terrible conditions of Theresienstadt. Theresienstadt records reported that in December 1942, 363 doctors were employed to treat about 58,000 prisoners, about 3,500 of them children between the ages of three and eighteen. The required work schedule was oppressive, between seventy-five and eighty-five hours per week plus twenty night shift hours for various caregivers. By July 1943 the number of doctors employed in the ghetto had increased to 635. In September 1944 that total had risen to 710. The number of medical practitioners fell when mass deportations to Auschwitz began

---

330 Munish Menashe Mautner, testimony, quoted in "Transport 42, Train Da 519," Yad Vashem.

331 Ilse Aichinger, *The Greater Hope*, trans. by Geoff Wilkes (Germany: Konigshausen and Neuman, 2016), 233.

in late September 1944, after footage had been shot for a propaganda movie (never released) showcasing Theresienstadt as a "model ghetto." Once Theresienstadt was no longer needed for propaganda, the SS began to eliminate the German, Austrian, and Czech inmates, regardless of their professional skills, and replaced them with prisoners from Hungary and points east.[332]

Few details remain about Martha Müller's work at Theresienstadt. Unusually for a woman and a non-Czech German-speaker, she was assigned to work as a pediatrician, rather than a lower-level caregiver, in the Hamburg Barracks.[333] Then after more than two years in Theresienstadt, she was deported to Auschwitz on October 19, 1944, in a transport of 1,500 prisoners (of whom only fifty-one survived). The standard process was to pack seventy to eighty prisoners into each cattle car.[334] During the month of October 1944, nine "liquidation transports" carried 14,404 prisoners from Theresienstadt to Auschwitz, where only 940 (about 6.5 percent) survived.[335] Sensing Germany's approaching defeat, Heinrich Himmler ordered an end to the gassing of Jewish prisoners in Auschwitz a few days after the last of these transports left from Theresienstadt, on November 2, 1944.[336] That was too late for Müller and the overwhelming majority of the final deportees from Theresienstadt. Müller was only thirty-eight when she was killed.

Tante Lotte—Deportation from Berlin

On the same day that Martha Müller was deported from Vienna, September 24, 1942, Antoinette's sister Charlotte (née Feder) Degner, Tante Lotte to the family, was deported from Berlin to

---

332   Adler, *Theresienstadt 1941–1945*, 613–619.

333   Hajkova, "Medicine in Theresienstadt," 90n64.

334   Adler, *Theresienstadt 1941–1945*, 247, 617.

335   Adler, *Theresienstadt 1941–1945*, 617.

336   Adler, *Theresienstadt 1941–1945*, 617; "Auschwitz Concentration Camp," Wikipedia, accessed January 24, 2022, https://en.wikipedia.org/wiki/Auschwitz_concentration_camp#cite_ref-284.

Theresienstadt in a small transport of about a hundred prisoners.[337] Tante Lotte survived in Theresienstadt for a year and a half before being deported from there to Auschwitz on May 16, 1944, on a large transport of 2,500 souls, of whom only five survived.[338] Lotte was seventy years old.

There is no way to know if Antoinette and Paula knew at the time of Lotte's imprisonment, or if they were able to exchange correspondence with Lotte and Martha Müller in Theresienstadt, even if it was perforce stilted and censored, during the short windows when it was allowed.[339] The rules for mail were restrictive and arbitrary. As of September 1942, prisoners could send correspondence from Theresienstadt, though it was limited to thirty words, including salutation and signature, written on one side of a postcard. Content was strictly controlled:

> As a general rule, caution was necessary. It was at times forbidden, and never advisable, to mention people by name. One could point out that receiving packages was permitted, but one could not make specific requests.[340]

When parcels, particularly of food, were sent to Theresienstadt, they were routinely pilfered by Czech gendarmes and the camp's "Jewish postal services." To prevent news and forbidden messages from reaching prisoners, "anything printed or written was removed from parcels, even sheets of old newspaper" that had been used as packing materials.[341]

---

337 "List of Transports to/from Theresienstadt," Porges.net, last modified 2002, http://www.porges.net/Terezin/TransportsToFromTerezin.html.

338 Adler, *Theresienstadt 1941–1945*, 616.

339 Adler, *Theresienstadt 1941–1945*, 509–510.

340 Adler, *Theresienstadt 1941–1945*, 509.

341 Adler, *Theresienstadt 1941–1945*, 509–511.

Deportations Further East

During the years when there were no letters from Vienna, many more family members disappeared into the East. I had never heard of any of them before beginning this project.

Helene Wilheim and Charlotte (Née Wilheim) Schneider— Deportation to Lodz

The Haims' and Kurzes' extended circles in Vienna included two of Mathilde's younger sisters, Paul and Olga's aunts Helene Wilheim and Charlotte (née Wilheim) Schneider. Their situation seemed stable for the first war years. In a letter dated April 29, 1940, Paula sent Walter Helene Wilheim's address, Leichtensteinstrasse 38 in the 9th District. In March 1941 Paula reported that Helene, along with her sister Charlotte and Charlotte's husband, Karl Schneider, had visited them the previous evening.

Then it all ended. On October 23, 1941, two and a half weeks after Antoinette's last postcard to Walter, Helene, Charlotte, and Karl were deported from Vienna on transport no. 8, Train Da 9, to Lodz ghetto in Poland.[342] The Schneiders' last address in Vienna was recorded as Grünentorgasse 10 in the 9th District, only six house numbers away from the former Landsmann-Neuhaus family apartment.

Some records survive from the chaotic and overcrowded conditions in the Lodz ghetto. Helene, Charlotte, and Karl lived together, initially at Reiter Strasse 11, flat 8, later at Alexanderhof Strasse 28. Perhaps Helene and Charlotte were able to keep up some correspondence with the remaining family in Vienna or receive parcels from them, but again there is no way to know. Eight months after being deported, on June 28, 1942, Karl died in the Lodz ghetto hospital. The cause of death was officially recorded as malnutrition, the acceptable medical euphemism for starvation. Six weeks later, on September 9, Paul's aunts Charlotte and Helene were "relocated,"

---

342 "Transport 42, Train Da 519," Yad Vashem.

a Nazi usage, from Lodz. They were taken about fifty miles west to Chelmno, an extermination camp, where they were murdered, probably in mobile gas vans. Helene was sixty years old, Charlotte sixty-six.

While Charlotte and Karl Schneider were prisoners in the Lodz ghetto, their daughter Else (Paul and Olga's cousin), their son-in-law Felix Preis, and their two young grandchildren, Eva and Peter Preis, were deported in August 1942 from Vienna to Theresienstadt. After nearly two years there, in May 1944, the Preis family were all transported from Theresienstadt to Auschwitz. None survived.

Caecilie (Nee) Kurz Vielgut—Deportation to Maly Trostinets

Mathilde Kurz's sister-in-law Caecilie (Tante Cilli, née Kurz) Vielgut, one of Ignaz Kurz's two sisters, thus another of Paul and Olga's aunts, was also an outer member of the Haim family circle. In April 1940 Martin included greetings from "Mrs. Vielgut" in his letter. Tante Cilli was deported from Vienna on August 17, 1942, to Maly Trostinets, near Minsk in what is now Belarus. Unlike Lodz or Theresienstadt, Maly Trostinets was not a ghetto or transit camp; it was an extermination camp. Four days after leaving Vienna, on August 21, Caecilie was murdered at Maly Trostinets. She was sixty-four years old.

Endless Insecurity

After the large-scale deportations ended in the fall of 1942, threats to the Jews remaining in Vienna continued. The fact that Paula and Hans were employed by the IKG and its successor Council of Elders would have shielded them at times against deportation, but this was not reliable. Martha Müller and the IKG's leadership were all deported to Theresienstadt. Protection for Jews who were married to "Germans," like Hans and Malvine, depended on both parties remaining alive and the marriage continuing intact. Even then, it was subject to changeable official policies. In January 1945, while German forces were being pushed back on two fronts, Berlin issued orders to deport to Theresienstadt all Jewish partners in "mixed" marriages and people who were "considered" Jews. In Vienna a transport for these groups was planned for the end of February 1945. Local Nazi authorities canceled it at the last moment as the Red Army drew closer to Vienna.[343]

---

343 Hecht, Raggam-Blesch, and Uhl, *Letzte Orte*, 168–169.

CHAPTER 21

The End of the War in Vienna

Surviving letters from the Haim family in Vienna resume only in late 1946, over a year after the war had ended, and they do not look back to the end of the fighting. What does exist are two firsthand accounts from the Neuhaus side of the family about the last days of the war. Coincidentally, both of these snapshot narratives focus on the northwestern area of Ottakring (16th District), a primarily working-class outer suburb of Vienna that includes the Sandleiten public housing complex.

Heroism at Sandleiten

Sandleiten is not as well known to visitors as its contemporary housing project, the more memorably named Karl Marx Hof. Both were built in the 1920s, during the "Red Vienna" period, to help ease the city's perpetual shortage of housing for workers and their families. Like Karl Marx Hof, Sandleiten's buildings were modern and practical. Various segments were designed by architects who had been students of Otto Wagner, a leading figure of the Austrian art nouveau style. Sandleiten was a massive facility, encompassing over 1,500 apartments that originally housed about 5,000 people. As a planned socialist community, Sandleiten was designed to include all imaginable services: "baths, kindergartens, laundry rooms, maternity advice centers, outpatient clinics, tuberculosis centers, gyms, libraries," and more.[344] Sandleiten's political origins are reflected in the surrounding streets, which were named for international Socialist martyrs, Rosa Luxemburg being the most widely known.[345]

Archway entrance to Sandleiten from Nietzscheplatz, 2023.[346]

Sandleiten twice escaped the destruction that marked many parts of Vienna.[347] During the short Austrian civil war in February

---

344 "Wohnhausanlage Sandleiten," Stadt Wien, accessed March 2023, https://www.wienerwohnen.at/hof/193/Wohnhausanlage-Sandleiten.html.

345 "Sandleitenhof," Wikipedia.de, accessed January 24, 2022, https://de.wikipedia.org/wiki/Sandleitenhof.

346 "Sandleitenhof," Wikipedia.de, accessed January 24, 2022, https://second.wiki/wiki/sandleitenhof.

347 "Wohnhausanlage Sandleiten," Wine Geschichte Wiki, accessed July 2023, https://www.geschichtewiki.wien.gv.at/Sandleiten_(Wohnhausanlage).

1934, police and military units occupied Sandleiten after an initial skirmish that inflicted only minimal damage.[348] A decade later, the complex sustained some damage from Allied air raids in January 1945 but continued to be inhabited.

The Red Army Approaches

Vienna had been a target of concerted Allied air raids since the beginning of 1945. At midday on March 12, an Allied air raid destroyed the opera and the vestry of St. Stephen's Cathedral. It also damaged major city icons along the Ring—the art museum, the imperial stables, the Spanish riding school, the Academy of Fine Arts, the stock exchange, and part of the Hofburg (the imperial palace), including the balcony where Hitler had addressed ecstatic crowds in March 1938.[349]

On March 30, 1945, which happened to be Good Friday, the Red Army reached the Hungarian border at Burgenland, less than fifty miles southeast of Vienna. The next day, April 1, the war closed in on Vienna, and residents prepared for a siege. An American historian described the situation:

> Allied air attacks on railroad yards, bridges over the Danube, and important intersections caused fires to spring up in so many places that the overworked fire brigades could not begin to cope with them. The Viennese took beds into their cellars or shelters, and began to live underground. Traffic could not move through the rubble-filled streets; the city railroad service was discontinued and streetcars ran on few routes. Gas and electricity were available only a few hours a day, and in many districts there was no water.[350]

---

348 "Sandleiten," Weblexikon der Wiener Sozialdemokratie, accessed September 12, 2022, http://www.dasrotewien.at/seite/sandleiten.

349 Thomas Weyr, *The Setting of the Pearl: Vienna under Hitler* (Oxford, UK: Oxford University Press, 2005), 270.

350 John Toland, *The Last 100 Days: The Tumultuous and Controversial Story of the Final Days of World War II in Europe* (New York: Random House, 1965), 340.

This local chaos was a prelude to anticipated annihilation. Nazi Gauleiter Baldur von Schirach ordered Vienna, like Budapest before it, to be treated as a "Festung," a fortress to be defended to the last man and bullet, and he forbade any surrender or retreat.[351]

As this was happening, nascent Austrian resistance groups, collectively known as "O-5," made contact with the approaching Red Army. They offered to assist the Russians, asking in return for an end to Allied bombing and Vienna's being treated as an open city. (Neither of these requests was met.) The O-5 representative offered a tactical plan. Instead of approaching the city from the east, where Nazi defenders anticipated the Soviet assault, the Red Army should "march straight through the Vienna Woods at Baden, then turn and enter the capital from the west"—in effect, arriving unexpectedly through the back door.[352] The Soviets agreed, and the Red Army advanced towards Vienna from the west.

The city's northwestern working-class districts, including the 18th, had suffered some damage from Allied bombs, but they surrendered relatively peacefully to the Russian conquerors. They thus escaped the street-to-street and house-to-house fighting between the advancing Red Army and retreating Wehrmacht that destroyed much of the 2nd District and Inner City.

Heroism at Sandleiten—"Vienna Must Not Become Another Budapest!"

Helene (Helli) Arent, the future wife of Lilly's cousin Walter Neuhaus, was a member of an underground Communist youth resistance group known as Kommunistischen Jungendverband (KJV) 44. In April 1945 Helli and her comrades' bravery and quick thinking helped to save the lives of residents of the Ottakring district and avoid further destruction of the area as the war finally drew to a close.

---

[351] Toland, *The Last 100 Days*, 340.

[352] Toland, *The Last 100 Days*, 340–342.

Helli's KJV group learned in early April from a contact in the O-5 resistance that the Red Army would be approaching the city from the northwest, not from the southeast where they had crossed the Hungarian border. The unarmed young people stationed themselves near the cinema at Sandleiten. This was a key crossroad for intercepting the retreating German forces because "everyone who came into town had to pass there." The retreating soldiers were a mixture of regular Wehrmacht troops and motley Volkssturm (home guard), the latter mainly old men and teenagers. Helli and her group's idealistic mission was to try to persuade them not to fight any longer, to drop their weapons and go home. "In the beginning it was difficult," Helli told an interviewer in 2015. "We didn't have rifles, but the soldiers did." Moreover, the Nazi government had ordered that anyone who behaved "disreputably," that is, who was "defeatist" or refused to fight to the end, should be shot summarily.[353]

Looking back after seventy years, Helli recalled her group's inspiration: "Vienna must not become a second Budapest."[354] In the spring of 1945, the siege and destruction of Budapest was a recent cautionary tale. For fifty days, from late December 1944 through February 13, 1945, the Red Army and its allied Romanian forces had encircled and besieged Budapest. Occupying Nazi defenders followed orders to hold "Fortress Budapest" to the end. An estimated 80 percent of Budapest's buildings were destroyed during the siege and 38,000 civilians died, 25,000 of them from starvation.[355] Helli recounted the horrors of the end of the war in Budapest, "People couldn't leave their cellars for ten days. Many, especially children and the elderly, starved to death or died of thirst." The prospect of a second useless siege in Vienna motivated Helli and her comrades; there was nothing left to lose. In Helli's words, "You choose the

---

353 Alexander Maurer, "Schmeißt die Waffen hin, geht's z'haus," Wiener Zeitung Online, last modified October 29, 2015, https://www.wienerzeitung.at/nachrichten/chronik/wien/781816-Schmeisst-die-Waffen-hin-gehts-zhaus.html.

354 Maurer, "Schmeißt die Waffen hin."

355 "Siege of Budapest," Wikipedia, accessed January 25, 2022, https://en.wikipedia.org/wiki/Siege_of_Budapest#Impact_on_civilians, citing Krisztian Ungvary, Ladislaus Lob, and John Lukacs, *The Battle For Budapest: One Hundred Days in World War II* (London: I. B. Tauris, 2005), 512.

lesser of two evils. When faced with the choice between being killed by bombs or shot by soldiers, you at least try to do something to end the fighting."

In 2015 Helli told the story to a newspaper interviewer:

The campaign went really well at the beginning. "Maybe we were also lucky that the first soldiers who streamed back were Viennese and Austrians. Of course, they didn't have far to go home and handed in their weapons, even machine guns....We piled up a mountain of weapons in front of the Sandleiten cinema in less than half an hour."

The soldiers who hesitated were afraid of being shot as traitors if they were found without a weapon but in uniform:

"That's when the idea hit us that we should break into a [neighboring] clothing warehouse,"...The "textile collection points" were clothing stashes belonging to the National Socialist Welfare Association. There was one across from the Sandleiten cinema.

"We said: 'Get yourself civilian clothes, but give up the guns.' That was much easier for the soldiers. We succeeded so well that Ottakring and Hernals [the neighboring district] fell without a fight. The fierce fighting only started again at the Gürtel [the outer ring road around Vienna], where the SS had withdrawn."[356]

In 2015 the City of Vienna erected a memorial at the Sandleiten housing complex commemorating the "nonviolent liberation" of this portion of the city. It consists of a bench and plaque fitted with a port where interested passersby can plug in headphones and listen to a recording of local middle school students interviewing two "contemporary witnesses," one of them Helene Neuhaus, about their

---

356 Maurer, "Schmeißt die Waffen hin."

roles in the liberation of the Ottakring district from Nazi rule.[357] Helli attended the memorial's dedication, then a white-haired lady in a wheelchair.

"Hitlerism Is Finally Dead!"

While Helli and her resistance group were disarming retreating soldiers, another Neuhaus connection was living in the 16th District and kept a journal account of the last days of the war. As the conflict finally came to an end, he witnessed surrender flags flying at Sandleiten and the entry of Soviet troops into Vienna's outer suburbs.

Robert Kolb was the husband of Julia "Julla" Neuhaus, the oldest child of Arthur Neuhaus's older brother Rudolf. Robert remained in Vienna during the war while Julla and their young son Hannes were in "semi-hiding" in the country. All of Julla's family were in exile because of their political affiliations and "racial" background: Julla's parents Rudolf and Minna Neuhaus (Social Democrats) first in Sweden then in Mexico City, her younger sister Friedl (described to me as a "fierce Trotskyite") in Sweden then Southern California, and her brother Walter (a committed young Communist) in Sweden.

Robert and Julla's younger son, Roberto Kolb-Neuhaus, who now has his father's diaries, summarized the political, social, and "racial" situation of his parents during the war. His father Robert was considered "German" under the Nazi "racial" laws and his mother Julla a person of mixed "race," with two Jewish grandparents and two "German" ones, though within Rudolf Neuhaus's family, identity was defined by political affiliation, not religion. Roberto recounted about his parents:

> My father [Robert Kolb] was trained as a pianist and school teacher. He had a job as a public school teacher at the time

---

357 Maurer, "Schmeißt die Waffen hin."

of the annexation. Due to the fact that he was married to a Mischling [Nazi term for a person of mixed "race"], he immediately lost his job. I don't know if they attempted to leave the country and couldn't or if they didn't attempt. Or if it was at some point too late to try. Part of the time, it was my mother [Julla] who provided the food by teaching English to Jewish people.[358] She was not as politically active as her brother and sister. She grew up, like all of them, in the Socialist Youth....

At some point during the occupation [that is, after the German annexation of Austria], my father got a third [academic] degree, this time as an electrical engineer. And he got a job in a car workshop in which they converted cars from gasoline to wood as a source of power. It was apparently owned by a German. After the war a Russian took over.

In '43, my mother went into semi-hiding in a little village (Schmelz) to protect herself and her baby son from the bombs. Robert stayed in Vienna, working. On the weekends, when possible, he would walk to Schmelz and on the way help farmers by fixing their machines in exchange for food that he then brought to my mother.[359]

Allied air raids, artillery fire, machine guns, flak, and tanks were

---

358 This is a coincidental parallel to Alice Haim, many if not all of whose students were hopeful intending emigrants, including her own parents and the Neuhauses, Walter's in-laws.

  Shortly before the war, the saying "Are you Aryan, or are you learning English?" became common among middle-class Jewish families in Pressburg (now Bratislava, Slovakia). This captures the centrality of learning English for those hoping to escape from the Fascist states. (Josef Tancer, "Lichtblicke im Dasein." Kommunikationsstrategien und Spracheflexion in den Holocaust-Briefen der Bratislaver Familie Sachsel, in Gabriela Dudeková, Daniela Kodajová [eds.]: V supermarkete dejín: podoby moderných dejín a spoločnosti v stredoeurópskom priestore. Pocta Elene Mannovej [Bratislava, 2021], 479, 493.)

  Forty years earlier, the connotations of learning English had been quite different. The protagonist in one of Stefan Zweig's novellas, a young German coming of age well before the twentieth century's wars, chose to study English at the university because it was "the language of the sea." (Stefan Zweig, "Confusion," in *The Collected Novellas of Stefan Zweig* [Pushkin Press, London 2021], 231.)

359 Roberto Kolb-Neuhaus, email to author, July 24, 2020.

daily realities in the 16th District where Robert Kolb lived. Here is what he recorded about the final days of the war:

Sunday, April 1, 1945

We are all terribly impatient and torn up. The sun shines over our quiet neighborhood and after a good night we gather together and all begin—tie up flowers, clean, cook—then suddenly: crash! New strike very close! And already there is the hellish noise from rolling wheels.…The bullets whistle and above all that, the arcing front fighter planes drone.—We are cut off from the surroundings. There is no radio because of lack of power. Our only news is what we see: and what do we see?

In the morning I discovered a red flag on Sandleiten and next to that a lot of small white cloths in the windows. In the afternoon a white flag was raised over the Jubiläumswarte [a lookout tower in Vienna's 16th District dating back to 1889]!

How will we find out about the end?

Since yesterday evening our flak hasn't been shooting any more.

The large Luftwaffe camp at Georgenberg is burnt away. Stragglers are seen in the streets. They have had enough. We've heard that the officers chase the troops forward with pistols!

Civilians could readily fashion ad hoc white surrender flags from sheets, and Nazi banners could be repurposed as red flags. One diarist recorded what she saw on April 9 outside the cellar in Vienna where she had been hiding during the siege. She emerged when she heard someone call, "Ivan is here":

We walked down the street. A Russian soldier stood outside the house next door surrounded by laughing, gesticulating people. Russians stood on the corners. All the houses had white and red flags on them. On some you could see the circle where the swastika had been cut out.[360]

Eight days after Robert Kolb saw the impromptu flags at Sandleiten, the Red Army was right there in his neighborhood. He went outside to meet them:

Monday, April 9, 1945

Today towards 10 a.m. 3 Russian soldiers in fur caps promenaded through Hasner Street [a main street in Ottakring]. During the night the German occupation disappeared, leaving behind, among other things, a loaded truck which was immediately plundered by the crowd.

Later, I was right on the street just as [Soviet] officers with maps came and called to me and asked about the route. With some difficulties, I was able to give information about how to get to the city center from Mauer [a village bordering the Vienna woods]. The officer pressed my hand, and generally one had the impression of these Red soldiers' great courage. Their equipment is simple but solid. They gave baked goods to children, but they would not take anything for themselves. A heavy nightmare for a lot of us. Artillery passed by. Everything in the direction of Mauer. The women breathed more easily. What rumors had gone around.

Those rumors weren't merely German propaganda. After the fall of Budapest, Red Army soldiers engaged in uncontrolled looting and mass rape, and the same was reasonably anticipated in Vienna.[361]

---

360 Weyr, *The Setting of the Pearl*, 282.

361 See, e.g., "Vienna Offensive," Wikipedia, accessed January 25, 2022, https://en.wikipedia.org/wiki/Vienna_Offensive, citing Peter Gosztony, *Endkampf an der Donau 1944/45* (Wien: Molden Taschenbuch, 1978), 263.

Robert Kolb continued his observations of the Soviets' arrival at Vienna. The date, April 9, was a significant anniversary. On April 9, 1938, the new Nazi government had held a referendum in which 99.7 percent of eligible voters (Jews were barred from voting) cast ballots affirming the fait accompli of Austria's absorption into Nazi Germany.[362] Seven years later, it was finally over:

> April 9
>
> This is the same day that the referendum took place in Vienna 7 years ago! What a difference and what serious consequences of this day! For us this terrible war is over. The guns only rumble from afar, only occasional machine gun fire. No tanks facing us. We can sleep peacefully again and don't have to fear aircraft—we can begin!
>
> Now let's begin to build our life! Hitlerism is finally dead!

Postwar Chaos and Privation

Vienna remained chaotic after the fighting stopped. Soviet battle forces moved westward towards Germany proper and were replaced by less disciplined troops. There was no civil order, and civilians had to scramble for the very limited food and water. Toland summarized the Hobbesian aftermath:

> The streets were littered with burned-out tanks and dead horses; thousands of dead Germans, Viennese and Russians lay side by side. Sick and wounded were trundled to emergency hospitals in baby carriages and wheelbarrows. Apartment buildings and

---

362 Eric D. Weitz, *Weimar Germany: Promise and Tragedy* (New Haven, NJ: Princeton University Press, 2013), 75. This referendum in April 1938 must be distinguished from the referendum that had been scheduled for March 13 on maintaining Austria's independence. The latter was cancelled after Chancellor Schuschnigg resigned and ordered the Austrian military not to resist Germany's armed takeover of Austria. See above, Part I, Chapter 3, Some History: The End of Austria

homes were barricaded to keep away Russians, liberated slave laborers and Viennese—all bent on loot and rape....

Though the reservoirs were intact, water pipes all over the city had been destroyed by bombs and shells, and people stood for hours at the few springs still flowing. The food problem was even worse. Those storage houses not destroyed had been plundered by civilians. Almost nothing was available; ration cards were useless, and a barter system flourished.

On April 12 St. Stephen's Cathedral, Vienna's most recognizable symbol, was set on fire (probably unintentionally, though some blamed the Soviets) and burned for two days. Its roof was destroyed along with the bell towers and their bells, the organ, Gothic choir stalls, statuary, and even a monument to the liberation from the Turkish siege of 1683.[363]

The toll of the battle for Vienna is estimated at three thousand civilians and thirty-seven thousand soldiers dead.[364] No one counted the injured. As Toland noted, the streets were ruled by the "law of club and fist."[365]

Thomas Weyr, in his history of Vienna under Nazi rule, gave a similar picture of the first chaotic weeks after the Russian victory:

Law and order was a distant dream. With no police on the streets, looting and crime continued. Men claimed authority based on nothing more than a red-white-red armband [the Austrian national colors]. The streets were unsafe during daylight, and after the 8 p.m. curfew they were unsafer still. Some 12,000 corpses lay on the streets. Many were buried in

---

363 Christian Fürst, "Schlacht um Wien brachte Tod und Zestorung," *Frankfurter Rundschau*, April 13, 2005, https://www.fr.de/politik/schlacht-wien-brachte-zerstoerung-11731852.html. See also https://www.visitingvienna.com/sights/stefansdom/.

364 Fürst, "Schlacht um Wien."

365 Toland, *The Last 100 Days*, 354–355, quoting a local politician.

parks or private gardens, others left on the pavement. Phones and telegraphs did not work.[366]

There are no Haim family letters from those first few months, but here is what one woman in Vienna described (after cataloguing relatives who had not survived) in a letter dated August 4, 1945, that she sent to family in the United States:

> As for us, we've had a terrible time of it ever since the Russians arrived. There is a great famine. There aren't even any potatoes. For months now, we've had no vegetables, fruit, milk, eggs, cooking fat, meat: in short, we've had nothing. Our rations consist of ½ kilo of bread per day, ½ kilo of dried peas and ½ liter of oil per month....
>
> It was awful. First the monstrous bombing and then the terrible plundering and rapes by the Russians....Whether we will survive the winter is still very questionable. All the windows are broken, no heating fuel, no gas.[367]

By February 1946 when Austrian writer and journalist Hilde Spiel returned to Vienna as a British press correspondent, even old Slavophiles who had hailed the Red Army as "our saviors, our liberators," had come to hate them. A painter Spiel had known before the war described the "disenchantment":

> The screams and cries for help from the cellars, the incessant shooting, heard even more loudly at night from the other side of the Danube, where warehouses were being looted, women hunted down, men [stripped] naked and robbed.[368]

---

366 Weyr, *The Setting of the Pearl*, 286.

367 Quoted in Jürgen Matthäus, Leah Anne Wolfson, and Mark Roseman, *Jewish Responses to Persecution 1944–1946: Documenting Life and Destruction: Holocaust Sources in Context* (New York: Rowman & Littlefield, 2015), 247–248.

368 Spiel, *Return to Vienna*, 74.

CHAPTER 22

Survivors in Vienna

Signs of Life and the *Aufbau*

In the spring of 1945, as parts of Greater Germany and occupied lands fell to the Allies, the *Aufbau* began publishing lists of Jews who had survived in various cities, including Vienna. Under the heading "The First Sign of Life" (Das erste Lebenszeichen), the *Aufbau*'s edition of Friday, May 25, 1945,[369] printed a short list that it had received from the World Jewish Congress in Geneva of Jews who had registered their residence in Vienna as of November 1944. The list included "Antonie Haim" (on a roster of persons recently cared for at the hospital at Malzgasse) and a "Paul Kurtz" (a resident or employee of the old age home at Malzgasse 7). This was an early flicker of life, though not entirely reliable, as the information was already six months old when the *Aufbau* printed it. Nearly a year later, on May 17, 1946, the *Aufbau* published a far longer list (half a page) of "Juden in Wien" (Jews in Vienna) that also included "Antonie Haim" (although she had died in January of that year) and Johann Haim.[370] Walter cut out and saved these lists.

While survivors in post-war Vienna struggled for dried peas, stunted potatoes, and scraps of coal, former Viennese who had had the good fortune to reach America were reasonably housed and fed, though many still needed to be frugal. The *Aufbau*'s advertisements offer an unintended

---

369 "Das erste Lebenszeichen," *Aufbau*, May 25, 1945, http://www.archive.org/stream/aufbau111945germ #page/n339/mode/1up.

370 The following month, on June 7, 1946, Paula Kurz's name appeared on another list of Vienna survivors.

time capsule. The *Aufbau*'s page from May 1945 containing the first list of surviving Jews in Vienna was filled with ads aimed at immigrants who were making their way in New York. Advertisers touted upholstered furniture, both new and refurbished, related services like furniture polishing and repairs, and carpet cleaning. Dealers offered to buy and sell porcelain figures, with one ad specifically mentioning Meissen groups and individual figurines. Some ads proclaimed that the buyers paid the "highest cash price" for antique jewelry, Leica and Rolleiflex cameras, and antiquities of all sorts. The Cross Stamp Co. (an Anglo name) on Fifth Avenue offered, in German, to buy and sell stamp collections, as did at least two other ads. Jack's Furniture Co. on Broadway advertised "modern furniture" for readers who had achieved a status that entitled them to furnish their own apartments. The ad pictured bedroom sets with two beds (evidence that the fashion for twin beds began before the more inhibited 1950s), as well as sofas, club chairs, and coffee and end tables.

Law professor Monroe Price, who emigrated from Vienna as an infant with his parents, started the chapter of his memoirs titled "New York City" with an informal paean to the *Aufbau*. He called it "the source for information about refugee life, refugee aspirations, news about the missing, news about reparations, news about Austria," a representation of "civilized Jewish Europe transplanted to New York." He recalled that "the *Aufbau* could be purchased at every newsstand on the Upper West Side" and was a "fixture of coffee houses on Seventy-Second Street,"[371] like the Eclair Bakery. The Eclair is a firsthand memory for me. Only a couple of blocks south of my grandmother's store on Broadway, the family would buy Danish pastries and rainbow cookies at the Éclair for special occasions.

War in Europe officially ended in May 1945, when the *Aufbau*'s first Lebenszeichen list appeared, but international correspondence remained impossible for months. On September 1 Paula and Antoinette sent letters to Paul, which he forwarded from Melbourne to Walter in New York. They arrived in October according to Paul's later letter, but I have not located them, and they likely no longer exist. Most improbably, the two women were alive. So was Walter's

---

371 Price, *Objects of Remembrance*, 55–57.

brother, Hans. They had survived seven years of the Nazi regime, six years of war, more than three years without mail to or from Walter and Paul, the mass deportations of Jews from Vienna during the summer and fall of 1942, months of air raids, the Red Army's conquest of the city, and post-battle chaos.

The earliest postwar letters from Vienna that I have found date from early 1946. They are from Paula and Hans, two from their aunt Malvine, and one from Hansi Dockerl, Paula and Alice's friend and a fellow English teacher. Walter put them in a folder that he labeled "Paula." This is the only separate group of letters; the others were all kept unsorted in the red manila folders.

Photos "For Walter"

Photo of Paula sent to Walter dated December 1945.

Amid Vienna's disorder and privations, photographers remained in business. At the end of 1945, Antoinette and Paula had photos taken of themselves and sent them to Walter as signs of life. The picture of Paula is inscribed on the back: "For Walter, December 1945." She looks exhausted and haunted, focused on some middle distance, her hair gone half gray. Still she managed to wear what looks like a tailored jacket over a white-collared blouse with an onyx and silver pin (that I now have) at the collar.

There is a companion photo of Antoinette, also inscribed "For Walter! December 1945." She appears tired but firm, sitting up in a bed with a pillow behind her back, wearing a sweater and headscarf, with a tea kettle on the table next to her, all suggesting that the room was

Photo of Antoinette sent to Walter dated December 1945.

not well heated. This could have been taken in the apartment at Zeltgasse 1, Paula and Antoinette's official address at the time. I haven't found any letter that would have accompanied these photos, so there is no written voice to help elucidate the images.

Antoinette

Antoinette died the month after the photo was taken, on January 15, 1946, in the Lainz Hospital, out in the 13th District near the Vienna Woods. She was buried in the Vienna Central Cemetery with her husband and daughter Alice. She was seventy-eight years old. The first seventy years of her life remain shadowy for me since no earlier letters and very few stories about her survive. The final seven years were unimaginably hard and marked by a succession of losses, but her voice in the letters always remained clear and purposeful, filled with realism, balance, and tempered optimism. She was a hospitable, centripetal center, maintaining ties with closer and more extended family even as they dispersed throughout Europe and beyond to Asia and the Americas.

Looking back in January 1947, Hans wrote about their mother:

So it is a year since Mama's death and so I will go and visit her in the Sephardic section [of the Vienna Central Cemetery]. About Mama's departure I still cannot be comforted. The thought still oppresses me that she was not allowed to enjoy some years of happiness and quiet without fear.

That fear is something that Antoinette never allowed to appear in her letters.

At the end of 1947, Hans wrote again about their mother, offering a glimpse of their closeness during the war years:

I can't tell you how much Mama is still missed by me daily. Every day I had something to discuss with her. The Hitler years brought and drove us so much together; I was at her house several times a day.

Letters from Vienna Resume

The extant letters from Vienna resume in December 1946. By then, Olga had returned to Vienna from London, and she and Paula were sharing an apartment. With no parents left to look after, Paula was focused on traveling to Paul in Australia.

Life in Vienna remained difficult, with endless shortages of food, clothing, and other consumer goods. Austria suffered from record cold winters in 1945 and 1946, and Paula's and Hans's letters consistently discuss machinations to obtain coal or other fuel. Vienna (like Berlin) was subject to a four-power military occupation, though neither Paula nor Hans mentioned it directly. This was the Vienna of *The Third Man*, the dark, expressionistic film written by Graham Greene and starring the still young Orson Welles. It immortalized what a Viennese film reviewer called the defeated city's "insecurity, poverty, and post-war immorality."[372]

A recurring theme in Paula's letters is how difficult writing was for her. For example, Paula wrote on December 15, 1946, in the earliest postwar letter in Walter's folder:

> Yes, it has really already been months that I have not written any letter to you [pl.]. There is no excuse for that and if I tell you [pl.] that I think of you daily and really in closest love, so that is first true and second still a cruel disgrace for me, despite not writing.
>
> Also for your [sing.] really dear and well-meant telegram, I have not thanked you until today but it is taken to heart. Writing is so difficult for me.

---

372 This description is from a review of the film published in Vienna's *Arbeiter Zeitung* (Worker's Journal) on March 12, 1950, accessed September 23, 2022, https://web.archive.org/web/20130617113752/

Hans and Lisl

Paula brought Walter up to date about Hans's health and general situation. All in all, Hans was doing well under the circumstances:

> You would still recognize him [Hans], but he has become very old and sometimes looks curiously like Uncle Julius.[373] Life is quite hard.

Paula captured Hans's characteristic stubbornness. He dealt with his doctor's recommendation to stop smoking by ceasing to see the doctor.

The saved letters from Hans also resume in December 1946. Surprisingly, Hans typed them, possibly taking advantage of a typewriter in the IKG offices for his personal correspondence. (Jews had been ordered to surrender their typewriters to the Gestapo five years earlier, in November 1941, along with other relics of former middle-class lives such as adding machines and cameras.[374])

At around this time, Hans and Lisl also sent studio photos of themselves to Walter, though they are not dated. The pair look distinguished, both well dressed and coiffed. Hans has something of a smile, while Lisl seems focused inward, with worry lines between her eyebrows.

Lisl, whom I met when she was an old lady, must have been a charmer when she was young. A photo from 1918 shows Lisl with huge dark eyes and bobbed hair, looking over her shoulder with an alluring smile. The caption on the back reads, "As a reminder of your Lisl, who loves you very much. Vienna, February 1918."

Unlike ever-prickly Malvine, Paula accepted the relationship as it was with her sister-in-law Lisl, commenting that during the past thirty years Hans and Lisl had each "polished" the rough edges off the other so that they lived together smoothly. Paula gave Lisl credit for having

---

373 Julius Feder was Antoinette's only brother. Like Paul he had the university title "Ingineur," and made a career with the Vienna suburban and regional railroads. One week after the war began, Julius and his wife Paula Feder committed suicide, gassing themselves in their apartment. The Haim parents and Paula successfully hid this news from Walter for nearly a near, until Tante Helene inadvertently disclosed it in a letter from Manila.

374 Hecht, Raggam-Blesch, and Uhl, *Letzte Orte*, 255; Rabinovici, *Eichmann's Jews*, 115.

stuck with Hans during the Nazi years despite the unrelenting pressure on her as a "German"[375]:

> Lisl looks relatively good, despite that she has become much much more slender. I get along with both very well....During the Hitler times she always conducted herself in a first-class manner towards him and always held 100% with the Jews. So far things are going quite well for them. They have food and a quite nice apartment; he does not have strenuous work and no boss.

Hans and Lisl, about 1945–46.

---

375 The Nazi "racial" laws characterized the marriage between a "German" or "Aryan" woman and a Jewish husband with no children from the marriage, like Lisl and Hans's situation, as a "non-privileged" mixed marriage. In addition to leaving their former apartment on Salmgasse for a communal apartment in the 2nd District, Lisl would have been forced to "subsist on reduced rations and shop during restricted hours." Once the war began, both Hans and Lisl would also have been required to abide by an eight o'clock curfew, while Lisl would regularly have been "urged to file [divorce] papers in order to rejoin 'the community of German blood'" (Bukey, *Jews and Intermarriage*, 30–32, 94).

Still, even a "non-privileged" mixed marriage provided most Jewish spouses with an incalculable advantage in terms of survival because they were not subject to deportation. Bukey estimates that "85 to 87 percent of intermarried Jews living in Vienna survived Nazi rule" (Bukey, *Jews and Intermarriage*, 22). This statistic seems surprisingly high, though specific instances in the extended family support it. Hans and Lisl Haim and Otto and Malvine Jahn (a "German" man married to a Jewish wife with no children from the marriage) all survived in Vienna. So did Rudolf Neuhaus's daughter Julla, considered a "half Jew," who was married to Robert Kolb, a "German." In contrast, Jewish widows, like Paul's mother Mathilde Kurz and Lilly's grandmother Regine Landsmann, Jewish married couples like Martin's cousin Adolf and Regina de Majo (who returned to Vienna in 1941 when they could no longer remain in Italy), and numerous Feder, Wilheim, and Kurz aunts and their families, were deported from Vienna in 1942 and did not survive.

Lisl, 1918.

Hans's self-consciously upright character remained intact. Throughout the years of postwar food, fuel, and clothing shortages, he generally disdained resorting to the black market. Sometimes, however, the black market could not be avoided. Paula wrote that during the winter of 1946–47, she and Hans had been cheated out of five hundred schillings by a "black market coal dealer" who subsequently went bankrupt.

Descriptions of Vienna's ubiquitous black market made good reading for Allied occupiers. A newspaper for American military personnel called *Yank* reported about the black market on October 5, 1945, in a story titled "This Is Vienna":

> In the Karlsplatz near the Opera House there is a bustling black market. Every day several thousand Viennese can be seen milling about the big square, offering their personal possessions for sale to Russian soldiers and Russian Wacs. The market is illegal, but local Austrian police and Red Army MPs seem to look the other way.
>
> Any article small enough to be carried in the pocket or a shopping bag is likely to change hands.

Yank also detailed the dire food shortages: "Full daily rations for a worker are 10 ½ ounces of bread, 1 ¼ ounces of meat, ¼ ounce of cooking oil, 2 ounces of beans and 1 ounce of sugar. Non-workers get even less."

Years of privation were visible in the population. The *Yank* article goes on:

> The Viennese have been undernourished for years, and they look it. Now they are close to starvation....The schools have been shut for at least a month because of malnutrition and disease among the pupils. Viennese get an average of 900 calories contrasted with the 2,000 required daily for health.... Added to the shortage of food and transport is a lack of coal, which also means no cooking gas.[376]

Early in 1947 Paula wrote that Hans's heart condition, a Haim family affliction, was "not so bad." This was a comforting overestimation. Hans continued to smoke and suffered from chronic angina; any sort of exertion had become a problem. Half a year later, in July 1947, Hans reported to Walter on his own medical status, typically making light of the cardiac symptoms:

> What my cadaver is doing is already too boring for me to write about and would not give you any peace. I really feel very well if I don't have to walk. The angina cramps are very seldom, never at night, mostly only before going to sleep. For weeks now they [the angina cramps] have been afraid of me and have not come!

A year after this letter, on July 26, 1948, Hans suffered a fatal heart attack on Augustinergasse in the 1st District while returning home from work. Hans was only fifty-nine.

---

376 Cpl. Ira H. Freeman, "GIs are Popular with Civilians, but the Capital of Austria Is a Far Cry Today from Its Storied Past of Gaiety, Love and Song," *Yank: The Army Weekly* 4, no. 15 (September 28, 1945), 7, accessed September 14, 2022, http://www.ibiblio.org/hyperwar/NHC/NewPDFs/USArmy/Yank%20Magazine/Yank%20Vol.%204%20no.%2015%201945-09-28.pdf.

Winter 1946–1947—"Life Is Very Hard at Present"

In December 1946 Haim family friend Hansi Dockerl wrote a letter (laden with exclamation marks) in English to Lilly recounting their situation in Vienna during the second postwar winter: bare survival amid perpetual food and fuel shortages. Hansi, who lived near the former Kurz apartment on Novaragasse, was still tutoring English pupils. She wrote more candidly than Paula or Hans about daily living conditions, though always reminding herself to maintain perspective as other people had it far worse:

> As I see by it [Lilly's letter], you live a quiet, pleasant life although you have also to work rather much. But you have all the conveniences that we know only from hearsay now—life is very hard at present and we all here are rather afraid of this winter, much more than we were a year ago. We have no fuel! I heat my second room, that one where I give lessons, by an oilstove! The first room, which I have to cross when I am answering the bell, is not heated and so I always run the risk to catch a severe cold—which is a great danger now when we are underfed and have no warm room and no nurse! But I will not complain, for I know I shall get over this winter and there are other people who are all worse than I am. They have not such good friends in New York as I have who send them parcels as you do!!!

Hansi described to Lilly how conditions had deteriorated although the war had been over for a year and a half:

> How difficult life is now. Worse than a year ago! We have not electric light till 6, yesterday till 8 o'clock p.m.—and some pupils did not come, being dark in the streets, too! Gas is also restricted and since 2 days I have no warm meal only a bit lukewarm given it a boil up on my oil stove! But things will improve, I am sure! If I come to think of all the misery that

had been, and all the cruelties and the wrong that so many people had to suffer, I am quiet.—Things here are still not so bad compared to all that happened!

The winter of 1946–47 became known as the "hunger winter" in occupied Austria, and the conditions that followed were even worse. During the summer of 1947, the potato crop failed. The United Nations Refugee Relief Agency (UNRRA) had been providing about two thirds of the civilian rations in occupied Austria since March 1946, but that ceased in June 1947. Food riots broke out first in Vienna in May 1947, and then in August in the resort town of Bad Ischl, and "turned into a pogrom of local Jews."[377]

Cold War politics contributed to the shortages. Two-thirds of Austrian agricultural output and nearly all oil production lay in the Soviet-occupied zone. The Soviets sent a large proportion of Austrian food and oil back to the USSR, leaving far too little for the Austrian population. Many Viennese, like Hansi, depended on food parcels food sent by relatives abroad.

Relief Parcels

Relief parcels were not a postwar invention. During the first year of the war, Walter, Lilly, and other relatives abroad mailed packages of necessities to Vienna. No detail survives about their contents, which were likely food, clothing, or some of both. Antoinette wrote in April 1940:

> Anna, Berta, and Trude Mayer have already sent us the second parcel with things which we can really use, and Malvine and I divide it according to our needs. Next month a parcel from you will come again, hopefully nothing will happen in between.

---

377 "Allied-occupied Austria," Wikipedia, accessed January 25, 2022, https://en.wikipedia.org/wiki/Allied-occupied_Austria#Hunger; Jill Lewis, "Dancing on a Tight Rope: The Beginning of the Marshall Plan," in *The Marshall Plan in Austria*, eds. Günter Bischof, Anton Pelinka, Dieter Stiefel vol 8 (New York: Routledge, 2000), 138–155; Thomas A. Bailey, *The Marshall Plan Summer: An Eyewitness Report on Europe and the Russians in 1947* (Stanford, CA: Hoover Press, 1977).

This practice resumed after the end of the war once international mail reopened.

Relief parcels were a constant topic in Paula's and Hans's letters from the end of 1946 and through 1947. Walter shipped packages directly from New York, while Paul sent some from Australia via Jerusalem and Stockholm. Relatives in the UK, Paul and Olga's Tante Grete and their uncle Rudolf Wilheim, were able to send parcels as well even though the UK was still rationing food and clothing. Tante Helene and Geza Frieder in Manila sent money to help underwrite Walter and Lilly's efforts.

Paula's and Hans's letters do not touch on the Cold War politics driving the food and fuel shortages, both because they would have expected Walter to keep up with news about occupied Europe from newspaper and radio accounts, and because it would have been thoroughly impolitic. Mail leaving and entering Austria continued to be opened and reviewed by the censors for almost a decade after the end of the war. In a continuation of wartime procedures, each page of the postwar letters bore a purple inked stamp and penciled identification number. The difference was that a new agency, the Austrian Censorship Office, was in charge rather than the defeated Wehrmacht.

A letter that Hans sent in December 1946 included an inventory of parcels numbers 5 and 6 from Lilly and Walter. They contained:

> ...2 tins of cocoa, 4 tins of condensed milk, 1 tin of dried milk, 1 tin of butter, 1 tin of coffee, 2 tins of Nescafe, 2 tins of sardines, 1 tin of anchovies, 2 tins of ____ [? illegible], 1 peppermints, 5 small tablets of table [eating] chocolate, 1 of the same large, 2 packets of tea, 1 box of fleckerl [small flat square noodles], and 1 of macaroni. The announced "*turkey fat*" was not in the two parcels. Thank you for the shipment!!

Hans then offered a considerate return:

Further I ask you to get some lovely flowers as Lilly's Christmas present or some little thing in our (Lisl's and my) name and here are 10 dollars to use for it. The rest will turn up.

Between endless details about relief parcels, there was some back and forth about whether the Haim siblings would still recognize each other after all the intervening years. Hans must have written to Walter that the remaining family in Vienna was still recognizable, or perhaps barely so. When Walter responded with some anxiety, Hans replied by downplaying his previous statements:

As to your question referring to recognition, that was only my ineptly chosen expression. We <u>really</u> don't look bad! I would only like to say about that that I have stopped getting older, older than my corresponding years, and certainly the Nazi years are much to blame for that. All your other conjectures are false, and we are really and truly doing well.

Hans tried to be reassuring about their food situation as well, emphasizing to Walter that things were manageable. A sign of improving times, Hans wrote at the end of 1946, was that ration cards were no longer completely worthless:

Of course, one does not always (always is an exaggeration) have what one would like immediately, but that will happen one way or the other. But as we have told you often enough already, we already have enough, thanks to the Joint [the Jewish Joint Distribution Committee] and American Red Cross, and thanks to many private shipments we are really doing very well, and every concern is completely unfounded. And finally we also receive something for our food [ration] cards! Bread really in a sufficient quantity.

Hans dismissed as overwrought and unnecessary their aunt Malvine's complaints about lack of food. He acknowledged in

December 1946 that Malvine had lost weight but blamed her earlier medical problems, not present food shortages:

> That Malvine goes scrounging around and writes such alarming letters is not entirely necessary. Because they always have sources of help and are in the situation of being able to buy things and also do so. Now she has been physically reduced a lot, but it cannot be attributed to the current bad nutritional conditions alone but to the previous difficult stomach surgery, and that's the reason.

A telling detail allows a glimpse beneath the assurances that things were well. Malvine wrote to Walter in November 1946 that she suffered from "starvation edema." Hans responded with a big-brotherly lecture about this condition. The fact was that malnutrition was so widespread in Vienna that what would normally be a bit of medical arcana had become common knowledge:

> I will explain famine edema [Hungeroedem] to you! Edema is also called anasarca and manifests itself as swelling and puffiness of the skin. Fact: different illnesses, e.g., kidney illness, heart ailments, etc., and also, as in this case, inadequate and insufficient food. In these days sadly a very widely seen condition.

Paula praised the contents of the parcels from New York and their secure packaging, but she was concerned that Walter and Lilly were spending more than they could spare on them. She had mixed feelings about Walter's propensity to save money for the future rather than use it for immediate things. Paula's and the family's experience with the post-World War I hyperinflation, followed by the Nazis' confiscation of Jews' assets like securities and insurance policies, had left her with an indelible mistrust of the value of saving money.[378] She wrote on December 15, 1946:

---

378 See Bukey, *Hitler's Austria*, 149.

All parcels have arrived faultlessly and will be confirmed in detail by Hans. We have divided them, like all the earlier ones. I would like to know if you have used the money that Geza sent [from Manila] for that. Please answer me that in particular. The little packets were so well packaged that the post office official told me, yes, if everyone would pack so orderly, the other parcels would also arrive in good condition. The contents were also very nice and well chosen. It sticks in my throat though, Bibolein, because I know that sometimes what you [pl.] send you did not buy for yourself because of the increase in price, and I would ask you not to send any more parcels. It is no longer so bad, and we will now receive parcels from England from Rudolf, Grete, etc. We have already received one from Sigi Winkler [a cousin of Paul and Olga] and two more are under way. This week a 10 kilogram parcel came from Paul via Jerusalem-Stockholm. That also was very nice. It had been en route since the beginning of September. We are all in a materially better situation than you [pl.] and because of the social situation where you are [that is, the lack in the United States of what would be called a social safety net, at least in comparison to Austrian labor and welfare systems], you certainly must still put money away for emergencies. Although this is also quite a thing. Save it from the mouth and then it suddenly becomes worth nothing in the bank. I was never in favor of saving, as you know. Rather buy things. And that worked well for us. If only we could exchange these years. But I understand that one should save.

Not all the parcels were delivered in "flawless condition." Malvine seems to have had bad luck with some of them. Hans wrote in January 1947 about one incident:

Malvine's parcel was damaged and it was missing the 6 packets of cigarettes as well as a tablet of chocolate. Otto [Malvine's husband] fetched it back from the post office and naturally he didn't do anything about it! One doesn't know where something like this would be robbed, but in any case, I would have had a report submitted and requested an investigation. But such things happen only to Malvine. Without exception, other people receive all shipments in flawless condition. She is really unlucky. [added in pencil] (Or suffers from persecution mania?)

Malvine and Otto Jahn

The earliest letter in the folder marked "Paula" is from their aunt Malvine, dated November 1, 1946. Although both Paula and Hans could write with something of an edge, Malvine's letter is different. Her letters typically are more barbed and less empathetic than those from the Haim family parents and siblings.

Malvine began her letter unexceptionally, with thanks for the parcel that "arrived here on October 29th in very good condition." Like Paula and Hans, Malvine wrote that Walter should "send nothing other than what Helene [in Manila] has sent you the money for," and that he and Lilly "must not deprive yourselves" or spend their own money on relief parcels until they were "better established." Then Malvine added with a snarky twist, "I hope, of course, that we will not have starved or frozen to death by then." Her comments about Hans and Paula also seem two-edged:

> Things are going well for Hans and Lisl thank God. He was always someone who makes the best of things [Lebenskünstler[379]] and she his assistant! Paula currently has a tooth marrow problem, but that also will soon be over. Unfortunately she cannot go to her husband at the moment. But she doesn't live badly here, thank God, as she has her accommodation and a charming apartment together with Olga.

---

379 Literally a "life artist." The word can carry a range of connotations, including a sybarite, hedonist, or someone who always lands on their feet, as well as one who makes the best of a situation, or a connoisseur of the art of living. Paul used the same word to describe his Tante Grete in a letter dated January 5, 1940.

Malvine continued more straightforwardly:

> You can hardly imagine how joyful Otto [her husband] was about the cigarettes. He sends his heartfelt thanks to you.

I don't recall my father ever mentioning Malvine, Otto, or Otto's brother Gustav Jahn, but the name retained some resonance for him. We had a slim book of Gustav Jahn's landscape paintings in the bookcase. Otto was an amateur photographer who captured many of his brother Gustav's mountaineering exploits.[380] In the early 1960s, an ice cream parlor opened in Jackson Heights that specialized in elaborate sundaes and faux 1890s style called "Jahn's," with the pronunciation anglicized to "Jan's." My father told me, maybe more than once, that the name would have been pronounced "Yahn's" in some unspecified ur-world.

Malvine wrote that she had lost so much weight that she was down to forty-five kilos, just under one hundred pounds. She complained that the available food was a "frightful plague" for her, though not for her husband Otto, who "eats the same as I but it suits him better and doesn't disagree with him."

Otto's Decline and Steinhof

What Malvine did not mention was that Otto was showing symptoms of dementia. Hans described the situation and its dismal prognosis in a letter to Walter from late December 1946:

> Otto has no suffering and has a clear mind, as far as he ever had much of that. But in one second he forgets what he just said or what one told him, does not notice the smallest thing, and for this reason does not need anything at all, and her

---

380 See, e.g., http://retours.eu/nl/33-Staatsbahnen-posters-Jahn-Barth/enlarge/jahn-barth.jpg and https://historiek.net/het-spoor-van-twee-alpinisten-oostenrijkse-spoorwegaffiches-rond-1910/55626/, accessed July 16, 2023.

[Malvine's] nervousness and anxiety is a serious thing. He knows about his former profession [Otto's stationery gave his title as Oberrechnungsrat, some sort of senior accounting advisor] and also many other subjects which he ever knew or learned, and one can speak and converse with him about all the past. But if he gives the tram ticket to Malvine to validate, he immediately looks for the card 20 times a minute, and if one tells him and shows him 20 times that she has it, he cannot recall it. So begins senility. There is no remedy against it.

A couple of months later, in early February 1947, Otto's condition had worsened. Hans wrote that the doctors suspected Otto may have had a stroke:

Otto Jahn has been sick for a couple of days, one doesn't know what he has. A sudden case of weakness. He is out of bed, however very decayed mentally. The doctor thinks it is perhaps a blood clot in his brain; he has to be observed for a couple of days. In any case, things are going very downhill with him. Certainly not necessary for Malvine's health and mental status.

Despite Malvine's difficult personality, a hypochondriac who instigated intrigues and imagined plots being carried out against her, Hans fulfilled his role as family elder during Otto's last illness. In mid-February Otto was hospitalized because of continued mental deterioration. As always, Hans reported the facts objectively and stated his conclusions:

Still to recount would be that since Friday, Otto has been in the hospital for examination. He had already been mentally very weak for several months, then last Monday at midday he came home from the club and suffered a sort of physical breakdown after lunch, which began with vomiting and complete weakness. Since then he has also declined more mentally. He responds to repeated questions but is usually wrong, as Malvine says. He cannot dress or undress himself, can neither sit or rise alone, and also cannot lie down or get up himself. The neurologist, who was new to her [Malvine], suggested that he be kept for observation in his department (in Elizabeth Hospital) and will report the examination results in a few days. Not much is to be expected, it doesn't appear that his mental state can improve, and the physical restrictions after such a brain event, according to my lay opinion, cannot be reversed. But she is decidedly not normal either and has been severely brought down by these physical and health issues and has no one to help, so this will be a lovely development! I am afraid it will end with his going to an institution.

Otto continued to deteriorate, and the doctors at the Elisabeth Hospital seemed to be giving Malvine and Hans misleading information. Finally, Hans reported, the doctors had Otto removed to the psychiatric hospital at Steinhof without advance notice to the family, much less their consent:

Since my last letter (a couple of days ago), Otto's condition has turned much for the worse. On Monday (Feb. 17) he went to the psychiatric clinic at Elizabeth Hospital, and they transferred him on Wednesday (19th) to Steinhof. This development is unheard of nonsense and hogwash. I visited him on Tuesday afternoon at the clinic, spoke with the treating physician in the office, and he told me an essential improvement can be expected in several days, and Malvine should come to on Wednesday at 11 a.m. during his office hours for exact information. She was there already at 10 a.m. and learned that he [Otto] had been taken away at 9 a.m.! In the afternoon he was at Steinhof, still at the corridor of the receiving office because there was no free bed. Yesterday he could not leave, and today at noon I will go there with her. Then we will see how things stand.

Hans continued the following day:

Yesterday I went with Malvine to Steinhof, and we found Otto very bad. The chief doctor described his illness as hardening of the brain arteries and doesn't see any possibility for improvement. Final stage. He can't speak, or barely understandable or just a lot of nonsense, can't eat without his false teeth, he won't last long. What will happen to her I also don't know yet, because she is physically a wreck.

Hans was proved right. Otto died the following week, on February 28, 1947.

The involvement of Steinhof brings what otherwise would be a private family story of an elderly man's mental decay into a more public realm and a view of the abyss. During the Nazi era, Steinhof had been a center for the mass deportation and euthanasia (using carbon monoxide) of disabled children and mental patients.[381] Thousands of adult psychiatric patients and disabled children at Steinhoff were murdered right there. Thousands more were taken from Steinhof to an extermination facility and crematorium at Hartheim Castle outside Linz. All told, about 7,500 Steinhof patients were killed between 1938 and 1941, about 800 of them children.[382] This was no secret. The public knew and some objected, at least at first. The Steinhof memorial website records that "the very first deportations from Steinhof led to demonstrations in front of the institution, to which the authorities reacted by deploying police and SS forces." Nearly contemporaneous news about the mass deportations and murders emanating from Steinhof reached England, where the doctor in charge of the child euthanasia program was identified by name. This was Erwin Jekelius, previously a psychiatrist for the City of Vienna.[383] In September 1941 the Royal Air Force

---

381 See, e.g., "Memorial Steinhof," Information Portal to European Sites of Remembrance, https://www.memorialmuseums.org/eng/denkmaeler/view/716/Memorial-Steinhof.

382 "Memorial Steinhof," Information Portal to European Sites of Remembrance.

383 See "Erwin Jekelius," Wikipedia.de, https://de.wikipedia.org/wiki/Erwin_Jekelius.

(RAF) "dropped fliers…that reported on Dr. Jekelius' murderous activities at Steinhof,"[384] though the killings continued.

If Hans knew of the atrocities committed at Steinhof, or if Olga had learned of them as a returning pediatrician, none of that awareness appears in the letters. The Viennese medical and political establishments buried this history in the postwar rush to return to "normalcy." Into the 1980s researchers at Steinhof continued to use body parts of the euthanasia victims, depersonalized as "anatomical specimens." Only in 2002, more than sixty years after the last murders of Steinhof patients, were their remains buried in the Vienna's Central Cemetery and a belated memorial erected for them.[385] Ironically, for all the horrors carried out there, Steinhof was and is known for its ethereally beautiful, early twentieth-century art nouveau church designed by Otto Wagner, the architecture illuminated by stained glass and mosaics by Koloman Moser of the Wiener Werkstätte.

Ongoing Friction between Hans and Malvine

Shortly after Otto's death, Malvine wrote to Walter thanking him for parcel no. 8, in particular the soup packets and cigarettes that used to make Otto "childishly happy," and lamenting her "sad and lonely existence" now that Otto was gone. Malvine wrote that she looked forward to her sister Helene's possible return to Vienna from Manila the following year, and perhaps a visit from Helene's daughter Margit and her two children who were then living in England.

That summer, Malvine sniped about Hans and Lisl's lack of warmth towards her. She was particularly insulted that Lisl had nothing to say to her during the few times that she visited them, and made no effort to hide her slighted feelings.

---

384 "Opposition and Resistance to Nazi Euthanasia," Der Krieg Gegen die "Minderwertigen," accessed January 25, 2022, http://gedenkstaettesteinhof.at/en/exibition/12-opposition-and-resistance-nazi-euthanasia; "Operation T4," Der Krieg Gegen die "Minderwertigen," accessed July 16, 2023, http://gedenkstaettesteinhof.at/en/exibition/08-operation-t4.

385 "Memorial Steinhof," Information Portal to European Sites of Remembrance, accessed July 16, 2023, https://www.memorialmuseums.org/denkmaeler/view/716/Memorial-Steinhof.

The situation did not improve. Hans wrote in December 1947 on the same subject with overt sarcasm:

> Malvine looks quite well and is always as dear as earlier. Unfortunately we have the pleasure of her visits often. She is always offended that Lisl hardly says anything when she is here. If you know Lisl, one could roast her and she would not open her mouth if she doesn't want to. It is high time that Helene were here, then M[alvine] could not always say that I am the only person and relative whom she has and that she must express herself to me.

Malvine was further miffed that Hans and Lisl did not invite her to accompany them on their vacation to the Austrian countryside in July 1947. Hans wrote again with heavy sarcasm:

> Your beloved aunt [i.e., Malvine] is very offended that we have not asked her to go on the vacation with us! Also I am very put out that I did not realize this in time, it would have been the only thing that was missing from my happiness! So one spoils the greatest chances through one's own fault, and so I must necessarily go on vacation alone with Lisl and with Boy [their dog]! I hope that you will empathize with our pain. By the way she was with us yesterday. (She brightens us up now and then on Sunday, so that we are not so completely abandoned.)

The vacation worked out well for Hans, Lisl, and their dog despite the challenge of providing for food. Hans wrote in September 1947:

> The main question in Austria today is whether the increased number of vacationers must buy their provisions in the Vienna black market and take them to the vacation spot if they don't want to starve at that place.

Hans's Views of America

Hans distrusted American holidays. When Walter sent greetings for Thanksgiving in November 1947, Hans responded critically:

> Yesterday I received your lines about *Thanksgiving Day*, and we respond to your dear wishes. I believe there is also such a harvest thanksgiving festival, which first had a damn Nazi aftertaste, and second this can't mean much for us city dwellers. All these things are artificially yoked together. However if it means a paid day off where you [pl.] are, then at least it has some value.

As for American food, Hans remained suspicious of it while expressing wholehearted gratitude for the food parcels. He was partial to American canned soup and instant coffee. In his earliest surviving postwar letter from December 1946, Hans commended the canned turkey fat that Walter had included in two parcels and proclaimed that he would be happy to receive "a separate shipment which contained nothing other than: the famous canned soup and Nescafé! Then I can live on soup, which is the main thing to me!" He also asked for pins, which were unobtainable in Vienna, and said that they were eagerly awaiting a promised rubber bone for the dog.

Despite relishing Nescafé and canned soup, six months later, Hans wrote a slashing indictment of the American diet:

> I acknowledge your chatter about shopping and cooking. American cooking can simply be stolen from me [i.e., I don't like it a bit]! The intolerable spices with which all this meat is preserved are an abomination to me! And cooking cannot be so easy and wholesome there if Americans must always be at spas with their stomach complaints!

Walter apparently responded by defending American cuisine, and Hans softened a bit. In a reply sent in July 1947, Hans allowed himself to think about a possible visit to the United States two years hence:

> I have gladly taken note of your clarification about the justification for American cooking. I hope to be able to taste it in the year 1949?!?!? Until then some miracles will have to happen. One of them is that I finally find a respectable position, because things here [at the IKG] will not last much longer.

Hans's job had become a problem. He was at odds with his supervisor and the IKG board, but he resolved to stick it out, comparing the IKG to his former mortal adversaries:

> I am so popular with them [IKG management] that this certainly cannot be a lasting marriage. Unfortunately the economic conditions are such that a change of position is almost an impossibility. For the time being, I have made up my mind to endure it. If I succeeded in outlasting the Nazis and the SS, so I will succeed with them also.

1947—Squabbles about Relief Packages and an Entrepreneurial Alternative

The letters from 1946 and 1947 are filled with incessant minutiae about the relief packages: which parcel had arrived, when had it been received, whether the contents were intact, who sent the parcel, who had paid for it, how was it to be distributed. The primary source of the brouhaha was Aunt Malvine. She suspected, or fantasized, elaborate machinations intended to deprive her of what she thought of as her due. She reacted badly if she felt she had been slighted when a parcel's contents were distributed, or if any part of the money that Helene and Geza in Manila had sent to Walter for Malvine's benefit had been used for Hans instead. In June 1947 Hans described one such scene, beginning by telling Walter, "Just now your Aunt Malvine was visiting here."

Suddenly in mid-1947, a practical alternative appeared. The Meinl Company, a venerable Austrian food and coffee business, began offering gift certificates as a replacement for food parcels.[386] It was significantly easier for families overseas to use their relief budget to buy Meinl certificates for recipients in Vienna than to run around New York (or Melbourne or Cardiff) to purchase individual items, cart them home, round up cartons and tape, pack the goods securely, take the boxes to the post office, stand in line there, and then wait to see if the parcels made it through the sea journey and inspection by questionably honest Austrian customs officials and postal clerks.

Meinl's website does not mention the innovative postwar gift certificates, though it was a clever business move. Customers abroad, Jewish and non-Jewish alike, could buy Meinl certificates for relatives in Austria while avoiding the burdens of sending traditional food parcels.

Hans initially welcomed the Julius Meinl gift certificates as a way to ease the strain on Walter and avoid endless bickering with Malvine over how the funds that their aunt Helene sent were being used. Malvine would be happier making her own choices, and so would Hans. He wrote in unusual detail:

> I suggest now a new process for Malvine and Helene, which will spare you time and trouble and has the greatest advantage

---

386 The Meinl Company has a "complicated" recent history. It had been established in 1862 and was a byword for good, solid coffee. The history timeline on the company's website boasts that Julius Meinl II (1869–1944), the son of the founder, expanded and modernized his father's grocery and coffee store until it became the "largest importer of coffee and tea in Central Europe" ("Julius Meinl: Now and Then," Julius Meinl, accessed July 16, 2023, https://juliusmeinl.com/about-julius-meinl/our-history). Julius II continued to operate the company after the Anschluss and through the war years, selling goods throughout Greater Germany and the occupied territories and supplying provisions to the German military. Meinl's internal company newsletters volubly supported the Nazi regime ("Julius Meinl, German Grocery Conglomerate, Meinl Rundpost, Company Magazines 1936–December 1944," USM Books, accessed July 16, 2023, https://usmbooks.com/julius_meinl_rundpost.html. See also "Rare Nazi Era Book on the House of Meinl Grocery Conglomerate," USM Books, https://usmbooks.com/julius_meinl_company_history.html). At the same time, his son Julius III (1903–1991), whose wife was Jewish, spent the war years in England, returning to Vienna in 1947 to take over the company.

that Malvine can choose what she wants for the money here in Vienna. The firm of Julius Meinl, A.G., in Vienna has...sent me an agreement with which one in New York can deposit any amount of dollars with this above mentioned firm and receive a gift certificate which the favored recipient then can use to choose what he will purchase from a fixed price list. This process would have the hugely beneficial effect for you that you would not first have to shop for the items to be shipped and then pack them and that also save postage expenses. Secondly, this would have the advantage for you that if you receive an amount from Helene you could purchase a gift certificate, and with it the whole matter can be resolved without bother and at one blow. Further, you would have with that a clear confirmation that the entire sum that you received was used immediately. Malvine brought this thought to my attention. It would be very good for her if she could freely choose the items herself here in Vienna and get them at Meinl, and so this would be best for all parties....I understand that you will gladly accept this suggestion from Malvine and will do that in the future because it will be easier for you....You can imagine what a clamor I had to listen to so that I decided to write this to you in such detail.

For himself, Hans requested only "some salt in a small packet...also milk in any form...and Nescafé!"

In his next letter, sent on June 25, Hans acknowledged the receipt of more parcels for him and Malvine:

As usual heartfelt thanks for your shipments, someone will repay you sometime, and if no one else then God!

Paula also weighed in on the problems with Malvine. Malvine had long been a trial to her, she wrote Walter, though after all this time, her anger at Malvine had devolved into something like pity.[387] Paula also endorsed the solution of Meinl gift certificates:

> I have nothing more to say about Malvine. Now I don't get upset any more about what she does or says. Remarkable. And still I hated her so that I really and actually felt ill if I saw her with us. Now she is a complete wreck and I am almost sorry. But I would write to Helene* in your place that she should send you the money to pay for the Meinl certificates directly.
>
> Only to honor Mama one didn't tell those two what they had coming to them.
>
> *By the way, Helene is not bad. Only stupid and believes just what M[alvine] writes to her.

Meinl used the gift certificate program to charge top dollar for their goods. Hans, who disdained using the black market, kept tabs on it sufficiently to compare black market prices to Meinl's. He wrote in August 1947:

> I have determined through a review of their [Meinl's] price list that the various offered things are priced very high. On the basis of the dollar black market exchange, the particular goods are higher there than what one could get them for on the black market. You will be astonished that I am so well informed about the clandestine exchange, but I can reassure you, I know this only through hearsay.

The following month, September 1947, Hans reported that he

---

387 Malvine apparently continued to foment dissension until the end. When Malvine died on February 4, 1965, Lisl did not attend Malvine's burial, first because it was very cold and snowy and Lisl had recently fallen and broken two fingers, and second, "there was an intrigue engineered against Lisl [by Malvine] even from the hospital bed, and that became too much for even the patient and upstanding Lisl.—This chapter is now ended forever." Paula, letter dated February 12, 1965.

would attempt to follow the legitimate channels and use newly issued shoe ration coupons to obtain his first new pair of shoes since the Anschluss:

> This afternoon we will go into the city to see if after a nine-year interval we finally can get a pair of useful shoes for the shoe coupons. For those not here, it can't be grasped how impossible it is to obtain necessities by reputable means (and not on the sly [through the black market]).

One can't imagine what Hans and Lisl's shoes must have looked like after nine years of daily use and patching.

Coal

Coal could not be sent to Vienna like food and cigarettes, so the family in Vienna suffered through shortages of heating fuel during the winters of 1945–46 and 1946–47. In December 1946 Paula tried to reassure Walter that they were comfortable because Olga had received a fuel allotment to heat the room in their apartment that she used for her medical practice:

> Here is has already become winter. It is already less than zero [i.e., below freezing]. But it is very nicely warm because Olga receives enough coal that is assigned for her consulting room. But I cannot bear the cold. Our apartment is really very very dear and comfortable and pleases everyone. Olga's private practice begins slowly, already all the children in Neustiftgasse and the surrounding neighborhood come to her.

Two days after Christmas 1946, Hans wrote about an unanticipated benefit of Vienna's fuel shortage. He did not have to go to work because offices and factories were closed:

Christmas Eve Paula and Olga were with us. We are off work from the 21st to the 30th, all because luckily there is no coal for heating. Industries are also closed from December 21st for two or three weeks for the same reason, to save electricity.

In June 1947 Paula asked Walter, "Have you heard of any sort of coal-CARE program for Vienna? There should be something like that. If you can learn anything about that, please write to me. That would be hugely important if it were possible." Unfortunately there seems to have been none.

That October, as heating season approached, Hans began to get in stores of fuel. He anticipated another difficult winter:

For several days we have had lovely weather yet already premonitions of winter. During the night it has already been a few degrees of cold, today in the morning minus 2 degrees. During the day magnificently sunny and warm, but one already thinks with pleasure of the coming no-heat times. By the way, an acquaintance has promised me 3 cubic meters of wood, now I only need to receive the wood, then I can already start heating. But we did not freeze to death in earlier years, and it will be nothing this year. In completeness I must say that we have already received 100 kilograms of briquettes that are in the coal cart in the winter storeroom. Things there [i.e., in New York] are somewhat better for you [pl.].

When Walter wrote that their apartment had central heat, and Hans responded with his usual wry realism, "There are a few houses here with central heating, but they have no heating fuel." Each apartment in Vienna typically had a heating stove in the main room where all that dearly bought coal, coke, and wood was burnt.

CHAPTER 23

Paul and Paula—Refocus

1945—Lichtblick: A Ray of Light Reaches Australia

Here is a short recap: In May 1945 New York's *Aufbau* printed a six-month-old list of Jews who had been registered as living in Vienna in November 1944, Antoinette and Paula among them. Two months later, in July 1945, there was a steadier bit of light. Walter somehow learned that Paula was alive and cabled Paul. Paul responded immediately by wire, telling Walter:

> Thanks for cable is there possibility to communicate with Paula Red Cross cannot help stop need her address.

Five days later, on July 24, Paul followed up with a letter:

> Since six years the first bit of a *Lichtblick*. When I came home from work on Thursday the 19th I found your wire on my table. I immediately went to our General Post Office and answered by cable....Through our Red Cross one can still only send those Red Cross messages to Vienna. I wonder whether they ever reach the addressee. Have you over there other possibilities if so then send them my love please. Last week I also had your letter of June 4th. If this mail business only would improve a bit. Such a letter takes an awful long time. I am all right that means much better than I was one week ago. Give my love to Lilly. Once more many thanks, you are a good boy.

In his otherwise English letter, Paul used the German word for ray of light, "Lichtblick," metaphorically a ray of hope.

Then that ray of light flickered maddeningly. According to Paul's letter sent August 5:

> One week ago I received your letter of June 21st, yesterday your letter of June 14th and two days ago your air mail letter of July 20th. Then things are not as bright as I saw them when I received your wire. In short "There is something fishy in the state of Danemark's." And I still do not like this business over there. Wait and see, that is all I can do.

Lilly and Walter were at a new address, this time in Queens, and they had been able to go on a vacation:

> Then you moved to a new apartment. What is it like? How about your trip to Canada? As to me, I am all-right so far. Still at the same place and still at the same job. Nothing has changed for me during the past two years besides getting older and grey haired.
>
> Keep well old boy. Give my love to Lilly.

A week later, Paul received third-hand news from an unidentified "lady in Prague." The core remaining Haim family had survived, but Paul's mother and most of his extended family had perished:

> May God bless you. I have your second air mail letter of July 26th. Sorry there is no air-mail service from here to USA. otherwise I would post by air mail. I had an air-mail letter from Olga of the same date as yours in which she informed me that Rudolf (my uncle in Cardiff)[388] had a letter from a lady in Prague saying that Toni, Paula, Hans and Lisl are

---

388 Rudolf Wilheim was the only brother of Mathilde (née Wilheim) Kurz and Grete (née Wilheim) Weisz.

all-right. The lady got this information on June 15th. But all my other relatives are gone except two cousins. That is all for today. Keep well old boy. Give my love to Lilly.

Later in August Paul learned from Walter that Helene and Geza Frieder were still in Manila, having survived three years of Japanese occupation followed by the US and Filipino forces' street-to-street battle to retake Manila. Paul's mood had lifted enough so that he could joke with Walter about which of them had the worst weather:

> The air mail service from here to your country has been opened a few days ago. I will make use of it on Friday when I go to the city. But as I feel like writing to you I write today and post by ordinary mail. I received two letters from you, June 29th and July 3rd. Of course I have more recent messages from you but nevertheless I was glad to get those letters as well. Then Helen and Geza are in Manila. Where is their son? I think Robert was his name. The other day I had a letter from Dr. Martha Müller's mother, Irma Müller who lives in Sydney. She has not heard from Martha yet. It was hard for me to answer her letter. I myself would very much like to know about Martha.
>
> Do not grumble about humid weather and temperature. In this respect your country is no competitor for us. We here make it much better. How about 140° at 2 p.m. and 60° at 2 a.m. But all this does not matter. I only want some new news from Vienna and should the temperature be 190°.
>
> Give my love to Lilly.

In September 1945 the mail had become a bit more reliable. Walter asked about Paul's plans for Paula, but Paul was not making any. The lesson he had learned over and over during the past six years was not to build any "fairy-castles." Paul acknowledged the low moods that had showed through his previous letters, but this time his letter filled the page:

> Within the last three days I received three letters from you, July 17th, 18th and August 3rd. I know I am a scum of the earth. My last letter to you was of August 21st. In that I promised to send you an airmail letter very soon. And...I did not keep my promise. Why? I do not know. When I received your cable, so about two months ago, I breathed a little bit after six years and then came again a black-out. It is a bit trying this waiting for direct news from our old country. Anyhow I will try to answer your letters as good as I can....Bobili you asked whether I have any plans for me and for A [Paula]. No I have none and I won't make any until I can get in direct touch with her and even then I won't make any plans. Look dear boy, I went through quite a different school during this last six years than you did and the result of my schooling was: not to plan anything anymore.—....
>
> Yes I know the Red Cross does not take any messages anymore for Austria and the ordinary mail is still in the moon. By the way, Olga wrote in her last letter of August 29th that according to a rumour in London it should be possible to wire to Austria from USA. I think that is rubbish. There is really nothing I could report from my part. One day like the other. Give my love to Lilly.

On October 26 Paul could spar lightheartedly with Walter over which of them was more blame as an irregular correspondent. The war was officially over, but mail remained erratic, six to eight weeks or more from New York to Melbourne, and censorship continued. Paul wrote that he received letters dated September 1, 1945, from Antoinette and Paula and that he copied them into two successive airmail letters to Walter. Unfortunately, none of those copied letters survived.

I am awfully sorry but you are unjust in putting the whole blame on to me. Of course it is the easier way to abuse me. It would not help and it wouldn't give you any relief would you abuse the postmaster. Now listen: Yesterday, <u>25th October</u>, I received two letters from you one of <u>August 24th</u> the other of <u>September 4th</u>. The last letter from you I received just one month ago on <u>23rd September</u> it was dated <u>August 12th</u>. That letter I answered on 25th September and then I sent you two airmail letters in close intervals. One on <u>3rd October</u> the other on <u>10th October</u>. In those airmail letters I gave you copies of your mother's and Paula's letters of September 1st. Now you dirty mug what-else do you want. I acknowledged your two air-mail letters of July at least ten times. Most probably I am suspected and the censor does not want to forward my letters.

Bobi now be a good boy do not ask too many questions as I am unable of answering them. For the time being I am here (see address above) and how things will look tomorrow no one knows, not even I.

Give my love to Lilly if she cares to get it, if not, pour it out.

Yours innocent
Paul

More news about survivors in Vienna became available in the fall of 1945. In September Paula's friend Henriette Nettel, who had been able to leave Japan for San Francisco in time—that is, before Pearl Harbor—wrote to Walter and Lilly, "I am so happy that your dear family is Vienna is together and healthy." The "family" would have been the remaining core of Paula and Antoinette, Hans, and Lisl. Nettel noted that there was not yet any direct postal connection with Vienna, but:

How glad I would be to help those who fortunately were saved from that hell. I hope that in a foreseeable time we will be able to send food and perhaps also clothing.

Information about individual victims of what was not yet called the Holocaust continued to emerge. Paula sent letters to Olga in London on September 14 and 24, 1945, advising her of the deaths of Paul's and Olga's mother and of Martha Müller. Olga copied the letters and sent them on to Paul, who forwarded their gist to Walter in November.

Paul, like Nettel, was eager to begin sending food to Vienna once that became possible. He wrote to Walter on November 4:

> Now a very peculiar question. How is your mail service to Vienna? Is there by any chance a permission to send food parcels to them? Should you be short of money to manage any parcel then please let me know. I'll manage to send you some.

Paul also wrote about the limitations of the mail service and a surviving cousin:

> It is possible to send letters from here through the Jewish Welfare Society (although I do not use that possibility as it goes quicker via my sister) but no food parcels can go yet. Perhaps the following information can be of some use to you. A genuine cousin of mine: HERBERT SCHWARZWALD, C.S.R., BRNO, PRICNIC UL. 30, who survived miraculously several concentration camps plus Flecktyphus [literally spotted typhus] was during the whole time and still is in contact with Paula. Honestly Bobi should there be a money question in sending things to them be sure I will come up for it.

> The mail business to the States can't be called business any more. It is absolutely out of order. I have no mail from you since ages and I do not know whether you ever get any of mine.

Three days later Paul wrote a follow-up letter repeating some of the information about his cousin Herbert Schwarzwald and complaints about the mail. Based on Walter's tally of letters received from Paul, "There are at least still ten missing." Paul declined to respond to Walter's questions about the fates of his family or Martha Müller:

> Bobi look what would be the sense of telling you those stories or counting all those from my family who perished. Be sure Bobi they were quite a number and the method was a quite efficient one. I think that is sufficient information. As to Dr. Martha Müller, her story is too holy to be told. I wished I could humbly believe in heaven then I would be sure she is an angel now. By now I have written to her mother.

Paul then turned to the location of the US military in Austria and Czechoslovakia, which could be expected to provide more for civilian populations than the Soviets. Russia occupied the state of Lower Austria, which contained Vienna, and one-fourth of the city. Paul stated the fact simply, "They need food over there." Paul also had positive news about his immigration status in Australia:

> Now Bobi I am also able to satisfy your curiosity in the following respect. You very often asked me in your letter whether I'll get the permission of staying here. On the 5th inst. I received so to say my second paper according to which I am now considered as a permanent resident in Australia. That means I soon can apply for bringing Paula here, provided she wants to.

In December 1945 mail from the United States was still slow but dribbling in. Paul was feeling expansive enough to respond self-deprecatingly to Lilly's letter and one-up her report about an elevator operators' strike in New York, which meant that she had to climb up nineteen floors to the office of Paramount Pictures near Times Square where she worked. Walter asked what the family in

Vienna were planning to do, and Paul countered that he was waiting for their decisions:

> It is an eternity since I wrote you last. But I really have nothing to report. No news whatsoever from Vienna since one month. Last week I received three letters from you in the following order: October 15th (Walter), October 9th (Walter), September 27th (Lilly). And as Lilly let herself down to write to me, muck, Nut-House convict, etc. I feel so proud that I will answer your letters.
>
> Lilly: First of all I very much doubt that you are interested in me, why should you be, there is no reason for it. Then writing about things does not help me, therefore I do not write about things. Thirdly until now they did not find out here that I am nuts. I even can say the contrary, funny, they find out that I am quite clever. Fourthly I already told you in my last letters that I got the permission of staying here. Your elevator-operators strike does not impress me, we know it much better here, what are nineteen floors. No Lilly, next time write a better letter; with that one of September 27th you failed, nichtgenugend [insufficient, a failing school grade].
>
> Walter or better Bobi: Thanks for your letters of October 9th and 15th.
>
> Bobi: Once I know what they have decided over there in Vienna I will make my decisions and I'll let you know then.

And so 1945 ended. The war was over, and a remnant of the family had survived, though scattered across three continents. Whether Paula and Paul would be reunited was an open question.

Becoming Naturalized in Australia

In 1944 Australia finally backtracked from its refusal to accept the *Dunera* internees for permanent resettlement. Once Paul was released from internment, he began the long process of regularizing his immigration status. That process made only the barest appearance in the letters but has been preserved in the administrative amber of the National Archives of Australia.[389]

The first step was obtaining a "landing permit." On September 19, 1944, the government's Naturalization Section informed Paul that his application had been approved and his "permanent admission to Australia" was authorized. This was significant progress out of the limbo of statelessness. The following month, Paul took the next step towards naturalization. He completed the required Statutory Declaration of Intent and had notices printed in two Melbourne newspapers, the *Age* and the *Argus*, to inform the population at large:

> I, Paul Kurz, of Stateless, former Austrian nationality, born in Vienna, Austria, and resident over four years in Australia, now residing at 38 Denbigh Road, Armadale, Victoria, intend to apply for Naturalization under the Nationality Act, 1920–1936.

The declaration identified his occupation as "industrial chemist" and his employer for the past fourteen months as Lanolin Products at Trenerry Crescent, Abbotsford, an inner industrial area of Melbourne. (Paul was to spend the remainder of his career at that firm.) The company's owner, Bill Barry, signed a Householder's Certificate in support of Paul's application for Australian citizenship, attesting that he had known Paul for one year and that Paul was "a person of good repute" with "an adequate knowledge of the English language."

The Statutory Declaration of Intent also asked about marital status. Paul wrote in Paula's name, date and place of birth, and the

---

389 All the information and quotations in this section are from "Kurz, Paul," National Archives of Australia, https://recordsearch.naa.gov.au/SearchNRetrieve/NAAMedia/ShowImage.aspx?B=6990757&T=PDF. Information courtesy of the National Archives of Australia. NAA: A435, 1946/4/2361.

date of their marriage. In the space for her residence, he entered the chilling answer: "unknown."

The next step was the equivalent of a background check. A local "Assistant Inquiry Officer" completed a "Report on Application for Naturalization" in October 1944. This official gave a solidly affirmative response to the question about Paul's ability to "read and write the English language"—"Yes, fluently." The inquiry officer explained why Paul lacked an address for Paula: "When last heard of in 1943, she was then in Vienna." A final note added:

> If his wife is alive after the cessation of hostilities in Europe, he will make an application for her admission to Australia.

Unlike many of the Dunera internees, whose goal was to return to the UK, Paul affirmed that he had "no intention of leaving Australia."

In February 1945 the Commonwealth Investigation Branch in Victoria approved the Assistant Inquiry Officer's report on Paul's application for naturalization. Nine months later on November 7, 1945, Paul signed an Oath of Allegiance form before the Clerk of Petty Sessions in Melbourne. In it he swore to be "faithful and bear true allegiance to His Majesty King George the Sixth and his heirs and successors according to law." A block on the form for "Renunciation of Nationality" was crossed out. As a stateless person, Paul had no nationality to renounce.

After all that there was a final glitch, a bureaucratic comedy over the color of Paul's hair. On November 23, 1945, an acting secretary in the Department of Immigration in Canberra sent Paul a letter stating:

> With reference to the application for naturalization made by you, would you please advise the colour of your hair.
>
> On your statutory declaration the colour is set out as "going grey", but it is desired to learn the actual colour.

Paul sent a deadpan reply on November 27:

> In response to your letter of 23rd inst. I wish to state that the colour of my hair is basically—**dark brown**—but now greying.

Nothing happened for several more months. Finally in March 1946, Paul sent a follow-up letter to the Department of Immigration with a copy of his letter from the previous November identifying his hair color. He ended the letter with a personal observation:

> In my case, I would be only too grateful to have my naturalization finalized as the lot of a stateless person is not an enviable one.

Paul's statement and restatement about his hair color eventually appeased officialdom. On April 5, 1946, the Australian Department of Naturalization issued a letter informing Paul that his "application for a Certificate of Naturalization has been submitted to the minister and has been approved." Six days later, on April 11, Paul signed a receipt for the certificate. The last two paragraphs of the letter of April 5 addressed Paula's situation. She had not automatically obtained Australian citizenship along with Paul because she was not living in Australia. However, if and when she were to arrive, she could acquire British nationality by submitting the proper form.

1946—The View from Australia

Paul's letters from 1946 began with the difficulties of sending food parcels from Australia to Vienna. He could send packages from Australia to England, where Olga was able to forward them to Vienna, but the permitted weight was quite limited. Alternatively, Walter could send larger food parcels directly from the United States to Vienna, but transmitting the funds from Australia to the States to help pay for them was slow and required circumventing

Australian currency restrictions. As he had in earlier years, Paul rejected Walter's expression of "sentiments" and refused to make pipe dream plans for an uncertain future. Financially, he was doing well enough working for the lanolin factory to assure Walter in January 1946 that money would not be a hindrance to sending relief parcels or even a possible reunion:

> I send this letter by air mail in order to clear or so to say to clean things up....
>
> Facts: For the time being it is not possible to send any food parcels to Paul [i.e., Paula; Paul continued to use this thin wartime code to avoid naming her] from here out. All I am officially allowed to do is: to send one 7 lbs food parcel a month to Olga [in England]. Olga forwards as much as possible through friends to Paul [i.e., Paula] as also there is no open Verkehr [trade or market] yet. Therefore I asked you in at least ten letters as to be so kind and to let me know whether you can send food. By your above mentioned letter of 16th pto [unknown abbreviation] I got now to know that you can. Now I will try and to transmit some money to you. This will take at least three months, but be sure you will get it. Who ever will give you the money from me, Bank, private, Committee etc., do not ask about me. The food needed is little bit otherwise than you put it: <u>tinned meat</u> (corned beef or so), <u>sweetened condensed milk, sugar, rice, chocolate, cheese</u> (tinned), cigarettes as a means of exchange. Stockings (silk or rayon) for Toni[390] and Paul [i.e., Paula]. I hope you will understand this letter. Be sure as soon as I get to know by our organization here that I can send directly I will do it. Another request Bobi, please skip all the sentiments. I own ship-loads of them and I am not in need of additional ones. Die Sorgen kommen der Reihe nach. [Troubles come one

---

390 Paul would not have been aware that Antoinette had died in Vienna on January 15, 1946, a week before he wrote this letter.

after the other.] And whether we will see each other again is, as for my part, certainly not a question of money.

...yours very old Paul

Emigration Snares and Transportation Shortages

In 1946 Paula began efforts to leave Austria for Australia and reunite with Paul. It was frustrating. As in 1938–39, western diplomatic missions in Vienna were besieged by endless lines of people who, having survived the war, hoped at last to join relatives in the UK, America, Australia, and beyond. They encountered bureaucratic obstacles comparable to those that had frustrated supplicants during the Nazi-era scramble to leave Vienna, though without the express threats of physical and financial devastation.

Even for those fortunate enough to obtain the necessary visas, little or no civilian transportation was available between Europe and Australia. Talk was going around that ageing ships were being hauled out of storage and refitted for the masses of hopeful Jewish migrants, but nothing was immediate or certain. Paula registered with the Joint Distribution Committee's transportation service in November 1946 and wrote to Walter:

> I am so disappointed that things are still going so slowly with my emigration, and I was advised in a friendly way that there is 12 to 18 months waiting time. I would like so much to be with Paul already. But I don't need to tell you [pl.] that, you know that also. There is a *vague* possibility that in January the Joint [i.e., the Jewish Joint Distribution Committee] will have a ship to Australia and I can get a place. The ship will probably be a scrapped wreck from a French ship line, but hopefully it will arrive, and that suits me.

Paula was still waiting for her Austrian passport to be issued, which she would then take to the Australian consulate for a visa. She reported that there had been a "visa closure for Australia" during the summer, but "now it is lifted" so she could apply again.

Paul had forwarded official paperwork in support of Paula's request for an Australian landing permit to the Hebrew Immigrant Aid Society (HIAS), but it was caught in a monumental bureaucratic morass:

> In the meantime my original permit swims somewhere around in the world. Paul sent it to HIAS in Paris, and they were supposed to send it to HIAS in Vienna. After many urgent telegrams, they let it be known that the Parisian office had "erroneously" sent it to HIAS in Munich, where it is still sitting. If I am lucky, it will not become lost in the mail between Munich and Vienna. There are neither registered letters nor telephone or telegraph connection to and from Germany. A small taste of the difficulties against which it is impossible to struggle.

Even with a visa, few transportation options were available. Travel to Australia via North America had the disadvantages of being expensive and requiring a US transit visa. Paula had been advised by a helpful source in Sweden that berths on ships sailing from the US West Coast to Australia were booked out about a year in advance. Most passenger shipping to Australia originated in the UK, but as a matter of official policy, that route was closed to people from Europe (i.e., Jewish refugees) to prevent them from "competing" for scarce transportation with the preferred migrants. The Australian Department of Immigration offered this bloodless explanation of a desperate situation: Britons, not women and children, came first:

> In view of the heavy demand in England for transport to Australia it was decided that aliens in Europe whose entry into Australia has been approved should not be permitted to travel to England and compete with Australians and other British subjects who have been waiting for transport to Australia for some considerable time.[391]

---

391 NAA, letter from Australian Department of Immigration to Ernst Morgen, January 23, 1947.

As a backup measure, once she had an Austrian passport and Australian landing permit, Paula tried to apply for an Australian passport in Vienna based on Paul's status as a naturalized Australian citizen. If approved, this would have allowed her to travel to Australia from England. In January 1947 the Australian consular staff in Vienna asked the Foreign Office in London for guidance on how to handle Paula's case. A consular official explained that despite Paula's having an Austrian passport and an Australian visa, she had additionally submitted a copy of Paul's naturalization certificate and "now desires to proceed to Australia via the United Kingdom and has applied to me for British passport facilities [sic] and for repatriation."[392] That application was eventually denied, for reasons showing officialdom at its worst: Paul's original naturalization certificate did not include his wife; there was no authorized Australian official in Vienna before whom Paula could sign the necessary naturalization paperwork; thus nothing could be done.

Back in Australia, Paul asked his friend and fellow former internee Ernst "Ernie" Morgen (or perhaps Ernie volunteered) to write to the Australian Department of Immigration on his behalf to help facilitate Paula's emigration. A Department of Immigration secretary in Canberra responded on January 23, 1947. The letter coolly restated the reasons that one door after another was shut to her. The most intractable one was that to become an Australian citizen, Paula would have to submit a Declaration of Acquisition for British Nationality that was signed before an Australian justice of the peace or similar authorized official. However, that was impossible because "so far as the Department [of Immigration] is concerned, there is no such Australian official in Austria."[393] The Department confirmed that even with her Austrian passport and Australian visa, Paula would not be allowed to go to the UK to try to obtain passage from there to Australia because she was an "alien," and there were already too many Australians and other British nationals waiting in line for passage ahead of her. The Department of Immigration

---

392 NAA, letter from Consular Branch, Political Division ACA, Vienna, January 9, 1947, to Foreign Office, London.

393 NAA, letter from Australian Department of Immigration to Ernst Morgen, January 23, 1947.

washed its hands of the matter with the superficially bland suggestion that "the Hebrew Immigration Aid Society which functions in Europe may be able to assist Mrs. Kurz to obtain a passage on a vessel or plane leaving for Australia from Europe."[394] In other words, maybe the Jews would help a fellow Jew, but the Australian government would not.

At about the same time, Paul, or perhaps Ernie Morgen on his behalf, wrote to Viscount Addison, Britain's secretary of state for Dominion Affairs and a member of the House of Lords, asking for assistance. Addison's office passed the request on to the Office of the High Commissioner for the Commonwealth of Australia in London and inquired whether Paula had made the required Declaration of Australian Nationality and so could be regarded as a British subject.[395] The office of the Australian Deputy High Commissioner responded on February 28, and the Deputy High Commissioner in London shortly after. Both repeated the same syllogism: Paul's citizenship certificate did not include Paula so she would need to make a Declaration of Acquisition of British Nationality before an authorized Australian official to be eligible for an Australian passport; there was no such authorized official in Austria; ergo, she could not acquire Australian nationality while in Austria.[396]

Paula's Travel Plans Come Together

At the beginning of 1947, Paula seemed to be stuck. Britons-first migration policies meant that she was not allowed to travel to the UK and sail to Australia from there, while ships from Europe to Australia were just hypotheses. A few ships sailed from the US West Coast to Australia, but they had too many people vying for too few places. Some civilian air transport had resumed, but it was limited and

---

394 NAA, letter from Australian Department of Immigration to Ernst Morgen, January 23, 1947.

395 NAA, letter from Office of Viscount Addison, February 12, 1947.

396 NAA, letter via the Department of External Affairs to the Deputy High Commissioner, Australia House, London, April 1, 1947.

impossibly expensive. However, with the assistance of Cook, Britain's oldest travel agency with offices worldwide, it all came together.

Paula's journey can be traced by the telegrams that Walter kept in the file marked "Paula." In laconic telegraphese, they chronicle a frantic daily process of uncertain reservations, obtaining permits, and shifting money internationally.

The earliest telegram in the file is dated February 8, 1947. Paula wanted to travel via the United States, which would allow her to see Walter and Lilly for the first time in eight years. It was not certain whether airline seats would be available after she left New York, so there was a backup plan for surface travel. Paula cabled from Vienna to Walter that Cook had cabled her a reservation for a train berth from New York to San Francisco. From there, Paula had a tentative reservation on a converted troopship, the *Marine Phoenix*, which made several journeys from San Francisco to New Zealand and Sydney in 1947. International communications were still spotty, so Paula asked Walter to contact Cook in New York and ask them to telegraph the alternative train and ship fare information to Paul in Melbourne.

Then travel complications multiplied. The option of sailing from San Francisco to Australia was disrupted when Cook in San Francisco cabled the company's Vienna office that the *Marine Phoenix* had experienced "various difficulties." Paula cabled Walter on February 11: "Please find out about this and about other ship possibilities. Kisses—Paula."

Walter contacted Cook in New York and responded to Paula the same day. The result was inconclusive. His penciled telegram draft reads, "Even with an immediate payment, reservations for the ship *Phoenix* in March are practically closed. Cook's here recommends Paul contact Cook's in Melbourne. Wait for further instructions."

The following day, February 12, Paula cabled back to Walter. The possibility of a sea passage was fading, so Paula asked about airline seats, quite scarce and expensive. She reported:

Cooks in New York contacted Cooks in Vienna on the 11th through an employee named Askew. If the *Phoenix* is impossible and no other ship will leave then, I will have to fly from San Francisco. How long is the waiting time for an airplane place?

Later that day, Walter cabled back to Vienna:

Continuing my cable from yesterday. Inquire at the consulate or Cook's about obtaining an American transit visa. Paul is making reservations with some ship line. However much waiting time you can stay here. We are US citizens and can put up whatever guarantee is required. After this experience until now, everything else is inappropriate.

Even for a well-connected travel agency like Cook, scouting out alternative travel arrangements was slow. Two days later, on February 14, Walter cabled back to Paula: "Cook's downtown office here will have the result next week."

Four days later there was some definite news from Cook in New York. The outlook for sea travel was not encouraging, but suddenly a plane ticket, albeit a costly one, could be had. On February 18, Walter cabled to Paula:

The waiting time is about six months for reservations if a later ship is impossible. Reserved a plane ticket April 16 from San Francisco. The price from San Francisco is about 600 dollars. Paul should soonest contact Cook's in Melbourne to arrange to pay this by cable to Cook's office at 211 Broadway, NY. Pay for either a train or flight NY–San Francisco. If it is financially possible, pay this all together within a foreseeable time.

Six hundred dollars was a small fortune in 1947. The US federal minimum wage was 40 cents per hour, and Walter and Lilly paid rent of $51.75 a month, or $621 a year, for their apartment in Jackson Heights.

Paul had saved money after his release from Tatura, and in a generous gesture, his uncle Rudolf in Cardiff offered to pay the difference between the cost of surface travel and airfare for Paula. So it worked. On Lilly's birthday, February 25, Paula in Vienna cabled the good news to Walter in New York: "Paul paid Cook's in Melbourne the whole flight from Vienna to Sydney."

After several confusing telegraph exchanges, Paul cabled to Walter from Melbourne on March 8. Success at last. The entire trip via air was booked and paid for:

> …have paid Cooks here full air fare Vienna Sydney via Newyork [sic, to save word count] Frisco who have arranged for Panamerican Airways cable credit Panair Vienna and Cooks Vienna have already cable confirmed stop. Repeat whole trip flying is paid for and therefore no additional payment from you necessary. Stop. Cooks Newyork keeping hundredsixty [sic] dollars cash for Paula. Paul

Reunions

Two weeks later Paula's journey from Vienna finally began. On March 11, 1947, she cabled Walter: "Flying out Wednesday the 12th of March. See you soon if all goes well, Kisses." Walter confirmed in a cable to Paul in Melbourne: "Paula leaving today twelfth arriving New York tomorrow." He penciled in the time: "7:50 a.m."

Paula landed at New York's LaGuardia airport on schedule, where she and Walter met for the first time since 1939. She stayed with Walter and Lilly for about a week. There are photos of Paula, Walter, and Lilly standing in a playground in Jackson Heights and on top of the Empire State Building. New clothing was unavailable in Vienna, so Paula borrowed essentials from Lilly: a coat, scarf, and gloves. Lilly also helped her to find a hat (both their hats are strikingly unflattering).

Walter and Paula stop at the Empire State Building, March 1947.

Whether Paula met with the Neuhaus parents or Gustl, I don't know. Paula continued to include regards to Lilly's parents in her letters into the 1960s. I recall wanting to ask on one of their visits when I was a teenager whether Paula and Paul had known my grandparents when they were in Vienna, but the self-censor prevailed.

Paula and Lilly at a park in Jackson Heights, March 1947.

On March 22 Paula flew from New York to San Francisco, where she stayed overnight with her friend Nettel, who sent Walter a confirming telegram: "Paula arrived Thursday left Friday night good health."

Paula's next telegram to Walter came from Honolulu, the first stop for trans-Pacific flights from the US West Coast: "Safely arrived splendid trip. Love, Paula." (The route was the same when I traveled to Australia in 1968 and 1969—San Francisco, Honolulu, Nadi, Sydney. Even in the 1960s and early 1970s, there were no direct international flights into Melbourne's old Essendon airport.)

Two days later, on March 24, Paula sent another telegram from her next stop, Nadi airport in Fiji. A few words said all that was needed: "Safely arrived. Love, Paula."

The last item in Walter's file is a telegram dated March 25, 1947. It was sent from Sydney to Walter in Jackson Heights: "Paula arrived alright love Paula Paul." Paula and Paul were reunited after eight years.

Settling In

Since his release from Tatura, Paul had been renting a room in the house of an Austrian couple with the resonant names of Friedrich and Clara Schiller in Armadale, an inner Melbourne suburb. In anticipation of resuming their interrupted life together, and despite the housing shortage, in early 1947 Paul was able to rent a small flat in an art deco style building on Grey Street in East Melbourne. Paula answered Walter's questions about it in July 1947:

> No, our apartment is not larger than the one in the Wienzeile. Only the bath is larger, which in the Wienzeile was nice and dear! It is just a furnished apartment and must make do.

A couple of months after arriving in Melbourne, Paula assured Walter, "I am doing very very well as before. I lead the life 'of the King of France.'"[397] The Grey Street flat was in walking distance of Melbourne's world-class botanical garden and large public library, and Paula had time to rest: "I don't do anything the whole day except go shopping a bit and do a bit of house work," she wrote. During the southern hemisphere's winter days, she listened to the radio. Unlike radio in Nazi Vienna, the ABC (Australian Broadcasting Corporation) was not political:

---

397 This is a variation on the saying, "leben wie Gott in Frankreich," to live like God in France, that is, in the lap of luxury.

I listen to radio a lot when I am alone. Earlier in Vienna I could never endure the radio. Now I like to listen. Yesterday was the Rosenkavalier, which I like a lot. Also they frequently play my favorite Offenbach.

In Melbourne Paula became the primary correspondent with Walter and the family in New York. Paul added only a couple of words and his signature at the bottom of letters. Although no longer writing regularly to New York, Paul kept in close touch with local internee comrades, whom Paula termed his "children":

Paul comes now home somewhat early. Usually at 5 p.m. Then we eat and often in the evening his children come to him. They are young, dear young men who were interned with him.

Paula initially had difficulties with day-to-day spoken English, particularly the Australian version. As is common, it was easier for her to converse with former internees who spoke second-language English than with Australian native speakers. She wrote to Walter in April, after a bare month in Melbourne:

As for the language it goes a little better than you. But then I hardly understand true Australians. A very distinct dialect. I don't understand the most primitive sentences. So it must be for a lot of people. But with us, only English is spoken if people come to Paul, and a lot of his former camp-comrades come, and I understand almost every word. Sometimes I speak quite well, and sometimes I can't get out a single orderly sentence.

While Paul and the former internees conversed exclusively in English among themselves, it is likely that Paul and Paula continued to speak German with each other. Into the 1960s Paula continued to write to my father in German, though when Paula and Paul visited us in New York, they always spoke English, at least when the kids were present.

Chapter 23: Paul and Paula—Refocus   433

After eight years in English-speaking countries, Paul could savor reading and listening to Australian slang. In June Paula wrote in response from a question from Walter about comic strips, a characteristically American phenomenon:

> Yes, there also such "comics" here in the newspaper and also on the radio: Bluey and Curley. Paul sits there and laughs until he cries. And I sit and look at him and also must laugh. For the comics I myself lack *the sense of humour*.

Bluey and Curley, hitching a ride on an American jeep. Used with the kind permission of Margaret Gurney. [398]

Keepsakes

Allied air raids and postwar looting had destroyed much of Vienna, but Paula had managed to keep a few things safe. In July 1947 Paula wrote that she was waiting for delivery of some household items that Olga had shipped to her from Vienna, including a small suitcase with photographs:

---

398 "Bluey and Curley: Jeep Jeep," John Ryan Comic Collection, National Library of Australia, MS 6514, Box 63, https://nla.gov.au/nla.obj-234439973/view.

Tomorrow I will receive my two small crates which I sent from Vienna. A little linen and a couple of books and little things and my little suitcase with all my photographs. Those I always had with me in the cellar during air raids; people thought that I carried the family jewelry around with me that way. But this was the most important to me. And also now I am most happy about that. The crates have already been inspected by customs and released.

A month later, in August 1947, Paula sent one of the photos from this little suitcase to Walter and Lilly as a present for their eighth anniversary:

I also want to express my very very best and most heartfelt wedding anniversary wishes. As a wedding anniversary gift this year, I have enclosed the little picture that I found in my photo suitcase. This is my first wedding anniversary gift to you [pl.]! But it is beautiful! Do you remember it still? It was after a big battle in the Prater, and when we were reconciled again, we went directly to a quick photographer there and kept this rare historical moment for all times. One can only say we two look good in it. I was 17 years old then!! I hope that Lilly will laugh.

Walter and Paula at the Prater in 1913.

Here is the photo, which would have been taken in 1913. I do not recall seeing it while my father was alive, and it must have remained untouched for decades among the folders in his closet. Eleven-year-old Walter, appearing startled, perhaps by the flash, wears pants that look like riding breeches with a tailored jacket, white collared shirt, and tie. Paula looks serious and a bit stouter than at any other time.

Sending Coal to Vienna

For those back in Vienna, keeping warm through the upcoming winter of 1947–48 loomed as a huge burden. During Paula's first northern winter in Australia, she specified that if and when the money for coal finally came through, it was to go first to Hans and then the remainder to Olga, because Olga "wrote to me that she has received some from the allotment and he [Hans] has no supply at all." After complex international currency transfer gyrations, Paula could confirm at the end of December that she had managed to send funds from Australia via the United States that were intended to purchase one thousand kilograms of coal for Hans and Lisl and five hundred kilograms for Olga. Even then, there was an additional wrinkle when Paula mistakenly ordered coal instead of coke (the latter more desirable as fuel because it has fewer impurities and a higher carbon content than coal). Hans wrote about this glitch in November 1947, being careful not to make unnecessarily difficulties for either Paula or Walter:

> I must ask you to ask Paula, as she announced to me after submitting an order for coal, to order not coal but coke. This has been a possibility for several days, but the coke must be ordered from outside because the order cannot be changed from here. We will receive the first 500 kilograms in the next few days, we already have the notice from the local delivery firm. Certainly you will not ask Paula to make a new order, only for my request to be put into effect if she can have something changed on the existing order!!

On November 1 Hans thanked Paula and Paul for their coal purchase and sent a copy of his letter to Walter:

> I am up to date about the coal story through Walter, and he has already announced 500 kilograms from your account. When it will be warm we will think of you [pl.]! (I mean not in summer, but when it will be warm through your heating donation!)....

You took great care of us with the coal, because it is actually harder to order it now than in previous years. Again thanks for it.

Further Immigration Tangles—Paula Becomes an Australian

Paula's immigration situation remained uncertain. Two months after Paula landed in Australia, Paul followed the advice that he had given to Lilly in London in 1939 when her US visa application had stalled: get a lawyer. They turned the matter over to Laura Brennan, one of Melbourne's very few female solicitors at the time and a friend of the future wife of Paul's fellow internee Ernie Morgen.

In May 1947 Laura sent a lawyerly letter to the secretary of the Department of the Interior asking whether Paula had in fact submitted an application for naturalization as a British subject, and if not, to send her the required forms. The Department of Immigration promptly acknowledged receiving Laura Brennan's letter and then went silent. Laura followed up again. A junior official looked at the case and wrote a memo concluding that Paula's naturalization application would ordinarily be denied because it was time-barred. But then he found a loophole. The deadline for Paula to acquire derivative Australian nationality had not been previously communicated to the principals, and the statute contained an exception that could resolve the situation: "The Minister may grant an extension of time in which the declaration can be made." A recommendation to allow the exception was duly made and approved six days later with the minister's rubber stamp and a neat signature. Forms were sent to Laura, completed by Paula, signed before the requisite justice of the peace, then returned to Laura, who forwarded them to Canberra. So it was done. Less than six months after landing in Australia, Paula became a British subject and obtained an Australian passport. Paula, Paul, and

Laura Brennan remained friends bound by affection and mutual high regard for the remainders of their lives.

Paula sent Walter prints of their new passport photos, which she complained looked quite unnatural, some of the lines in her face having been retouched away.

Passport photos of Paul and Paula, Melbourne 1947.

1948—An Aunt, and Life in Melbourne

Then in November 1948, Paula became an aunt when I was born:

> Patricia Ann, the Sunday child, is here! Yesterday the telegram arrived as Paul came home; I grabbed him and danced through the room with him for joy. He also is hugely glad and congratulates me on my newest rank as aunt.

Paula and Paul had both grown up in families teeming with aunts, of whom only three remained.

During the same period, Paula wrote about the waves of strikes in Melbourne that had forced them to stock up on staples and make do:

> During the past 3 weeks we had a constant lot of strikes. First a bakers strike. No bread, no yeast for three weeks after that. After that one week of gas strike, and to crown the whole thing, there was a tram and bus strike the whole previous week. Because of that the [congratulatory] telegram could only be sent delayed. At the moment there is no strike, but it is very probable that towards the end of the week there will be a general strike. I bought an oil stove, oil, candles, and various kinds of food. I must also send off a quick letter so that it will not lie for too long in the post office.

Unlike Austrian labor unrest during the 1920s and 1930s, Paula did not perceive any of this as genuinely threatening. From what she saw, Australian workers were hardly oppressed and were not about to start a revolution. Rather, they were by and large "big capitalists":

> In fact no one here takes it [the general strike] very seriously. At the moment there are differences between the unions and the [Labour] government concerning a new law. Otherwise many want to have a 30-hour work week instead of the currently legal 40-hour week. The "workers" here are almost all house owners, have their own auto, etc., and need more free time to be able to work in their gardens. Only the ones who drink and gamble away their money at the *races* are poor devils, all the others are themselves more or less big capitalists. It is unbelievable but true. I believe in no other country is the population so *"well off."*

Savings and Insurance—Trust in a Future?

Australia after the war was a land of plenty and reasonable stability, with nearly every worker at heart a home- and car-owning bourgeois. Still, after a lifetime of watching what had seemed to be rock-solid financial security evaporate, Paula remained deeply skeptical of saving for the future at the expense of the present. When Paula and Paul sent some money in late 1948 to Walter for their newborn niece (me), telling them to use it for some little necessity or luxury, Walter's instinct was to stash it away as savings. Paula disagreed forcefully, as she had two years earlier when Walter wrote about saving money rather than spending it for current needs. She backed her argument with a unique window into the family's history and survival:

> Your intention to save the money for Penny together with yours has upset us both. It is so difficult for us to believe that you or she will ever have something from that. We have already often spoken about that, how saving was punished. For years Papa invested his hard earned money in the "Gisella-Association" [a life and dowry insurance society established in 1869 under the patronage of the Archduchess Gisela, a daughter of Emperor Franz Joseph I] for Alice and then lost it all. Every month he bought state savings shares and Red Cross shares and always wrote our names on them in pencil. When I left, I showed Hans a packet of those shares and asked what I should do with them. He said: throw them away. And in the same way Paul's father completely lost his savings that he had worked in blood to save. And you also work hard enough for your money. But I don't know how one can advise you in a reasonable manner to buy something for your money. I know that one often needs money that one can instantly make liquid. Please, think about it yourself, perhaps something better will come to your mind. You already pay for life insurance which of course, against

all experience, is also a risk, but I see that that is necessary in your case. The only things that Papa bought and that kept their value were a couple of pieces of jewelry. We really lived on those in the time of need, and that always kept its purchasing power when no one took money any more. Genuine art objects seemingly keep their worth, good stamps, etc. Please, dear Bibo, think about it.

This is one of the few glimpses of what the family in Vienna went through during the economic disruptions of the 1920s and later wartime and postwar shortages. Money, bank accounts, securities, and insurance policies all became worthless—"saving was punished." Once the people with goods to sell refused to accept worthless cash, the family had scrambled to barter jewelry, art, and stamps for subsistence food.

Discussing this letter, longtime family friend Edith Liebenthal (who was sent to England on a Kindertransport from Vienna at the end of 1938) wrote to me in June 2017: "Interesting, how Paula reacted to saving the money for you. I believe that whole generation was traumatized by the horrors they experienced and unable to believe in a more normal world where such common things as savings and insurance have their value." This was the cosmic wager that both Edith's and my parents made, that the United States would provide a "more normal world" for foreseeable generations.

Insurance in particular had been a bedrock foundation of the nineteenth-century Habsburg Empire's "age of security," as Stefan Zweig recognized:

The century of security became the golden age of insurance. One's house was insured against fire and theft, one's field against hail and storm, one's person against accident and sickness. Annuities were purchased for one's old age, and a policy was laid in a girl's cradle for her future dowry [this was the Gisela Association]. Finally even the workers organized, and won standard wages and workmen's compensation. Servants saved up for old age insurance and paid in advance into a burial fund for their own interment.[399]

No doubt the reality had not been quite so tidy. (Historian Steven Beller characterized Zweig's evocation of a "world of security" as part of the latter's nostalgic retelling of the "Habsburg myth."[400]) But there had been acute people who had believed in it, at least to some extent. Martin Haim's years of buying insurance policies, public bonds, and Gisela Association annuities represented something deeper than a mathematical calculation; it manifested his confidence in the rational course of an "orderly" world. Long before the end of the war, Paula and Hans had been divested of that faith. Not so Walter who, despite the immigrant's inevitable hardships, trusted the promises of life in the United States. He bought insurance, deposited money in savings banks, and did not scoff at US savings bonds.

Building a House

Only a few months after Paula's arrival, Paul began thinking about their becoming homeowners. In November 1947 Paula wrote:

> Paul turns the question about in his head whether he should buy a little house. You will think that he had hit the jackpot. But here it is often handled like that. One pays a couple of hundred pounds on account and pays the remainder weekly in an amount that is a little higher than we are paying in rent, for example, for our rather inadequate apartment, 4

---

399 Zweig, *The World of Yesterday*, 3. For a more double-edged view than Zweig's, see, e.g., Price, *Objects of Remembrance*, 150. Price discerned a wary subtext to his mother's stories about Rumpelstiltskin and Rapunzel; the fairy tale heroines had invited their own plights through "complacency in the face of predictable and cyclical oppression."

400 See Steven Beller, *The Habsburg Monarchy 1815–1918* (Cambridge, UK: Cambridge University Press, 2018), 17. This myth idealized the old monarchy as "an orderly, spiritually settled, safe world, where people knew their place and also could trust in the loyalty and faith of the whole Hapsburg community." There bank deposits were safe, insurance policies solid, and bonds prudent investments for a predictable future.

pounds—weekly! Oddly I have, in fact, absolutely no opinion in this respect. I don't believe that we will always remain here, and we have no children. In any case in 2–3 years the little house would be completely paid for, and in the meantime the rent being paid would not be thrown out but capitalized. We will see. In fact it is not at all so easy to find an appropriate house (about 3–4 small rooms, kitchen, bath, garden).

They must have mulled it over for years, but by 1953, with a return to Europe looking quite unlikely, Paula and Paul commissioned plans from a young Australian architect named Alistair Knox, who had been influenced by European Bauhaus design. The house was sited on a sloping corner lot in a newly laid out suburb northwest of the city center. It had a living area on one main story and a carport and wood-working shop for Paul underneath. Two bedrooms looked out over the raw space that would become the garden. The plans provided for the addition of another bedroom if Olga should retire and come to live with them in Australia.

By late 1956 Paula and Paul were at home at 32 Sunburst Avenue in North Balwyn. In January 1957 Paula reported about the local social mores:

Because North Balwyn is like a small English provincial city, we were invited by most of the surrounding neighbors and also invited them to us. At these get-togethers one talked about garden, garden, garden and weather, and according to the English manners the conversation never took the least personal turn. We, then, weren't brought up to be effusive and loquacious, but at the end I am still always "*puzzled*" by such a "*party*," how these people manage to avoid in conversation everything which could halfway interest (me!).

Looking back in 1964, Paula described herself as "an experienced house-grow-watcher." She encouraged Walter as my family acquired our first house:

When we first moved into our house it looked like a weather station in a desert. But since then the trees & shrubs have grown & make the house look homier.

Paula and Paul's North Balwyn neighbors, whose wives chatted only about gardens and weather, favored English-style gardens featuring roses and lawns. Paul planted Australian natives, tall gum trees and mounding wattles.

Travels

Life was good, and Paula and Paul traveled. They visited Sydney, Tasmania, and points of natural interest in Victoria. Every four or five years, they journeyed around the globe, stopping in New York and then flying onward to see the remains of family and friends in Cardiff, London, and Vienna, and often going with Olga for a vacation in the Alps.

In April 1964 Paula wrote merrily that she had read about the opening of the World's Fair, just a few miles away from where we lived in Jackson Heights:

> I would love to come to NY to see the fair. And I wouldn't mind having to put up with seeing all the Haims. How I am longing to see you all again. Perhaps, perhaps—

Her health must have been declining, but she did not write about it, only that she had been cleared to travel:

> At my last check up (electrocardiogram etc. etc.) my doctor was very satisfied with me. Everything is O.K. & she gave me the green light for a round the world trip!!

Paul was okay as well, working hard at the lanolin factory and on fall cleanup in their garden.

In June 1965 they left for a three-month trip, this time going west, first to Europe. They began with an excursion to Switzerland with Olga, where Paul hiked Mount Rigi ("Queen of the Mountains") and the Jungfrau. Paula reported that "the meals are a catastrophe: it is delicious & I am putting on 1 kg per day!" Afterwards they stayed with Olga in Vienna, then made stops in Paris and London. In August they arrived in New York. After visits to the new Guggenheim Museum and the World's Fair, we all stayed in a cottage on Cape Cod for a week. I was in junior high school, and Paula and Paul were a window onto a dream world of art, culture, and domestic harmony. They were my antipodean ideals.

Darkness Again

That visit marked the end of an era that, with the protective deception of youth, I had expected to be eternal. Paula died in February 1966 in Melbourne, a few months short of her seventieth birthday. She succumbed to the familial cardiac illness. The death certificate identifies "coronary atherosclerosis with myocardial ischaemia" as cause of death and "duration of last illness" as "years."

Paul was devastated. Three months later he flew to Europe. Though always reticent and sensitive to others' feelings, Lisl, Hans's widow, gave the clearest picture. She wrote on May 20 from Vienna:

> Yesterday morning Paul arrived at the airport. He is very nervous. He can't talk about Paula at all, then he begins to cry immediately. On the 23rd it will already be 3 months. From what I know, he is on leave here and will fly back again. You know I am not the proper person to ask questions of people. I know what people tell me, but I won't ask them. If I learn anything, I will let you know.

Paul stayed with Olga as a retreat from an unbearable world. He had brought Paula's ashes home to Vienna, where they were buried in the Central Cemetery with her parents, Martin and Antoinette, and her sister, Alice.

With Paula gone, Paul had to resume correspondence with Walter and family. My parents wrote to him in Vienna and urged him to visit in New York. I began writing to him as well. After two months in Europe, he returned to Australia, writing to my parents:

> Lilly I really thank you for your kind invitation. But I can't. I am still not fit for human consumption. It would not work. It does not work here either.
>
> I go back to Melbourne on the 23rd and will try to bury myself in work, hard work. Maybe it will work. Maybe not. Time does not help and Vienna did not help.

In September 1966 Paul wrote to Walter in tones reminiscent of the wartime days:

> My other life is not existent. I exist, that is all. My neighbours, a Scotch family, are personified angels. Every Saturday and Sunday I am eating at their place. I reciprocate a tiny wee bit by taking them out now and then for a meal. Otherwise I am on my own.
>
> And so are millions and millions of others. Some get along all right, some don't. Some pull through, some don't. Some don't at the start, some do later. Some run away into dope and alcohol, some don't. That is life.
>
> Cruel.

In November he wrote to Lilly:

> Not much to write about me. I am working, reading, writing. People write to me from Vienna and I answer. At the factory

they are pathetically kind and nice to me, the toughest rogue there treats me like a kitten.

Time does nothing but makes me used to...

Lilly of course I cannot tell when I will go again overseas. But I sincerely will do my best to go via New York. Only I don't think you will recognize me.

And then, and then...I was a teenager, just beginning my freshman year as a commuter at Barnard College, an hour-plus each way on the subway. Ironically, Barnard was only a few blocks from my parents' former furnished room with the ogreish Mr. Stern. I had extravagant hopes but no sense of direction. I began writing to Paul once, twice a week. The words flowed, and he responded with wonderful letters, his dearly earned sense of fatality and experience shining through.

A year later Paul was beginning to emerge from the darkness. He traveled to New York, Britain, and Vienna in March 1967. He cautioned Lilly that his control was still fragile:

And please just be casual (that applies especially to Walter) or I'll collapse. That strong sex is not worth a cracker.

CONCLUSION

New Light

After talking to my parents about the fantastical notion of my spending a year studying in Australia, Paul arranged for the University of Melbourne to accept me as an exchange student. I left for Melbourne in February 1968, my mother accompanying me to San Francisco for a few days there as tourists.

Being with Paul and attending university in Melbourne were life-shaping for me and to an extent, transformative for him. I brought home some of my new friends from the honors English program. They became a next generation of "children" for Paul, his old camp friends having become middle-aged men with families and businesses. Paul made Liptauer, a Hungarian soft, spiced cheese spread, and sometimes fed us filet steaks. His cucumber salad tasted quite like my mother's and grandmother's. He got us to talk about our studies as well as life and history and began himself to read some of our texts—the metaphysical poets, T. S. Eliot, and James Joyce come to mind. As one of our literary circle recalled fifty years later:

> We are Paul's age now, and it is hard to face how ignorant and unconscious I was when we knew him and benefited so much from his generosity. The only upside of that is that it was only two years after Paula died that his life was filled with us bright young lively noisy (if ignorant and unconscious as in my case) creatures.

I did unexpectedly well at university and stayed three years instead of the planned one, a blow to my parents back in New York. Then after graduation, having no better idea of what to do with myself, with the invincible self-absorption of youth, I applied to US graduate schools and left in early 1971. Paul continued as a sort of father figure for several of my friends after I'd gone, in particular Tim McNamara. Paul and I continued to write to each other. He returned to Vienna every year or two to visit Olga and the diminishing family circle.

Closing Days

Nearly forty years after leaving Austria, Paul continued to associate my father with the mountains they both had loved, but to confirm over and over, in the words of Thomas Wolfe, "You can't go home again." They had been adults and fully formed when they were forced into exile. My mother, in contrast, had been a teenager with her adult development ahead of her. In January 1968 Paul sent my father a picture postcard of the Dachstein massif, a nearly ten thousand-foot glaciated peak not far from Salzburg, writing:

> Walter! I did not want to first but now I do send you this picture. It is a lovely country, even more than that, and still one cannot live here anymore.
>
> Love to Lilly, she does not know this country.

In September 1972 he and Olga were again in the Alps. He sent Walter a postcard of the Grossglockner, Austria's highest peak at well over twelve thousand feet, writing: "Whenever I see a high mountain I think of you Bibo."

Life continued to flow on. I was in graduate school in North Carolina. My parents remained in Jackson Heights. After college, my brother was posted to Karlsruhe with the US Army. Then in

1976 Paul wrote that he was ill, though no details, no drama. In early November Olga wrote to my father:

> I don't know whether someone from Melbourne has let you know that Paul died on October 22. He had liver cancer and was not sick for very long. The last weeks he was in a hospital where one did not let him suffer, his doctor was a friend—
>
> If there is any consolation for me, it is just this, that he did not suffer and fell asleep peacefully.
>
> Throughout it he did not want me to go there—

Paul's ashes lie in a Melbourne cemetery. He wanted to spare Olga the bureaucratic procedures that he had to go through to bring Paula's remains back to Vienna.

This was the end of Paul's admirable, fully integrated life. Two years later, I named my first child after him. My brother named his daughter, born six years later, Paula. Paul's pessimistic view, that in fifty years no one will remember what he and the families lived through, is not the final word.

APPENDIX: WHO WAS WHO

This section lists the main individuals who are mentioned in the letters and text. Included are maiden names and commonly used names (where applicable), years and places of birth and death—with both the contemporaneous place names and their current designations—and notes about professions.

Haim Family
Martin Haim, Walter's father and pater familias (1859, Vienna–1941, Vienna). In 1938 he was a retired accountant, auditor, and financial advisor.

Antoinette (née Feder) Haim, Walter's mother and mater familias (1868, Vienna–1946, Vienna). They were married in Vienna in 1888.

Their children:
  Johann Jochanan (Hans) Haim, oldest brother (1889, Vienna–1948, Vienna), bank worker, businessman, cashier for the IKG.
    Elisabeth Auguste (Lisl, née Ricker) Haim, Hans's wife (ca. 1888–1973, Vienna). They were married in Vienna in 1915 in what was then a relatively rare civil ceremony, as neither of them had renounced their different religious affiliations.

  Alice Haim, oldest sister (1891, Vienna–1940, Vienna), a private English teacher.

Paula (née Haim) Kurz, next sister (1896, Bucharest–1966, Melbourne), an accountant and auditor, worked as a nurse or caregiver during the war.

Paul Kurz, Paula's husband (1901, Vienna–1976, Melbourne), a chemical engineer specializing in lanolin chemistry.

Walter Haim, my father (1902, Vienna–1979, New York). He, too, worked as an accountant.

Julianne (Lilly, née Neuhaus) Haim, daughter of Arthur and Pauline Neuhaus, Walter's wife, my mother (1919, Vienna–2002, New York). They married in New York in 1939. In the early 1960s, Lilly began working for a small import company as a bilingual bookkeeper and rose to become its secretary-treasurer. After retiring, she resumed her long-interrupted studies and earned a bachelor's degree "with high distinction."

Some Feder Aunts and Uncles—A Selection of Antoinette's Siblings

Charlotte (Lotte, née Feder) Degner, Antionette's sister (1872, Vienna–1944, Auschwitz). Lotte married Albert Hermann Degner in 1909 in Vienna, and thereafter they lived in Berlin with their son Paul.

Julius Feder, Antoinette's only brother (1876, Vienna–1939, Vienna), a university-trained engineer specializing in local and suburban railroad maintenance.

Paula Feder, Julius's wife (ca. 1890–1939, Vienna). They had one daughter.

Malvine (née Feder) Jahn, Antoinette's sister (1882, Vienna–1964, Vienna).

Otto Jahn, Malvine's husband (1877, Austria–1947, Vienna). Otto had the title of senior accounting consultant. As a young man, he had been an amateur alpine photographer. They had no children.

Helene (née Feder) Frieder, Antoinette's youngest sister (1885, Vienna–1985, Sydney). Helene and her family spent the war in Manila and remained in the Philippines for many years after, eventually moving to Australia in the 1970s.

Ignacz (Geza) Frieder, Helene's husband (1878, Varanno, Hungary–1958, ?). They had two children, Robert Frieder (1915, Vienna–1989, Sydney) and Margit (Margaret, née Frieder) Hammond (1911, Vienna–?).

Kurz Family

Mathilde (née Wilheim) Kurz, Paul and Olga's mother (1875, Gross Meseritsch, Moravia [now Velke Mezirici, Czech Republic]–1942, Theresienstadt).

Ignaz Kurz, a grocer (1869, Schaffa, Moravia [now Safov, Czech Republic]–1935, Vienna). They had two children: Dr. Olga Kurz, a pediatrician (1898, Vienna–1989, Vienna), and Paul Kurz, Paula's husband (see above, Paula Kurz).

Some Wilheims—Mathilde Kurz's Relatives

Rudolf Wilheim, Mathilde Kurz's only brother (1887, Gross Meseritsch, Moravia [now Velke Mezirici, Czech Republic]–1947, Cardiff, Wales), owner of a paper products factory. He and his family emigrated to the United Kingdom in about 1938 and settled in Cardiff.

Rosa (née Korani) Wilheim, Rudolf's wife (1892, Vienna–1967, Cardiff, Wales). They were married in Vienna in 1917. They had a daughter Gertrud (née Wilheim) Scheier (1917, Vienna–1997, Prague). A cousin of Paul and Olga Kurz, Gertrud lived for a time in England, then Sao Paolo, Brazil, and later in Germany.

Gretta (Grete, née Wilheim) Weisz, Mathilde Kurz's youngest sister (1890, Gross Meseritsch, Moravia [now Velke Mezirici, Czech Republic]–1984, Cardiff, Wales), "Tante Grete" to Paul and Olga. For a time before the war, she attempted to make a career as an opera singer.

Paul/Pavel ("S" or Sam) Weisz, Grete's husband (ca. 1897, ?–1981, Cardiff, Wales). They had no children.

Landsmann and Neuhaus Families

Regina (née Schefranek) Landsmann, Pauline's mother and Lilly's grandmother (1859, Skalitz, Hungary [now Szakolca, Slovakia]–1942, Theresienstadt), owned a glass and gift shop in the 9th District.

Adolf (Angelm) Landsmann, Regina's husband and Pauline's father (1857, Piesling, Moravia [now Písečné, Czech Republic]–1921, Vienna), a glazier. They had three children:

> Gustav (Gustl) Landsmann, Lilly's uncle (1888, Vienna–1953, New York), a glazier like his father. Gustl married twice and had no children:
> > Stella (née Popper) Landsmann, Gustl's first wife (1901, Vienna–1929, Vienna). They married in Vienna in 1924, and Stella died five years later of tuberculosis.
> >
> > Stella (née Herzl, Beller) Landsmann, Gustl's second wife (1904, Vienna–1995, New York). This Stella emigrated to New York in 1939, where she and Gustl married in 1941.
>
> Siegfried (Sigl) Landsmann, Lilly's uncle (1891, Vienna–1970, Philadelphia), trained as an engineer, worked as a draftsman in the US.
> > Irma (née Brügel) Landsmann, Sigl's wife (1894, Vienna–1989, Philadelphia). Sigl and Irma had one daughter, Anneliese (Lissy, née Landsmann) Reif, Lilly's cousin (1923, Vienna–2007,

Philadelphia). Lissy and her husband Martin Reif had two sons, Gerald and Robert.

Pauline (née Landsmann) Neuhaus, Lilly's mother, my grandmother (1896, Vienna–1964, New York). In New York, she had a dress shop, Pauline Originals, on Broadway.
Arthur Neuhaus, son of Heinrich and Julia Neuhaus (see below), Pauline's husband, Lilly's father, my grandfather (1889, Vienna–1969, New York). They married in 1917. Arthur retired in 1938 as a major in the Austrian army. They had one daughter, Julianne (Lilly, née Neuhaus) Haim, my mother (see above, Walter Haim).

More Neuhauses
Heinrich Neuhaus (1854, Szenitz, Hungary (?) [now Senica, Slovakia]–1926, Vienna), Lilly's paternal grandfather. Heinrich owned a brandy distillery and working men's pub in the Vienna suburbs. He was married three times:
Julia (née Nussbaum) Neuhaus (1856, Holleschau, Moravia [now Holesov, Czech Republic]–1911, Vienna). Julia and Heinrich had four children, Rudolf, Bertha, Arthur (see above, Pauline Neuhaus), and another son who died as an infant.

Jeanette (née Schefranek, Askenasy) Neuhaus, Heinrich's second wife (ca. 1860, Skalitz, Hungary [now Szakolca, Slovakia]–1921, Vienna). They married in 1912. Jeanette, a widow, was a younger sister of Regine (née Schefranek) Landsmann (Omama).

Marie (née Nussbaum, Deutsch) Neuhaus, Heinrich's third wife (1865, Holleschau, Moravia [now Holesov, Czech Republic]–1938, Vienna). They married shortly after Jeanette died. Marie, also a widow, was a younger sister of Julia (Nussbaum) Neuhaus, Heinrich's first wife.

Rudolf Neuhaus, the oldest child of Heinrich and Julia, and Lilly's uncle (1878, Vienna–1969, Vienna) was a Social Democrat and adult education activist before and after the war. While in Mexico City from 1941 to 1947, he opened a bookstore, the Libreria Internacional, and organized a group of Austrians in exile.

Hermine (Minna, née Neubauer) Neuhaus, Rudolf's wife (1891, Vienna–1982, Vienna). They had three children:

> Julia (Julla, née Neuhaus) Kolb, Rudolf and Minna's older daughter, Lilly's cousin (1913, Vienna–?, Mexico City). Julla and her husband and their young son emigrated to Mexico in 1947.
> Robert Kolb (ca. 1907, Vienna–1993, Mexico City), Julla's husband.
>
> Elfriede (Friedl, née Neuhaus) Lvoff, Rudolf and Minna's second daughter, Lilly's cousin (1915, Vienna–1952, Santa Barbara, California).
>
> Walter Neuhaus, Rudolf and Minna's son, Lilly's cousin (1919, Vienna–1990, Vienna).
> Helene (Helli, née Arent) Neuhaus, Walter Neuhaus's wife (1922, Vienna–2016, Vienna).

Bertha (née Neuhaus) Bandler (later Magyarized to Barta), Julia and Heinrich Neuhaus's daughter and Lilly's aunt (1883, Vienna–1964, Budapest).

Moritz Bandler (later Magyarized to Mor Barta), Bertha's husband (1876, ?–1945, Budapest). They married in Vienna in 1905 then moved to Budapest, where they had four sons.

Liebenthals
Robert Friedler, Edith's father (1893, Pilgram, Bohemia [now Pelhřimov, Czech Republic]–1967, New York).
Margit (Grete, née Steiner) Friedler, Robert's wife and Edith's mother (1897, Hasprunka, Slovakia–1985, New York). Grete, a corsetiere, owned a custom corset shop on Lexington Avenue in Manhattan. They had one daughter:

Edith (née Friedler) Liebenthal (1924, Vienna–2020, Houston).
Kurt Liebenthal, Edith's husband (1922, Bremerhaven, Germany–2009, Houston). Edith and Kurt had three children.

Friends of Paula and Paul
In Vienna
Dr. Martha Müller, a pediatrician (1906, Vienna–1944, Auschwitz). Martha was a former colleague of Olga Kurz, and apartment-mate of the Haim parents and Paula Kurz from 1939 until she was deported to Theresienstadt in 1942.

Henriette Nettel, close friend of Paula's (1884, Bohemia [now Czech Republic]–1978, Berkeley, California). She escaped first to Japan, where she worked as a dietician, and then settled in San Francisco.

In Australia
Ernest (Ernie) Morgen (originally Morgenstern), *Dunera* internee (1912, Vienna–1983, Melbourne). In 1951, Ernie, an engineer, married Kathleen (née Merrillees), a solicitor and friend of Laura Brennan. They had one daughter.

Peter Tikotin, *Dunera* internee (1920, Dresden, Germany–2003,

Melbourne). In 1945, he married Lilian (née Cooper), a nurse from Canada, and they had four children.

Kurt (Bob) Vogel, *Dunera* internee (1924, Vienna–2000, Sydney). Bob married Ilona (née Balog, 1924, Germany [Hungarian citizen]–2015, Sydney) in 1947, and they had three children.

Laura Brennan, friend of Kathleen Morgen (1907, Victoria, Australia–1989, Victoria, Australia), solicitor.

ACKNOWLEDGMENTS

This book would not have been possible without the support and encouragement of so many people during its long gestation. In particular, I would like to thank the following:

Edith Liebenthal (1924, Vienna–2020, Houston), a supporter of the project and source of inspiration from the beginning. Edith generously shared her recollections and knowledge, and transcribed many letters that otherwise would have remained illegible, closed books.

Tim McNamara (1949, Melbourne–2023, Melbourne), University of Melbourne professor emeritus and Redmond Barry Distinguished Professor of applied linguistics and Member of the Order of Australia. Tim, a primum mobile for this project, knew and admired my uncle Paul since our days at uni. Tim's final work, titled *Paul and Paula: A Story of Separation, Survival and Belonging*, was published by Monash University in 2024.

My cousins Eva Thorpe and Roberto Kolb-Neuhaus, who generously shared stories of their parents from this era. Many thanks also to Eva for her most generous hospitality in Vienna.

Brigitta and Thomas Busch, whose generous hospitality at Illmitz in the Austrian countryside provided the setting for Tim and me to begin writing our "Paul projects."

Anneliese Rohrer, who demonstrated her journalistic chutzpah on a busy Saturday morning in February 2020, driving me through Vienna's 4th, 7th, 9th, and 2nd Districts and boldly ringing apartment bells at old family addresses.

Wolf-Erich Eckstein, former archivist at the IKG in Vienna, for his help in unearthing and organizing family names and addresses early in the project.

National Archives of Australia and the Leo Baeck Institute in New York, for their kindness in granting permission to reprint artwork and documents.

Margaret Gurney, the daughter of Australian cartoonist Alex Gurney, creator of Bluey and Curley, for kind permission to use one of her father's images.

Sarah B. Munro, who accompanied me on early research trips to Melbourne.

Carol L. Couch, a friend since our law school days, who read the project piece by piece, created the map of Vienna addresses, and always discerned light at the end of the tunnel. Also Carol's sister Joan Julian, who most generously designed the cover.

Dorothy Freudenberg, who brought her artist's eye to the author photo.

Friends in Bend, especially Elina Harper and Alison Hamway, who read drafts of the project, and James Cagney for invaluable tech advice.

My children Paul, Alice, and Ruth, who listened to so many of the old stories.

ABOUT THE AUTHOR

Patricia Haim was born and raised in New York City. She lived in Melbourne for three years with her uncle Paul Kurz and graduated from the University of Melbourne's honors program in English language and literature. After that, she returned to the United States for graduate school at Duke University and, eventually, Notre Dame University Law School. She retired after a career specializing in employment, labor, and immigration law, and lives in Bend, Oregon. In addition to visits to Austria and Australia to research and write this book, Pat has been able to indulge in some adventure travel, from trekking to Mount Everest base camp to kayaking in Fiji and Antarctica.

www.ingramcontent.com/pod-product-compliance
Lightning Source LLC
LaVergne TN
LVHW042253070526
838201LV00106B/307/J